The Legitimacy of Medical Treatment

Whenever the legitimacy of a new or ethically contentious medical intervention is considered, a range of influences will determine whether the treatment becomes accepted as lawful medical treatment. The development and introduction of abortion, organ donation, gender reassignment, and non-therapeutic cosmetic surgery have, for example, all raised ethical, legal, and clinical issues. This book examines the various factors that legitimatise a medical procedure.

Bringing together a range of internationally and nationally recognised academics from law, philosophy, medicine, health, economics, and sociology, the book explores the notion of a treatment, practice, or procedure being proper medical treatment, and considers the range of diverse factors which might influence the acceptance of a particular procedure as appropriate in the medical context. Contributors address such issues as clinical judgement and professional autonomy, the role of public interest, and the influence of resource allocation in decision-making. In doing so, the book explores how the law, the medical profession, and the public interact in determining whether a new or ethically contentious procedure should be regarded as legitimate.

This book will be of interest and use to researchers and students of bioethics, medical law, criminal law, and the sociology of medicine.

Sara Fovargue is Reader in Law, at Lancaster University, and Co-Director of the Lancaster Centre for Bioethics and Medical Law.

Alexandra Mullock is a Lecturer in Medical Law at the University of Manchester, and a member of the Centre for Social Ethics and Policy at the University.

Biomedical Law and Ethics Library
Series Editor: Sheila A. M. McLean

Scientific and clinical advances, social and political developments and the impact of healthcare on our lives raise profound ethical and legal questions. Medical law and ethics have become central to our understanding of these problems, and are important tools for the analysis and resolution of problems – real or imagined.

In this series, scholars at the forefront of biomedical law and ethics contribute to the debates in this area, with accessible, thought-provoking, and sometimes controversial, ideas. Each book in the series develops an independent hypothesis and argues cogently for a particular position. One of the major contributions of this series is the extent to which both law and ethics are utilised in the content of the books, and the shape of the series itself.

The books in this series are analytical, with a key target audience of lawyers, doctors, nurses, and the intelligent lay public.

Available titles:

Human Fertilisation and Embryology
Reproducing regulation
Kirsty Horsey & Hazel Biggs

Intention and Causation in Medical Non-killing
The impact of criminal law concepts on euthanasia and assisted suicide
Glenys Williams

Impairment and Disability
Law and Ethics at the Beginning and End of Life
Sheila McLean & Laura Williamson

Bioethics and the Humanities
Attitudes and Perceptions
Robin Downie & Jane Macnaughton

Defending the Genetic Supermarket
The law and ethics of selection the next generation
Colin Gavagham

The Harm Paradox
Tort law and the unwanted child in an era of choice
Nicolette Priaulx

Assisted Dying
Reflections on the Need for Law Reform
Sheila McLean

Medicine, Malpractice and Misapprehensions
V. H. Harpwood

Euthanasia, Ethics and the Law
From the conflict to compromise
Richard Huxtable

The Best Interests of the Child in Healthcare
Sarah Elliston

Values in Medicine
What are we really doing to patients?
Donald Evans

Autonomy, Consent and the Law
Sheila A.M. McLean

Healthcare Research Ethics and Law
Regulation, review and responsibility
Hazel Biggs

The Body in Bioethics
Alastair V. Campbell

Genomic Negligence
An interest in autonomy as the basis for novel negligence claims generated by genetic technology
Victoria Chico

Health Professionals and Trust
The cure for healthcare law and policy
Mark Henaghan

Medical Ethics in China
A transcultural interpretation
Jing-Bao Nie

Law, Ethics and Compromise at the Limits of Life
To treat or not to treat?
Richard Huxtable

Regulating Pre-Implantation Genetic Diagnosis
A comparative and theoretical analysis
Sheila A.M. McLean & Sarah Elliston

Bioethics
Methods, theories, domains
Marcus Düwell

Human Population Genetic Research in Developing Countries
The Issue of Group Protection
Yue Wang

Coercive Care
Rights, law and policy
Bernadette McSherry & Ian Freckelton

Saviour Siblings
A relational approach to the welfare of the child in selective reproduction
Michelle Taylor-Sands

Human Population Genetic Research in Developing Countries
The issue of group protection
Yue Wang

Stem Cell Research and the Collaborative Regulation of Innovation
Sarah Devaney

The Voices and Rooms of European Bioethics
Richard Huxtable and Ruud Ter Meulen

The Legitimacy of Medical Treatment
What role for the medical exception?
Sara Fovargue and Alexandra Mullock

Forthcoming titles include:

Autonomy and Pregnancy
A comparative analysis of compelled obstetric intervention
Samantha Halliday

The Jurisprudence of Pregnancy
Concepts of conflict, persons and property
Mary Neal

Regulating Risk
Values in health research governance
Shawn Harmon

The Umbilical Cord Blood Controversies in Medical Law
Karen Devine

Revisiting Landmark Cases in Medical Law
Shaun D. Pattinson

Revisiting the Regulation of Human Fertilisation and Embryology
Kirsty Horsey

The Ethical and Legal Consequences of Posthumous Reproduction
Lewis Browne

Pioneering Healthcare Law
Essays in honour of Margaret Brazier
Catherine Stanton, Sarah Devaney, Anne-Marree Farrell and Alexandra Mullock

End of Life Decision Making for Critically Impaired Infants
Resource allocation and difficult decisions
Neera Bhatia

Birth, Harm and the Role of Distributive Justice
Burdens, blessings, need and desert
Alasdair Maclean

About the series editor

Professor Sheila McLean is International Bar Association Professor of Law and Ethics in Medicine and Director of the Institute of Law and Ethics in Medicine at the University of Glasgow.

The Legitimacy of Medical Treatment

What role for the medical exception?

Edited by Sara Fovargue and Alexandra Mullock

Routledge
Taylor & Francis Group
LONDON AND NEW YORK

First published 2016
by Routledge
2 Park Square, Milton Park, Abingdon, Oxon, OX14 4RN

and by Routledge
711 Third Avenue, New York, NY 10017

First issued in paperback 2017

Routledge is an imprint of the Taylor & Francis Group, an informa business

British Library Cataloguing in Publication Data
A catalogue record for this book is available from the British Library

Library of Congress Cataloging-in-Publication Data
A catalog record for this book has been requested

ISBN 13: 978-1-138-09817-6 (pbk)
ISBN 13: 978-1-138-81963-4 (hbk)

Typeset in Baskerville
by Apex CoVantage, LLC

For Mia, Amelia, and Mary

Contents

Acknowledgements

We would first like to thank the Society and Ethics stream of the Wellcome Trust for generously funding the seminar ('Transforming wrong(s) into right(s): The power of proper medical treatment') which was held in Manchester in September 2013 and was the genesis for this edited collection. We are grateful to all the participants and attendees for their interest in the seminar, and for their insightful contributions at the seminar and subsequently. Many of the contributors to this collection presented at that seminar (Brazier and Fovargue, Coggon, Donaldson, Griffiths and Mullock, Huxtable, and Lyons), others attended it (Frith, Laing, and Miola), and we are delighted to include chapters from other interested colleagues (Neal and Syrett). We would like to thank the University of Manchester for granting Alex research leave which enabled her to work on this collection, and the team at Routledge, in particular Mark Sapwell and Sheila McLean, the Biomedical Law and Ethics Library series editor, for supporting this project.

As well as the contributors to this collection, we would like to thank our friends and colleagues within the health care law and ethics community for their encouragement, especially Margot Brazier, Hazel Biggs, Bobbie Farsides, and Penney Lewis. As will be clear from this collection, Penney has been enormously influential in this field, and we are very grateful to her for helping us develop our thinking and for her collaboration and support. Our friends and family continue to be patient and tolerant, and we thank Ciaran and Tony for bearing with us as deadlines loomed and tempers frayed. The support of Janet and Eric Stacey and Adele Richards has, as always, been important to Alex, who would also like to say a special thanks to Sara for being such a brilliant colleague and dear friend. Sara would like to thank Caroline Mitchell, Sian Slater, Gemma Gordon, Jayne Hall, Jo Elliott, and Karen Atherton who have vicariously (and with much bemusement) enjoyed the highs and lows of editing a book. Last but not least, Sara would like to thank Alex for making this project such fun.

Notes on contributors

Sara Fovargue is Reader in Law at Lancaster University, and Co-Director of the Lancaster Centre for Bioethics and Medical Law. Her research mainly centres around two areas, biotechnology and reproduction, and she has explored legal and ethical aspects of clinical research, regulation, and risk. She has published on the legal regulation of xenotransplantation, and issues surrounding consenting to risk, and is interested also in decision-making processes and practices with regard to the 'vulnerable'.

Alexandra Mullock is a Lecturer in Medical Law at the University of Manchester, and joined the School of Law in 2011 after completing her PhD at Manchester, which was funded by the AHRC project on the Impact of the Criminal Law on Health Care Practice and Ethics. Her research has primarily focused on end-of-life law and ethics, and criminal issues in health care law.

Margaret Brazier, OBE, FBA, FMedSci is a Professor of Law at the University of Manchester. She was Editor of the *Medical Law Review* from 2004–2011, and President of the Society of Public Teachers of Law, 1997–1999. Her research focuses on the criminal process and health care, the use of human tissue, patients' responsibilities, the history of medical law, and the ethics of prolonging life in severely disabled fetuses and newborn infants.

Lucy Frith is Programme Director for the MSc, PG Diploma, PG Cert and CPD programmes in health care ethics at the Department of Health Services Research, University of Liverpool. Her research interests are in the ethical and social aspects and implications of health care. Her current research is in the following areas: organisational culture and ethics; knowledge transfer and implementation research; ethical decision-making in practice; reproductive technologies (particularly gamete donor anonymity; embryo disposition; welfare of the child issues); social and ethical aspects of maternity care; and empirical ethics.

Barry Lyons is Clinical Senior Lecturer in Medical Ethics at the School of Medicine, Trinity College Dublin. He is also is a Consultant in Anaesthesia at Our Lady's Children's Hospital. He obtained his PhD in 2011 and has published in a wide range of journals, particularly on the subject of children, law, and ethics.

José Miola is Professor of Medical Law at the University of Leicester. His research interest is in medical law and ethics, and he has published a book with Hart Publishing, entitled *Medical Ethics and Medical Law: A Symbiotic Relationship*. He is Assistant Editor of the *Medical Law Review* and a member of the Editorial Board of *Clinical Ethics*, and a member of the UK Clinical Ethics Network.

Celia Kitzinger is a Professor in the Department of Sociology, University of York, and Co-Director (with Jenny Kitzinger) of the Chronic Disorders of Consciousness Research Centre (cdoc.org.uk), a transdiscliplinary centre exploring social, ethical, philosophical, and legal issues related to the vegetative and minimally conscious states. Their research has been translated into an award-winning multi-media online resource for family support and practitioner training: Family Experiences of Vegetative and Minimally Conscious States (www.healthtalk.org, search 'coma'). Celia is also researching the theory and practice of advance decisions.

Jenny Kitzinger is a Professor and Director of Research, Impact and Engagement in the School of Journalism, Media and Cultural Studies at Cardiff University. She is Co-Director (with Celia Kitzinger) of the Chronic Disorders of Consciousness Research Centre (cdoc.org.uk). She has researched a range of health issues from AIDS to health inequalities, including work around sexual violence which examined the emergence of child sexual abuse as a public issue, the representation of social work intervention scandals, the discovery of 'false memory syndrome', responses to a feminist social awareness advertising campaign, and the development of anti-violence initiatives in schools.

Danielle Griffiths is a Research Fellow in Interdisciplinary Bioethics and Law in the Institute for Science, Ethics and Innovation (iSEI) at the University of Manchester. She joined the Law School at Manchester in 2009 as a Research Fellow on an AHRC funded project examining 'The Impact of the Criminal Process on Health Care Ethics and Practice'.

Mary Neal is Senior Lecturer and Director of Teaching and Learning in the School of Law, University of Strathclyde. She teaches and co-ordinates two Honours classes, Law, Persons and Property (Honours) and Issues in Healthcare Law and Ethics (Honours), in addition to legal theory. Her main research interests are in healthcare law, bioethics, and legal theory, focusing at present on beginning and end of life issues, theories of property, and meta-disciplinary concepts such as dignity, sanctity, and love.

Richard Huxtable is Professor of Medical Ethics and Law, and Director of the Centre for Ethics in Medicine at the University of Bristol. He has held visiting positions at the Ethox Centre in the University of Oxford, the Centre for Biomedical Ethics in the National University of Singapore, and the Hastings Center, New York. A long-standing participant in clinical ethics consultation, Richard is a member of the UHBT Clinical Ethics Advisory Group and a Trustee of the National Council for Palliative Care.

Judy Laing is a Senior Lecturer in the School of Law at the University of Bristol. She has previously taught at Leeds, Liverpool, and Cardiff universities. Her main research and teaching interests are in medical and mental health law and criminal law and justice. Her monograph, *Care or Custody? Mentally Disordered Offenders in the Criminal Justice System* (Oxford University Press, 1999), was awarded the SLS prize for Outstanding Legal Scholarship by a Younger Scholar in 2000. More recently, Judy has assisted with editing and co-authored a chapter in the third edition of *Principles of Medical Law*, which was published by Oxford University Press in 2011.

Cam Donaldson holds the Yunus Chair in Social Business and Health at Glasgow Caledonian University. From 2002–2009, he held the Health Foundation Chair in Health Economics at Newcastle University, where he was founding Director of the Institute of Health and Society and a Professor in the Newcastle University Business School. He held the Svare Chair in Health Economics at the University of Calgary from 1998 to 2002, having first become a Professor of Health Economics in 1996 whilst at the Health Economics Research Unit at the University of Aberdeen.

Rachel Baker is Professor of Health Economics and Deputy Director of the Yunus Centre for Social Business and Health at Glasgow Caledonian University. Her research interests focus on societal values with respect to health care resource allocation and understanding choice. With funding from the Medical Research Council, from 2011–2014 she led research exploring societal perspectives on the relative value of life-extending treatments for people with terminal illnesses.

Neil McHugh is a researcher at the Yunus Centre for Social Business and Health at Glasgow Caledonian University. He is currently completing his PhD on the potential use and impact (particularly health impacts) of microcredit for enterprise in the UK. Alongside his PhD, he was the main researcher on a Medical Research Council funded project exploring societal perspectives on the relative value of life-extending treatments for people with terminal illnesses. He is currently the main researcher on a Chief Scientist Office (NHS Scotland) funded project which aims to provide more definitive evidence of societal preferences in relation to quality adjusted life years (QALYs) gained at the end-of-life relative to QALYs gained from non-terminal health problems, and on the relative value of different types of QALYs gained at the end-of-life.

Keith Syrett is Professor of Law at Cardiff University. His research lies at the intersection of health policy, bioethics, politics, and law. He has a particular interest in decision-making on the allocation of scarce health care resources, and the law's response to this. This was the subject of his 2007 book, *Law, Legitimacy and the Rationing of Health Care* (Cambridge University Press), and is also reflected in extensive work which he has undertaken on institutions and processes of health technology assessment, especially the activities of the National Institute for Health and Care Excellence (NICE).

John Coggon is Professor in Law and the Philosophy of Public Health at the University of Southampton. He is a member of the Research Centre in Health, Ethics and Law, with particular interests in public health ethics and law. His research and teaching interests lie in legal, moral, and political theory, primarily as these concern health and health policy.

1 Introduction

Sara Fovargue and Alexandra Mullock

When a surgeon amputates a diseased leg or removes an inflamed appendix with her patient's consent, she may worry about legal consequences if she makes a serious error and bungles the operation. She may fear being sued, or reported to the General Medical Council, or, in an extreme case and the patient dies, she may be prosecuted for gross negligence manslaughter. But if she does her job well she need not fear any of these possibilities, and so a surgeon should not be concerned about the criminal law. Neither she nor her patients will see the amputation or removal of the appendix as an assault. Yet were it not for the existence of the 'medical exception' which takes 'proper medical treatment' outside the remit of the criminal law, doctors (and surgeons in particular) might be serial criminals. Indeed, the relationship between medical practice and the criminal law is much closer than many realise. The legal justification for bodily invasions in the medical context has developed according to the medical exception to the criminal law discussed by the House of Lords in *R v Brown*[1] and *Airedale NHS Trust v Bland*,[2] and by the Law Commission in 1994.[3] Without the exception, medical and surgical activities may fall within the remit of the Offences Against the Person Act 1861. While the phrase 'proper medical treatment' is seductively simple, the chapters in this collection show that it is, in reality, more complex in its meaning, justification, and application to evolving developments in medicine and changing social attitudes to the body. In fact, it conceals a plethora of issues and influences which combine to determine whether a particular treatment *is* legitimate.

The contributors to this collection explore the notion of a treatment, practice, or procedure being proper medical treatment, and consider the range of diverse factors which might influence whether a particular procedure *is* regarded as acceptable and appropriate in the medical context. Whenever the legitimacy of a new or ethically contentious medical intervention is considered, a range of influences will determine whether the treatment becomes accepted *as* proper medical treatment

1 *R v Brown* [1994] 1 AC 212, HL.
2 *Airedale NHS Trust v Bland* [1993] AC 789, 891, HL.
3 Law Commission, *Criminal Law: Consent and Offences Against the Person: A Consultation Paper*, Consultation Paper No 134 (HMSO, 1994).

and, thus, lawful. The development and introduction of abortion, organ donation, gender reassignment, and non-therapeutic cosmetic surgery have, for example, all raised ethical, legal, and clinical issues. The chapters in this collection encourage the reader to question the way the law, the medical profession, and society interact in order to determine whether a new or ethically contentious procedure is and should be regarded as proper medical treatment. Legal, historical, social, ethical, and professional influences which contribute to the acceptance of a particular procedure are thus considered. A number of issues are addressed, including why some ethically contentious treatments are accepted as 'proper' and others are not, and whether if a doctor is willing to perform a procedure it should be regarded as legitimate simply because it has gained professional approval. The role of patient demand in this regard is considered, as is the balance between doctors as merely servants of the public (and their wants and desires), and their professional autonomy and clinical judgement. The motivations for performing certain treatments are explored, as is whether some medical treatments have become accepted as proper through custom and practice and because some doctors believe that it is better for them, rather than someone else less qualified, to do it. In that case, do doctors believe that *they have* to perform the surgery or provide the treatment, rather than it being a clinical judgement to do so? The financial implications of certain treatments are also noted, in that if the state is willing to fund a treatment, does that automatically make it proper or appropriate?

Penney Lewis has examined the way in which the medical exception to the criminal law regulates medical practice generally,[4] and, in relation to the legitimisation of contraceptive sterilisation, she highlights how applications of the medical exception change over time, sometimes quite rapidly.[5] For example, just over 60 years ago Lord Denning was horrified by the prospect of a man having a vasectomy, declaring it degrading;[6] yet today vasectomy is a common, even mundane, procedure. Judicial conceptions of morality, of what is proper, are important, but, as José Miola explains in Chapter 5, judges have generally been willing to defer to the professional medical assessment of what should be permissible, even when there are obvious risks for patients.[7] Indeed, he suggests that in doing so, a medical exception over ethical matters has, essentially, been created within the civil law. This exception has enabled the medical profession to make decisions about ethical matters, decisions which were outside its sphere of expertise, but Miola contends that the judicial mood has now changed so that decisions are now more patient than doctor focused.

An example of judicial deference to medical practice is living organ donation. The legality (criminality?) of this type of donation was once at issue, until it

4 P. Lewis, 'The medical exception' (2012) 65 *Current Legal Problems* 355.

5 P. Lewis, 'Legal change on contraceptive sterilisation' (2011) 32 *Journal of Legal History* 295.

6 *Bravery v Bravery* [1954] 1 WLR 1169, 1180, CA.

7 J. Miola, 'Moralising medicine: "Proper medical treatment" and the role of ethics and law in medical decision-making' in this collection.

became accepted as a proper practice *by* the relevant professionals, and long before the Human Tissue Act 2004 gave such donation statutory blessing. As Margaret Brazier and Sara Fovargue discuss in Chapter 2, when the meaning of proper medical treatment is dissected, the focus is principally on what *doctors* consider to be within good medical practice, with the state and the courts taking a secondary role in assessing how proper the profession's views are.[8] Yet, as Lucy Frith explores in Chapter 3, the concept of proper medical treatment fluctuates over time and is related to both the internal morality of medicine and the moralities of the social context in which medicine operates.[9] Focusing on the notion of (im)proper medical treatment, she suggests that an evolutionary theory of the internal morality of medicine based on the goals of medicine and concepts of medical professionalism can help to answer the question of what is proper medical treatment.

Clues as to how we arrived at the current balance of power (between the state, the judiciary, and the medical profession) can be found in Chapter 4, where Barry Lyons explores medicine in history and early attempts to gain control over who could do what to whom.[10] Historically, medicine was a purely commercial endeavour, and discerning a clear distinction between a qualified health professional and a 'quack' was difficult if not impossible. As Lyons discusses, if our ancestors had conducted empirical studies at the time they would almost certainly have concluded that medicine was dangerous, if not lethal, and that doctors should be avoided. Fortunately for us, the lack of scrutiny and regulation, together with the high rewards (often financial, but also altruistic) available for practitioners, has propelled developments in medicine to a point where, on balance, the benefits outweigh the risks. Accordingly, the doctor has come to be regarded as a figure deserving not only great respect but also wielding significant power within society. Although, as Miola discusses in Chapter 5, levels of deference to the medical profession have declined in the last few decades, doctors still often have the loudest voice when it comes to persuading the judiciary what should, and should not, be regarded as proper medical treatment, as Brazier and Fovargue also note.

The relationship between fluctuating concepts of proper medical treatment and the inner morality of medicine is further considered by Danielle Griffiths and Alexandra Mullock in Chapter 7, in their exploration of non-therapeutic cosmetic surgery and the medical exception.[11] The evolution of cosmetic surgery from a therapeutic intervention into a non-therapeutic surgical choice, facilitated by doctors working within a rapidly growing commercial industry that is risky yet poorly regulated, raises legal and ethical concerns. Griffiths and Mullock argue that there are compelling reasons to make a distinction between medically necessary surgery,

8 M. Brazier, S. Fovargue, 'Transforming wrong into right: What is "proper medical treatment"?' in this collection.

9 L. Frith, 'What do we mean by "proper" medical treatment?' in this collection.

10 B. Lyons, 'Papist potions and electric sex: A historical perspective on "proper medical treatment"' in this collection.

11 D. Griffiths, A. Mullock, 'The medical exception and cosmetic surgery: Culpable doctors and harmful enhancement?' in this collection.

where the risks and any consequent harm may be justified on public policy grounds, and medically unnecessary cosmetic surgery, where the risks and harms are not justifiable according to *medical* public policy grounds. Considering the influence and authority of the medical profession, a theme which runs throughout this collection, they also explore the influence of the medical profession in perpetuating the evolution of non-therapeutic cosmetic surgery, and question the power accorded to the profession under the medical exception. Griffiths and Mullock thus question whether the medical exception, which renders serious harmful acts lawful in the medical context, should apply to non-therapeutic cosmetic surgery, and they argue that a more robust approach to informed consent is necessary to better safeguard consumers of non-therapeutic cosmetic surgery.

The balance of power between the law and medicine in relation to the acceptance of contentious treatments is explored by Judy Laing in Chapter 10, in the context of mental health treatment.[12] Here, the law talks of 'appropriate' treatment, which is interpreted broadly and subjectively, and there is a lack of clarity concerning the appropriateness of certain treatments. The law permitting compulsory treatment is particularly contentious, and Laing explores how the evolution of the legal framework and consequent medical practices have developed according to the swing of a "pendulum" which sways between legalism and medicalism. She suggests that while the current legal framework aims to balance these alternatives, medical discretion, again, emerges victorious from the battle for power.

Once a procedure is endorsed *as* proper medical treatment it may cease to be wrong, but it does not necessarily and immediately become a right that patients can claim. Indeed, *patient* autonomy may be invisible at this stage, and there may, in fact, be a conflict between what patients want and what they are permitted to receive. The application of the medical exception could, thus, be viewed as a process that may first lead to an intervention which was once seen as wrong becoming permissible, often via changing views among doctors, especially about what constitutes treatment, and then evolving via practice, case law, and, possibly, statute into being a right that patients may claim. There are examples of this across the spectrum of medical treatment. For example, in England and Wales, abortion, at least on grounds of risk to the woman's physical or mental health, is seen by some as a right, and, in much of Europe, there is a broader right to terminate a pregnancy, in the first trimester at least.[13] The practice of medical professionals in England for centuries was to prefer the life of the woman to that of the foetus in extreme cases, and so, to a limited extent, *good* medical practice legalised abortion at the discretion of the doctor and when the life of the woman was at stake.[14] The acquittal

12 J. Laing, 'Doctors' orders? Analysing appropriate medical treatment in mental health law' in this collection.

13 R. Sifris, 'Restrictive regulation of abortion and the right to health' (2010) 18 *Medical Law Review* 185.

14 M. Brazier, 'Can the common law accommodate moral controversy in medicine?: The case of abortion' in A. Alghrani, R. Bennett, S. Ost (eds), *The Criminal Law and Bioethical Conflicts; Walking the Tightrope* (Cambridge University Press, 2012).

of Aleck Bourne in 1938 for terminating the pregnancy of a young victim of rape has been seen by many as crucial to broadening the grounds for lawful abortion in England and Wales, and as a key step to the eventual enactment of the Abortion Act 1967.[15] Yet, the decision paid no regard to the notion of rights. Indeed, Mr Bourne's defence rested on the argument that *good medical practice allowed, even mandated,* his action. Notably, Mr Bourne deplored the view that any police officer could dictate to *him* what he, as a *surgeon,* might do.

In summing up the case to the jury, Macnaughten J was careful to distinguish Bourne's case from another being heard by the court at the same time, where 'a woman without any medical skill or medical qualifications . . . unlawfully used an instrument for the purpose of procuring the miscarriage of a pregnant girl; she did it for money'.[16] In contrast, Mr Bourne was:

> [a] man of the highest skill, [who] openly, in one of our great hospitals, performs the operation . . . as an act of charity, without fee or reward, and *unquestionably believing that he was doing the right thing, and that he ought, in the performance of his duty as a member of the profession devoted to the alleviation of human suffering, to do it.*[17]

The evolution and presentation of abortion in terms of rights, rights that a woman could assert *against* her doctor, and its acceptance *as* proper medical treatment might have resulted in consequences that would dismay Dr Bourne and his colleagues. In Chapter 8, Mary Neal examines the concept of proper medical treatment in relation to lawful abortion, focusing, in particular, on the campaign to decriminalise abortion.[18] Arguing that there is a spectrum of proper medical treatment, she suggests that the status of abortion *as* proper medical treatment depends on a range of factors, including the grounds on which it is performed and public interests considerations. Its status as proper medical treatment can, thus, only be determined on a case-by-case basis. With regards to decriminalising abortion, Neal argues that, at least so far as surgical interventions are concerned, it is impossible to exclude the criminal law completely because the legality of all surgery rests on the medical exception. Thus, caution is required when seeking to amend or abolish the current statutory framework which regulates the provision of abortion.

Similarly, proper medical treatment may, rightly, be a formula to be feared by those opposed to changes in the law with regards to assisted dying, because it may be used to ensure that wrong becomes right, and there is but a short step from there to the point at which what is medicalised then becomes a right. As Richard Huxtable explores in Chapter 9, the ways in which public interest arguments (*my*

15 *R v Bourne* [1939] 1 KB 687.

16 *Bourne* (n 15) 689. Also, 691–692.

17 *Bourne* (n 15) 690, emphasis supplied.

18 M. Neal, 'Locating lawful abortion on the spectrum of "proper medical treatment"' in this collection.

interests, *your* interests, *our* interests?) are explicitly and implicitly deployed to bolster arguments in the 'death on demand' debates present challenges when seeking to balancing these conflicting appeals.[19] He suggests that while these different accounts could all support assisted dying, the courts have so far been resistant to this, and concerns about the intrinsic value of life and claims about the proper role of health professionals trump arguments premised on autonomy. Celia Kitzinger and Jenny Kitzinger also consider the particular challenges of end of life dilemmas in Chapter 6, where they examine the question of what is proper treatment for people with chronic disorders of consciousness (such as those in vegetative or minimally conscious states) from the perspective of the family.[20] In many cases, families' deference to medical opinion soon after the precipitating incident gives way to lay expertise, based on internet research, media accounts, and information sought from personal contacts, and family and medical versions of proper medical treatment can then come to, quite markedly, diverge. They discuss how those closest to the patient may suffer from the responsibility of contributing to medical decision-making over what is 'proper' for their relative, often experiencing terrible conflict over which treatment within the parameters of acceptability (and legitimacy) is the least worst option.

In end of life cases, proper medical treatment may thus be a means of granting the cloak of legality to conduct that which the criminal law has traditionally condemned. For example, in *Airedale NHS Trust v Bland*, for three of the judges the most powerful factor in granting the declaration that it was lawful to withdraw artificial nutrition and hydration was the evidence that medical professional guidelines deemed such a course to be in the best interests of Anthony Bland.[21] It *was* proper treatment when confined within the medical exception. But if the relatives of someone in a permanent vegetative state decided that the doctors were slow in implementing the withdrawal of life support from their relative, and so removed the tubes themselves, they may well face trial for murder even though they would have performed the same act as the doctor. The power of medical practice can also be seen in debates on assisted dying, with some proponents of legalisation arguing for *physician* assisted dying because this falls within the *duty* of the doctor to care. The argument here is that the doctor's duty is to help the patient achieve the death that is the only remaining means of assisting her when pain or grievous disability cannot be alleviated.[22] In this way, medicalisation of the end of life, via the application of proper medical treatment in the medical exception, can be used to make what has been seen as a wrong right.

19 R. Huxtable, 'Death on demand: "Proper medical treatment"?' in this collection.

20 C. Kitzinger, J. Kitzinger, 'Family perspectives on "proper medical treatment" for people in prolonged vegetative and minimally conscious states' in this collection.

21 *Bland* (n 2) 870–871, *per* Lord Goff, 885, *per* Lord Browne-Wilkinson.

22 For example, in the Netherlands euthanasia and physician-assisted suicide were legalised on the basis of falling within a doctor's duty to relieve intractable suffering by providing assisted dying on request when other means of relieving suffering had proved inadequate. See J. Griffiths, H. Weyers, M. Adams, *Euthanasia and the Law in Europe* (Hart, 2008).

Yet, for this very reason opponents of assisted dying equally vehemently reject any case that health professionals' active assistance to help a patient to die *can* be seen as proper medical treatment.[23] They deny claims that palliative care might be inadequate in relieving suffering, and they argue that allowing doctors to help bring about death would, in more than the literal sense, fatally undermine the doctor patient relationship. Proper medical treatment is thus a card that can be, and is, played by both sides of the assisted dying debate. It is notable that in his 2010 guidance on prosecuting assisted suicide cases, the Director of Public Prosecutions (DPP) stated that the fact that the assistor was a health professional *may* be a factor in favour of prosecution.[24] In so doing, the DPP may have sought to distance a policy of compassionate pragmatism from contentions that assisted dying might be seen as part and parcel of good medicine. However, a recent update to the policy by the current DPP,[25] following the *Nicklinson* appeals,[26] confirms that provided a health professional has not exerted pressure on the so-called victim, prosecution is unlikely.[27]

The process of movement from wrong to right can also be observed with interventions which sit on the border of treatment and innovation. As Brazier and Fovargue discuss in Chapter 2, it *does* matter whether a procedure is deemed to be treatment, research, or a new interventional procedure, even though the distinctions between these are not clear cut. Once something is reported as a treatment, on the internet and in the media, there may be pressure or a push to provide that treatment *now* and, even, as a *right*. Some patients, their families, and health interest groups, particularly those with limited treatment choices, may lobby for access to experimental procedures or drugs in development *as treatments* because they represent their only hope of survival or an improved quality of life.[28] While this may be understandable, there are issues with this,[29] and permitting such access may minimise the number of clinical trial participants available and so undermine

23 See e.g. I. G. Finlay, V. J. Wheatley, C. Izdebski, 'The House of Lords Select Committee on the Assisted Dying for the Terminally Ill Bill: Implications for specialist palliative care' (2005) 19 *Palliative Medicine* 444.

24 Director of Public Prosecutions, *Policy for Prosecutors in Respect of Cases of Encouraging or Assisting Suicide* (Crown Prosecution Service, February 2010).

25 DPP (n 24), updated October 2014.

26 *R (on the application of Nicklinson and another) (Apellants) v Ministry of Justice (Respondent); R(on the application of AM)(AP)(Respondent) v The Director of Public Prosecutions (Apellant); R(on the application of AM)(AP) (Respondent) v The Director of Public Prosecutions (Apellant)* [2014] UKSC 38.

27 See further A. Mullock, 'The Supreme Court decision in *Nicklinson*: Human rights, criminal wrongs and the dilemma of death' (2015) 31 *Journal of Professional Negligence* 18.

28 On the involvement of patients in setting the research agenda see S. Woods, P. McCormack, 'Disputing the ethics of research: The challenge from bioethics and patient activism to the interpretation of the Declaration of Helsinki in clinical trials' (2013) 27 *Bioethics* 243; L. Halpin, J. Savulescu, K. Talbot, M. Turner, P. Talman, 'Improving access to medicines: Empowering patients in the quest to improve treatment for rare lethal diseases' (2013) *Journal of Medical Ethics* (advance access online, DOI:10.1136/medethics-2013-101427).

29 See further S. Fovargue, 'The (ab)use of those with no other hope? Ethical and legal safeguards for recipients of experimental procedures' (2013) 22 *Cambridge Quarterly of Healthcare Ethics* 181.

the clinical trial process.[30] Nevertheless, a citizens' jury convened by the University of Glamorgan and supported by Genetic Alliance UK recommended that when determining the risks and benefits of new medicines for serious conditions, *more* weight should be given to psychosocial factors as opposed to primary reliance on biomedical evidence and clinical outcomes.[31] Furthermore, regulators should be *more* permissive for treatments for people with rare and/or serious conditions, especially where there are little or no other treatments available. Such calls have not gone unheard by the government, and in March 2014 the Early Access to Medicines Scheme was announced to 'give patients with life threatening or seriously debilitating conditions access to medications that do not yet have a marketing authorisation when there is a defined unmet medical need'.[32] Similarly, the US Food and Drug Administration has published guidance to 'facilitate and expedite development and review of new drugs, to address unmet medical need in the treatment of a serious or life-threatening condition: fast track designation, breakthrough therapy designation, accelerated approval, and priority review designation', and 'to help ensure that therapies for serious conditions are approved and available to patients as soon as it can be concluded that the therapies' benefits justify their risks'.[33]

In the light of this, it is important to consider the *process* by which it is determined that something *is* proper medical treatment, and can thus be provided to patients, particularly on the National Health Service. This may be another point at which wrongs are transformed into rights. Treatment X may start off as something which society, including medical professionals, thinks of as not acceptable, not something which should be offered to patients or is something that patients should not be able to access themselves. Think of the initial reactions to treatments now (largely) considered as standard, such as organ transplants, gender reassignment, or abortion. But gradually, opinions change, particularly within the medical profession and (nowadays) patients themselves and their supporters/health interest groups. Combined together, these voices can help to shift the view within society regarding treatment X, which starts to become something which it *is* acceptable for doctors to offer, something which it is not always wrong for them to do. The point at which it is acceptable and appropriate for doctors to offer treatment X is not always clear, and so it may not be uniformly offered for

30 M. Chahal, 'Off-trial access to experimental cancer agents for the terminally ill: Balancing the needs of individuals and society' (2010) 36 *Journal of Medical Ethics* 367.

31 Genetic Alliance UK, *New Medicines for Serious Conditions: Weighing the Risks and Benefits – The Verdict of a Jury of Patients* (Genetic Alliance UK, 2011).

32 Medicines and Healthcare Products Regulatory Agency, 'Early Access to Medicines Scheme (EAMS)', available at http://www.mhra.gov.uk/Howweregulate/Innovation/EarlyaccesstomedicinesschemeEAMS/index.htm (accessed 11 December 2014).

33 US Department of Health and Human Services, Food and Drug Administration, Center for Drug Evaluation and Research, Center for Biologics Evaluation and Research, *Guidance for Industry Expedited Programs for Serious Conditions – Drugs and Biologics* (2014) OMB Control No. 0910–0765, 1, references removed.

some time. It may, instead, be something which individual patients must request or push for.[34]

When this shift in thinking and practice is established, the issue for the patient changes and the question becomes *why* is the provision of treatment X something for the *doctor* to decide? Why can the patient not decide for herself whether she has treatment X? If the stamp of approval and respectability has been awarded to treatment X, via its determination *as* proper medical treatment, it becomes debatable why patients are dependent on their doctor's decision as to whether they can have it. This is especially so when notions of what is proper and what is medical may not be a wholly medical opinion or decision, but may be tied up with social and cultural norms, such as with regards to circumcision.

The troubled issue of *who* should get *what* and according to *whom* (and how the *what* is defined) links into wider and ever-pressing concerns regarding health economics. In Chapter 11, Cam Donaldson, Rachel Baker, and Neil McHugh consider how, from an economics perspective, the term proper can be equated to achieving the most benefit from limited resources.[35] They use two principles from economics, opportunity cost and marginal analysis, to assess whether the principles can usefully be brought to bear in deciding on the appropriateness of health interventions. Outlining the challenges for clinicians and health care managers posed by implementing these principles, Donaldson, Baker, and McHugh consider the potential limitations of economists' efficiency-based frameworks. The question of appropriateness also provides the focus for Keith Syrett's discussion in Chapter 12, where he explores how defining certain services and treatments as *inappropriate* offers a means of managing the inevitable and increasingly fraught mismatch between demand and supply.[36] He analyses how English courts have understood the notion of appropriateness against a backdrop of scarce healthcare resources, drawing on insights from systems theory to illuminate the court's evolving approach to determining which treatments should be funded.

The question of what is appropriate, and so worth funding, thus links to the wider determination of what is proper medical treatment. From the question of what the state is willing to pay for (because it is appropriate and satisfies the opportunity costs and marginal analysis tests), to the question of what the state is willing to permit as an exception to the criminal law (because the public policy justification in relation to the value of the treatment demands it), there are a range of private, public, and professional interests which influence whether any particular medical treatment *will* be regarded as legitimate. While the private and public interests engaged by a treatment may vary and be issue-specific, the power of the medical profession in determining what is legitimate is constant and significant.

34 See e.g. the litigation surrounding the provision of Herceptin in England: *R (Rogers) v Swindon NHS PCT* [2006] EWCA Civ 392.

35 C. Donaldson, R Baker, N McHugh, 'The economics of "proper medical treatment"' in this collection.

36 K. Syrett, 'Rationing, resource allocation, and appropriate medical treatment' in this collection.

Where medical expertise is essential, the influence of the profession is necessary and desirable, but, as Miola argues in Chapter 5, when moral, ethical, or social issues are more crucial to the question of whether a treatment should be legitimate, the influence of the profession should be less authoritative.

In Chapter 13, John Coggon reflects on the preceding chapters and identifies four themes which emerge from the interdisciplinary research contained in this collection.[37] First, how assessing the *medical* is often a comparative question in relation to the non-medical *something else*. Second, that what emerges from explorations of the meaning of proper medical treatment reaches beyond the technical legal concept, expanding to a broader medico-legal journey into analysing diverse influences upon the determination and acceptance of a legitimate medical treatment. Third, how different approaches to considering the question of what constitutes proper medical treatment can enrich our understanding of this issue, and, finally, how the objectives of diverse approaches to legal governance are explained and understood. Having identified and explored these themes, Coggon then discusses the importance of this collection, setting it alongside earlier works in the field, in developing a greater understanding of the legitimising influences and complex interests which speak to the question not only of what is proper medical treatment but also to wider concerns in medical law and ethics. He highlights the importance of Lewis's contribution to this field,[38] and reflects on the earlier, significant influence of Ian Kennedy's examination of medical legitimacy.[39]

Coggon also advances some of the key themes emerging in this collection by reference to two associated fields, the philosophy of health and rights theory. He draws out and develops some of the ideas expressed in this collection, in order to add his own valuable contribution to our collective exploration of proper medical treatment. Suggesting that much can be gained by both building on philosophical analyses (such as Kennedy's) and engaging with rights theory in order to categorise conflicting claims, Coggon argues that a plurality of approaches and understandings to the concept of proper medical treatment is necessary. We agree and hope that this collection succeeds in illustrating that no single concept of proper medical treatment will suffice or is, indeed, possible. The multitude and complexity of issues pervading any analysis of the legitimacy of contentious or innovative medical treatment demands an interdisciplinary approach and, as Coggon suggests, one that embraces a subtle range of concepts.

Indeed, as Brazier and Fovargue make clear in Chapter 2, many of the difficult questions in medical and health care law and bioethics involve engaging with what is 'medical' and what is 'proper' or 'appropriate' treatment according

37 J. Coggon, 'Comments and reflections on "proper medical treatment": A case for coherent inconsistency' in this collection.

38 Lewis (n 4).

39 I. Kennedy, 'What is a medical decision?' in I. Kennedy, *Treat Me Right: Essays in Medical Law and Ethics* (Clarendon Press, 1988).

to the particular context of any given health dilemma. Thus, the determination of what is legitimate (and not criminal) and thus 'proper medical treatment' has a profound influence on broader questions beyond the criminal law. Exploring the force and nature of professional medical power which is exerted upon the law and, relatedly, how society values an intervention according to the (sometimes conflicting) interests which are examined through legal, medical, and ethical lenses is thus a valuable exercise, and one which we hope will prompt further interrogation.

2 Transforming wrong into right: What is 'proper medical treatment'?

Margaret Brazier and Sara Fovargue

Introduction

As indicated in the Introduction to this book, many of the things that doctors, particularly surgeons, do would be crimes in England and Wales if performed by someone not medically qualified. Cutting open a patient to check if an organ is diseased, removing that organ, and drawing blood are all activities that cause bodily harm, even grievous bodily harm. For doctors, the law has endorsed a magic mantra that makes these potential wrongs right: the medical exception of 'proper medical treatment'. If a colleague asked us to amputate her left arm and we did so competently and safely, we are likely to face prosecution for causing grievous bodily harm, despite our care and skill, unless we acted in dire necessity to save her from, for example, being trapped in a burning building. Indeed, in *Airedale NHS Trust v Bland*, Lord Mustill said that '[i]f one person cuts off the hand of another it is no answer to say that the amputee consented to what was done'.[1] Yet, if our colleague persuaded a surgeon to do the same and remove her left arm, *he* may be able to invoke the medical exception to shield him from such charges. A surgeon is, of course, better placed than we are to assess our colleague's condition and offer less radical alternatives to amputation. And even if we suppose that our colleague has capacity, her consent to us removing her arm would not change anything; we would still be committing a crime, while a surgeon who acted with her consent does not appear to be doing so.[2] Does this mean, then, that *doctors* who are asked to undertake life-changing, or even life-limiting, procedures can do so without, on the whole, fear of sanction or punishment, whereas legal academics who (competently and safely) perform the same activity must 'go straight to jail'?

In this chapter, we explore the elusive meaning(s) of proper medical treatment, its elements and applications, including distinctions between treatment and innovative therapy, and how far the stance of medical professionals determines such

1 [1993] AC 789, 891, HL.

2 R. C. Smith, 'Body Integrity Identity Disorder: A Problem of Perception?' in A. Alghrani, R. Bennett, S. Ost (eds), *Bioethics, Medicine and the Criminal Law Volume 1: The Criminal Law and Bioethical Conflict: Walking the Tightrope* (Cambridge University Press, 2013); T. Elliott, 'Body dysmorphic disorder, surgery and the limits of consent' (2009) 17 *Medical Law Review* 149.

boundaries. What these three words mean is crucial not only because they transform something 'wrong' into something 'right', but also because, as suggested in the Introduction, a claim of proper medical treatment may go further and affect how society and the law regard not only what is 'right' in society but also what sorts of treatments *become* 'rights' that patients may assert. Thus, for example non-therapeutic sterilisation was once considered unlawful, became viewed as proper medical treatment, and, finally, as an intervention to which women and men might demand as a right.

What is 'proper medical treatment'?

The consent of a person with capacity is a necessary but not sufficient condition for lawful contact with her body.[3] In *R v Brown*, the House of Lords reaffirmed that consent *alone* cannot make lawful the infliction of actual bodily harm,[4] although it might make minor assaults (touching that results in minimal harm) lawful. In that case, convictions for assault occasioning actual bodily harm contrary to section 47 of the Offences against the Person Act 1861 were upheld by the House of Lords (by a majority of three to two) for a group of men who engaged in consensual sadomasochistic practices, for which none required medical treatment for any injury. This was on the basis that, as Lord Lane CJ said in the *Attorney-General's Reference (No. 6 of 1980)*, it was 'not in the *public interest* that people should try to cause or should cause each other actual bodily harm *for no good reason*'.[5] Thus, exceptions to the general rule that consent cannot legitimise the infliction of actual bodily harm centre around this notion of 'good reason', and in *Bland* Lord Mustill stated that a surgeon amputating a diseased hand commits no crime because 'bodily invasions *in the course of proper medical treatment* stand completely outside the criminal law'.[6] Furthermore, the 'category of proper medical treatment . . . *already* stands outside the criminal law',[7] and, for example, operations such as the sterilisation of patients who permanently lack the capacity to consent would amount to 'a most serious crime . . . *unless* the acts of the doctors fell into the *special category of proper medical treatment*'.[8] And in *Brown*, Lord Mustill suggested that if treatment, and surgery in particular, did not constitute a good reason for bodily harm then medicine would risk being a largely criminal enterprise, because 'much of the bodily invasion involved in surgery lies well above the point at which consent could even arguably be regarded as furnishing a defence'.[9] But no crime is committed because '*proper medical treatment*, for which

3 Law Commission, *Criminal Law: Consent and Offences Against the Person: A Consultation Paper*, Consultation Paper No 134 (HMSO, 1994) para. 2.4.
4 [1994] 1 AC 212, HL.
5 [1981] 1 QB 715, 719, CA, emphasis supplied. *Brown* (n 4) 233 (Lord Templeman), 243 (Lord Jauncey), 253 (Lord Lowry), 270 (Lord Mustill), and 278 (Lord Slynn).
6 *Bland* (n 1) 891. Also, 889.
7 *Bland* (n 1) 889, *per* Lord Mustill, emphasis supplied.
8 *Bland* (n 1) 891, emphasis supplied, referring to *Re F (Mental Patient: Sterilisation)* [1990] 2 AC 1.
9 *Brown* (n 4) 266.

actual or deemed consent is a pre-requisite, *is in a category of its own*'.[10] Thus, Lord Mustill makes it clear that proper medical treatment is a specific exception to the norms of criminal liability; so, 'surgical treatment which requires a degree of bodily invasion well on the upper side of the critical level will nevertheless be legitimate *if performed in accordance with good medical practice and* with the consent of the patient'.[11]

Therefore, the criminal law requires that for an intervention to be lawful, and thus not a criminal wrong, significant bodily harm must be more than consensual; it must also be justifiable in the broader public interest. Indeed, in 1925, Lord Atkin opined that 'the mere consent of the patient to an operation which may be considered contrary to *public policy*, or likely to be an *injury to the public generally*, is not such an operation as would relieve the surgeon from [criminal] responsibility'.[12] Nevertheless, consent *is* important 'because it is usually essential to the propriety of medical treatment',[13] and in its 1994 consultation paper on consent and offences against the person, the Law Commission (over)stated that 'doctors are *undoubtedly* exempt from criminal liability for acts done in the course of *lawful* medical or surgical treatment that would otherwise be serious assaults, for instance the amputation of a limb'.[14]

While the medical exception is well established within English and Welsh law, it remains unclear *what* exactly constitutes proper medical treatment which, when coupled with consent, takes the bodily invasion *outside* of the criminal law.[15] In their 1994 consultation paper, the Law Commission referred to Lord Lane CJ in the *Attorney-General's Reference (No 6 of 1980)*, who acknowledged the '*accepted legality* of . . . *reasonable* surgical interference . . . [which] can be justified as . . . [being] needed in the *public interest*'.[16] There appears to be two elements to the medical exception: first, the reasonableness of the activity under consideration, and, second, whether that activity is in the public interest. These elements were not, however, further considered in the Law Commission's 1994 paper, because the Commission did not believe that the exemption of 'lawful medical treatment' depended on consent, and considered that the exemption raised policy issues beyond those that it could address.[17] However, following representations from respondents to that consultation,[18] in their 1995 consultation on consent in the

10 *Brown* (n 4) 266, emphasis supplied. Also, 258–259.

11 *Brown* (n 4) 259, emphasis supplied. Also, see Lord Jauncey and Lord Templeman 245 and 231, respectively.

12 Lord Justice Atkin responding to Lord Riddell, 'The legal responsibility of the surgeon' (1924–25) 19 *Transactions of the Medico-Legal Society* 93, 95, emphasis supplied.

13 *Bland* (n 1) 891, *per* Lord Mustill.

14 Law Commission (n 3) para. 2.4, emphasis supplied.

15 For a historical perspective on the notion of proper medical treatment see B. Lyons, 'Papist potions and electric sex: a historical perspective on "proper medical treatment"' in this collection.

16 *Attorney-General's Reference* (n 5) 719, emphasis supplied; Law Commission, (n 3) para. 1.3.

17 Law Commission (n 3) para. 2.7.

18 Law Commission, *Criminal Law: Consent in the Criminal Law: Consultation Paper No. 139* (HMSO, 1995), para. 8.5. For a discussion on this consultation paper see e.g. P. Alldridge, 'Consent to medical and surgical treatment – The Law Commission's recommendations' (1996) 4 *Medical Law Review* 129.

criminal law the Law Commission confirmed that 'proper' medical treatment or 'reasonable' surgery constituted a defence to charges of causing bodily harm of any degree, *and* even to an intervention resulting in death.[19] Furthermore, 'the exemption for *lawful* medical treatment . . . turns on other matters unrelated to consent, and, in particular, the identification of the *purpose* for which the "treatment" is administered'.[20] The *reason* for the treatment thus appears central to the medical exception. The Commission considered the composition of the medical exception in other jurisdictions,[21] and proposed that statute should provide that 'a person should not be guilty of an offence, notwithstanding that he or she causes injury to another, of whatever degree of seriousness, *if such injury is caused during the course of proper medical treatment or care administered with the consent of the other person*'.[22] While the term proper medical treatment as a whole was not defined, the Commission proposed that 'medical treatment or care':

(a) should mean medical treatment or care administered by or under the direction of a duly qualified medical practitioner;
(b) should include not only surgical and dental treatment or care, but also procedures taken for the purposes of diagnosis, the prevention of disease, the prevention of pregnancy or as ancillary to treatment; and
(c) without limiting the meaning of the term, should also include the following;

 (i) surgical operations performed for the purpose of rendering a patient sterile;
 (ii) surgical operations performed for the purposes of enabling a person to change his or her sex;
 (iii) lawful abortions;
 (iv) surgical operations performed for cosmetic purposes; and
 (v) any treatment or procedure to facilitate the donation of regenerative tissue, or the donation of non-regenerative tissue not essential for life.[23]

The medical exception would, therefore, have two elements: first, the *nature* of the act (proper medical treatment), and, second, *who* performed it (a duly qualified medical practitioner). The Law Commission's proposals to give statutory authority to the medical exception have never been implemented, and while the Commission stated that '[c]*onventional* medical and surgical treatment for a *therapeutic purpose* by *qualified practitioners* gives rise to no particular difficulties',[24] we need to examine, 20 years later, what the elements of the medical exception ('proper',

19 Law Commission (n 18) paras 8.2–8.4.
20 Law Commission (n 18) para. 8.5, emphasis supplied.
21 Law Commission (n 18) paras 8.7–8.11.
22 Law Commission (n 18) provisional proposal 31(1), 206, emphasis supplied. In provisional proposal 32, a similar exception for 'properly approved medical research' was proposed, 206.
23 Law Commission (n 18) provisional proposal 31, 206.
24 Law Commission (n 18) para. 8.25, emphasis supplied.

'medical', 'treatment') mean, as the number of controversial and contested health technologies, practices, and treatments increase, and the boundaries of the medical exception are thereby challenged.

'Proper'

The elements of the medical exception are to some extent interdependent, but breaking them down enables us to question their applicability and usefulness today. 'Proper' could mean that which is performed by someone with the appropriate medical qualifications and/or is a registered medical practitioner, so that *who* performs the act is what matters. In England and Wales, someone without medical qualifications or registered as a medical practitioner *does not* commit a crime simply by practising medicine or even surgery *so long as* she does not represent herself to be a registered and licensed medical practitioner.[25] But, if she extends her 'practice' to surgery involving bodily harm (so, if we amputated our colleague's arm at her request), she, unlike the registered medical practitioner, cannot rely on the medical exception to protect her from a criminal charge.

If this definition of proper is adopted, then only activities which fall within the definition of medical practice or surgery *and* are performed by someone who is medically qualified would be proper medical treatment, and, on the face of it, covered by the medical exception. If these two elements are not met, the activity, procedure, or practice would not (*could not*) be 'proper' medical treatment. Support for this can be found in Gerald Dworkin's suggestion that for surgery to be lawful four conditions should be met, with the fourth one being that the operation is performed by someone with the '*appropriate medical skills*'.[26] And the Law Commission could also 'see no reason at present why unqualified persons should have the benefit of any medical exception, at least so far as surgery is concerned'.[27] We would go further. The *medical* exception should cover *only* the activities of those who are medically qualified. Excluding charlatans and unqualified people from the protection the law gives to those trained and qualified to do the job seems a reasonable intervention in the public good. Whether people should be free to consent to any intervention that they desire performed by anyone they choose is a different matter.

But are we actually starting at the wrong point, that is, asking the wrong question? Should we, instead, be considering whether the criminal law should be involved in this area *at all*? Considering cosmetic surgery in 1995, the Law Commission queried whether this *was* an area in which 'English law unconsciously recognises that the criminal law has no acceptable place in controlling operations

25 Medical Act 1983, ss 49, 49A.

26 G. Dworkin, 'The law relating to organ transplantation in England' (1970) 33 *Modern Law Review* 353, 356–357, emphasis supplied. The other three conditions are that (i) full and free informed consent must be given by the patient, (ii) the operation must be therapeutic, and (iii) there must be a lawful justification for the surgery,

27 Law Commission (n 18) para. 8.14.

performed by qualified practitioners upon adults of sound mind with their consent'.[28] But what of more 'extreme' surgery which is possible today?[29] Commenting on what was, in 1988, highly controversial gender reassignment surgery, Ian Kennedy suggested that while the criminal law was, at that time, unclear on the legality of an operation to reassign a person's gender, the surgery *was* lawful if a number of conditions were fulfilled, including that it was '*performed by experienced practitioners*'.[30] And, for Kennedy, the role of the criminal law should be limited, and this position had long been shared by Glanville Williams, who stated that:

> [i]t may be questioned whether the criminal law has any place in controlling operations performed by qualified practitioners upon adults of sound mind with their consent, whether for reasons of therapy, charity or experiment. *Controls exercised by the medical profession itself should be accepted as sufficient.* If any particularly serious problems arise they should be left for the consideration of Parliament.[31]

Williams contended that provided 'medical procedures' were 'undertaken for genuine therapeutic purposes',[32] the criminal law should not be involved because the decision fell to the patient and her doctor *alone*.[33] Ormrod J in *Corbett v Corbett* agreed with regard to gender reassignment surgery,[34] seemingly arguing that 'the law should be kept out of decision-making'.[35] Nevertheless, long after the decision in *Corbett*, questions have continued to be raised about whether certain medical advances fall within the ambit of proper medical treatment. Such concerns may have inhibited the development of such advances, most notably and for many years, living organ donation where the donor receives no therapeutic benefit.[36] That question is now resolved by statute, and the legality of live donations in England and Wales is unquestionable, provided the legal regime set out in the Human Tissue Act 2004 is complied with. And now that the legality of living

28 Law Commission (n 18) para. 8.30. Also, para. 8.15.

29 See D. Griffiths, A. Mullock, 'The medical exception and cosmetic surgery: Culpable doctors and harmful enhancement?' in this collection.

30 I. Kennedy, 'Transsexualism and single-sex marriage' in *Treat Me Right: Essays in Medical Law and Ethics* (Clarendon Press, 1988) 262, emphasis supplied.

31 G. Williams, *Textbook of Criminal Law* (Stevens & Sons, 1978) 544–545, emphasis supplied.

32 We explore 'therapeutic purposes' further below with regard to ideas of beneficence.

33 Williams (n 31) 545.

34 [1971] P 83.

35 P. Healey, J. Samanta, 'When does the "learning curve" of innovative interventions become questionable practice?' (2008) 36 *European Journal of Vascular and Endovascular Surgery* 253, 256.

36 See e.g. I. Kennedy, A. Grubb, *Medical Law* (3rd edn, Butterworths, 2000) 1755–1759; D Price, *Legal and Ethical Aspects of Organ Transplantation* (Cambridge University Press, 2000) ch. 6; P.D.G. Skegg, 'Medical procedures and two offences against the person' (1976) 16 *Medicine, Science and the Law* 264; P.D.G. Skegg, 'Medical procedures and the crime of battery' [1974] *Crim LR* 693; Dworkin (n 26); E. Davies LJ, 'A legal look at transplants' (1969) 62 *Proceedings of the Royal Society of Medicine* 23.

organ donation is beyond dispute, since the 2004 Act came into force, the number of living donations has risen dramatically.[37]

In seeking to restrict the role of the criminal law in the medical sphere, the Law Commission and others might have been trying to avoid moral and cultural judgements of the sort that led Denning LJ, *obiter*, to contend in *Bravery v Bravery* that non-therapeutic vasectomy was unlawful because it was performed 'so as to enable a man to have the pleasure of sexual intercourse, without shouldering the responsibilities attaching to it'.[38] Such surgery was '*plainly* injurious to the public interest . . . degrading to the man himself . . . injurious to his wife and to any woman whom he may marry, to say nothing of the way it opens to licentiousness'.[39] There was thus 'no just cause or excuse for this operation at all'.[40] In contrast to Denning, Williams was clear that the notion of law as moral policeman was an uncomfortable one;[41] indeed, 'cases in which the moral indignation of the judge is aroused frequently make bad law'.[42]

If we accept, as the law currently does, that the involvement of the criminal law in this matter *is* appropriate, then is *any* procedure carried out by a qualified doctor proper, or does (should?) proper mean more than *who* performs it? We could, instead, define proper as 'appropriate' to the patient, as of benefit to her. Lord Mustill's comments in *Brown* suggest that for English law the crucial issue is beneficence, and the Law Commission declared that:

> [i]t is understandable that the [medical] exemption should not apply, for example, in the case of a surgeon who with an adult patient's consent amputates the patient's arm or leg when there is *no conceivable benefit to be derived from doing so*, and the professionally qualified surgeon would not be permitted to do this by the professional standards by which he or she is bound.[43]

The surgeon who amputates the gangrenous leg acts lawfully because, in so doing, she does a greater good to her patient and society than the harm she causes in the course of surgery. In *Bravery*, Denning LJ was content that '[a]n ordinary surgical operation, *which is done for the sake of a man's health*, with his consent, is, of course, perfectly lawful *because there is just cause for it*'.[44] And in *Corbett*, Ormrod J said that 'if [gender reassignment surgery is] undertaken for *genuine therapeutic purposes*, it is a matter for the decision of the patient and the doctors concerned in his case'.[45] As we have noted, Kennedy argued that the operation *was* lawful as long as it

37 For the latest statistics see NHS Blood and Transplant, 'Statistics', available at http://www.organdonation.nhs.uk/statistics/ (accessed 11 December 2014).
38 [1954] 1 WLR 1169, 1180, CA. Sir Raymond Evershed and Hodson LJ did not agree, 1175.
39 *Bravery* (n 38) 1180, emphasis supplied.
40 *Bravery* (n 38) 1179.
41 G. Williams, 'Consent and public policy' [1962] *Crim LR* 74 and [1962] *Crim LR* 154.
42 G. Williams, *The Sanctity of Life and the Criminal Law* (Faber and Faber, 1958) 103–104.
43 Law Commission (n 3) para. 8.23, emphasis supplied.
44 *Bravery* (n 38) 1180, emphasis supplied. Also see Hodson LJ, 1172.
45 *Corbett* (n 34) 99, emphasis supplied.

was performed by 'experienced practitioners' who concluded 'that there is *at least some risk of harm to the patient if surgery is not performed*',[46] suggesting that the purpose of the surgery is to benefit the patient.[47]

Linking proper medical treatment to beneficence is superficially attractive, but one problem is that it requires the 'good' to be identified and identifiable, and this raises other questions, including who determines whether there is benefit, what benefit means, and from whose perspective the benefit is determined? It is also difficult to define 'health'. When a surgeon removes an inflamed appendix the (therapeutic) benefit to health is obvious. If a surgeon amputates a healthy limb to relieve the acute mental distress of a patient who threatens to chop her own arm off, the benefit may be more disputed. Indeed, Kennedy argued that:

> [t]herapy means more than curing a physical illness, though much more depends on views of social policy than on medical evidence . . . Abortions and sterilizations . . . raise difficulties. They are performed for the most part on healthy patients. They are justified not on the ground of physical illness, but of mental well-being. The decision is made that the patient needs the operation, that it is 'good' for him. The question is what limits exist on this view of what constitutes therapy. The issue comes down to who should decide what is 'good' for the patient, the patient himself, his doctor, or the public through the courts.[48]

In her consideration of the medical exception, Penney Lewis identifies three types of public policy justifications, one of which must be present (along with the patient's consent) for the medical exception to apply. She proposes that ideas of beneficence are identifiable in her first category of 'patient-focused' public policy justifications for allowing someone to consent to a particular medical treatment or procedure.[49] Lewis contends that '[p]atient-focused justifications mandate that the procedure be intended to benefit the patient *or* be therapeutic for the patient', suggesting there is a difference between benefit and therapy which she does not explore further.[50] She draws attention to the use of this patient-focused public policy justification in Criminal Codes in Canada, New Zealand, and some Australian States, noting that while there are variations in this category, the focus is on the patient, with the court's role being to assess whether the procedure was 'reasonable'.[51] In contrast, in England and Wales the role of the court has been different, that is, to decide whether a procedure is intended to benefit the patient, with Ormrod J's comments in *Corbett*, noted above, an example.[52] Benefit is not

46 Kennedy (n 30) 262.
47 See also Lord Atkin (n 12) 95.
48 Kennedy (n 30) 267–268 n 34.
49 P. Lewis, 'The medical exception' (2012) 65 *Current Legal Problems* 355, 357–359.
50 Lewis (n 49) 357, emphasis supplied.
51 Lewis (n 49) 357–359.
52 *Corbett* (n 34).

determined by the patient; rather, '[t]he benefit must be to the patient's life or physical or mental health . . . [and] the focus must be on the *doctor's* intention to benefit the patient rather than actual benefit'.[53] So, 'proper' could be determined in relation to the benefit to the patient which is determined by the intention of the doctor. Doctors would thus be the ultimate arbiters of whether a procedure or treatment *is* proper medical treatment, and this, in some ways, brings us back to the first possible definition of proper.

This may seem relatively unproblematic, but with controversial and contested procedures, liminal treatments at the edge of medical practice, there will be doubts as to whether *that* procedure *is* therapeutic for *that* patient or whether the benefit goes (and can go) wider, to another person or society.[54] If benefit is stretched to include the latter, then the public policy justification for allowing a patient to consent to bodily harm has moved from being patient focused to being 'public focused'.[55] This then moves us into Lewis's second type of public policy justification, which is 'generally broader than a patient-focused justification, ranging from "just cause or excuse" to "lawful purpose" to the "public interest"'.[56] The medical exception is thus just one strand of a broader notion of public good legitimising what would otherwise be criminal assaults. Recall Lord Lane CJ's comments above in the *Attorney-General's Reference (No 6 of 1980)*,[57] and he confirmed that while 'ordinarily an act consented to will not constitute an assault', the question to be decided was 'at what point does the *public interest* require the court to hold otherwise?'[58] The answer was that 'it is not in the *public interest* that people should try to cause, or should cause, each other actual bodily harm *for no good reason*'.[59] Thus, there might be a good reason, a just cause or excuse, to allow a patient to consent to a medical procedure which is not based on the benefit which may accrue to her individually, such as when we permit healthy volunteers to participate in non-therapeutic research.

'Proper' would then be determined by considering whether there was some wider public interest or public good which would ensue from allowing a patient to consent to a particular type of bodily harm, such as live organ donation. It would align medical and surgical treatment with other activities for which the common law allows that public interest justifies consensual bodily harm. So, despite the fact they involve people inflicting violent contact on each other, neither boxing nor rugby are illegal because sports such as these have been deemed to confer benefits (public and personal) which outweigh any harm or risk of harm.[60] They *are* in the public interest *and* proper. One of us has questioned the justification for boxing,

53 Lewis (n 49) 358, emphasis supplied.
54 Lewis (n 49) 358.
55 Lewis (n 49) 359.
56 Lewis (n 49) 359, references removed. Also, 359–362.
57 *Attorney-General's Reference* (n 5). Also, see Denning LJ in *Bravery* (n 38) 1180.
58 *Attorney-General's Reference* (n 5) 719, emphasis supplied.
59 *Attorney-General's Reference* (n 5) 719, emphasis supplied.
60 *Attorney-General's Reference* (n 5).

in particular, as being in the public interest elsewhere,[61] but the idea that public interest can be used to *prevent* an autonomous choice and to police the way in which we can exercise choices, as occurred in *Brown*, requires consideration. It is inconsistent that contact sports, despite the damage they may cause, are deemed acceptable in the public interest, while obtaining sexual pleasure via sadomasochistic practices, conducted in private spaces and requiring no medical treatment, are not. Once we mount the unruly horse of public policy the need for any sort of justification for consensual harm comes into question.

Lewis's final category for allowing someone to consent to a particular procedure or treatment under the medical exception is professionally focused public policy justifications which rely on notions of '*proper* medical treatment', '*reasonable* surgical interference', and '*necessary* surgery'.[62] Such adjectives suggest 'some role for a court in evaluating medical practice', and that a 'more professionally focused justification simply reflects "good" or "accepted" medical practice'.[63] So how may good medical practice be evidenced? We suggest there are two ways. First, as Lewis notes,[64] the General Medical Council's guidance document *Good Medical Practice* describes in broad terms what is expected of doctors registered with the Council.[65] Second, the oft-cited statement of McNair J in *Bolam v Friern Hospital Management Committee* that '[a] doctor is not guilty of negligence if he has acted in accordance with a practice accepted as proper by a responsible body of medical men skilled in that particular art',[66] concedes to the profession the definition of good practice.[67] Proper could thus be defined with regard to the *Bolam* test, as refined by the House of Lords in *Bolitho*.[68] Thus, provided a body of medical opinion agrees that the proposed procedure *is* proper then this element of the medical exception will be fulfilled. Jonathan Montgomery has suggested that '[i]t is . . . probable that surgical procedures *accepted by the medical profession* may legitimately be consented to unless there is an express statutory legal prohibition'.[69] We consider the use of the *Bolam* test below, with regards to the meaning of 'treatment'; here we note that adopting this definition of proper would largely entrust this element of the medical exception to the judgement of the medical profession itself, and the implications of adopting this approach would need careful consideration.

61 M. Brazier, S. Ost, *Bioethics, Medicine and the Criminal Law, Volume 3: Bioethics and Medicine in the Theatre of the Criminal Process* (Cambridge University Press, 2013) 45–52.

62 Lewis (n 49) 362–364, emphasis supplied for latter.

63 Lewis (n 49) 362–363. Also, see Lord Mustill in *Brown* (n 4) 258–259.

64 Lewis (n 49) 363.

65 General Medical Council (GMC), *Good Medical Practice* (GMC, 2013), updated 29 April 2014.

66 [1957] 2 All ER 118, 122.

67 For a fascinating exploration into the role of the medical profession in effecting legal change see P. Lewis, 'Legal change on contraceptive sterilisation' (2011) 32 *Journal of Legal History* 295.

68 The House of Lords held that a doctor did not automatically escape liability for negligence just by producing evidence from other experts who confirmed that the doctor's opinion accorded with 'sound medical practice'. That opinion must also have a 'logical basis', and the experts must have reached 'a defensible conclusion': *Bolitho v City and Hackney Health Authority* [1998] AC 232, 241–242, HL, *per* Lord Browne-Wilkinson.

69 J. Montgomery, *Health Care Law* (2nd edn, Oxford University Press, 2003) 232, emphasis supplied.

Kennedy suggests that:

> we in the United Kingdom . . . have had a tradition of leaving the regulation and control of medical practice largely to the medical profession. Regarding the problems [caused by medical technology] as merely technical, we have trusted the profession, and been unwilling to interfere too closely at decisions arrived at.[70]

Indeed, the *civil* law has been reluctant to interfere with doctor's decisions, and relies on the *Bolam* test and doctors to set the legal standard of care. Additionally:

> in the case of the *criminal* law, it is rare in the extreme to see a doctor prosecuted for practising what other people regard as valid treatment. *If responsible, reputable doctors are prepared to say that some procedure is adequate or proper treatment, then that is normally sufficient for the law.*[71]

Thus, medicine in general, and proper medical treatment in particular, could be seen as a private matter, that is, one for discussion between doctor and patient, with the law (especially the criminal law) limited in its involvement.[72] However, as Kennedy neatly charts, medicine as a whole is no longer seen in this way, because the ethical and social implications and effects of medical procedures have come to be more widely recognised and acknowledged.[73] It is, therefore, unsurprising that we are no longer prepared to leave such decisions to medical professionals (or the medical profession) alone, or in conjunction with their professional bodies, and/or their patients.

'Medical'

We have considered how 'proper' can be determined and have canvassed the possibilities of looking at who performs the treatment, the intended outcome, notions of public policy and public interest, or using the *Bolam* test, but how do 'proper' and 'medical' sit or fit together? Does 'medical' add anything to the debate, or does it simply reinforce the simplistic argument that if it is done by a doctor and permitted by the patient, then there is no crime. The Law Commission's recommendation that 'proper medical treatment or care . . . administered by or under the direction of a *duly qualified medical practitioner*' and with consent would be privileged, did just that.[74] The Law Commission thus distinguished between 'those whom [the Commission] trusts to engage in the consensual infliction of

70 I. Kennedy, 'Emerging problems of medicine, technology, and the law' in *Treat Me Right: Essays in Medical Law and Ethics* (Clarendon Press, 1988) 5.

71 Kennedy (n 70) 6, emphasis supplied.

72 Williams (n 31).

73 Kennedy (n 70) 6–8.

74 Law Commission (n 18) Recommendation 31, emphasis supplied.

harm and those who are not trusted'.[75] Those with medical qualifications *could* be trusted, and so 'the cases in which there is no necessary benefit to the patient are resolved by making lawful what the registered medical practitioner currently does, and unlawful what he/she does not do'.[76] The *profession* of the person doing the act seems to be crucial, rather than any benefit which may ensue from that act. On this interpretation, medicalisation relates to and means something performed by someone with a medical qualification, and operates to legitimise otherwise prohibited conduct. Patient autonomy is secondary. It matters not what the patient is willing, able, or demanding to consent to; *only* procedures performed by a doctor and approved by doctors lie within the medical exception.

But such a proposition cannot withstand analysis. First, if the law were to free us from any limitations on what we may do to our bodies this may not be unduly problematic for many patients, and most bioethicists, because the emphasis should be on the free choice of the individual, and not the beneficence or status of the doctor. Imagine an actress who believes that if she is a partial amputee she will obtain more roles; why should she not have the right to seek this end? And if she may do so lawfully, why can she not then commission the 'technician' of her choice to remove that limb? She *may* choose an orthopaedic surgeon, but the surgeon's role is merely as a technician, as a plumber working on flesh instead of blocked pipes. There is no need for this to be seen as a medical matter, beyond the actual technical physical act of the amputation.[77] The actress *could*, in theory, select anyone she believes is qualified to remove her limb, even legal academics.

Second, a claim of 'if it's done by a doctor then it's OK' ignores the fact that there are a number of bodily (quasi-medical) interventions not (as yet) banned in England and Wales but which entail bodily harm and *are not performed by doctors*. The recent report by Sir Bruce Keogh on the regulation of cosmetic procedures details the administration of assorted substances by unqualified practitioners, and seeks to bring most cosmetic procedures back to the domain of medicine so that they would only be proper *and* lawful if performed by a doctor.[78] And infant male circumcision is currently carried out by non-medical practitioners;[79] therefore, an exception limited to doctors would mean that all circumcisions were medicalised, even if they were carried out for cultural or religious reasons. Requiring a doctor to administer Botox or circumcise a baby may seem to be a safety measure and to fit within the Law Commission's rationale that doctors may be trusted to do what is proper, but what would the consequences be? It could be that once confined to the medical exception, the procedure would cease to be seen as proper, and thus be deemed unlawful.

75 Alldridge (n 18) 137.

76 Alldridge (n 18) 137–138.

77 On 'medical' matters see I. Kennedy, 'What is a medical decision?' in *Treat Me Right: Essays in Medical Law and Ethics* (Clarendon Press, 1988). Also, Montgomery (n 69) 16.

78 Review Committee, *Review of the Regulation of Cosmetic Interventions: Final Report* (Department of Health (DH), 2013).

79 As discussed in e.g. Brazier and Ost (n 61) 51–52; M. Fox, M. Thomson, 'Short changed? The law and ethics of male circumcision' (2005) 13 *International Journal of Children's Rights* 161.

Imagine that June (5′ 6″ tall and weighing 7 stone) asks for a gastric band to become a size zero. National Health Service criteria classify June as underweight.[80] Will such a procedure be regarded as medical as long as a registered medical practitioner performs it? We suggest that it must not be if it may significantly endanger June's life or health for no good reason. A gastric band for June for vanity only may be seen as not medical or not proper; it would not be good practice according to the views of the profession. *Doctors* offering radical cosmetic interventions should thus not be free (or at least not protected by the medical exception) to give patients what they want when an intervention creates a risk of harm not balanced by any objective benefit, *even if* patients can pay for what they want. Consider a procedure which is sought by a patient with compromised physical health (so the risks of any surgery are greater) but who is willing to consent to that surgery in order to achieve the desired result. Most doctors would refuse to perform it on the basis of risk, but Dr Slash agrees to the request, claiming that the benefit to the patient's mental health justifies those risks (and the request, of course, increases Dr Slash's profits).[81] Dr Slash's status as a medical practitioner alone will not render the procedure medical if professional practice deems it not to be proper. Dr Slash must make out her case that *for this patient*, despite the risks, the medical benefit justifies the risk of harm. She cannot simply do what the patient wants and pocket the cheque. On this reading then, if it is performed by a medically qualified professional, *and* it is within professional norms, *and* the patient may benefit from the procedure, then the procedure can be interpreted as proper 'medical' treatment, and so falls within the medical exception. However, if certain treatments or procedures currently carried out by non-medical practitioners are (re)located within the domain of medicine, practices tacitly accepted today might be deemed *not* to be properly medical (by health professionals), and thus not lawful, or not lawful within the medical exception.

Of course, the boundaries of proper medical treatment and the medical exception are not set by an exclusively physical assessment of risk and benefit. At the turn of this century there was an outcry when it was made public that a surgeon, Robert Smith, had amputated healthy limbs at the request of the patients. Smith argued that in so acting he was meeting the patients' mental health needs and *preventing* greater harm from the person attempting to remove their own limb or allowing someone less qualified to do so.[82] In making this argument, Smith could have relied on Peter Skegg, who argues that 'conduct which benefits bodily health should not be regarded as causing bodily harm',[83] noting that it was held in *Miller* that injury to a person's 'state of mind for the time being' comes within

80 NHS Choices, 'Height/weight chart', available at http://www.nhs.uk/Livewell/healthy-living/Pages/height-weight-chart.aspx (accessed 11 December 2014).

81 Elliott (n 2) 178–181.

82 Smith (n 2). For similar arguments with regard to gender reassignment when such procedures were not common or widely accepted, see e.g. D. Meyers, *The Human Body and the Law: A Medico-Legal Study* (Edinburgh University Press, 1970) 66–67.

83 P.D.G. Skegg, *Law, Ethics and Medicine: Studies in Medical Law* (Clarendon Press, 1984) 31.

the definition of actual bodily harm.[84] Thus, 'a medical procedure should not be regarded as causing bodily harm if physical detriment is outweighed by psychological benefit'.[85] Does this mean that no firm boundary may be applied to medical procedures? What if someone wanted both of their eyes removed, on the basis that this would meet their mental health needs? Could Smith's argument prevail there too? We allow people to consent to and undergo procedures which may carry with them immediate and/or long-term significant risks, including from the surgical procedure itself and the accompanying anaesthesia. Indeed, cosmetic surgery is seen by many as proper medical treatment, and those faced with requests for such interventions are unlikely to require that the patient must prove that they will benefit from it, despite the risks involved. Are such procedures legitimate, then, because they fall within the boundaries of reasonable and responsible practice?[86] If this is so, what are limits of such practices and treatments, and who decides this and how? Do we go back to the idea that proper medical treatment must be endorsed by reasonable and responsible medical opinion, with, in essence, the *Bolam* test being met?[87]

Remember June. If a surgeon agreed to give her the desired, but not medically needed, gastric band and June consented to the surgery, might this constitute a criminal assault if the majority of the surgeon's peers disagreed with his clinical judgement that the band was in June's best interests and he could not advance a logical and defensible case why in this instance the surgery was justified by exceptional factors? If the men in *Brown* could not consent to harm for their sexual pleasure, can June consent to interventions that clearly fall outside any objective definition of proper medical treatment, in her search for beauty as a size zero? Simply dressing her case up as medical will not, and cannot, surely suffice.

'Treatment'

Finally, what does the word 'treatment' add to our understanding of the medical exception? The extent to which doctors define treatment echoes debates about the meaning of 'proper' and 'medical'. As Kennedy stated, 'the assumption was made that, if something was described as treatment, it was *ipso facto* justified. The word 'treatment' was enough. And treatment was what the doctor said was treatment. The law did not enquire further.'[88] This is now unlikely to be accepted as a sufficient justification or explanation because 'we are not as ready as we once were to accept the doctor's, or the doctor's and patient's, words, or simply the use of the word "treatment", as conclusive of the propriety of any particular form of conduct'.[89] Indeed, 'the word "treatment" is not only descriptive, it is also prescriptive;

84 [1954] 2 QB 282, 292.
85 Skegg (n 83) 31.
86 See further Griffiths and Mullock (n 29).
87 *Bolam* (n 66).
88 Kennedy (n 70) 8.
89 Kennedy (n 70) 8.

it has a normative quality';[90] as such, more than just the stamp of the medical profession is needed to determine that something *is* treatment.

If we deem June's gastric band to be *treatment* for her obsession with being a size zero and thinner than Victoria Beckham, then who are we to say that the gastric band does not fall within the medical exception of proper medical treatment and that she cannot have it if a surgeon agrees to perform it? The boundary of treatment is as unclear as boundaries regarding proper and medical, and it generates additional problems when we are concerned with new cutting edge procedures and techniques. This is because once the boundary between treatment and research is crossed, external regulation of what is legitimate kicks in. But this boundary is also not well defined. We can say with some confidence that a doctor who engages in a randomised control trial to test her hypothesis that removing the appendix cures bulimia would fall outside any treatment exception, even if she has the participants' consent. However, in reality, cases are unlikely to be this clear, but rather are likely to sit in the grey area which is notoriously harder to classify.

The words 'treatment', 'therapy', and 'practice' are often used to cover 'standard', 'innovative', 'novel', 'experimental', or 'new' procedures and techniques,[91] but we have to distinguish between these terms because of the regulatory consequences of falling within a particular category.[92] Indeed, Patricia Healey and Jo Samanta note that '[i]nnovation . . . sits in a perceptible lacuna, in that regulation exists largely at a personal, professional level'.[93] The terms treatment and therapy suggest that a procedure has been *shown* to benefit the recipient, and if a procedure is deemed to be treatment then it will fall within an individual doctor's clinical judgement and discretion as to whether to provide it; this is a discretion which the courts are reluctant to interfere with.[94] Furthermore, a doctor providing treatment may be able to exercise her therapeutic privilege with regards to information disclosure,[95] whereas that privilege is unlikely to be held to operate in situations of innovation or research. Importantly, 'labelling a procedure only as therapy tends to evade prospective independent evaluation, regulation and on-going monitoring'.[96]

The aim of treatment and therapy is to benefit *that particular patient*, with research seeking to 'derive *generalizable* new knowledge by addressing clearly

90 Kennedy (n 70) 8.

91 On the legal and ethical issues raised by innovative surgery see e.g. J. Johnson, W. Rogers, 'Innovative surgery: the ethical challenges' (2012) 38 *Journal of Medical Ethics* 9; Healey and Samanta (n 35).

92 For further discussion see S. Fovargue, *Xenotransplantation and Risk: Regulating a Developing Biotechnology* (Cambridge University Press, 2012) ch. 3; T. E. Chan, 'Legal and regulatory responses to innovative treatment' (2013) 21 *Medical Law Review* 92.

93 Healey and Samanta (n 35) 257.

94 See e.g. *R (Burke) v General Medical Council* [2005] EWCA Civ 1003; *Portsmouth Hospitals NHS Trust v Wyatt and another* [2005] EWCA Civ 1181 (Fam); *Re J (A Minor) (Child in Care: Medical Treatment)* [1992] 3 WLR 507, CA.

95 As recognised in, e.g. *Sidaway* [1985] AC 871, HL; *Smith v Tunbridge Wells Health Authority* [1994] 5 Med. LR 334; *Pearce v United Bristol Healthcare NHS Trust* [1999] PIQR 53, CA; *Chester v Afshar* [2004] UKHL 41.

96 D. Price, 'Remodelling the regulation of postmodern innovation in medicine' (2005) 1 *International Journal of Law in Context* 121, 130.

defined questions with systematic rigorous methods'.[97] The focus is not on the individual patient/participant per se but on what can be learnt from the group of research participants of which the patient/participant is a part. As a research participant, the patient stands outside of the traditional doctor patient relationship, even if her doctor is involved in the research. The research will also be subject to ethical approval prior to beginning, and the project will be monitored and evaluated during its lifetime. Specific legal rules and ethical guidelines regulate how research is conducted.[98] What, then, of 'experimental medicine' or 'innovative practice'? Such terms have no settled definition in England and Wales, but the Medical Research Council states that experimental medicine is 'a broad term' which refers to '[i]nvestigation[s] undertaken in humans, relating where appropriate to model systems, to identify mechanisms of pathophysiology or disease, or to demonstrate proof-of-concept evidence of the validity and importance of new discoveries or treatments'.[99] Experimental medicine 'precedes and informs the development of late phase clinical trials'.[100] The Royal College of Physicians suggests that 'the distinction between medical research and innovative medical practice derives from intent',[101] and that:

> [w]hen a clinician departs in a *significant way* from standard or accepted practice entirely for the benefit of a particular individual patient, and with the patient's consent, *the innovation need not constitute research, though it may be described as an experiment in the sense that it is novel and unvalidated.*[102]

If this is so, how can experiments on people outside of the regulatory system ever be seen as proper, and if not proper or validated in the research context, may such experiments be criminal?

In *Simms v Simms*, Butler-Sloss P used the terms 'untried *treatment*', 'pioneering *treatment*', 'experimental *treatment*', and 'innovative *treatment*' to describe using Pentosan Polysulphate (PPS) for two patients with probable variant CJD who lacked capacity.[103] The High Court declared that it was lawful, and in their best interests,

97 DH, *Research Governance Framework for Health and Social Care* (2nd edn, DH, 2005) para. 1.10, emphasis supplied.

98 See e.g. World Medical Association, *Declaration of Helsinki Ethical Principles for Medical Research Involving Humans* (1964, amended 2013); Council for International Organizations of Medical Sciences, World Health Organization, *International Ethical Guidelines for Biomedical Research Involving Human Subjects* (Council for International Organizations of Medical Sciences, 2002); GMC, *Good Practice in Research and Consent to Research* (GMC, 2010, updated 2013); Royal College of Physicians (RCP), *Guidelines on the Practice of Ethics Committees in Medical Research with Human Participants* (4th edn, Royal College of Physicians, 2007).

99 Medical Research Council (MRC), 'Experimental Medicine', available at http://www.mrc.ac.uk/research/initiatives/experimental-medicine/ (accessed 11 December 2014).

100 MRC (n 99).

101 RCP (n 98) para. 3.4.

102 RCP (n 98) para. 3.5, emphasis supplied.

103 *Simms v Simms and another; A v A and another* [2002] EWHC 2734 (Fam), paras 48, 51, 57, emphasis supplied.

to provide PPS to these patients, even though it was not licensed for this purpose and pre-clinical research had not yet been validated.[104] Butler-Sloss P stated that it was 'in one sense unclear' whether using PPS in this situation came within the *Bolam* test because it was untried and the pre-clinical research was unvalidated,[105] and so it could not be said to be treatment which a responsible body of medical practitioners would endorse. However, she was adamant that the *Bolam* test

> 'ought not to be allowed to inhibit medical progress. And it is clear that if one waited for the "*Bolam* test" to be complied with to its fullest extent, no innovative work such as the use of penicillin or performing heart transplant surgery would ever be attempted'.[106]

As the High Court had 'evidence from responsible medical opinion which does not reject the [unvalidated pre-clinical] research',[107] Butler-Sloss P was satisfied that 'consistent with the philosophy that underpins the "*Bolam* test", . . . there *is* a responsible body of relevant professional opinion which supports this innovative *treatment*'.[108] Thus:

> it [could not] be said that in principle this is *treatment* which is clearly futile or that it would not, in suitable cases be proper to give the PPS *treatment* to those suffering from prion disease, and I am therefore satisfied that the proposed PPS *treatment* complies with the '*Bolam* test'.[109]

The use of PPS was, however, subject to analysis of the seriousness of the risks and the degree of potential benefit.[110]

Although the precedent value of *Simms* is unclear,[111] in *An NHS Trust v J*, the High Court was asked to authorise the use of zolpidem, a sleeping pill, on a patient in a permanent vegetative state (PVS) prior to the withdrawal of artificial nutrition and hydration.[112] The Official Solicitor, representing J, objected to the withdrawal but requested the use of zolpidem following the publication of an article which described three patients in PVS who showed temporary increases in consciousness after receiving zolpidem.[113] Sir Mark Potter, then President of the Family Division, approved this request and, along with the only expert consulted by the court, spoke of it in terms of a 'possible course of *treatment*',[114] and as a '*trial*

104 *Simms* (n 103) para. 48.
105 *Simms* (n 103) para. 48.
106 *Simms* (n 103) para. 48.
107 *Simms* (n 103) para. 48.
108 *Simms* (n 103) para. 51, emphasis supplied.
109 *Simms* (n 103) para. 58, emphasis supplied.
110 *Simms* (n 103) para. 51.
111 J.K. Mason, G.T. Laurie, *Mason and McCall Smith's Law and Medical Ethics* (9th edn, Oxford University Press, 2013) 667.
112 [2006] EWHC 3152 (Fam).
113 *An NHS Trust v J* (n 112) para. 15; R. Clauss, W. Nel, 'Drug induced arousal from the permanent vegetative state' (2006) 21 *NeuroRehabilitation* 23.
114 *An NHS Trust v J* (n 112) para. 20, emphasis supplied. Also, paras 18, 23, 30, 31.

of treatment'.[115] Yet, it is hard to see that zolpidem could be said to meet the usual understanding of the *Bolam* test, with only one expert consulted and one report on its use published. Indeed, as Lewis suggests, the expert's support for proceeding with zolpidem appears to be 'based more on the absence of risk to J than on any positive opinion about the research'.[116] As such, it exemplifies a patient-focused approach to the meaning of proper medical treatment.[117]

These cases suggest that experimental treatment (which is focused on a particular patient) *can* be offered in England and Wales without a significant risk of criminal or civil liability, provided that the clinician judges that it is appropriate to do so, the *Bolam* test as interpreted in *Simms* is met, and, presumably, that the patient consents or, if they lack capacity, it is in their best interests to receive it. It is thus legal to provide such treatments *outside* the regulatory framework which exists for clinical trials and other forms of medical research, and so, for example, research ethics committee approval is not required, and, of course, in many cases time constraints would make an application for such approval practically unfeasible. This seems to be going beyond the Law Commission's statement that 'conventional medical . . . treatment for a therapeutic purpose by qualified practitioners gives rise to no particular difficulties'.[118] Rather, if *doctors* think the proposed new or innovative or experimental treatment *is* 'proper', that is enough. Does that mean that doctors can simply classify experimental procedures *as* treatment and avoid the regulations governing research at will? That cannot be right.

Let us envisage an experimental treatment for motor neuron disease that a reasonably large number of neurologists and neurosurgeons believe is effective, but they are advised that approval for a clinical trial will require prior non-human animal studies and may take at least three years. The procedure is, however, invasive, painful, and likely to fail in 10 per cent of patients. With the consent of the patients, the doctors press ahead. In assessing if the procedure is a criminal assault or within the medical exception, even a responsible body of opinion *cannot* de facto frame the law.[119] To bring an innovative or experimental procedure within the medical exception, objective evidence *must* exist which demonstrates that the procedure *is* the best course of action for *that* particular patient. It appears that this was the aim of Lord Saatchi's Medical Innovation Bill which was working its way through the parliamentary process during 2014–15. Saatchi was concerned that the threat of a medical negligence claim inhibited doctors from offering patients a last hope of innovative treatment. The fear of criminal liability would, if real, undoubtedly have a greater effect. But we suggest that these fears are misguided and that the Bill is unnecessary. The criminal law, via the medical exception, prioritises the duty of beneficence to patients, and a proper interpretation of the *Bolam* test and existing best practice already *allows* responsible innovation. It is thus difficult

115 *An NHS Trust v J* (n 112) para. 23, emphasis supplied. Also, paras 18, 21, 22, 30–32.

116 P. Lewis, 'Withdrawal of treatment from a patient in a permanent vegetative state: judicial involvement and innovative "treatment"' (2007) 15 *Medical Law Review* 392, 398.

117 Lewis (n 49).

118 Law Commission (n 24).

119 See further S. Fovargue, 'Oh pick me, pick me: selecting participants for xenotransplant clinical trials' (2007) 15 *Medical Law Review* 176.

to understand the mischief the Bill was designed to address. Moreover, the Bill might have been dangerous for patients if it gave the impression that research regulations could be overridden at will.

Where are we now?

Possible definitions of the elements of the medical exception in the form of proper medical treatment are, we suggest, circular, and all roads lead us to the medical profession and medical professionals themselves. While this may be acceptable in some circumstances, it may, on occasion, leave patients unprotected. And what if patients are *demanding* certain treatments or procedures?[120] Although there is a general sense that the criminal law should not be involved in medical practice ('a well-intentioned doctor should not be treated as a common criminal'),[121] could we look to an older, less well-known offence to assist us here? In *Brown*, Lord Mustill explicitly rejected limiting the capacity to consent to self-harm on the basis of the ancient crime of maim/mayhem, declaring that crime 'obsolete'.[122] Maim was committed whenever the infliction of bodily harm resulted in 'such a hurt of any part of a man's body whereby he is rendered less able, in fighting, either to defend himself or to annoy his adversary'.[123] A third party or the person himself could commit the offence of maim. As one of us has noted elsewhere, while this offence may not sit well in today's society as a justification for not allowing consent as a defence to assault, it is at least transparent.[124] It would also have the additional benefit of setting a higher bar to limit consent than that of public interest as espoused in *Brown*. Indeed, '[t]he men convicted in *Brown* suffered no loss of body part or permanent disability; they remained fit to fight'.[125]

The parameters of maim thus might allow some clearer delineation of the limits of the medical exception. Kennedy noted that maim was not raised as a possible charge when gender reassignment surgeries were first performed in the 1950s, even though '[r]emoving surgically various parts of the body such that the patient is thereafter irreparably changed, and some would say disabled, seems to me to be basically a question of maim'.[126] Nevertheless, we suggest that 'it is useful to bear the past existence of this offence in mind in any analysis of the limits of the ability to consent to treatment that has no apparent justification'.[127] So, for example, cosmetic surgery even of a highly invasive and risky nature might be lawful

120 The courts are currently clear on this, see *Burke* (n 94). Alternatively, for discussion of *families'* perspectives on what is proper medical treatment see C. Kitzinger, J. Kitzinger, 'Family perspectives on "proper medical treatment" for people in prolonged vegetative and minimally conscious states' in this collection.

121 Lewis (n 49) 371.

122 *Brown* (n 4) 262.

123 *Hawkins' Pleas of the Crown*, 8th edn, vol. 1, ch. 15, 107.

124 Brazier and Ost (n 61) 46.

125 Brazier and Ost (n 61) 46.

126 Kennedy (n 70) 7.

127 Law Commission (n 18) para. 8.23.

but limited from the point it risked permanent disabling injury. The psychological benefit of certain forms of elective amputation could justify the surgical removal of a limb but not quadrilateral amputation or elective blinding. The emphasis, however, would be what may *we* agree to and not so much what can be done *to* us.

Conclusion

Contested and unclear as it may, at times, be, the doctrine (dogma even) of proper medical treatment is the means by which doctors are protected from criminal liability for simply doing their job. Judges have made it clear that doctors are granted special dispensation to perform acts which would for everyone else be criminal assaults. The exception derives from, but is discrete from, the more general public interest defence for certain sorts of consensual bodily harm, such as those inherent in rugby and boxing. But the relationship of the medical exception to the more amorphous notion of public interest means that we cannot wholly ignore the latter. In 2015, any argument that we may lawfully consent to being brain injured while boxing but not to fairly minor injuries in sadomasochistic sexual practices is hard to defend. But the boundaries and scope of this broader public interest are unknown. The core questions seem to be *how* much 'bodily harm' to ourselves we are permitted to authorise, and *what* good ends outweigh the physical harm?

Restoring the offence of maim is unlikely, and many would argue that, instead, the decision in *Brown* should be overturned. What would be key, then, is a person's voluntary and informed consent so that no offence could be committed where consent is present, even to the most serious levels of non-fatal harm. The notion of proper medical treatment would thus become otiose. This may be no bad thing, for while the medical exception is designed 'to identify procedures which should not be permitted and effectively prohibit them',[128] as Lewis correctly notes, in practice it 'fails to pick up procedures which in retrospect we can see as problematic but which were nonetheless accepted by the medical profession at the time they were "new"'.[129] But what would this mean, then, for the role of doctors? Would they be no more than technicians acting as their patients request or demand? This is, undoubtedly, a question for another day.

128 Lewis (n 49) 371.
129 Lewis (n 49) 372.

3 What do we mean by 'proper' medical treatment?

Lucy Frith

Introduction

In this chapter I explore how the term 'proper' medical treatment is used, and what work it does in legitimising or delegitimising a particular practice, a particular individual's role in carrying it out, or the funding or provision of a practice. Drawing on debates in bioethical and the philosophy of medicine literature, I consider whether the question 'what is "proper" medical treatment?' can be answered by appealing to some idea of the appropriate norms governing medical practice. Some accounts suggest that there is an inherent morality of medicine based on the goals of medicine and concepts of medical professionalism, and this could be used to determine what is proper medical treatment. I examine these contentions, and advance an evolutionary theory of the internal morality of medicine based on the work of Franklin Miller and Howard Brody, and apply this theory to contested areas of practice. I argue that what constitutes proper medical treatment fluctuates over time, and is an interplay between the internal morality of medicine and the moralities of the social context in which medicine operates.

Before undertaking these tasks, I want to clarify the different ways a treatment or intervention[1] can be viewed as *not* properly part of medical practice:

1 Types of activity that should not be part of proper medical practice are those in which the responsibilities and duties that doctors have *as* doctors might prohibit medical involvement in any circumstances. For example, doctors participating in torture or capital punishment.
2 In some cases a treatment or activity should not be part of medical practice if it medicalises a part of life that had hitherto not been part of medical practice. Medicine has over the course of the last century brought many features of life under its umbrella. Areas that might previously have been addressed by religion or folk beliefs, or simply been seen as moral failings, are now seen as medical conditions, and, therefore, suitable for some form of treatment. For example, bereavement was once seen as part of everyday life and concerns about it discussed in a religious context, but now it has become a disorder and

1 I use 'treatment' to include any medical intervention, be that drugs, surgery, or medical management.

people are often advised to see their GP if they are not coping with the death of a loved one.

3 A third type of improper medical treatment involves procedures that are appropriate in one context, for example amputation for gangrene, but not appropriate when applied in another context, for example amputation for personal preference. This overlaps to some extent with the second type of improper treatment, as we could argue that it is not the surgeon's job to amputate to make someone feel better emotionally. The patient should come to terms with feelings about the unwanted limb, and distress should not be medicalised but dealt with in another way.

4 Certain treatments should not be part of the offer of a publicly funded health service and so, in this sense, are not proper medical treatments.[2] Here the procedure and expertise needed are medical but that expertise is being directed at something that is a merely a want rather than a need. For example, desiring bigger breasts is a *want* whereas people *need* blood transfusions in certain situations. This is a demarcation between what is a necessary and important part of health care provision, the central function of medicine, and the unnecessary and peripheral parts, the application of medical techniques to non-essential or social problems.

5 Proper medical treatment also includes the legitimisation of *who* can carry out certain procedures.[3] Something is not proper medical treatment if it is carried out by a lay person, and medicine has done much to consolidate its power over the right to be sole custodians of certain practices. The professional accreditation of the General Medical Council to determine who can practice medicine, to remove doctors from the medical register, and to set the appropriate training qualifications required to practise medicine are forms of control over who can 'do' proper medical treatment. Indeed, the legal status of medical practitioners separates them from alternative therapists who, for example, have looser and non-legally binding practitioner accreditation.[4]

6 The final type of meaning of proper medical treatment is employed by Celia Kitzinger and Jenny Kitzinger in this collection,[5] and relates to treatment that is appropriate for the condition but not for that particular patient. This might be because that patient is not benefiting from that treatment and so, in this case, the treatment is futile. But this can also include debates over what particular treatment to give a patient; what is the proper medical treatment in a

2 See the discussions by D. Griffiths, A. Mullock, 'The medical exception and cosmetic surgery: Culpable doctors and harmful enhancement?', and K. Syrett, 'Rationing, resource allocation and appropriate medical treatment', in this collection.

3 See further M. Brazier, S. Fovargue, 'Transforming wrong into right: What is "proper medical treatment"?' in this collection.

4 The Complementary and Natural Healthcare Council maintains a register of accredited practitioners in this area, available at http://www.cnhc.org.uk/ (accessed 2 January 2015).

5 C. Kitzinger, J. Kitzinger, 'Family perspectives on 'proper medical treatment' for people in prolonged vegetative and minimally conscious states' in this collection.

particular situation? In the recent case of Ashya King, who has brain cancer, his parents removed him from Southampton General Hospital in order to obtain treatment overseas.[6] In this case, the treatment that the family thought *was* the proper medical treatment for their son, proton beam treatment, was not available at that hospital and so the medical staff were unable to provide it. There were thus conflicting views between the parents and the hospital on what was the 'proper' treatment.

In this chapter, I concentrate on the first four types of improper medical treatment, as these raise important issues about the acceptable limits of medical practice, what areas of life we want to bring into the medical domain,[7] and the proper role and remit of medicine in modern society. I focus here on *how* we determine what medicine *should* or *should not* be doing in the moral sense, rather than in the technical or expedient sense.[8] I consider the view that medicine has an internal morality of medicine, and develop an evolutionary account of the internal medical morality based on Miller and Brody's work,[9] to answer the question of what is proper medical treatment.

Medicalisation and 'too much medicine'

An important issue facing modern society is the overuse of medicine. How to determine what is and what is not proper medical treatment is thus a critical endeavour. This question has come to fore recently when discussing issues such as whether enhancement technologies,[10] 'wish-fulfilling procedures',[11] or certain types of cosmetic surgery should be part of medical practice.[12] The *British Medical Journal* runs a 'Too much medicine' campaign which seeks to reign in medical excess in overdiagnosis and treatment.[13] This concern about the encroachment of medicine into

6 J. Halliday, N. Vekaria, 'Ashya King to have cancer treatment with 70% chance of survival' (*The Guardian*, 9 September 2014), available at http://www.theguardian.com/uk-news/2014/sep/09/ashya-king-cancer-treatment-70-per-cent-chance-survival (accessed 2 January 2015).

7 Note that the medical domain is no longer the sole preserve of the medical profession. The economic aspects of medicine, pharmaceutical companies, governments, and patient groups also influence what is determined to be appropriate areas for medical practice.

8 For discussion of how the law has addressed this issue see J. Miola, 'Moralising medicine: "Proper medical treatment" and the role of ethics and law in medical decision-making' in this collection.

9 H. Brody, F. Miller, 'The internal morality of medicine: Explication and application to managed care' (1998) 23 *Journal of Medicine and Philosophy* 384; F. Miller, H. Brody, 'The internal morality of medicine: An evolutionary perspective' (2001) 26 *Journal of Medicine and Philosophy* 581.

10 F. Miller, H. Brody, 'Enhancement technologies and professional integrity' (2005) 5 *American Journal of Bioethics* 15.

11 A. Buyx, 'Be careful for what you wish for: Theoretical and ethical aspects of wish-fulfilling medicine' (2008) 11 *Medicine, Health Care and Philosophy* 133, 133.

12 Discussed by Griffiths and Mullock (n 2).

13 See British Medical Journal (BMJ), 'Too much medicine', available at http://www.bmj.com/too-much-medicine (accessed 2 January 2015), and the special issue on too much medicine: (2002) 324(7342) *British Medical Journal*.

almost every area of life, and the medicalisation of human existence, has been a dominant theme in popular and sociological literature since the middle of the last century. Ivan Illich's *The Limits of Medicine* is a seminal text on how medicine has taken over many aspects of life and death, and he drew attention to iatrogensis (doctor created harm).[14] Illich claimed that '[t]he medical establishment has become the major threat to health',[15] and that in an industrial society we are taught to get things rather than do things and to value what can be purchased rather than what we create. In a medical context, we are guided and treated rather than healed; 'healing ceases to be considered the task for the sick. It first becomes the duty of the body repair men and then soon changes from a personal service into the output of an anonymous agency'.[16] He uses the example of death to show how medicine has colonised a previously inevitable and natural part of human existence, arguing that we are now a death defying society.[17] Old age is seen as a disease, and extreme (even cruel) measures are used to prevent or postpone death. Lifestyles have now become medicalised risk factors to be managed by 'health information' and advice from doctors on how to minimise risk. Health promotion and screening bring elements of human existence under the medical gaze; those who do not feel sick can now become concerned that they *might* become sick.

Iona Heath has recently reiterated many of Illich's concerns,[18] and she cites Susan Sontag, who talks about kingdoms of the sick and kingdoms of the well.[19] Heath argues that:

> ever more are corralled into the kingdom of the sick earlier than ever, and residency there becomes longer and longer. All this is legitimised by being described as an epidemic of chronic illness, although many of those affected have no symptoms whatsoever.[20]

Heath's reasons for this increasing medicalisation mirror some of Illich's arguments that health has become a commodity and fears of sickness are exploited to sell this product. She suggests that '[t]he principal weapons deployed are detaching notions of disease from the experience of suffering, broadening the definitions of diseases, turning risk factors into diseases, and, most potent of all, fear'.[21] This fear, among patients and doctors, drives over treatment and the increasing remit of medicine.[22]

14 I. Illich, *Limits to Medicine – Medical Nemesis: The Expropriation of Health* (Marion Boyars, 1976).
15 Illich (n 14) 11.
16 Illich (n 14) 217–218.
17 I. Illich, 'Medical nemesis' (1974) 303 *The Lancet* 918.
18 I. Heath, 'Role of fear in over diagnosis and over treatment' (2014) *British Medical Journal* 349:g6123 (online advance access, DOI: 10.1136/bmj.g6123).
19 S. Sontag, *Illness As Metaphor* (McGraw-Hill Ryerson, 1978).
20 Heath (n 18).
21 Heath (n 18).
22 Discussed in, for example G. Welch, L. Schwartz, S. Woloshin, *Over-Diagnosed: Making People Sick in the Pursuit of Health* (Beacon Press, 2011); D. Healy, *Pharmageddon* (University of California Press, 2013).

Modern life can thus now be seen as dominated by the 'medical', but Illich's portrayal of medicine producing largely negative effects can be countered by arguing that he overstates his claims and ignores the positive benefits that medicine has achieved. However, the question remains, how can we determine what the proper domain of medicine is? And, conversely, how can we judge when medicine has overstepped the mark? One way of approaching these questions is by appealing to some idea of the inherent morality of medicine based on the goals of medicine and concepts of medical professionalism.

The internal morality of medicine

The debate over whether there is an internal morality of medicine was stimulated by Alisdair MacIntyre's concept of 'practice' and the claim that practices have virtues that are internal to them. A practice is:

> a coherent and complex form of socially established cooperative human activity through which goods internal to that form of activity are realized in the course of trying to achieve those standards of excellence which are appropriate to, and partially definitive of, that form of activity.[23]

A practice has its own goals or telos, and internal goods are generated by successfully engaging in the practice and by realising and pursuing its unique telos.

This notion of a unique good or telos of an activity has been applied, by others, to the practice of medicine. The accounts that build on this idea of a unique, unchanging telos of medicine have been termed essentialist,[24] and they have two central tenets. First, that medicine has an essential character, ends, or goals that are distinctive to it; for instance, the healing aim of medicine is a distinctive goal. Second, from such conclusions about the nature of medicine and a reflection on its ends and goals, it is possible to decide what should be done, what is proper medical treatment, and how to construct a medical ethic for the profession. Leon Kass was one of the first to advance this approach, and he adopted an Aristotelian view that medicine had a particular end of producing health and the morality of medicine depended on the advancement of that end.[25] Edmund Pellegrino developed this further and is one of the main exponents of the essentialist account of the internal morality of medicine.[26] He argues that the ethics of medicine has its source in the nature of the profession,[27] in what is distinctive about the medical

23 A. MacIntyre, *After Virtue* (Notre Dame Press, 1981) 175.

24 See R. Veatch, 'The impossibility of a morality internal to medicine' (2001) 26 *Journal of Medicine and Philosophy* 621.

25 L. Kass, 'Regarding the end of medicine and the pursuit of health' (1975) 40 *The Public Interest* 11.

26 E. Pellegrino, 'The internal morality of clinical medicine: A paradigm for the ethics of the helping and healing professions' (2001) 26 *Journal of Medicine and Philosophy* 559.

27 Pellegrino includes other healing professions in this analysis. So nursing, clinical psychology, and dentistry, for example, would all be classed as professions with a distinctive telos: Pellegrino (n 26).

profession, and in the good for which it aims. Medical practitioners have generic obligations as healers and aim at health as a good.[28] These goods are conceptualised as unchanging. This essentialist element is important for Pellegrino to guard against abuses committed by the medical profession, such as the Nazi medical experiments, that could be justified on the grounds that they were a reflection of the social context at the time. Unless medical goods are held to be set apart from such a social context, we have no leverage to argue against them.

This kind of essentialist account has been criticised by, for example, Robert Veatch.[29] One issue is that in seeing the goals of medicine as unchanging, ahistorical entities; medicine becomes an inherently conservative enterprise and any change would be morally suspect simply on the grounds that it is a change.[30] Brody and Miller have advanced a version of internalism that seeks to overcome this kind of difficulty encountered by essentialist accounts.[31] They propose what has been called an evolutionary account which sees the gradual evolution of an internal ethic of medicine in concert with wider society. John Arras sums up this evolutionary approach:

> Miller and Brody propose a theory of professional medical goals and duties conditioned by the evolving demands of history and (external) social/cultural influences. They thus want to argue that there is indeed a core ethic developed on the basis of reflection on medicine's specific goals and duties, but that this core ethic develops historically as a result of a dialectic or conversation between the medical profession and the larger society.[32]

There are two key elements in this account: first, how the internal morality of medicine is constructed, and, second, its relationship to wider society.

The construction of the internal morality

Miller and Brody contend that medicine is 'a professional practice governed by a moral framework consisting of goals proper to medicine, role-specific duties, and clinical virtues'.[33] They set out the goals proper to medicine based on the Hastings Center's goals of medicine project:[34] (i) the prevention of disease and injury and promotion and maintenance of health, (ii) the relief of pain and suffering,

28 Pellegrino (n 26).
29 Veatch (n 24).
30 Miller and Brody (n 9).
31 Brody and Miller (n 9); Miller and Brody (n 9).
32 J. Arras, 'A method in search of a purpose: The internal morality of medicine' (2001) 26 *Journal of Medicine and Philosophy* 643, 648.
33 Miller and Brody (n 9) 582.
34 An International Project of the Hastings Center, 'The goals of medicine: Setting new priorities' (1996) 26 *Hastings Center Report* S1. See also the discussion in M. Neal, 'Locating lawful abortion on the spectrum of "proper medical treatment"' in this collection.

(iii) the care and cure of those with a malady, and (iv) the avoidance of premature death and the pursuit of a peaceful death.[35] A further element of Miller and Brody's evolutionary account is a concept of professional integrity that follows from medicine's goals.[36] There are four internal duties of a doctor to ensure integrity: (i) to possess competence in technical and humanistic skills, (ii) to avoid disproportionate harm, (iii) to refrain from fraudulent misrepresentations of medicine as a scientific practice and clinical art, and (iv) fidelity to the therapeutic relationship with patients.[37]

So how is this translated into a theory of medical professionalism? My account of medical professionalism is broadly based on a view that there *are* specific moral responsibilities and obligations required of doctors qua their membership of the profession of medicine, that arise out of the internal morality of medicine. This is a form of 'practical precondition account', which says there are specific ethical precepts that all doctors have to broadly share to be able to practise medicine. This gives the medical profession a degree of moral cohesion upon which a view of proper medical treatment can be based. Rosamund Rhodes uses John Rawls's theory[38] to explain this distinctive form of professional morality.[39] She argues that in medicine the concept of political liberalism and the success of public reason are often more apparent than in political deliberation. This notion of public reason is central to Rhodes's and Rawls's accounts. While Rawls separates his claims about political liberalism from his theory of justice, the Rawlsian foundations do not have to be accepted in order to advance this account of medical professionalism. In this context, we are not talking about hypothetical formulations of principles but actual ethical professional codes which doctors must adhere to in their professional practice. It is enough to say that there is a social practice (medicine) that has professional ethical codes that doctors have to follow on moral and legal grounds, and that these have arisen out of the social context that medicine operates in. Rawls argues that there must be a capacity for reason and reasonableness in order for people to participate in the hypothetical construction of political justice; 'all ways of reasoning . . . must acknowledge certain common elements: the concept of judgment, principles of inference, and rules of evidence . . . and include standards of correctness and criteria of justification'.[40] The idea that there can be a common standard of reason is coupled with Rawls's recognition that there are some elements in society that have a distinctive character and autonomy and,

35 Hastings Center (n 34) S10–14.

36 See also the discussion of integrity of medicine in R Huxtable, 'Death on demand: "Proper medical treatment"?' in this collection.

37 Miller and Brody (n 9) 583.

38 Rhodes draws on Rawls's later work *Political Liberalism* (Columbia University Press, 1993) to ground her account, and the quotes from Rawls are the ones that Rhodes has used to substantiate her account.

39 R. Rhodes, 'Two concepts of medical ethics and their implications for medical ethics education' (2002) 27 *Journal of Medicine and Philosophy* 493.

40 J. Rawls, *Political Liberalism* (Columbia University Press, 1993), as quoted in Rhodes (n 39) 500.

therefore, act from their own principles. Rhodes argues that while Rawls may not have had medicine in mind, 'medicine is clearly a part of society that is ethically autonomous'.[41]

Building on these two elements, Rhodes attempts to construct the principles that should govern the social institution of medicine. These principles are drawn from 'the distinctive character and autonomy of the profession [of medicine]'.[42] She argues that 'there is genuine consensus on the core content of the professional responsibilities of physicians',[43] and gives the example of the consistency of the principles she lists to those found in 'The Medical Professionalism Project', an international charter on professional ethical values in medicine.[44] Rhodes's two foundational principles are, first, the fiduciary responsibility of doctors that they should act for the good of their patients, and, second, 'physicians and the institutions and profession of medicine must *seek trust and make themselves deserving of trust*'.[45] From these two foundational principles come the principles of caring, confidentiality, non-judgemental regard, non-sexual regard, and respect for the patient's values. Hence, for Rhodes, these principles arise out of the distinctive character of medicine, and place moral duties on doctors qua their being doctors. These duties are different from the kind of moral duties that the person in the street might have, 'because of its distinctive position in society, medicine has its own ethical principles that are in some notable respects different from the rules of ordinary morality, and they have a distinctive rationale'.[46]

The relationship between internal and external morality

These features internal to medicine operate within a society, and the morality of medicine depends 'in part on concepts in the social context outside of medicine'.[47] For Miller and Brody, there is an important interaction between medical values and societal norms. They argue that their account cannot properly be seen as truly internalist due to the recognition that the morality of medicine is an interplay between both internal and external factors, which together form the morality of medicine.[48] But can this evolutionary account and its conception of

41 Rhodes (n 39) 499.

42 Rhodes (n 39) 500. See also Charles Bosk, who argues that medical training is above all an ethical training where doctors inculcate the ethical values of their profession: C. Bosk, *Forgive and Remember: Managing Medical Failure* (University of Chicago Press, 1979).

43 Rhodes (n 39) 505.

44 ABIM Foundation, 'Medical professionalism in the new millennium' (2002) 136 *Annals of Internal Medicine* 243. Such values are also consistent with those outlined in the Royal College of Physicians' report on medical professionalism: Royal College of Physicians (RCP), *Doctors in Society: Medical Professionalism in a Changing World* (RCP, 2005).

45 Rhodes (n 39) 501.

46 Rhodes (n 39) 499.

47 Miller and Brody (n 9) 590.

48 Miller and Brody (n 9) 590.

the morality of medicine be shared by the wider community in which clinicians practise? While medical practitioners might agree on the internal morality that governs their decision-making, other people, such as patients, might not adhere to this. The evolutionary account of medical morality that I propose holds that both the internal and external morality are linked; they are symbiotically related, both informing each other. While there are specific moral obligations and duties on doctors that do not pertain to other members of society, these *have* to be in step with wider societal norms and arise out of them.

However, the problem is that patient groups, for example, have historically been at variance with the medical profession's approach to many issues.[49] This has been well documented and disparate, including patient dissatisfaction with childbirth practices in the 1970s, and the practices of organ retention in many hospitals that came to light at Alder Hey hospital towards the end of the 1990s.[50] So it would be overstating the case to say that everyone in society holds the same moral beliefs because morality is inherently pluralistic. For example, Tristram Engelhardt argues that the secularisation of western societies has had a profound effect on the ability of a society to institute any widespread moral advice or policies.[51] As there is no general moral vision or position, any agreement will only be partial to those who uphold the underlying position. Those who hold another position will be left out, and what comes to be the prevailing consensus is largely a matter of power and politics rather than morals. This lack of a shared moral vision makes moral decision-making difficult and contentious, and Engelhardt argues that there are moral communities ('moral friends') who share values, such as particular religious groups, whereas moral strangers who do not share the same values 'will not see the world in the same way'.[52] Therefore, there are no commonly agreed standards on which to base decisions over what is proper medical treatment.

Hence, the medical profession may become inculcated into a particular ethical viewpoint that is not generally shared. However, two counterarguments can be raised. First, medical decision-making is no longer the sole preserve of doctors.[53] Other disciplines, patient groups,[54] committees that include lay members (such as research ethics committees), for example, now contribute to both decision-making and the construction of the morality of the medical profession, or, at least, there are moves to try and bring this about. The values and processes of medical professionalism could thus be said to include not just doctors but all health care

49 See D. Lupton, *Medicine as Culture: Illness, Disease and the Body in Western Societies* (Sage, 2003) 122–127, for a discussion of patients' resistance to medical dominance.

50 See T. McIntosh, *A Social History of Maternity and Childbirth* (Routledge, 2013); *The Royal Liverpool Children's Inquiry* (Stationary Office, 2001), respectively.

51 T. Engelhardt, *The Foundations of Bioethics* (2nd edn, Oxford University Press, 1996).

52 T. Engelhardt, K. Wildes, 'The four principles of health care ethics and post-modernity' in R. Gillon (ed.), *Principles of Health Care Ethics* (Wiley, 1994) 136.

53 See further Miola (n 8).

54 See NHS England, Transforming Participation in Health Care (2013), available at http://www.england.nhs.uk/wp-content/uploads/2013/09/trans-part-hc-guid1.pdf (accessed 2 January 2015).

professionals. Furthermore, members of the medical profession are now publicly scrutinised, and their decisions and professional ethics are matters for general debate.[55] Therefore, professional ethics have to be in step with and informed by a more general consensus, and so are less likely to impose an alien morality on wider society.

Additionally, this kind of medical morality is dependent on a wider societal acceptance as, at root, it is about the medical profession being trustworthy in the eyes of the community it practices in. Therefore, the morality of medicine both reflects and is reflected in the morality of the wider community. Medicine was traditionally seen as a *moral profession*, in the work of Everett Hughes for example.[56] The medical profession was seen as having a set of moral values that it adhered to, and this was what gave it its status and prestige.[57] Medical practice was, on the whole, an altruistic and moral enterprise, and doctors were granted their privileged status on the grounds that they would be moral in their everyday undertakings.[58] However, this notion of medical professionalism began to be criticised in the 1960s and 1970s, and it was argued that any notion of professional ethics was a cynical ploy; doctors' supposed altruism was really a mask for their own self-interest.[59] However, since the 1990s there has been a change in the tenor of sociological literature, and medical professionalism has begun to be reunited with the notion that medicine has certain values (such as altruism) that are central to its functioning in society. For example, Eliot Freidson has argued that medical professionalism serves an important social function in ensuring that the profession maintains high standards of work and trustworthiness.[60]

William Sullivan exemplifies this trend, and contends that medicine cannot function unless the public has trust in it as an institution; 'the root of the public's trust is the confidence that physicians will put patients' welfare ahead of all other considerations . . . It is the function of medicine as a profession to safeguard and promote this trust in the society at large'.[61] In its report in 2005, the Royal College of Physicians defined medical professionalism as 'signif[ying] a set of values, behaviours and relationships that underpins the trust that the public has in doctors'.[62] The College argued that 'these values, which underpin the science and practice of medicine, form the basis of a moral contract between

55 See e.g. *Mid Staffordshire NHS Foundation Trust Public Inquiry* (2013), available at http://www.midstaffspublicinquiry.com/ (accessed 2 January 2015).

56 E. C. Hughes, *Men and their Work* (Gencoe Free Press, 1958).

57 T. Parsons, *The Social System* (Routledge & Kegan Paul, 1951).

58 S. Cruess, R. Cruess, 'Professionalism: A contract between medicine and society' (2000) 162 *Canadian Medical Association Journal* 668.

59 See e.g. E. Krause, *Death of the Guilds: Professions, States, and the Advance of Capitalism, 1930 to the Present* (Yale University Press, 1996); P. Starr, *The Social Transformation of American Medicine* (Basic Books, 1982); E. Freidson, *Professional Dominance: The Social Structure of Medical Care* (Aldine, 1970).

60 E. Freidson, *Professionalism Reborn: Theory, Prophecy and Policy* (Polity Press, 1994).

61 W. Sullivan, 'Medicine under threat: Professionalism and professional identity' (2000) 162 *Canadian Medical Association Journal* 673, 675.

62 RCP (n 44) 14.

the medical profession and society'.[63] Professionalism becomes associated with the ethical values of practice, and those values are ones that encourage and facilitate public trust in the medical profession. This medical professionalism account, which is an articulation of the values without which 'medicine would cease to be a going concern',[64] are values that necessarily link the medical profession with the wider community. This is essential because the medical profession must be trustworthy; medicine could not be 'a going concern' if it did not have the public's trust.

The external and internal moralities of medicine thus have a symbiotic relationship, and changes in public attitudes influence the acceptability of medical practice and vice versa. So, what is proper medical treatment may change over time, and determining whether these changes are within the spirit of the morality of medicine is a matter of judgement, to balance change with fidelity to previous iterations of the internal morality of medicine.[65] The changing fortunes of medical involvement in fertility treatment can be used as an example of how the two elements of medical morality, internal and external, are inextricably linked. Infertility treatment has traditionally been on the boundaries of proper medical treatment and provides a useful case study of activities that are contested, and the implications this has for what is considered as proper medical practice. The medical profession's involvement in infertility treatment has long been questioned, from religious objections to feminist writings in the 1980s.[66] Techniques such as artificial insemination (AI) had been used in animal breeding for centuries, and there is mention of surrogacy arrangements in the Bible where the servant girl Hagar has a child for Sarah, Abraham's wife. However, the medical profession was not been involved in any systematic way in seeking to address issues of infertility until the middle of the last century. The practice of artificial insemination by donor (AID) or husband (AIH) was something that was not considered to be an appropriate part of medical practice, with particular concern over the use of donor sperm to create families.[67] Donor insemination was first used in clinical practice in England in the late 1930s, but was generally practised in secret.[68] In 1945 Mary Barton, a gynaecologist, and her colleagues published an article in the *British Medical Journal* about her AID programme.[69] This was greeted with outrage and wholesale condemnation of the practice.[70] Furthermore, sperm donors were

63 RCP (n 44) 15.
64 Arras (n 32) 646.
65 Miller and Brody (n 9).
66 M. Warnock, *A Question of Life: The Warnock Report* (Basil Blackwell, 1985).
67 R. Snowdon, G. D. Mitchell, E. M. Snowdon, *Artificial Reproduction: A Social Investigation* (George Allen and Unwin, 1983).
68 R. Nachtigall, 'Secrecy: An unresolved issue in the practice of donor insemination' (1993) 168 *American Journal of Obstetrics and Gynecology* 1846.
69 M. Barton, K. Walker, B. Wiesner, 'Artificial insemination' (1945) 1 *British Medical Journal* 40.
70 N. Pfeffer, 'Artificial insemination, in-vitro fertilisation and the stigma of infertility' in M. Stanworth (ed.), *Reproductive Technologies: Gender, Motherhood and Medicine* (Polity Press, 1987).

generally regarded with suspicion,[71] and the 1960 Feversham Committee, which was set up by the government to look into the legal aspects of AID and AIH, said that donating sperm was 'an activity which might be expected to attract more than the usual proportion of psychopaths'.[72] The Committee concluded that while AID might be an acceptable treatment for some couples, 'in the interests of the child alone . . . the practice should be discouraged'.[73]

Yet attitudes to AID began to change during the 1960s, and the demand for AID continued to grow. In 1968 it became available on the National Health Service (NHS) if recommended on medical grounds.[74] Subsequently, the 1973 Peel Committee, a committee of the British Medical Association set up to consider human AI, reiterated the position that AID *was* an acceptable medical procedure.[75] Infertility treatment thus began to become more acceptable to wider society, and in 1978 developments in embryology and embryo transfer culminated in the birth of Louise Brown, the world's first baby born as a result of in vitro fertilisation (IVF) in Britain. This event prompted extensive ethical debate over the acceptability of this new form of infertility treatment, with opinions ranging from wholehearted support to condemnation. In the light of Louise's birth and the responses to it, the Warnock Committee was set up by the UK government in 1982 to examine the ethical implications of reproductive technologies, and it reported in 1984.[76] The Committee broadly supported IVF, AID, and embryo research, recommending that the manipulation of gametes and embryos outside the body should be allowed to operate within a regulated framework, with clinics licensed.[77] These laboratory-based procedures were far removed from the days of AID and its associations with animal breeding and masturbation. Not being able to have a child if you wanted one, had thus shifted from being something that had to be accepted, to a condition for which medical help could be sought. Changes in public attitudes influenced the acceptability of infertility treatment and scientific developments, and medical views, in turn, influenced public opinion. Thus, by the 1990s the perceptions of the practice (which itself had developed) changed from one thought of as immoral and not part of medicine, to gradual acceptance, to regulation, and then being accepted *as* proper medical treatment. This illustrates the symbiotic relationship between the external and internal moralities of medicine, with both playing a part in constructing the morality of medicine.

71 Pfeffer (n 70).

72 The Earl of Feversham, *Report of Departmental Committee on Human Artificial Insemination*, Cmnd 1105 (HMSO, 1960) 59.

73 Earl of Feversham (n 72) 46.

74 D. S. Irvine, A. Templeton, 'Donor insemination' in T. B. Hargreaves (ed.), *Male Infertility* (Springer, 1994).

75 The Peel Committee, 'Annual report of the council: Appendix V: Report of the Panel on Human Artificial Insemination' (1973) Suppl. 2 *British Medical Journal* 3.

76 Department of Health and Social Security, *Report of the Committee of Inquiry into Human Fertilisation and Embryology*, Cmnd 9314 (Stationery Office, 1984); Warnock (n 66).

77 D. Morgan, R. Lee, *Blackstone's Guide to the Human Fertilisation and Embryology Act 1990* (Blackstone Press, 1991).

Criticisms of the evolutionary theory

This evolutionary theory has not gone unchallenged, and one problem is that, in contrast to internalist accounts of the morality of medicine, externalist accounts suggest that medicine does not have its own morality and that morality is external to medicine. Veatch advances an externalist account of the morality of medicine and suggests that there are many medicines, each has its own morality, and, that even within those different medicines, doctors will not agree on what is morally right.[78] Medical morality is determined *solely* by the doctor's moral views and not by any aspect of medical practice itself. There can be a Catholic medicine, a Buddhist medicine, a libertarian medicine, and so on. There is no such thing as medicine per se. This is a common criticism of theories that posit some form of distinctive medical morality, and Mary Wurm-Schaar and Michelina Fato have argued that 'the medical profession itself appears to lack consensus regarding its core values . . . is fragmented into various sub-speciality organizations with their own codes of ethics and conduct'.[79]

Veatch argues that medical morality comes from *outside* the practice of medicine; we cannot get general answers to questions of what medicine should do, what is part of proper medical treatment, by appealing to some form of distinctive medical morality or a morality that is internal to medicine. Such an internal morality cannot be derived from a reflection on the practice of medicine because there are so many different medical roles that have different purposes or ends that 'they therefore have different moralities'.[80] Within these different roles there are differences in purpose and goals; thus, the ends of medicine must come from outside the practice. Veatch contends that, ultimately, any decision over what the ends of medicine should be are matters to be decided *externally* from medicine itself.[81] Using the example of the debate over doctors participating in capital punishment, he argues that:

> the question of whether a physician's behaviour is morally appropriate when he or she participates in an execution is surely not settled by the balancing of two competing goals of medicine. Surely it is settled by resolving the more fundamental societal moral question – the morality of capital punishment itself.[82]

In their response, Miller and Brody question whether if Veatch's contention that there are many different medicines all with a different morality is true, then 'by virtue of what are all these disparate practices . . . seen as *practices of*

78 Veatch (n 24).

79 M. Wurm-Schaar, M. Fato, 'The professionalism movement: A pause might not be sufficient' (2004) 4 *The American Journal of Bioethics* W1, W1.

80 Veatch (n 24) 629.

81 Veatch (n 24).

82 Veatch (n 24) 634.

medicine'.[83] They contend that there *are* similarities between different forms of medicine (such as Western and Chinese) that involve some notion of caring for the sick, and, therefore, both types of medicine share key elements that distinguish them as practices of medicine. In contrast, Veatch's position reinstates the dichotomy between medicine as pure technique and medicine as a moral practice, that there is one medicine from a technical point of view but many medicines from a moral the point of view. Miller and Brody suggest that '[p]ure technique forms a vessel into which we must pour a morality which originates elsewhere',[84] and that this dichotomy is questioned by the very existence of medical ethics which 'is predicated on the need to break down any perceived dichotomy between medicine as "pure" technique and medicine as moral practice'.[85] Medicine *cannot* be morally empty as medicine itself *is* a moral practice.

Furthermore, accounts of the morality of medicine based on a cohesive list of goals have been criticised on the grounds that there is no general agreement over what the goals of medicine are. If the goals of medicine are construed too broadly then they fail to differentiate medicine from other activities, and if too narrowly then much of what is considered modern medicine might fall outside what should properly be seen to be medical activity. To have the main focus as healing does not capture all of what modern medicine *does* or, indeed, *should* do. Alena Buyx has considered the ethical status of 'wish-fulfilling procedures',[86] which she defines as 'doctors and other health professionals using medical means (medical technology, drugs etc.) in a medical setting to fulfil the explicitly stated, prima facie non-medical wish of a patient'.[87] She argues that 'referring to medical goals does not help to evaluate the ethical status of wish-fulfilling medical procedures, since the construal of the pivotal concept *goals of medicine* is so controversial'.[88]

Clearly, this is a problem with accounts that rely on some conception of the goals of medicine to determine *what* should be part of medical practice, and there is a plethora of accounts of such goals. Nevertheless, Buyx appeals to some loose conception of goals, and argues that working towards a consensus on the goals of medicine is important; '[e]ven without an uncontested list of goals as reference it is quite apparent that some of the goals aimed for by wish-fulfilling interventions are further away from medicine and less benign than others'.[89] This indicates that while unanimity is unlikely to be gained on the goals of medicine, there are key elements that characterise the practice of medicine (such as healing, care, doing no harm, and promoting beneficence), and that these can be used as a starting point for discussion. We are able to broadly recognise the difference between,

83 Miller and Brody (n 9) 590.
84 Miller and Brody (n 9) 592.
85 Miller and Brody (n 9) 592.
86 Buyx (n 11) 133.
87 Buyx (n 11) 134.
88 Buyx (n 11) 137.
89 Buyx (n 11) 138.

for example, medicine and the beauty industry, and determine what distinguishes appropriate practice in each.[90]

Applying the theory

Having proposed an evolutionary account of the internal morality of medicine, I will now consider how this framework can help us answer the question of whether something *is* proper medical treatment. I will apply the theory of an evolutionary medical morality to four of the examples of improper medical treatment that were outlined at the beginning of this chapter: (i) claims that certain practices are outside the proper remit of medicine, (ii) medicalising an aspect of human life, (iii) applying medical techniques in areas where they are not warranted, and (iv) what parts of medicine should be publicly funded.

(i) Certain practices are **outside** *the proper remit of medicine*

Doctors are, and have been, involved in certain practices that are argued to be *outside* the remit of proper medicine *under any circumstances*. Medical involvement in torture and capital punishment are often given as examples of this sort of practice. To make a case that doctors should not be involved in torture is not hard as it contravenes all formulations of the goals of medicine and theories of medical professionalism. Doctors' involvement in torture is also prohibited by codes of ethics such as the World Medical Association's Declaration of Tokyo.[91] However, doctors do participate in torture, and a Task Force report funded by the Institute on Medicine as a Profession and the Open Society Foundations and published in 2013 found that doctors and other health care workers working in US military detention centres had been involved in 'designing, participating in, and enabling torture and cruel, inhumane and degrading treatment of detainees'.[92] With regard to capital punishment, where this is permitted it might be argued that it is *better* if doctors are involved to ensure that prisoners' suffering is minimised;[93] however, the American Medical Association (AMA) has stated that it:

> is troubled by continuous refusal of many state courts and legislatures to acknowledge the ethical obligations of physicians, which strictly prohibit

90 On this see Griffiths and Mullock (n 2).

91 World Medical Association, *Guidelines for Physicians Concerning Torture and other Cruel, Inhuman or Degrading Treatment or Punishment in Relation to Detention and Imprisonment*, Adopted by the 29th World Medical Assembly, Tokyo, Japan, October 1975, and editorially revised by the 170th WMA Council Session, Divonne-les-Bains, France, May 2005 and the 173rd WMA Council Session, Divonne-les-Bains, France, May 2006.

92 A Task Force Report funded by IMAP (The Institute on Medicine as a Profession)/OSF (The Open Society Foundations), *Ethics Abandoned: Medical Professionalism and Detainee Abuse in the War on Terror* (2013), available at http://imapny.org/wp-content/themes/imapny/File%20Library/Documents/IMAP-EthicsTextFinal2.pdf (accessed 15 December 2014).

93 For discussion of a similar argument relating to elective amputation see Brazier and Fovargue (n 3).

> physician involvement in a legally authorized execution. The AMA's policy is clear and unambiguous – requiring physicians to participate in executions violates their oath to protect lives and erodes public confidence in the medical profession.[94]

With regard to both torture and capital punishment, the arguments against doctors' involvement are appeals to the goals of medicine and medical professionalism, and that such practices contravene these at a fundamental level. Therefore, on these grounds the evolutionary theory of the morality of medicine gives clear reasons why these practices should not be part of proper medical practice.

(ii) Medicalisation

I have already noted that one of the issues facing societies in the developed world is the increasing medicalisation of aspects of life previously outside the medical domain. This has been an issue in debates over the status of infertility treatment, for example. Is infertility treatment *treating* a medical condition? Is infertility an illness or is it a social problem that is outside the remit of medicine? Infertility treatment can be said to relieve the suffering of those unable to have children, the involuntarily childless, and, thus, fulfil one of the goals of medicine. Robert Winston, a prominent British fertility specialist, has said that '[i]nfertility is actually a terrible disease affecting our sexuality and well-being'.[95] As Miller and Brody recognise, there is ambiguity over the term medical, and 'it is harder to distinguish "medical" goals, risks and benefits clearly from questions about how well or how poorly patients function in all dimensions of their lives'.[96] Medical techniques *can* alleviate the condition of infertility by enabling people to have a child, and there are many 'acceptable' medical interventions which ameliorate the effects of physical malfunctions. For example, diabetes cannot, as yet, be cured, but its unpleasant side effects can be and are managed. Therefore, infertility treatment appears to fit with medicine's goals of relieving suffering, and on these grounds could be said to be part of proper medical treatment.

However, if we consider the criterion of professional integrity, we could argue that the benefit of infertility treatment is outweighed by the risks. For the woman an IVF cycle is an invasive and possibly dangerous procedure, with the live birth rate per IVF cycle 25.8 per cent in 2012.[97] However, to those who want a child the risk benefit ratio could be viewed to be acceptable *as long as* they are informed

94 American Medical Association, 'Physician Participation in Lethal Injection Violates Medical Ethics', Press Release, July 17 2006.

95 R. Winston, 'Why we need to experiment' (*The Observer*, 10 February 1985).

96 Miller and Brody (n 10) 16.

97 Human Fertilisation and Embryology Authority (HFEA), 'Fertility Treatment in 2013: Trends and Figures' (2014), available at www.hfea.gov.uk/docs/HFEA_Fertility_Trends_and_Figures_2013.pdf (accessed 15 December 2014).

and clear about the success rates and the possible risks.[98] On balance, a case that infertility treatment should be part of proper medical treatment can be advanced on the grounds that it can relive suffering by addressing an important need and help fulfil this need without compromising professional integrity.

(iii) Applying medical techniques into areas where they are not *warranted*

With regards to the third example of improper medical treatment, how do we determine when medical techniques that are acceptable in one area should not be used in another? Enhancement technologies are examples of medical treatments (usually drugs) that have been developed for one condition and then applied to a non-medical condition. For example, sildenafil (Viagra) was developed for high blood pressure and angina, and then was found to have other (side) effects. Miller and Brody argue that enhancement technologies, such as methylphenidate for concentration or modafinil for alertness, are *contrary* to the goals of medicine and professional integrity.[99] This is because the medical risk–benefit assessment suggests that they should not be part of medical practice because while the risks are clear, the medical benefit is not. As they note, what is within the medical domain is ambiguous and, due to this, they do not call for banning enhancement technologies entirely but for a recognition that such interventions *can* challenge professional integrity and need to be carefully considered.[100] The more clearly an enhancement intervention meets a medical goal and the less risk it poses, the easier it is to justify it as part of medical practice, and vice versa.

Miller and Brody use contraception as an example to illustrate this point. Contraception does not treat a disease and, therefore, might be thought of as outside proper medical practice. But they argue that the risks, both physical and mental, of unwanted pregnancies mean that contraception provides a clear medical benefit, and, therefore, 'prescribing contraceptives is much closer to the goals of medicine than prescribing sildenafil to enhance sexual performance in males with normal sexual functioning'.[101] Thus, on the grounds of not fulfilling the goals of medicine and being contrary to 'proper professional duties', enhancement technologies are on the boundaries of proper medical practice, if not outside it.[102]

98 There has been criticism that clinics, particularly in the US, misrepresent success rates: L. Frith, E. Blyth, 'Assisted reproductive technologies in the US: Is more regulation needed?' (2014) 29 *Reproductive Biomedicine Online* 516. In the UK, the HFEA attempts to provide clear and accurate data on clinics: HFEA (n 97).

99 Miller and Brody (n 9).

100 Miller and Brody (n 9).

101 Miller and Brody (n 10) 16.

102 For discussion of the boundaries of proper medical treatment in relation to abortion, see Neal (n 34).

(iv) What should be publicly funded?

Infertility treatment is also a good example to consider in this final category. Whether such treatment should be provided on the NHS has been a longstanding debate in the UK. As I have already discussed, there are debates over whether infertility treatment *is* part of proper medical practice, and even if it is accepted that it is, it might not be seen to be addressing the core goals of medicine. This ambiguity over the status of infertility has contributed to a lack of public funding in the UK for infertility treatment. Only 41.3 per cent of IVF treatment is provided on the NHS, as are 15.4 per cent of donor insemination cycles.[103] A recent report by the National Infertility Awareness Campaign (NIAC) highlights how few Clinical Commissioning Groups (CCGs), the bodies responsible for commissioning infertility treatment in England, follow the guidance set out by the National Institute for Health and Care Excellence (NICE) regarding such treatment.[104] NICE guidelines recommend that three full cycles of IVF should be offered;[105] however, the NIAC reported that only 24 per cent of CCGs funded three cycles, 24 per cent two cycles, and 49 per cent only funded one cycle of IVF, in their survey period of 2013.[106] Thus, the majority of CCGs who responded to the survey (204, with no data from 7 CCGs) do not follow NICE's guidance.[107] On the face of it then, CCGs appear to view infertility as less important than other areas of medicine, and often infertility treatment is not part of the core services offered.

These arguments over whether infertility treatment should be publicly funded illustrate the difficulties in drawing boundaries between what might be seen as interventions which are a key part of medical provision, and those that appear to be on the periphery of proper medical practice. Priority setting has been approached in some cases by considering the goals of medicine, and this was the original purpose of the Hastings Center Report on the goals of medicine.[108] Funding issues force us to consider what we see as important, and while it has been established that infertility treatment is properly part of medical practice, whether it should be given the same priority as interventions that align more centrally with the goals of medicine and provide a clearer medical benefit is debatable.

103 HFEA (n 97).

104 NIAC, 'Assisted conception needs assisted implementation: A report into the status of fertility services in England' (NIAC, 2014), available at http://www.infertilitynetworkuk.com/uploaded/NIAC/Assisted%20Conception%20Needs%20Assisted%20Implementation.pdf (accessed 15 December 2014).

105 National Institute for Health and Care Excellence (NICE), *Fertility: Assessment and Treatment for People with Fertility Problems* (NICE, 2013, CG156), available at https://www.nice.org.uk/guidance/CG156 (accessed 2 January 2015).

106 NIAC (n 104).

107 NIAC (n 104).

108 Hastings Center (n 34). Also, D. Callahan, *The Troubled Dream of Life* (Simon and Schuster, 1993). On economic and rationing aspects of proper medical treatment see C. Donaldson, R. Baker, N. McHugh, 'The economics of 'proper medical treatment'', and K. Syrett, 'Rationing, resource allocation, and appropriate medical treatment' respectively, in this collection.

Conclusion

In this chapter I have advanced an evolutionary theory of the morality of medicine that seeks to guide us on what might be considered proper medical treatment. This theory of medical morality does not provide clear cut answers to what is or is not properly part of medical practice. As Miller and Brody state, 'it has never been our goal in invoking IMM [the internal morality of medicine] to claim that it *simplified* the resolution of difficult moral problems in medicine'.[109] Rather, it gives us tools that can be applied to consider whether something should be properly part of medicine. Does it violate the goals of medicine as torture does, or does it compromise medical professionalism, as certain types of enhancement technologies appear to? Considering these questions can stimulate a debate over what kind of medicine we *want* to foster, and what kind of medicine we wish to discourage.

109 Miller and Brody (n 9) 586, emphasis in original.

4 Papist potions and electric sex: A historical perspective on 'proper medical treatment'

Barry Lyons

Introduction

In Charlotte Brontë's *Jane Eyre*, Rochester's guest at Thornfield Hall, Mr Mason, is attacked with a knife and bitten. Shaken and bloodied, his wounds are attended to at the house by the local surgeon, Carter. Later, Rochester instructs the surgeon to take Mason with him and to care for him until healed, but, prior to their departure, he insists on medicating Mason himself. Rochester sends the eponymous heroine to fetch a vial of cordial, and proceeds to dispense the remedy despite the presence of a 'medical man':

> 'Now, doctor, I shall take the liberty of administering a dose myself; on my own responsibility. I got this cordial at Rome, of an Italian charlatan – a fellow you would have kicked, Carter. It is not a thing to be used indiscriminately, but it is good upon occasion: as now, for instance. Jane, a little water.'
>
> He held out the tiny glass, and I half filled it from the water-bottle on the washstand.
>
> 'That will do; – now wet the lip of the phial.' I did so; he measured twelve drops of a crimson liquid, and presented it to Mason.
>
> 'Drink, Richard: it will give you the heart you lack, for an hour or so.'
>
> 'But will it hurt me? – is it inflammatory?'
>
> 'Drink! drink! drink!'
>
> Mr Mason obeyed, because it was evidently useless to resist. He was dressed now: he still looked pale, but he was no longer gory and sullied. Mr Rochester let him sit three minutes after he had swallowed the liquid; he then took his arm –
>
> 'Now I am sure you can get on your feet', he said – 'try.'
>
> The patient rose.
>
> 'Carter, take him under the other shoulder. Be of good cheer, Richard; step out – that's it!'
>
> 'I do feel better', remarked Mr. Mason.[1]

1 C. Brontë, *Jane Eyre* (Service & Paton, 1897) 148–149.

In her analysis of this dramatic scene, Sylvia Pamboukian argues that Brontë uses the passage to allude to the dynamic relationship between Victorian medicine and quackery by distinguishing between Italian charlatanism and 'proper English medicine'.[2] The cordial comes specifically from Rome, and is thus both foreign and possesses a religious significance. Although Carter is awarded the elevated status of a practitioner in the scene, he still 'submits silently to being cast aside by this amateur physician in favour of an admitted quack remedy'.[3] Mason improves quickly after taking the cordial, and so it appears that this foreign papist potion is deemed more effective than alternative orthodox, English, Protestant treatments. As Pamboukian states, this incident raises questions about the conflicting roles of medical practitioners and 'amateurs' in the therapeutic and social hierarchy, and although she is concerned with Victorian medicine, many of her questions remain pertinent today:

> How can orthodox practitioners assert professional standards of care?
> How can one discriminate between a quack remedy and an orthodox remedy, if not on the basis of efficacy alone?
> What limitations should be placed on quack remedies without infringing upon patients' freedom of choice and the free market?
> From what viewpoint may one judge such matters fairly?[4]

In this chapter I examine a number of these issues from a historical perspective, and consider whether there were restrictions on who could deliver 'proper medical treatment' and whether the more pertinent question is whether a treatment is efficacious or harmful. I explore whether the patient/client/consumer should be the most important judge when it comes to deciding what proper medical treatment means for them, and, finally, whether the notion of 'proper' has any particular sense in the context of proper medical treatment.[5] Although I am substantially concerned with the seventeenth and eighteenth centuries, the material considered extends from the early fifteenth century physician's appeal to Parliament (seeking some means to control and regulate the practice of medicine), to the publication of F Scott Fitzgerald's *Tender is the Night* some 600 years later.

Who can deliver 'proper medical care'?

The matter of who can deliver proper medical care has been a vexed question throughout the history of medicine, exercising physicians who were in no doubt that *they* were only people qualified to provide correct medical treatment. Physicians' petition to Parliament in 1421 is among the earliest attempts (in Great Britain) to restrict medical practice. They requested that no unqualified persons

2 S. Pamboukian, *Doctoring the Novel: Medicine and Quackery from Shelley to Doyle* (Ohio University Press, 2012) 1.
3 Pamboukian (n 2) 1.
4 Pamboukian (n 2) 2–3.
5 On the patient as consumer see D. Griffiths, A. Mullock, 'The medical exception and cosmetic surgery: Culpable doctors and harmful enchancement?', and on 'proper' see L. Frith, 'What do we mean by "proper" medical treatment?', in this collection.

should be allowed to practise 'physic', claiming that the performance of untaught practitioners caused significant injury and frequent mortality.[6] The appeal was specific about the qualifications required to engage in medical practice, and also declaimed the capacity of women to perform such a role:

> But, worthy Soveraigns, as it is known to your high discretion, many uncunning and unapproved in the foresaid Science practises, and especially in Physic, so that in this Realm is every man, be he never so lewd, taking upon him practise, be suffered to use it, to great harm and slaughter of many men . . . Wherefore pleases to your excellent Wisdoms . . . to ordain and make in Statute perpetually to be straightly used and kept, that no man, of no manner, estate, degree, or condition, practise in Physic, from this time forward, but he have long time used the Schools of Physic within some University, and be graduated in the same; that is to say, but he be Bachelor or Doctor of Physic having Letters testimonials sufficience of one of those degrees of the University in the which he took his degree in; under pain of long imprisonment, and paying £40 to the King; and that no Woman use the practise of Physic under the same pain.[7]

However, it was not until the Physicians and Surgeons Act, 1511 (3 Hen. VIII, ch. 11) that the law attempted to limit medical practice to those who had been examined. The examination was conducted in each diocese by the jurisdictional bishop, except within seven miles of the City of London where the relevant cleric (usually either the Bishop of London or the Dean of St Paul's Cathedral) was assisted by four physicians or surgeons.[8] The function of the 1511 statute was to eliminate the:

> great multitude of ignorant persons . . . that . . . boldly and accustomably take upon them great cures and things of great difficulty, in the which they partly use sorcery and witchcraft, partly apply such medicines unto the disease as be very noxious and nothing meet therefore, to the high displeasure of God, great infamy of the faculty, and the grievous hurt, damage, and destruction of many of the King's liege people.[9]

The subsequent Royal Charter of 1518 permitted the newly formed Royal College of Physicians to take control of determining who was appropriately qualified,

6 J. Raach, 'English medical licensing in the early seventeenth century' (1944) 16 *Yale Journal of Biology and Medicine* 267.

7 Cited in Raach (n 6) 268–269.

8 D. Giesen, *International Medical Malpractice Law: A Comparative Study of Civil Responsibility Arising from Medical Care* (Martinus Nijhoff, 1988) 3–4.

9 3 Hen. VIII, ch.11, as cited in J. W. Willcock, *The Laws Relating to the Medical Profession* (J. & W. T. Clarke, 1830) Part Second, Records, vi. The Act lists among the dangerous practitioners 'common artificers, [such] as smiths, weavers, and women.'

along with sole rights of practice in the region around London and the right to protect this privilege through litigation. By law, nobody else would be able to treat patients without being instructed by a physician. Thus, the question of *who* could deliver proper medical treatment would seem to have been settled, in London at least, and the law only recognised three types of medical practitioners: apothecaries, surgeons, and physicians, in ascending order of importance. This strict hierarchical structure endowed physicians with the position of 'first class of medical practitioner in rank and legal pre-eminence'.[10] While they were entitled to perform the roles of surgeon and apothecary, they usually restricted themselves to the important and learned functions of diagnosis and prescription, instructing the apothecary as to the drugs that needed to be compounded for the particular patient, and overseeing the bleeding and operating of surgeons.[11] This seems to be an orderly system with primacy afforded to the physician, a secondary status to surgeons, and apothecaries occupying a tradesman-like position as dispensers.[12] Yet, as frequently occurs with such neatly packaged systems, the reality on the ground was somewhat different.

In the 1980s, historians started to conceptualise health care in early modern England as a 'medical marketplace'.[13] Roy Porter portrayed this market as a place 'where physicians, surgeons, and apothecaries . . . melted into each other along a spectrum that included thousands who dispensed medicine full- or part-time'.[14] Concurring, Mark Jenner and Patrick Wallis eschewed the notion that there was a strict hierarchy; rather, they argued that the legislation had limited effect resulting in boundaries that dissolved in the face of a commercial world where practitioners had to compete for custom, and 'where services were advertised and sold to those sufferers who cared to shop'.[15] Furthermore, patients had 'relative freedom to choose the medical practitioners they liked', and they were 'medically promiscuous', picking the therapists that provided the perceived most successful treatment for a specific ill, with cost-effectiveness and bedside manners being important considerations.[16] Thus, despite their apparent position in the hierarchy, physicians failed to achieve cultural pre-eminence until the late nineteenth century. The development of a monetised economy in Britain produced 'a commercial capitalist, spectacle-loving, consumer oriented society', which fed into a competitive

10 I. Waddington, 'General practitioners and consultants in early nineteenth century England: The sociology of an intra-professional conflict' in J. Woodward, D. Richards (eds), *Health Care and Popular Medicine in Nineteenth-Century England* (Croon Helm, 1977) 165.

11 I. Waddington, 'The struggle to reform the Royal College of Physicians, 1767–1771: A sociological analysis' (1973) 17 *Medical History* 107.

12 P. J. Corfield, *Power and the Professions in Britain 1700–1850* (Routledge, 1995) 149; W. J. Reader, *Professional Men: The Rise of the Professional Classes in Nineteenth-Century England* (Weidenfeld, 1966) 16.

13 M.S.R. Jenner, P. Wallis, 'The Medical Marketplace' in M.S.R. Jenner, P. Wallis (eds) *Medicine and the Market in England and its Colonies, c.1450–c.1850* (Palgrave McMillan, 2007).

14 R. Porter, 'The patient's view: Doing medical history from below' (1985) 14 *Theory and Society* 175, 188.

15 Jenner and Wallis (n 13) 2.

16 Jenner and Wallis (n 13) 2.

market for medical skills.[17] According to Porter, 'in any year a sick person might visit a wart-charmer, get a remedy from a neighbour or bookseller, pay for a surgeon and hire a horse-leech'.[18] Essentially, these social developments transformed medicine and served to 'eclipse the College of Physicians' dreams of regulation',[19] and to dilute the claim that they alone could provide proper medical treatment. As far as the public-at-large were inclined, physicians were *not* an absolute necessity in the world of early modern health care provision; rather, patients' personal medical needs could be serviced by a variety of providers.

In an attempt to protect their practice, physicians denigrated other healers as 'quacks', or charlatans, or empirics. However, exactly who was a quack, and what kinds of practices constituted quackery, was not settled. The etymology of 'quack' is uncertain, but it is frequently taken to be derived from a shortened version of the obsolete Dutch word *kwakzalver*. Lorenzo Servitje proposes that this term translates as a 'person who cures with home remedies', and is derived from the words for 'rubbish' and 'to cure with ointments.' The Middle Dutch *kwacken* means 'to brag, boast; literally to croak', thus referring to the tendency of quacks to loudly advertise their wares.[20] Essentially, a quack was a medical charlatan.[21] As Porter states, 'the term [quack] was polemically tossed around as an accusation: used to brand someone practising medicine in bad faith'.[22] By and large everybody agreed that quacks were a bad thing, frequently described as illiterate, ignorant, and foreign individuals whose 'much-trumpeted arts and arcana, pills and potions, were at best worthless, and, all too often, positively deadly draughts'.[23] They were branded cheats, liars, and impostors. Importantly, above all, a quack was always someone else.[24]

In order to safeguard their privilege, the fellows of the Royal College of Physicians frequently litigated against the unqualified who practised in the area around London. Such legal action, however, did not seem to have a chilling effect on many practitioners. One of the most notable examples of their diligence, and ultimate failure in this regard, was the case of William Trigge (c.1630–1656), an empiric who originally was a shoemaker yet went on to become one of the best-known unlicensed medical practitioners in London. The censors' board of the London College of Physicians first heard a complaint about his allegedly illicit practice in December 1630. He admitted to practising in a variety of cases, was admonished, but chose to ignore the warning not to practise again. There then followed a series of recorded complaints: from Mrs Goodridge that he had practised

17 R. Porter, *Health for Sale: Quackery in England, 1660–1850* (Manchester University Press, 1989) 55.
18 Porter (n 17) 55.
19 Jenner and Wallis (n 13) 4.
20 L. Servitje, 'If it looks like a duck' (2013) 34 *Journal of Medical Humanities* 407, 409.
21 Alternative terms for quack included mountebank and empiric. Although these were not necessarily identical, the difference is not relevant to the purposes of this chapter and thus need not be expounded upon.
22 R. Porter, *Quacks: Fakers & Charlatans in English Medicine* (Tempus Press, 2000) 9.
23 Porter (n 22) 16.
24 W. H. Helfand, *Quack, Quack, Quack: The Sellers of Nostrums in Prints, Posters, Ephemera & Books* (Grolier Club, 2002) 11.

on her husband and overcharged, from Mr Cooke (a surgeon) that he had treated one of Cooke's patients with an enema and a purgative and the patient had died, and from Dr Daniel Oxenbridge that Trigge had inserted a drain into the abdomen of Widow Thompson to treat hydropsy and she had died.[25] Despite multiple fines and incarcerations, Trigge continued to ply a medical trade. Ultimately, he was tried at the King's Bench (in 1639) where, despite excellent legal representation (by John Cooke, who subsequently argued the army's case against Charles I), Trigge was fined £115. He apparently continued to practise, however, since the College subsequently ordered him to come before them again on 2 December 1641.

After the Civil War, Trigge (now calling himself a 'Doctor of Physic') continued to be pursued by the College of Physicians. However, at his last trial in Guildhall (in 1656) Trigge (and several others) challenged the juridical authority of the College and won on the technicality that the King had not actually signed the relevant Parliamentary Act.[26] Trigge had persisted in practice for 30 years despite frequent brushes with the law. It would seem reasonable to hold that his insistence on continuing to practice, coupled with his ability to pay prominent lawyers and fines, indicates that he probably made a decent living out of providing medical care. At least some of the population of London must have been happy to attend him, despite his lowly start, and to purchase his proprietary treatment, the 'Golden Vatican-Pill', which was advertised as being 'Famous for the Cure of Most Diseases in Either Sex', and sold very well.[27]

But physicians did not necessarily reserve the label of quack for the sellers of potions and nostrums, strokers, herbalists, and astrologers; esteemed physicians such as William Withering were also sometimes denounced.[28] In part, it was difficult to even define who was a physician. James Graham (1745–1794), perhaps the most notorious of those condemned of quackery,[29] had received an excellent clinical education at Edinburgh although he had never submitted a thesis for his MD.[30] However, this was not unusual, as less than 10 per cent of students did so. Indeed, some physicians bought their MDs from Aberdeen and St Andrews without ever attending a lecture, while graduates of Oxford and Cambridge had a broad education in philosophy and the arts but no clinical training at all. In a world where academic honours could be purchased, or were no reflection of

25 H. J. Cook, 'Trigge, William (fl. 1630–1656)' in B. Harrisson (ed.), *Oxford Dictionary of National Biography* (Oxford University Press, 2004), available at http://www.oxforddnb.com/view/article/57252 (accessed 10 December 2014).

26 Cook (n 25).

27 After his death, his wife sold the secret recipe to a Benjamin Shrove, who then marketed the pills through 27 intermediaries: Cook (n 25).

28 In 1788, Withering, a pioneer of digitalis therapy for dropsy (heart failure), was accused by Dr Erasmus Darwin of the 'solemn quackery of large serious promises of a cure'. However, Porter suggests that Darwin was motivated by Withering poaching clients from his son, Dr Robert Waring Darwin: Porter (n 22) 16–17.

29 W. L. Whitwell, 'James Graham, Master Quack' (1977–8) 4 *Eighteenth-Century Life* 43. Graham's case is discussed further below.

30 Porter (n 22) 21.

clinical training or acumen, the possession of a medical degree was, thus, no indication of a capacity to provide proper medical treatment.[31] In fact, some of the most successful and honoured practitioners of the fifteenth to twentieth centuries had no medical qualifications at all.

It is instructive to consider the case of Graham a little further, most recently detailed in Lydia Syson's biography.[32] After leaving Edinburgh for America, he started a successful practice as an oculist (eye specialist). He seems to have been a talented doctor, later gaining the patronage of Lady Spencer (mother of Georgiana, Duchess of Devonshire) at Spa. While in America he was inspired by Benjamin Franklin's public demonstrations of electricity, and believed that it could be effectively harnessed to treat ill health. In May 1780 Graham opened the Temple of Health in a spectacular new building at the Adelphi in London, where he treated patients with electricity and magnetism, musical therapy, and pneumatic chemistry. The Temple of Health was very successful, although opinion was divided as to whether Graham was a true healer or the 'King of Quacks', and he was a regular subject of satirical plays, poems, and newspaper skits.[33]

Graham subsequently became a very public pioneer of sexology, and in June 1781 he launched the Temple of Hymen in Pall Mall and installed his newly built electro-magnetic Celestial Bed, which was designed to cause 'immediate conception' in those 'permitted to partake in its heavenly joys', as even the 'barren certainly must become fruitful, when they are powerfully agitated in the powers of love'.[34] Indeed:

> [m]arriages and families would no longer be ruined by infidelity and infertility. Britain could be populated with a race of superhumans, of the highest physical and mental calibre. In the Bed's final and most extraordinary incarnation, electricity, magnetism, mechanical musicians, fragrant airs, fresh flowers, seductive mirrors and miniature automata all came together to deliver sexual pleasures that were said to be sublime.[35]

The bed, which was 12 feet by 9 feet, was roofed by a canopy that contained fresh flowers and a pair of live turtledoves. Fragrances and 'ethereal gases' were diffused under the canopy, while the atmosphere crackled with electricity from 40 huge Leiden jars. Meanwhile, on the bed (under the sign 'Be fruitful, multiply and replenish the earth') the courting pair (hair standing on end from the electricity) coupled in positions best suited to conception (made easy by a tilting inner frame) to the sound of organ pipes whose music varied with the intensity of their activity, all the while suffused in a mixture of ether and oxygen.[36]

31 L. Syson, *Doctor of Love: James Graham and His Celestial Bed* (Alma Books, 2008).

32 Syson (n 31).

33 Syson (n 31).

34 J. Graham, *A Private Advice, Formerly Sold at the Temple of Hymen, By the Doctor Himself, For One Guinea* (London, 1783) 11.

35 Syson (n 31) 7.

36 Syson (n 31) 153–157.

Graham described the first patient to try out one of his earlier versions of the electric bed as 'a good stout-like Dutchwoman who came from Lancaster', childless after six or eight years 'united to a strong likely man'.[37] She 'laboured under a paralytic complaint', was incapable of speech, and had suffered a cessation of menstruation. Her mother and husband brought her to see Graham in the hope that he could cure her 'palsy'.[38] Graham attributed her problems to a lack of fresh air, exercise, and her bizarre and unvarying diet of very strong coffee in the morning and old tea leaves with salt and vinegar in the evening. For her therapy, she took daily exercise, slept (sometimes alone, sometimes with her husband) in the charged-up bed, preceded by an icy bath scented with herbs and flowers, followed by a firm massage 'with the whole strength of her worthy husband'. Within two months she was on her way back to Lancaster, 'in perfect health and high-spirits, and happily pregnant', and later enquiries proved her to be the 'healthy and happy mother of a pretty large family'.[39]

Although posterity has tended to view Graham as a charlatan, Porter has suggested that he 'was also a man of significant medical ideas . . . whose views . . . were actually highly typical of his age'.[40] The two characters of Trigge and Graham, both decried as quacks, one with a medical education, the other a shoemaker, made their living from attending to the health needs of the population. People consulted them for medical treatment rather than (or perhaps as well as) orthodox physicians. Why would the populace choose to attend quacks when regular practitioners were available? Perhaps it was their personality, or cost (although Graham was far from cheap, a night in the Celestial Bed cost £50),[41] or perhaps it was because the unorthodox were sometimes seen as delivering more efficacious treatments.

Is efficacy not more important than who prescribes?

As the above makes clear, sometimes it was difficult to decide who was a quack and who was a genuine health care provider. In the face of this failure to discriminate and decide who was a legitimate physician, and so capable of directing or providing proper medical treatment, perhaps the most rational method would be to choose different criteria for determining how a treatment might be regarded as proper medical care. One approach might be to look at the efficacy of the treatment provided rather than to focus on the provider. Under such scrutiny, one of the difficulties faced by orthodox physicians, had they claimed that they alone could deliver proper medical care, was the fact that their treatments were not very good. The historian David Wooton argues that not only were many treatments

37 J. Graham, *A Lecture on the Generation, Increase, and Improvement of the Human Species* (London, 1784) 61.

38 Graham (n 37) 61.

39 Graham (n 37) 60–63.

40 R. Porter, 'Graham, James (1745–1794)' in B. Harrisson (ed.), *Oxford Dictionary of National Biography* (Oxford University Press, 2004), available at http://www.oxforddnb.com/view/article/11199 (accessed 10 December 2014).

41 Graham (n 34) 11.

relatively simple and ineffective, but that, up until the middle of the nineteenth century, the therapies used by doctors 'must have done . . . more harm than good', with medicine becoming more, rather than less, dangerous over time.[42] Because of its safer profile, homeopathy, he argues, would most likely have outperformed Hippocratic medicine in a clinical trial.[43]

For most of the historical period between the Hippocratic and Victorian eras, there was a strong belief that excess fluids were the cause of many illnesses and should be eliminated from the body by inducing vomiting, diarrhoea, or, most commonly, by venesection. Bloodletting was a common medical treatment for millennia, and remained so well into the nineteenth century (and even persisted into the twentieth century).[44] But for someone who was already ill, being gradually exsanguinated over a short period of time could hardly be regarded as beneficial. Parapia contends that many deaths, including those of Queen Anne, Mozart, and George Washington, were greatly accelerated by overenthusiastic bloodletting.[45] Other common treatments appear to have been no more inspiring. This provoked many sixteenth to nineteenth century writers who satirised medicine to allude to its failure to cure and its propensity to kill.[46] In *Timon of Athens*, Shakespeare had Timon say to the banditti: 'Trust not the physician, his antidotes are poisons, and he slays more than you rob'.[47] Later, Voltaire described physic as the art of 'pouring drugs of which we know little into bodies of which we know less'.[48] And in *Gulliver's Travels*, Jonathan Swift jeers at the physician whom he defines as 'a sort of people bred up among us, in the profession, or pretence, of curing the sick'.[49] Swift's satirical attack on the medical practice of the day questions the humoral theories of medicine, finding them both inaccurate and irrational.[50] Perhaps most famously, Molière directly and repeatedly tackled medicine's failures and greed. For example in *Le Malade Imaginaire*, the surgeon discusses the utility of treatment:

> *Mr. Diafoirus:* To tell you the truth, I have never had any predilection to practice with the great; it never seemed pleasant to me, and I have found that it is better for us to confine ourselves to the ordinary public. Ordinary people are more convenient; you are accountable to nobody for your actions, and as long as

42 D. Wooton, *Bad Medicine: Doctors Doing Harm Since Hippocrates* (Oxford University Press, 2004) 2.
43 Wooton (n 42) 75
44 D. P. Thomas, 'The demise of bloodletting' (2014) 44 *J Royal College of Physicians of Edinburgh* 72, 75.
45 L. A. Parapia, 'History of bloodletting by phlebotomy' (2008) 143 *British Journal of Haematology* 490, 492.
46 E. M. Papper, 'Satire of medicine: The 18th century and beyond' (1990) 83 *Journal of the Royal Society of Medicine* 524.
47 Act IV, Scene III.
48 Cited in R. Quain, 'The harveian oration: On the history and progress of medicine' (1885) 2 *British Medical Journal* 775.
49 J. Swift, *Gulliver's Travels* (Jones & Company, 1826) 145.
50 Papper (n 46) 527.

you follow the common rules laid down by the faculty, there is no necessity to trouble yourself about the result. What is vexatious among people of rank is that, when they are ill, they positively expect their doctor to cure them.

Toinette: How very absurd! How impertinent of them to ask of you doctors to cure them! You are not placed near them for that, but only to receive your fees and to prescribe remedies. It is their own look-out to get well if they can.[51]

Earlier, Béralde tries to persuade his hypochondriac brother, Argan, from continuing to seek unnecessary treatment:

Béralde: I mean, brother, that I know of no man less sick than you, and that I should be quite satisfied with a constitution no worse than yours. One great proof that you are well, and that you have a body perfectly well made, is that with all the pains you have taken, you have failed as yet in injuring the soundness of your constitution, and that you have not died of all the medicine they have made you swallow.

Argan: But are you aware, brother, that it is these medicines which keep me in good health? Mr. Purgon says that I should go off if he were but three days without taking care of me.

Ber. If you are not careful, he will take such care of you that he will soon send you into the next world.

Arg. But let us reason together, brother; don't you believe at all in medicine?

Ber. No, brother; . . . I don't know of a more absurd piece of mummery, of anything more ridiculous, than a man who takes upon himself to cure another man.

Arg. Why will you not believe that a man can cure another? . . . according to you, the doctors know nothing at all.

Ber. Oh yes, brother. Most of them have some knowledge of the best classics, can talk fine Latin, can give a Greek name to every disease, can define and distinguish them; but as to curing these diseases, that's out of the question . . . All the excellency of their art consists in pompous gibberish, in a specious babbling, which gives you words instead of reasons, and promises instead of results.[52]

Molière's stance on the inefficacy, and downright harmfulness, of orthodox medical treatment brought him into direct conflict with physicians. But opprobrium was not reserved solely for the medically qualified, and unorthodox practitioners were as frequently reviled and satirised. The work of graphic satirist William Hogarth (1697–1764), in *A Consultation of Physicians or The Company of*

51 Scene VI.
52 Scene II.

Undertakers (which he presents as a coat of arms), ridicules the status of both physicians and the famous quacks of the time, finding little difference, if any, between them.[53] However, herbal remedies and simples,[54] although ineffective, were generally safe but not universally so. The enormously popular Dr James's Fever Powders (Robert James was medically qualified) were subscribed to by George III, Oliver Goldsmith (also medically qualified), and Horace Walpole, among many others. Walpole claimed the powders could cure most complaints, and that he had 'such faith in these powders that I believe I should take them if the house were on fire'.[55] Patented in 1746, the remedy was the subject of numerous attempts to establish its formula. A private analysis identified that the powder contained potentially toxic levels of antimony which, it was claimed, was responsible for the premature demise of Goldsmith and Laurence Sterne, among others.[56]

Wooton's thesis suggests that not only were physicians ineffective and frequently harmful, but also that (for a variety of reasons) they failed to introduce techniques that could have been beneficial. He cites the failure to embrace the microscope as a particular example.[57] In the 1670s Antoni van Leeuwenhoek made a series of simple microscopes and discovered a world of microorganisms almost everywhere he looked, including red blood cells and spermatozoa. Yet, despite the obvious (in hindsight) clinical possibilities, microscopes were not introduced into medical practice and were not used again as a serious research tool until the 1830s. Wooton attributes this lag between discovery and implementation to professional opposition, and argues that by delaying an effective understanding of germ theory, physicians prevented the introduction of antisepsis by 150 years and cost thousands of lives, particularly of women during childbirth.[58] In general, doctors saw no need to rethink their understanding of disease, which the microscope would have forced them to do, because they believed that the traditional account was fundamentally adequate. This conservative mindset was responsible for the delayed introduction of other beneficial technologies, including anaesthesia.[59]

It thus appears that many (if not most) therapies, quack or orthodox, lacked utility, but the former were less likely to cause harm than the latter. Some remedies were undoubtedly efficacious, but there were no randomised controlled trials, and no scientific data upon which to base a judgement. Doctors (and quacks) simply refused to record or reflect upon successes and failures. If they had made an effort to so do, to add up the number of people with a diagnosis of disease X who received treatment Y yet still died, then they would most certainly have abandoned procedures such as bloodletting centuries before they did. Instead,

53 H. R. Magee, 'Doctors in satirical prints and cartoons' (2007) 187 *Medical Journal of Australia* 596.
54 Powdered matter of a single vegetable, usually sold for medicinal purposes.
55 Cited in D. Porter, R. Porter, *Patient's Progress: Doctors and Doctoring in Eighteenth- Century England* (Stanford University Press, 1989) 49.
56 Porter (n 17) 9.
57 Wooton (n 42) 112.
58 Wooton (n 42) 143–147.
59 Wooton (n 42) 31–33.

there were competing claims of utility and efficacy (quacks advertised their wares widely) that were impossible for the patient to unravel. In a buyer's market perhaps an alternative way to settle what constitutes proper medical treatment would be to allow the consumer to choose.

Let the patient decide?

Given that patients might be best characterised (historically at least) as consumers, should they not be the most important judges when it comes to deciding what proper medical treatment means for them? As we have seen, the seventeenth and eighteenth centuries saw the rise of the medical marketplace in England, where physicians, surgeons, apothecaries, and other unorthodox practitioners plied their trade and competed for custom.[60] In addition to these practitioners, for any particular illness a person might also receive 'medical help' from friends, family, or neighbours using folk remedies, or from charitable clerics, astrologers, midwives, or sellers of simples. Part of the reason for the escalating nature of health care shopping was the rapid and unprecedented urbanisation which, as Loudon notes, created health problems for which the medical profession was woefully unprepared.[61] The waves of contagion (influenza, cholera, typhus, typhoid, smallpox, and scarlet fever) demonstrated in stark terms the impotence of the medical establishment when confronted with infectious disease.[62] Indeed, the burgeoning and increasingly literate middle class, with the disposable income to purchase a newspaper, were daily confronted with reports of disease, suffering, and death.[63] Thus, Tim Davies argues that the ubiquitous nature of such news concerned the middle class in a manner similar to modern day society:

> In the twenty-first century, the media is inundated with news reports about rising levels of obesity, higher risks of heart disease and the apparently unstoppable march of cancer. Faced with such a barrage of information, people, both today and in the nineteenth century can be forgiven for feeling at threat, and in need of getting a grip on their own personal health and hygiene. Therefore, amid the furore of information regarding public health throughout the nineteenth century, individuals grew more anxious about their personal health. Mass publicity about widespread public illness made people feel anxious about the maintenance of their personal health.[64]

Proprietary medicines, and often associated beauty products, dominated the advertising pages of newspapers from the late seventeenth century. The price for

60 Porter (n 17) 188.

61 I. Loudon, *Medical Care and the General Practitioner 1750–1850* (Clarendon Press, 1986) 130.

62 T. Davies, *The Promotion and Pursuit of Health, 1780–1880* (unpublished PhD thesis, University of Leicester, 2009) 4.

63 Davies (n 62) 5.

64 Davies (n 62) 7.

proprietary medicines was beyond the means of most working-class families, but the middle class could afford them, and became the biggest consumers of health and beauty products.[65] And by the nineteenth century the range of health and beauty products advertised in the press had grown substantially. Davies has calculated that the weekly issue of the *Leicester Journal* carried, on average, 3.67 health-related adverts in the 1780s, 8.17 by the 1830s, and 35.3 by the 1880s.[66]

There was also a shift in the scale of advertising in general, with proprietors of health and beauty products being the heaviest investors. One example is Thomas Holloway, the proprietor of Holloway's Pills. These were advertised as the 'Key to Health', useful 'for the treatment of many Diseases incident to the human frame'.[67] Holloway's annual expenditure on advertising rose from £5,000 in 1842 to £40,000 in 1864, and peaked at £50,000 in 1883, the year of his death.[68] Given his increasing outlay on advertising, it is likely that the revenue from his pills was substantial. Many people obviously believed that Holloway's Pills were the proper medical treatment that they needed for their ill. And Holloway was just one among many, with others including Thomas Beecham (of Beecham's Powders renown), and Dr de Jongh, owner of the famous Cod Liver Oil.[69]

However, if proper medical treatment simply consists of giving people what they want, then perhaps there is a salutary lesson to be learned from the case of Mrs Joanna Stephens. Kidney and bladder stones were a common and agonising complaint, and Mrs Stephens, an eighteenth century herbalist, had concocted 'Medicines for the Stone' which were supposed to work by dissolving the stones when taken orally according to specific instructions.[70] By 1737 her treatments had become widely known, and 'the Cures performed by these Medicines were so many and so well attested that the speedy Publication of them was judged to be of great Importance to Mankind'.[71] Despite repeated requests to publish the recipes she, unsurprisingly, declined. Following public pressure, a Parliamentary Commission was appointed to review her claims of efficacy.[72] Serving as Trustees of the Commission were the Archbishop of Canterbury, the Lord High Chancellor, the Lord Privy Seal, three dukes, two earls, two viscounts, the Speaker of the House of Commons, the Chancellor of the Exchequer, two Fellows of the Royal Society, five physicians (including Thomas Pellett, President of the Royal College of Physicians), and three surgeons. A clinical trial was designed, and four patients were

65 Davies (n 62) 15.
66 Davies (n 62) 16.
67 Anonymous, 'The composition of certain secret remedies' (1911) 1 *British Medical Journal* 1324, 1326.
68 Davies (n 62) 17–18.
69 Davies (n 62) 18.
70 L. Blum, 'An eighteenth century health care provider and medical entrepreneur' (1984) 60 *Bulletin of the New York Academy of Medicine* 944.
71 E. L. Keyes, 'The Joanna Stephens Medicines for the Stone: A faith that failed' (1942) 18 *Bulletin of the New York Academy of Medicine* 835, 838.
72 A. J. Viseltear, 'The last illnesses of Robert and Horace Walpole' (1983) 56 *Yale Journal of Biology and Medicine* 131.

treated with the medicine. On 5 March 1740, the Trustees signed a certificate attesting to the fact that Joanna Stephens's 'recipe for stone' had been examined and that they were 'convinced, by experience, of the Utility, Efficacy and dissolving power thereof'.[73] Mrs. Stephens's medicine was judged a success. Two weeks later, she received £5,000 from the Office of the Exchequer and the gratitude of the nation. She then published the details of her 'decoction', subsequently disappeared, and was never heard of again.[74] Perhaps unsurprisingly, it soon became apparent that her remedy did not work, and it is obvious to us today that a trial containing just four subjects provides little useful data. Giving consumers the medical treatment that they want does not necessarily make it proper, especially in the absence of proven efficacy and at the expense of the taxpayer.

The notion of 'proper'

While one notion of 'proper' in proper medical treatment might be interpreted as that which is correct for the patient, an alternative view might be to look at it in terms of propriety, or to consider what *improper* medical treatment might look like. The two subjects that I will briefly deal with here are the notion of the 'therapeutic lie', and what might be considered proper (or improper) doctor patient relationships.

In what Winifred Schleiner refers to as the first book on forensic medicine,[75] the Sicilian physician Fortunato Fidele (1550–1630) tells this story:

> a girl in her flourishing youth, who consulted her physician about aborting a fetus before its time. In order to foil her undertaking, the physician, in a pious misrepresentation (*pia simulatione*), promised her he would give her something that would fulfill her expectation expedition entirely: but in truth he mixed an antidote from ingredients that should make the fetus strong and healthy. However, the girl had hardly drunk it down, when she began to burn with the desire to bring forth, and hoping that what she had been promised falsely would certainly happen, entirely bent on this one concern, she before long felt the fetus dropped down; and to the disgrace (*ignominia*) of the physician, she aborted in spite of the resisting medication. For the image of the abortion, so strongly conceived, both overcame the power of the medication and foiled the physician's endeavor.[76]

This raises the question of whether it is acceptable or appropriate to lie to a patient for what the doctor considers good ends. Obviously, in this case the ends of the doctor and the patient were at odds, raising the further question of whether it is ever acceptable to impose the medical view of the good upon a patient, and

73 Viseltear (n 72) 134.
74 M. E. Moran, *Urolithiasis* (Springer, 2014) 67–78.
75 W. Schleiner, *Medical Ethics in the Renaissance* (Georgetown University Press, 1995) 5.
76 As cited in Schleiner (n 75) 5.

lie in the process. The latter clearly would not be acceptable today, but whether lying to patients is ever justified remains a contested notion.[77]

Historically, the therapeutic lie was an accepted part of medical practice. Antonio Carera (c.1652) stated that his Professors at Padua defined the art of medicine as 'the art of deceiving the world whereby the whole world is deceived'.[78] Schleiner argues that many physicians in the Renaissance assumed without question that pretence in the interest of curing was always allowed.[79] Those for whom the matter became important enough to warrant discussion pointed to Plato and Hippocrates, who appeared to have shared that assumption. For example, in *In Epidemiis* the Hippocratic term *apate* (deception, deceit, lie) was used, an allowance for the physician to gratify the patient by trickery.[80] The much-published medieval physician author Rodrigo agreed that deception had a place in medicine, and cited three reasons why certain types of untruthfulness should be allowed. First, at certain times lying is not only not blameworthy but sometimes even commendable. Second, while a lie that causes harm is always wrong, an effective one can be useful. Lies should be used discriminately, like a poisonous medication which can be salutary in certain circumstances. Finally, Rodrigo likens a therapeutic lie to a ruse used to good effect to cleverly defeat an enemy or robber.[81] This view was probably shared by the American physician and essayist Oliver Holmes, who contended that:

> Your patient has no more right to all the truth you know than he has to all the medicine in your saddlebags . . . He should get only just as much as is good for him . . . It is a terrible thing to take away hope, every earthly hope, from a fellow creature.[82]

But there is a distinction to be made between the deliberate lie as told in the story by Fidele, and the withholding of truth in order to prevent harm (sometimes known as the therapeutic privilege).[83] Although a discussion of the difference is beyond the scope of this chapter, if the patient is misled through either a falsehood or an incomplete rendition of the facts but derives a health care benefit from these actions, how might we think of this? It could be that we always regard anything short of disclosure of the full truth to be improper (principally because of the importance of autonomy and trust in medicine), or, alternatively, that veracity is

77 See e.g. B. Cox White, E. H. Gampel, 'Resolving moral dilemmas: A case-based method' (1996) 8 *Healthcare Ethics Committee Forum* 85; G. Mitchell, 'Therapeutic lying to assist people with dementia in maintaining medication adherence' (2014) 21 *Nursing Ethics* 844.

78 Schleiner (n 75) 5–6.

79 Schleiner (n 75) 8.

80 Schleiner (n 75) 9.

81 Schleiner (n 75) 11–12.

82 Cited in D. J. Rothman, *Strangers at the Bedside: A History of How Law and Bioethics Transformed Medical Decision Making* (Transaction Publishers, 1991) 123.

83 K. Hodkinson, 'The need to know – therapeutic privilege: A way forward' (2013) 21 *Health Care Analysis* 105.

an obligation that sometimes can be waived in order to improve a physical, psychological, or emotional outcome. The therapeutic lie, or (more euphemistically) privilege, remains a contested value.[84] Yet if we think that it might be acceptable in cases where there is clear evidence that the patient's welfare is improved through deception, does this in some way render dishonesty to be proper?

A second point I want to raise in this final section pertains to the doctor patient relationship. In general, intimate relations between doctors and patients are regarded as improper and, indeed, as a sanctionable offence. But what if the relationship holds a substantial therapeutic benefit for the patient? F Scott Fitzgerald's *Tender is the Night* invites us to consider this matter. The novel concerns Dick Diver, a doctor and psychoanalyst. He is asked by a colleague to review a complicated case of neuroses. Nicole Warren is a beautiful heiress whose mental ill health is apparently due to an incestuous relationship with her father. She becomes infatuated with Dick, who is encouraged to form a relationship with her as part of her treatment. They marry, and Nicole's money pays for Dick's partnership in a Swiss clinic and for their extravagant lifestyle. Nicole is presented to us as being vulnerable and unstable, while Dick is strong, although not always caring. As the book progresses, the roles change, and the story culminates with Nicole divorcing Dick to marry another. Nicole is cured of her mental illness, while Dick drifts into alcoholic decline and ever-diminishing circumstances. Nicole has become strong while Dick is destroyed. The point of the relationship being therapeutic for Nicole is emphasised cynically by Nicole's sister, who finally remarks, 'That was what he was educated for'.[85]

Clearly, those who regulate medical practice frown upon intimate doctor patient relationships as a policy matter to protect vulnerable patients. But where there is a therapeutic outcome, is such a relationship improper? Or perhaps another way of framing the question might be, as in the case of lying, can improper means ever be used for therapeutic ends?

Conclusion

Why should we pay any attention to history; why is it in any way illuminating to view the notion of proper medical treatment through the lens of the past? One reason might be encapsulated by the aphorisms of Machiavelli, Hume, or Santayana, which reflect the notion that we must study the past to learn from it.[86]

84 M. Brazier, E. Cave, *Medicine, Patients and the Law* (Penguin, 2011) 135–136.

85 F. Scott Fitzgerald, *Tender is the night* (Charles Scribner's Sons, 1934) 318.

86 M. Cesa (ed.), *Machiavelli on International Relations* (Oxford University Press, 2014) 44: 'it is easy, by diligent study of the past, to foresee what is likely to happen in the future in any republic, and to apply those remedies that were used by the ancients, or, not finding any that were employed by them, to devise new ones from the similarity of the events. But as such considerations are neglected or not understood by most of those who read, or, if understood by these, are unknown by those who govern, it follows that the same troubles generally recur in all republics'; D. Hume, *An Enquiry Concerning Human Understanding*, P. H. Nidditch (ed.) (Clarendon Press, 1975) 83: 'Mankind are so

However, there is more to history than simply this.[87] First, bioethics, professional conduct, and medical law are fundamentally concerned with human (doctor and patient) behaviour. History is, in large part, the study of how people and societies have behaved, and how these past actions have led to present situations. The laws of today have been developed as a reaction to events of the past, and history provides us with a perspective that allows us to understand these developments. Second, historical events provoke moral contemplation. The failure of doctors to assess their treatments and practices; the existence of quacks and their habit of widely advertising their pills, potions, and powders; the consumer choices of the literate eighteenth century middle classes; and the therapeutic lie or intimate relationship can contribute to our moral understanding of the biolegal complexities that face the courts, medical practitioners, and patients in contemporary society. Finally, when we look at the medical market of early modern Europe we see a place that is not so different from today. For example, a patient with a painful joint condition today is likely to attend a general practitioner and, perhaps, a rheumatologist or orthopaedic surgeon. However, some sufferers may also choose to attend a chiropractor, an osteopath, or an acupuncturist, or to engage in the consumption of a variety of herbal remedies. Some, perhaps many, individuals may find that these unorthodox practitioners and treatments do more to relieve their pain and increase their sense of wellness than do the orthodox. Much like the early modern era, we live in a medical marketplace where, as before, we mix and match our therapies and therapists to suit ourselves. When we come to consider what constitutes proper medical treatment we face similar difficulties to those that arose historically. Just because a treatment is prescribed or performed by a licensed practitioner does this automatically make it proper *regardless* of outcome?[88] If administered by a modern day quack or 'complementary' therapist, is it straightforwardly not proper medical treatment? And in the lexical assigning of proper, what status do we afford to what patients (or consumers) identify as being most efficacious or best for themselves?

much the same, in all times and places, that history informs us of nothing new or strange in this particular. Its chief use is only to discover the constant and universal principles of human nature'; G. Santayana, *The Life of Reason: Introduction and Reason in Common Sense* (MIT Press, 2011) 172: 'Progress, far from consisting in change, depends on retentiveness . . . when experience is not retained, as among savages, infancy is perpetual. Those who cannot remember the past are condemned to repeat it.'

87 B. Southgate, *What is History For?* (Routledge, 2006).

88 See further M. Brazier, S. Fovargue, 'Transforming wrong into right: What is "proper medical treatment"?' in this collection.

5 Moralising medicine: 'Proper medical treatment' and the role of ethics and law in medical decision-making

José Miola

Introduction

The medical exception provides that conduct that would normally be unlawful is lawful if performed by a qualified medical practitioner. This is quite a responsibility for a profession to have, and it is imperative that it is used wisely. This exception is contingent upon the act constituting 'proper medical treatment'; a term which, as others in this collection have highlighted, is fraught with complexity.[1] I do not propose to revisit these arguments here, as they are more than adequately dealt with by those others. Rather, in this chapter I shall explore the question of *how* English law has determined what decisions should properly be decided by medical professionals. As we shall see, there has been a significant change of approach by the courts from the 1980s and early 1990s (the 'old' cases), where medical discretion was allowed to run riot, to decisions made from the mid-1990s onwards (the 'new' cases), which are more patient oriented. The change in emphasis has implications for the notion of proper medical treatment and, indeed, the medical exception because when the law designates an act to constitute proper medical treatment there are at least two consequences which are relevant. First, that decisions with respect to that treatment should properly be made by the medical profession and its own standards. Second, a doctor exercising her clinical judgement in making decisions about proper medical treatment should benefit from the protection of the medical exception.

However, a number of complications arise when we consider how the law has protected medical discretion, and how it has (widely) interpreted what decisions it is proper to abrogate to the medical profession and its standards. As Margaret Brazier and Sara Fovargue make clear, the use of the *Bolam* test and the decision in *Bolitho*[2] to determine what is 'proper' and what is 'treatment' is unsatisfactory.[3] Indeed, it leads to a circular logic whereby a procedure is proper medical treatment when the medical profession says that it is; and the profession will say that

1 See e.g. M. Brazier, S. Fovargue, 'Transforming wrong into right: What is "proper medical treatment"?'; L. Frith, 'What do we mean by "proper" medical treatment?' in this collection.

2 *Bolam v Friern Hospital Management Committee* [1957] 1 WLR 582; *Bolitho v City and Hackney Health Authority* [1998] AC 232, HL.

3 Brazier and Fovargue (n 1).

it is so when it is proper medical treatment. This is similar to the logic employed by the courts in the old cases. A further difficulty arises when it is recognised that many of the issues that have been delegated in this way to the medical profession do not involve the procedures themselves but processes ancillary to them, such as informed consent and decisions regarding *whether* to act at all. These questions are, I argue, *outside* the ambit of medical expertise. They are, in essence, ethical. As Lucy Frith notes, there has been 'concern about the encroachment of medicine into almost every area of life, and the medicalisation of human existence',[4] and I agree and suggest that this process has not only included the *medicalisation* of life but also the (sometimes unnecessary) *ethicalisation* of medical practice. In other words, medical practice has increasingly come to include, particularly around these ancillary decisions, questions that, as I argue below, are *ethical* rather than *technical* in nature. As such, these are not necessarily matters which the medical profession are automatically and uniquely qualified to take or make.

If the medical exception is to be applied to these ethical matters, then it is vital that decisions relating to them are made correctly and in a fashion that is consistent with what we might define as 'acceptable ethical principles'. Medical morality must, therefore, be shown to be fit for purpose if it is to be given legal immunity. However, this is not always the case.

Is there a problem with medical morality?

I want to begin with two cautionary tales. The first concerns the report by Sir Robert Francis, QC into the treatment of patients at Mid Staffordshire Foundation Trust, which revealed a catalogue of care that was undoubtedly both immoral and unethical. The report's Executive Summary highlighted appalling care including that:

- Patients were left in excrement in soiled bed clothes for lengthy periods;
- Assistance was not provided with feeding for patients who could not eat without help;
- Water was left out of reach;
- In spite of persistent requests for help, patients were not assisted in their toileting;
- Wards and toilet facilities were left in a filthy condition;
- Privacy and dignity, even in death, were denied;
- Triage in A&E was undertaken by untrained staff;
- Staff treated patients and those close to them with what appeared to be callous indifference.[5]

4 Frith (n 1) 34–35.

5 Mid Staffordshire NHS Foundation Trust Public Inquiry, *Report of the Mid Staffordshire NHS Foundation Trust Public Inquiry – Executive Summary* (HC 947, 2013) para. 23, available at http://www.midstaffspublicinquiry.com/sites/default/files/report/Executive%20summary.pdf (accessed 9 January 2015).

These findings have shocked both the medical community and wider society, but medical practitioners are human too, and so the profession will include individuals who act well and others who do not. We should not, therefore, allow ourselves to lapse into the easy assumption that this behaviour is more unforgivable because it came from medical practitioners. Nevertheless, it is true that the medical profession *is* seen as different from other professions, and its regulatory system is supposed to ensure that its members are appropriately qualified *and* act in an ethically and legally appropriate manner.[6] It might thus be argued that supporting the medical exception is not just a reflection of the nature of medical practice, but it is also how the law has traditionally seen *the medical profession*. This will be evident in my discussion of the old law below, where judges entrusted ethical decisions to medical practitioners and justified this on the basis that the profession itself was 'respectable', and 'medical ethics' was seen as an internal, quasi-legal regulatory system for the medical profession.[7]

In some ways this position can be justified given the plethora of discourse and, in particular, ethical guidance published by professional bodies such as the General Medical Council (GMC), British Medical Association (BMA), and the Royal Colleges.[8] Yet the proof of the pudding is in the eating, and nobody would describe the acts listed in the Mid Staffordshire Report as ethical. Indeed, Sir Robert Francis highlighted the failure of the system of professional regulation and held it responsible for the events at the hospital because the regulatory system had not prevented the inadequate conduct:

> It is because not all professionals do live up to the high standards expected of them that we have professional regulators . . . It does not need a public inquiry to recognise that this elaborate system failed dramatically in the case of Stafford . . . the system as a whole failed in its most essential duty – to protect patients from unacceptable risks of harm and from unacceptable, and in some cases inhumane, treatment that should never be tolerated in any hospital.[9]

Bad behaviour by doctors, both within and without the course of their work, is nothing new.[10] In the recent past we have seen doctors who have killed their patients, in the form of Dr Harold Shipman,[11] clinicians routinely removing and

6 For example, all doctors have to conform to General Medical Council (GMC) guidance: GMC, *Good Medical Practice* (GMC, 2013), updated 29 April 2014.

7 See further J. Miola, *Medical Ethics and Medical Law: A Symbiotic Relationship* (Hart, 2007).

8 See e.g. GMC (n 6); British Medical Association (BMA), *Medical Ethics Today: The BMA's Handbook of Ethics and Law* (Wiley, 2012); Royal College of Physicians (RCP), *Guidelines on the Practice of Ethics Committees in Medical Research with Human Participants* (4th edn, RCP, 2007).

9 *Mid-Staffordshire Report* (n 5) para. 4.

10 For analysis of some recent examples see M. Dixon-Woods, K. Yeung, C. Bosk, 'Why is UK medicine no longer a self-regulating profession? The role of scandals involving "bad apple" doctors' (2011) 73 *Social Science and Medicine* 1452.

11 Shipman Inquiry, *Shipman: The Final Report* (TSO, 2005).

retaining organs from dead children without the knowledge or consent of their parents,[12] and doctors (albeit not in the UK) involved in torture, the force-feeding of prisoners, and even judicial executions.[13] And, of course, less than a century ago, doctors participated in war crimes including 'medical research' and genocide during the Holocaust.[14] The medical profession, just as any other group in society, contains individuals who should not be given the freedom to act as they might wish to. However, sometimes poor behaviour will not only be *within* the law, it may be sanctioned or encouraged by the state. For example, the removal and retention of organs in British hospitals during the 1990s was not actually unlawful because of the weak legislative framework which existed at that time.[15] And in the US there are instances of state involvement in what many would consider to be unethical behaviour; doctors are involved in judicial executions, and it has been alleged that in some cases they have to actually insert the catheters for lethal injections.[16] It has also been alleged that medical practitioners were, and perhaps still are, involved in the torture of terrorism suspects and the force-feeding of prisoners on hunger strike in Guantanamo Bay.[17] These activities are not just legal but are actively sanctioned by the state, and medical involvement in human experimentation and genocide during the Holocaust is but a further extreme example. In such situations, as Thomas Szasz noted in the context of mental health and psychiatrists, the doctor ceases to be an agent of the patient seeking to work for her benefit but, instead, becomes an instrument of the state working to further *its* interests. And these interests may well conflict with those of the patient.[18] For example, a doctor undertaking assessments for disability benefits may face pressure from her employer to declare as many patients as possible fit for work, even though this may be to the detriment of some patients who will not be able to cope with work.

It might be hoped, at least in modern times, that the profession as a whole and its ethics might prove an obstacle to such behaviour. But the above examples indicate that this is not the case. Doctors *are* involved in executions, force-feeding, and torture, despite the fact that the American Medical Association, for example, has

12 This was discovered as part of the work of the Retained Organs Commission, available at http://collections.europarchive.org/tna/20060802143339/nhs.uk/retainedorgans/ (accessed 9 January 2015). For an overview see S. Giordano, 'Is the body a republic?' (2005) *Journal of Medical Ethics* 470.

13 See e.g. R. J. Lifton, 'Doctors and torture' (2004) 351 *New England Journal of Medicine* 415.

14 There is extensive literature discussing this, but for an excellent and readable collection see A. Caplan (ed.), *When Medicine Went Mad – Bioethics and the Holocaust* (Humana Press, 1992).

15 D. Price, 'From Cosmos and Damien to Van Velzen: The human tissue saga continues' (2003) 11 *Medical Law Review* 1.

16 E. Pilkington, 'Doctor involved in botched execution "experimented" on inmate, suit claims' (*The Guardian*, 14 October 2014), available at http://www.theguardian.com/world/2014/oct/14/oklahoma-clayton-lockett-execution-doctor-experiment-oaths-lawsuit (accessed 9 January 2015).

17 See Lifton (n 13).

18 T. Szasz, *The Theology of Medicine: The Political-Philosophical Foundations of Medical Ethics* (Syracuse University Press, 1988). Also Miola (n 7) ch. 2.

denounced each of these practices.[19] Equally, ethical codes and guidance from the GMC failed to stop unconsented to organ removal and retention by doctors in the UK. Thus, as Sir Robert Francis noted with respect to the events at Mid Staffordshire, such behaviour at that hospital persisted despite the plethora of organisations offering advice and guidance on both the technical and ethical aspects of medical practice. Therefore, *more* ethics and ethical guidance does not automatically signify *better* guidance and more ethically appropriate professional practice and behaviour. This system of medical ethics, then, cannot be seen to be a successful regulator. If this is so, then it might provide other decision-making mechanisms, such as the law, with the justification it needs to intervene and ensure that reasonable decisions are made.[20] Indeed, a pattern of identifiably unacceptable ethical decision-making by medical professionals, such as at Mid Staffordshire, should alert the law to the fact that such ethical issues should *not* form part of any definition of proper medical treatment and should, therefore, not be covered by the medical exception.

Furthermore, the recent disclosure of the report into potential CIA torture of prisoners following the 9/11 attacks detailed what was referred to as the 'rectal rehydration' of at least five prisoners.[21] The *Guardian* report of that disclosure notes that:

> One CIA cable released in the report reveals that detainee Majid Khan was administered by enema his 'lunch tray' consisting of hummus, pasta with sauce, nuts and raisins was 'pureed and rectally infused'. One CIA officer's email was in the report quoted as saying 'we used the largest . . . tube we had'. Rectal feeding is of limited application in actually keeping a person alive or administering nutrients, since the colon and rectum cannot absorb much besides salt, glucose and a few minerals and vitamins. The CIA administered rectal rehydration to Khalid Sheikh Mohammed 'without a determination of medical need'.[22]

19 See American Medical Association (AMA), *Opinion 2.06 – Capital Punishment* (1980), updated June 2000, available at http://www.ama-assn.org/ama/pub/physician-resources/medical-ethics/code-medical-ethics/opinion206.page? (accessed 9 January 2015); AMA, *Opinion 2.067 – Torture* (1999), available at http://www.ama-assn.org/ama/pub/physician-resources/medical-ethics/code-medical-ethics/opinion2067.page? (accessed 9 January 2015). Force-feeding is not covered, but in 2013 the AMA wrote a letter condemning physician involvement in the practice at Guantanamo Bay to the then Secretary of State for Defence: see C. Rosenberg, 'AMA opposes forced feedings at Guantánamo' (*Miami Herald*, 30 April 2013), available at http://www.miamiherald.com/news/nation-world/world/americas/guantanamo/article1950859.html (accessed 9 January 2015).

20 See further C. Foster, J. Miola, 'Who's in charge? The relationship between medical law, medical ethics and medical morality' (online advance access, DOI: 10.1093/medlaw/fwv004). I do not consider here how we might determine whether individual decisions are good or bad, but would argue that some are self-evidently bad.

21 Senate Select Committee on Intelligence, *Committee Study of the Central Intelligence Agency's Detention and Interrogation Program: Findings and Conclusions* (SSCI, 2012) 4, available at http://www.intelligence.senate.gov/study2014/sscistudy1.pdf (accessed 9 January 2015).

22 See D. Rush, E. MacAskill, I. Cobain, A. Yuhas, O. Laughland, 'Rectal rehydration and waterboarding: The CIA Torture Report's grisliest findings' (*The Guardian*, 10 December 2014), available at http://www.theguardian.com/us-news/2014/dec/09/cia-torture-report-worst-findings-waterboard-rectal (accessed 9 January 2015).

Not only were these actions unnecessary but, as the report notes, there were risks to the prisoners in the procedure, including damage to the rectum and food rotting 'inside the recipients' digestive tracts'.[23] The CIA was informed that excessive force had been used and that at least one inmate had 'suffered from an anal fissure, chronic hemorrhoids and symptomatic rectal prolapse'.[24]

If we assume that such actions were either performed or supervised by qualified medical practitioners, then it is not difficult to see how this raises questions regarding the supervision and regulation of medical conduct. While rectal rehydration might have been carried out or supervised by medical professionals, the key decisions were not concerned with the execution of the procedure itself but *whether to provide it at all*. They were *ethical* and not *technical* in nature. Any doctors involved would undoubtedly have acted contrary to the ethical mores of their profession, and the profession failed to adequately regulate their conduct. The doctors would also have been acting as agents of the state, or at least believed that they were doing so. But I hope that we can agree that such conduct should not (cannot, must not) be governed by the medical exception. This may be even clearer here than with the events at Mid Staffordshire, where many of the staff failed to prevent harm rather than actively caused it. Yet these cases demonstrate some of the difficulties with defining the nature of proper medical treatment, and with applying the medical exception across the board simply to what doctors *do*. Unfortunately, decisions of the courts in the old cases indicate that this was a longstanding practice, in England and Wales at least.

The 'old' approach

Many, though not all, of the cases I analyse below involve the civil law; thus, the medical exception would not apply. Nevertheless, if we take medical law as a discrete area of law, non-intervention by judges in civil cases where proper medical treatment is identified as being at play is analogous to the application of the medical exception in the criminal law. Indeed, the civil courts in England and Wales have a long tradition of non-interference in decisions that they class as 'medical', and such reluctance to intervene may have facilitated the abuses described above. Ethical issues were routinely medicalised by the courts, which determined that such matters fell within the remit of medical treatment or medical matters and so justified delegating responsibility for decision-making to the medical profession's own ethics. An example of this is the decision of the House of Lords in *Gillick*.[25] At issue in this case was whether doctors could provide contraceptive advice and treatment to under 16s without the knowledge and/or consent of their parents. This issue was not a question of technical medical skill, but the House medicalised the issue and viewed this ethical decision as a medical matter. Responsibility for determining when it would be appropriate for doctors to provide contraceptive

23 Rush *et al.* (n 22).

24 Rush *et al.* (n 22).

25 *Gillick v West Norkolk and Wisbech Health Authority* [1985] 3 All ER 402, HL.

advice and treatment to under 16s was thus to be left to the judgement of doctors. As Lord Fraser stated:

> *[t]he medical profession have in modern times come to be entrusted with very wide discretionary powers going beyond the strict limits of clinical judgment* and, in my opinion, there is nothing strange about entrusting them with this further responsibility which *they alone are in a position to discharge satisfactorily.*[26]

Two points stand out in this quote. First, Lord Fraser was happy to medicalise something that he identified as an ethical issue. He recognised that the question of whether to provide treatment was beyond the unique expertise of the clinician, but he, nevertheless, passed on that responsibility. Second, what might be seen as the basis for the medical exception can be found in his latter italicised comment, which indicates his faith in the ability of the medical profession as a whole to make such decisions. The reference to the unique position of medical professionals could refer to the fact it is their responsibility to interact with the patient, but another comment, I suggest, makes it clear that that there is also an innate confidence in the ability of the medical profession to police its own decisions. Thus, having listed the criteria that doctors should consider when deciding whether to provide contraceptive advice and treatment, Lord Fraser stated:

> That result ought not to be regarded as a licence for doctors to disregard the wishes of parents on this matter whenever they find it convenient to do so. Any doctor who behaves in such a way would be failing to discharge his professional responsibilities, and I would expect him to be disciplined by his own professional body accordingly.[27]

Thus, his Lordship was prepared to abrogate responsibility to the medical profession for a decision that he acknowledged was *beyond* the strict scope of medical competence. Moreover, he also entrusted the medical profession with responsibility for policing and punishing transgressors. This seems, to all intents and purposes, to be a new medical exception created within the civil law, with the approach being to first medicalise ethical issues by redefining them as being medical in nature, and then refusing to intervene in such issues because of a desire not to interfere in the proper work of medical practitioners.

Such an approach was prevalent in cases during the 1980s and early 1990s, and was based on judges widely defining what constituted a medical decision and so what should be decided by the medical profession and its ethics. Indeed, for example, it was held that not only was the amount of information to be disclosed to a patient 'primarily a clinical judgment',[28] but also that it made no difference

26 *Gillick* (n 25) 413, emphasis supplied.
27 *Gillick* (n 25) 413.
28 *Sidaway v Board of Governors of Bethlem Royal Hospital* [1985] 1 All ER 643, HL.

whether disclosure was in relation to therapeutic or non-therapeutic treatment.[29] Similarly, the concept of what was in the best interests of a patient who lacks the capacity to make decisions for themselves was initially deemed to be a medical decision.[30] In both of these examples the process identified in *Gillick* was utilised. Thus, in *Blyth v Bloomsbury*,[31] which concerned consent to an elective sterilisation, Mrs Blyth argued that the disclosure of risks should be different, more extensive, in non-therapeutic cases because such procedures were elective. In these cases the disclosure of information should be determined by the patient. The Court of Appeal disagreed, stating that whatever doctors did in the course of their jobs constituted proper medical treatment, regardless of the context, and decisions relating to such treatment should thus be left to doctors:

> a doctor's duty of care in relation to diagnosis, treatment and advice, whether the doctor be a specialist or a general practitioner, is not to be dissected into its component parts. To dissect the doctor's advice into that given in a therapeutic context and that given in a contraceptive context would be to go against the whole thrust of [the law].[32]

The decision to disclose information on risks was thus viewed as medical decision. This displays a similar attitude to that in evidence in *Gillick*, where medicalisation was justified even though it was recognised that the issue at hand was not technically medical in nature, but, regardless, doctors could be allowed to make such decisions because they were inherently trustworthy.

Such reliance and trust clearly depends not only on the profession's good conscience, but also on the profession's ability to regulate itself and those practising medicine. But, obviously, not all decisions made by individual doctors are good decisions, and the myriad of regulatory bodies that provide advice and guidance to medical practitioners have not prevented the medical scandals noted above. Indeed, such scandals have occurred against a backdrop of the increasing ethicalisation of medical practice, where more matters are being drawn into the medical sphere, requiring *more* rather than *less* ethical decisions to be made. In large part, this ethicalisation is due to the rapid advances in medical technology over the course of the last century.[33] Without such technology we would not have to consider issues such as parentage in relation to artificial insemination using donor gametes, whether to remove artificial nutrition and hydration or ventilation

29 *Blyth v Bloomsbury Health Authority* [1993] 4 Med LR 151, CA. Although reported in 1993, this case was decided in 1987.

30 *F v West Berkshire Health Authority* [1990] 2 AC 1, HL. This is now interpreted more widely under the Mental Capacity Act 2005, and is, arguably, more respectful of patient autonomy.

31 *Blyth* (n 29).

32 *Blyth* (n 29) 156.

33 See R. H. Ebert, 'A twentieth century retrospective' in E. Ginzberg (ed.), *Medicine and Society – Clinical Decisions and Societal Values* (Westview Press, 1987).

from patients in a permanent vegetative state or even a minimally conscious state, or whether to strive to keep alive babies born after 23 weeks' gestation.[34] This increasing ethicalisation of medical practice, creating decisions relating to *whether* to treat rather than *how* to do so, combined with the courts' traditional abrogation of responsibility for ethical decisions to the medical profession, has led to criticisms that what had come to be defined as proper medical treatment, and decisions that were to be left for doctors to make, were too wide.[35]

Moreover, such decisions were beyond what was within the boundaries of medical expertise, and, for example, Ian Kennedy argued that:

> Doctors make decisions about what is to be done. Some, but only some, of these decisions are matters of technical skill. I submit that the majority of decisions taken by doctors are not technical. They are, instead, moral and ethical. They are decisions about what ought to be done, in light of certain values. Now, this creates a problem. Doctors claim a special, indeed unique, competence in a particular area, the practice of medicine. So medical judgements, medical decisions, are for them and them alone. But, if I am right that it is a fundamental feature of medical practice that doctors are making ethical judgements, it means that ethics, to the extent that they touch on how doctors choose to practice medicine, are something for them and them alone. This is a surprising and even dangerous notion.[36]

This quote encapsulates much of what I have discussed in this section: the (unnecessary) medicalisation of ethical issues, and the notion that such decision-making is claimed by the medical profession. But Kennedy does not identify the complicity of the law in this process. I have argued that the law has itself participated in the process of medicalisation, and the creation of what is, essentially, a medical exception within the civil law can be seen as a failure by the law to protect patients. This is disappointing because it might be thought that the *raison d'etre* of the law is such protection. As Sheila McLean argued:

> [n]o matter the quality of medicine practised, and no matter the doubts of doctors themselves about the appropriateness of their involvement, human life is increasingly medicalised. In part, this is the result of the growing professionalism of medicine, in part our responsibility for asking too much of doctors. In part, however, it is also because the buffer which might be expected to stand between medicalisation and human rights – namely the law – has proved unwilling, unable or inefficient when asked to adjudicate on or control issues which are at best tangentially medical.[37]

34 These issues are covered in most health care law textbooks. See e.g. E. Jackson, *Medical Law: Text, Cases and Materials* (3rd edn, Oxford University Press, 2013).

35 See further Brazier and Fovargue (n 1).

36 I. Kennedy, *The Unmasking of Medicine* (George Allen & Unwin, 1981) 78.

37 S. McLean, *Old Law, New Medicine: Medical Ethics and Human Rights* (Pandora Publishing, 1999) 2.

Like Kennedy, McLean identifies the *ethical* nature of a lot of medical decision-making, and identifies the law as being unwilling to take responsibility for decision-making. In this way, decisions that were not legitimately medical were redefined by the law *as* medical in nature, and the medical profession itself was tasked with policing decision-making with respect to them. In order for this system to work, medical ethics, which is relied upon to regulate decisions, must be effective at doing so. Unfortunately, this has not always been the case.

The (failing) relationship between law and ethics

I argue that the law's relationship with medical ethics has been, and remains, dysfunctional, as it assumes that medical ethics is similar to the law: a regulatory system of rules backed by sanctions and designed to police behaviour.[38] The dysfunction occurs because this assumption is incorrect, and so a 'regulatory vacuum results'.[39] Thus, a doctor may rely on her individual conscience or personal ethical or moral beliefs to fill this vacuum and influence her decision about an ethical matter. This may, on the face of it, not seem problematic, but reliance on individual conscience is something that modern medical law and ethics has, I suggest, tried to move away from.[40] Indeed, the conscience of individual practitioners is no better than that of the rest of us, and the central premise of post-Nuremberg medical ethics is the recognition of that fact, as well as the need for the regulation of medical behaviour to prevent abuses.[41] Furthermore, as I will show, there is evidence that the process of medicalisation described above continues, and that there is a leaking of the medical exception into the civil law and outside of what might be considered legitimately medical decisions.

An example of this dysfunction can be found in *Re W*, where the Court of Appeal held that it would be lawful for a doctor to provide medical treatment to an under 18-year-old if either a parent or a competent child consented to that treatment.[42] Lord Donaldson noted that:

> Hair-raising possibilities were canvassed of abortions being carried out by doctors in reliance upon the consent of the parents and despite the refusal of consent by 16 or 17 year olds. *Whilst this may be possible as a matter of law, I do not see any likelihood, taking account of medical ethics [that this would be allowed to occur].*[43]

38 J. Miola, 'Medical law and medical ethics: Complementary or corrosive?' (2004) 6 *Medical Law International* 251. Also Miola (n 7).

39 See further Miola (n 38).

40 Miola (n 7) particularly ch. 3.

41 See E. Schuster, 'Fifty years later: The significance of the Nuremberg Code' (1997) 337 *New England Journal of Medicine* 1436; G. Annas, M. Grodin (eds), *The Nazi Doctors and the Nuremberg Code: Human Rights in Human Experimentation* (Oxford University Press, 1995).

42 *Re W (A Minor) (Medical Treatment: Court's Jurisdiction)* [1992] 4 All E.R. 627, CA. See Miola (n 38) 261–269.

43 *Re W* (n 42) 635, emphasis supplied.

Again, the decision described by Lord Donaldson is *ethical* in nature. *Whether* to perform such an abortion is not a clinical decision for which doctors have a unique competence; *how* to perform that abortion is. And Lord Donaldson not only abrogated responsibility to the medical profession and medical ethics for the decision whether to terminate a pregnancy without the minor's consent, he also acknowledged that his 'hair-raising possibility' was *legally possible* but was content to place trust in medical ethics as a regulatory tool to prevent it from happening in practice. This confidence might have been because he assumed that medical ethics was a tangible entity that provided a clear set of rules for doctors, rather than the amorphous concept that it was and is. Perhaps he viewed it as an effective regulator of medical conduct, as a surrogate legal system, with medical ethics a form of internal 'law' for the medical profession. But in this context this was not the case. The relevant GMC guidance of the time merely restated the law, while the BMA recommended seeking legal advice if the situation arose.[44] Thus, the law passed decision-making responsibility in this matter to the medical profession and its ethics, and the profession returned it to the law. Essentially, what might then result is the decision being made on the basis of the conscience of the individual practitioners involved. So, in the absence of anyone else directing their decision, the doctor would most likely do what they were minded to before investigating the issue. And this may well be the situation today because while the relevant guidance accurately reflects the law, it does not prevent such abortions being performed in the way that Lord Donaldson appeared to assume that it would.[45]

Indeed, medical law and professional medical ethics have not been integrated or have not been working together, and this is of concern because of, as I have shown, the courts' traditional willingness to allow the medical profession to take decisions which it views to be of an ethical nature. Recall Lord Fraser's comments in the House of Lords in *Gillick*,[46] where he stated that if a doctor did not follow the five requirements that he set out as prerequisites to allow a doctor to treat minors without the knowledge or consent of their parents, he 'would expect him to be *disciplined* by *his own professional body accordingly*'.[47] The question of regulating medical conduct in relation to an ethical rather than a technical medical question is thus again seen as being the responsibility of the medical profession itself rather than the law.

But it is worth pausing here and considering what Lord Donaldson actually did in *Re W*. Essentially, he created a medical exception relating to the question of whether to provide treatment to an anorexic minor with the consent of only one of three parties required (W or either of her parents), with the court constituting

44 Miola (n 38). The guidance of the time was contained in GMC, *Good Medical Practice* (GMC, 1998); GMC, *Seeking Patients' Consent: The Ethical Considerations* (GMC, 1998); BMA, *Consent, Rights and Choices in Health Care for Children and Young People* (BMJ Books, 2001).

45 See BMA, *Children and Young People Tool Kit* (BMA, 2010) Card 4, available at http://bma.org.uk/practical-support-at-work/ethics/children/children-and-young-people-tool-kit (accessed 9 January 2015); GMC, *0–18 Years: Guidance for All Doctors* (GMC, 2007) paras 22–41.

46 *Gillick* (n 25).

47 *Gillick* (n 25) 413, emphasis supplied.

a fourth party that could still authorise treatment even if the others refused to do so. This surely cannot be deemed to be a *medical* question, and would fall squarely within Kennedy's description of ethical issues that have been medicalised.[48] Yet Lord Donaldson not only abrogates responsibility to medical ethics by noting that the doctor will have a *professional and ethical* but not *legal* problem; he left this legal possibility open on the assumption that medical ethics would prevent doctors from using it. While it is not unreasonable for the legal and ethical standards to be different, it should be remembered that Lord Donaldson referred to his scenario as 'hair raising', suggesting something that should not be allowed to occur. So, what if a doctor did propose to perform an abortion on a 17-year old without her consent but with that of her parent(s)? Since, as Lord Donaldson himself noted, this would be legally possible, then seemingly a doctor performing an abortion on a 17-year-old despite her refusal would not be *legally* liable. The medical exception would apply. However, it would be a breach of the medical ethics that Lord Donaldson referred to, and, as per Lord Fraser's comments in *Gillick*, the expectation would be that the poor conduct would lead to *professional* sanctions.[49] The fact that the ethical guidance does not do what Lord Donaldson assumes is incidental. The important point is that the court redefined an ethical decision as legitimately medical, thereby absolving itself of any responsibility to provide oversight of medical decision-making, even in relation to issues that are not, I suggest, legitimately medical.

The 'new' cases

Although the dysfunctional relationship between law and medical ethics is concerning given the increase in the ethicalisation of medical practice, since the mid-to-late 1990s medical law has undergone a process of change, and there has been legal modifications in key areas resulting in what can be seen as more patient-friendly rules. The process of legal change has thus demedicalised many of the issues raised in the old cases, and so the scale of the 'civil medical exception' has been circumscribed, albeit incidentally rather than by design. For example, in relation to information disclosure, patient autonomy is now placed at the centre of the law, and in *Chester v Afshar* the House of Lords even modified the rules relating to causation to allow a negligence claim by a patient, effectively on the basis that her autonomy had been compromised.[50] Furthermore, with regard to both sterilisation and the withdrawal of life-sustaining treatment, for example, the law remains based on the concept of the best interests of the patient, but the Mental Capacity Act 2005 now provides a statutory definition of this concept. And the 2005 Act aims, as much as possible, to enhance patient autonomy by seeking to ascertain

48 Kennedy (n 36). See also I. Kennedy, *Treat Me Right: Essays in Medical Law and Ethics* (Clarendon Press, 1988).

49 *Gillick* (n 25).

50 *Chester v Afshar* [2004] UKHL 41. For an excellent analysis of this decision see S. Devaney, 'Autonomy rules OK' (2005) 13 *Medical Law Review* 102.

what the patient would have wanted had she had capacity.[51] A notable exception, however, is the law relating to consent for minors, which has fundamentally remained the same. The courts' understandable desire to prioritise the welfare of children may have prevented any change to the law relating to consent in that area,[52] and so it could be considered an outlier rather than weakening the generally accepted view that the law has drifted into prioritising patient autonomy at the expense of medical paternalism.[53] Indeed, what these legal changes have in common is the prioritisation of autonomy as being seen as the purpose of the law. This is, perhaps, ironic given that, as Brazier and Fovargue identify, consent is in itself insufficient to justify the very actions to which the medical exception applies.[54] Another example is provided by Richard Huxtable, who notes that consent is also deemed insufficient by the law to allow assisted suicide.[55]

The new approach of the law, then, is to demedicalise issues, and to remove them from the legitimacy granted to decision-making by medical practitioners where they relate to ethical rather than technical decisions.[56] For example, *Ms B v An NHS Trust* involved a paralysed woman who was on a ventilator which was keeping her alive.[57] She wished to die and asked for it to be turned off. The doctors treating her refused because they viewed their role as being protective of life rather than to end it, and they argued that to do as Ms B demanded would be 'unethical'.[58] The court, however, disagreed, and ordered that another treatment team that would accede to her wishes be found and the ventilator switched off. Following Dame Butler-Sloss P's decision in the High Court, Ms B was transferred to another hospital and treatment team, and she died. Of note here is that the court was willing to intervene to protect what it saw as Ms B's autonomy, and Dame Butler-Sloss P quoted Lord Goff in *Bland*:

> *[T]he principle of the sanctity of human life must yield to the principle of self-determination* . . . and for present purposes perhaps most important, *the doctor's duty to act in the best interests of his patient must likewise be qualified.* On this basis, it has been held that a patient of sound mind may, if properly informed, require that life support should be discontinued . . . It is simply *that the patient has, as he is entitled to do, declined to consent to treatment* . . . and the doctor has, in accordance with his duty, complied with his patient's wishes.[59]

51 Mental Capacity Act 2005 ss 4(6)–(7).

52 See further S. Fovargue, S. Ost, 'Does the theoretical framework change the legal end result for mature minors refusing medical treatment or creating self-generated pornography?' (2013) 13 *Medical Law International* 6.

53 This is charted and critiqued in C. Foster, *Choosing Life, Choosing Death: The Tyranny of Autonomy in Medical Law* (Hart, 2009).

54 Brazier and Fovargue (n 1).

55 R. Huxtable, 'Death on demand: "Proper medical treatment"?' in this collection.

56 Foster and Miola (n 20).

57 *Ms B v An NHS Hospital Trust* [2002] EWHC 429.

58 *B* (n 57) para. 57, *per* Butler-Sloss P.

59 *B* (n 57) para. 23, quoting Lord Goff in *Airedale NHS Trust v Bland* [1993] AC 789, 864, emphasis supplied.

This case is an example of the court recognising the ethical content of the decision and taking control to give effect to the patient's wishes. It thus gave effect to what McLean demanded: a recognition of the patient's rights in relation to a question that was not one of technical medical skill, and an intervention to protect those rights.[60] Indeed, the court recognised that the decision in *Ms B* related not to whether the medical treatment was to be provided to or withdrawn from B, but to the question of whether to provide it at all. With regards to the medical–ethical boundary, this issue fell to *ethics* rather than *medicine*. There was thus no justification for leaving this decision to the medical profession as it was not a *legitimately* medical decision. Even if the treatment being provided here was proper, the question being asked and the answer sought lay outside the ambit of treatment, and the court was, therefore, justified in intervening in the decision-making process. At issue was the patient's autonomy, and so even though the decision related to a proper clinical interaction in terms of removing life-sustaining treatment, the court's determination of the issue as *ethical* meant that the decision was not properly the doctor's to make.

The courts might justify their intervention in medical decision-making based on the principle of self-determination, but implicit in this is the recognition that its protection is important because it does not involve fettering the doctor's ability to exercise her technical expertise. Perhaps the most explicit example of the court's use of the principle of autonomy as such a justification can be found in *Chester v Afshar*.[61] This is a classic 'informed consent' case. Ms Chester was not informed of a 1–2 per cent risk of partial paralysis prior to a pain-relieving back operation, a risk which subsequently materialised. The case rested on causation. Ms Chester admitted that had she been informed of the risk that had not been disclosed, she may have taken more time to think about things but would probably have consented to the surgery anyway.[62] Under the normal rules of causation this would mean that her claim failed because the breach of duty, not disclosing a material risk, had not *caused* the harm because she would have consented to the operation in any event. Nevertheless, the House of Lords found a way to compensate Ms Chester for what was, essentially, a loss of autonomy.[63] Lord Steyn stated that '[the] right to autonomy and dignity *can and ought to be vindicated*',[64] and Lord Walker noted (quoting Michael Jones) that the *purpose* of the law was to ensure that the patient was provided with sufficient information to exercise her autonomous choice because:

> [p]art of the imbalance between doctor and patient is due to the patient's lack of information, and, on one view, it is the function of the law to redress the imbalance by providing patients with the 'right' to be given that information, or perhaps more accurately imposing a duty on doctors to provide it.[65]

60 McLean (n 37).

61 *Chester* (n 50).

62 See further Devaney (n 50).

63 Devaney (n 50).

64 *Chester* (n 50) para. 41, emphasis supplied.

65 M. Jones, 'Informed consent and other fairy stories' (1999) 7 *Medical Law Review* 103, 129, as quoted in *Chester* (n 50) para. 58.

The court thus changed the law relating to causation to protect the principle of autonomy. Their Lordships appeared to begin by identifying the purpose of the law relating to informed consent as being the protection of patient autonomy, and then asked whether the law fulfilled that purpose. When they found that it did not, they declared the law to be deficient and so rectified the error. In this, the House was following the approach and philosophy taken by the High Court of Australia in the case of *Rogers v Whitaker*, which also began by so defining the purpose of the law, then proceeded to find the law deficient and change it.[66]

In both of these cases, we can see the court reject the legitimacy of medical decision-making in the relevant areas by using the concept of autonomy and refusing to medicalise what was identified as an ethical issue. Thus, in B's case, to provide and remove a ventilator requires an exercise of medical expertise but the decision *whether* to do so does not. The same is true for Ms Chester's back operation; performing that operation involves medical skill but providing information to enable her to make a choice whether to consent to the operation does not.[67] So, even though the treatments in *Ms B* and *Chester were* proper medical treatments, the law ensured that *it*, and not the medical profession, set out the boundaries of when that treatment started and ended. Outside of that boundary there is, I argue, a duty on the courts to protect patients from decisions made *about* them by people who do not have unique competence in making such decisions. Indeed, the most noticeable difference between the two approaches is the initial question that the courts ask. Instead of asking whether the issue is medical in nature, a doctor-centred question, the courts' current approach seems to be to begin by asking whether the patient's right to autonomy is sufficiently protected, which is a patient-centred question.

This approach rejects medicalisation and misplaced confidence in medical ethics to resolve ethical issues, and what could be seen as a civil law version of the medical exception does not seem to apply any more. The law is now patient facing rather than focused on doctors. Thus, whereas the old cases seemed to concentrate more on the duties of the doctor, making it more natural to abrogate decision-making responsibility to the medical profession, the new cases emphasise the rights of patients. Medicalisation is thus no longer a logical step. Indeed, what we can see in the new cases is that once decisions are identified as being ethical, the legitimacy of medical decision-making is *removed* rather than proved. Given this, there is no question of delegating decision-making responsibility to the medical profession, and the effective civil medical exception is thereby also removed.

Implications for proper medical treatment

This new, patient-focused approach has two noteworthy effects. First, by definition, it limits the space available for a doctor to rely on her conscience when

66 [1993] 4 Med LR 78. For discussion of this see J. Miola, 'On the materiality of risk: Paper tigers and panaceas' (2009) 17 *Medical Law Review* 76. This was also the approach of the Supreme Court in *Montgomery v Lanarkshire Health Board* [2015] UKSC 11.

67 The identification of this distinction was the basis of Lord Scarman's (essentially dissenting) judgment in *Sidaway* (n 28).

making decisions. The older approach provided that space through its overly wide definition of what constituted a medical decision, and the courts' reflexive reluctance to interfere in medical matters made that space even larger. The new legal landscape does much to close that space by aligning judicial activism with the interests of patients, in particular the principle of autonomy. Doctors are no longer routinely allowed by the law to be the decision-makers in relation to ethical questions. However, Jonathan Montgomery has highlighted the fact that this risks removing morality from medical practice:

> the discipline of healthcare law is at risk of being transformed – moving *from* a discipline in which the moral values of medical ethics (and those of the non-medical health professions) are a central concern, *to* one in which they are being supplanted by an amoral commitment to choice and consumerism. In other words, that the morality is being taken out of medicine by legal activity.[68]

Thus, it might be argued that only by allowing doctors to make ethical decisions can we encourage doctors to act ethically. If this *is* the result of the new legal landscape, then it is concerning. I am not suggesting that there are *no* decisions that are most appropriately made by individual doctors or the medical profession. Indeed, just as we must look at the boundaries of legitimate medical decision-making and assess what lies outside, we must also look at what is contained within it. If we are to argue that one reason for encouraging judicial involvement in decision-making is the fact that a decision lies outside the sphere of technical medical skill, this suggests that where a decision does relate to medical skill it should be for the medical profession itself to make. In *Sidaway* Lord Scarman suggested as such, stating that in matters of diagnosis and treatment the standards should be 'set by the medical profession'.[69] There are powerful arguments for holding to that line, and many would be uncomfortable with a situation where, for example, judges were routinely involving themselves in decisions regarding the correct place for an incision to be located or for an artery to be clamped. These *are* issues where doctors *do* have a unique competence, and it is not unreasonable to expect that *their own standards* should carry almost determinative weight. That said, the word 'almost' is critical because I contend that it is never right for a profession to police itself, it must always be subject to the law and legal oversight. Therefore, even if we agree with Lord Scarman's opinion in *Sidaway* in general terms, it is necessary for there to be a mechanism for patients to have recourse to judicial analysis of medical conduct and decisions.

In this respect, the law's current rules relating to negligence introduced by the House of Lords in *Bolitho* strike the correct balance.[70] A doctor will not be liable

68 J. Montgomery, 'Law and the demoralisation of medicine' (2006) 26 *Legal Studies* 185, 186, emphasis supplied.

69 *Sidaway* (n 28) 647.

70 *Bolitho* (n 2).

so long as she has the support of some other doctors, which is subject to judicial scrutiny as the court retains the right, in 'rare cases', to find liability even in the face of unanimous medical support for the defendant where the medical view is 'unable to withstand logical analysis'.[71] In this way, cases that concern the performance of proper medical treatment could benefit from a 'light touch' regulation by the law. A good example of this can be found in *Richards*, where a treatment team took an hour to perform a caesarean section after the decision to proceed had been made.[72] The guidelines, set by the medical profession itself, stated that good practice was to operate as soon as possible after the decision to perform a caesarean was made, with the aim of doing so within half an hour.[73] The High Court held that, in the absence of mitigating circumstances leading to the delay in treatment, the length of time taken was unreasonable, using the medical profession's own best practice document as its guide to what was reasonable.

Such an approach allows the medical profession to have a say in whether conduct will be legally sanctioned without the law ceding all control as occurred during the 1980s and early 1990s. The old law had identified the correct delineation; it *was* right to tread cautiously in matters of technical medical skill. However, it failed patients by defining 'medical' too widely, and being overly reluctant to intervene in ethical issues that were not legitimately medical decisions. The execution, rather than the principle, was faulty, and the interests of patients were forgotten. The new approach goes some way to correct that error. But, as Montgomery argues, the risk with it is that by closing the space for medical conscience, morality is removed from medical practice, and it would be equally undesirable to end up in a consumerist medical mindset where the patient acts as a consumer for whom anything goes. Autonomy would then indeed become a tyrant.[74]

The second noteworthy effect follows on from the first. The danger in the new approach is that we forget that it *is* proper for doctors to be the principle decision-makers in issues that are properly medical. If we close the door to medical decision-making too much, we risk swinging the pendulum too far the other way and demedicalising what are and should be medical decisions. This would particularly be the case if patients were to be able to demand treatment. Traditionally, English law has not allowed this,[75] but it is not such a large step to say that if patients are to be treated as consumers then they should be able to demand that their rights include a right to treatment, and treatment of their choice.[76] This might not be a positive development, as patients might demand unreasonable,

71 *Bolitho* (n 2) 243, *per* Lord Browne-Wilkinson.

72 *Richards v Swansea NHS Trust* [2007] EWHC 487 (QB).

73 *Richards* (n 72) para. 20. The judge cites clinical guidance published by National Institute for Health and Care Excellence and the Royal College of Obstetricians and Gynaecologists.

74 Charles Foster has argued the principle of autonomy has been so overused in contemporary medical law that it has become the eponymous tyrant: Foster (n 53).

75 See e.g. *R (Burke) v General Medical Council* [2005] EWCA Civ 1003; *Re Wyatt (A Child) (Medical Treatment: Parents' Consent)* [2005] EWHC 693 (Fam).

76 R. E. Ashcroft, 'Could human rights supersede bioethics?' (2010) 10 *Human Rights Law Review* 639.

inappropriate, ineffective, or even harmful treatments. Nevertheless, patients *are* entitled to make decisions that affect them, and this means that it is correct that the law takes patient self-determination seriously, and the de-medicalisation inherent in the new approach of the law is thus to be welcomed. Questions of autonomy *do* fall outside the remit of proper medical decisions because they relate to the question of *whether* to do something rather than *how* to do so. But we must not forget that technical decisions are principally for medical practitioners to make. We must not allow the law to creep too far into that sphere.

Conclusion

Individual doctors are moral agents, and their ability to act with regard to their own consciences is deserving of respect.[77] It is for this reason that I propose a system of allocation for decision-making that is based on the boundaries of medical expertise. By going back to Kennedy's notion of doctors making decisions that they are not uniquely qualified to make, I argue that if we can determine that a decision is outside the boundaries of this competence, then the law has an increased justification, and possibly even a duty, to intervene in the decision-making process. They are not legitimate medical decisions. The protection of patient autonomy is based not only on the principle of autonomy itself but also on its categorisation of the protection of autonomy as a non-medical decision. This autonomy applies to decisions made by doctors and patients, and thus, for example, a doctor's refusal to participate in abortion on the grounds of conscience must also be respected as an exercise in autonomy, so long as such refusals do not result in harm to the patient.

Medical decision-making must be based on legitimacy, and doctors should only make decisions that are thus properly medical. At one point the law failed to acknowledge this, but the more recent approach goes some way to rectifying that situation. This may be a somewhat inadvertent change, as the new law is based on autonomy rather than legitimacy, but, as Montgomery noted, this risks encouraging a consumerist mindset that might push things too far the other way. We must not forget that just as doctors have no legitimacy to make non-medical decisions, they must have the loudest voice in legitimately medical decisions. There is also a need to ensure a culture of ethical conduct on the part of doctors, and this was absent in the examples provided at the beginning of this chapter. The key is balance. The law must be able to be involved in medical decision-making but it must do so with care. There are times when law should be actively interventionist, and times when it should back off. The difficulty, of course, is determining when each of these is appropriate. Kennedy's distinction between legitimately medical decisions and ethical decisions which are *not* legitimately medical is a good place to start.[78]

77 Discussions of conscience and proper medical treatment can be found in 'Conscience and Proper Medical Treatment' (2015) 23(2) *Medical Law Review*, a special issue of the *Review*.

78 Kennedy (n 36).

6 Family perspectives on 'proper medical treatment' for people in prolonged vegetative and minimally conscious states

*Celia Kitzinger and Jenny Kitzinger**

Introduction

Proper medical treatment is routinely defined, in law and in practice, as requiring the consent of the patient. Patients with disorders of consciousness (long-term 'coma') are unable to give or withhold consent because they are completely unconscious ('vegetative') or have only fleeting and occasional moments of consciousness ('minimally conscious'). They are completely (or largely) unaware of themselves and their environment.[1] They cannot understand the situation they are in or the treatments on offer; they cannot retain information relevant to a decision to accept or to refuse a particular medical treatment, nor can they weigh up the pros and cons of any treatment.[2] In England and Wales these patients, like others who lack the capacity to make some or all decisions because of learning disabilities or dementia, fall under the remit of section 5 of the Mental Capacity Act 2005, which is designed to ensure that proper medical treatment can be provided to people who lack the capacity to consent to it without putting doctors at risk of criminal prosecution.

The initial impetus for the 2005 Act is usually traced to the decision in *F v West Berkshire*,[3] commonly identified as 'a turning point in English medical law'.[4] The House of Lords was asked to determine the legality of sterilising a 36-year-old woman with learning disabilities who was deemed incapable of giving consent

* This chapter was part-funded by an ESRC Knowledge Exchange Grant [ES/K00560X/1], which also supported the http://www.healthtalk.org module where extracts from the filmed interviews can be viewed. The work was also supported by Research Priming Funds provided by the Wellcome Trust [ref: 097829/Z/11/A] through the Centre for Chronic Diseases and Disorders (C2D2) at the University of York.

1 Royal College of Physicians (RCP), *Prolonged Disorders of Consciousness: National Clinical Guidelines* (RCP, 2013), available at https://www.rcplondon.ac.uk/resources/prolonged-disorders-consciousness-national-clinical-guidelines (accessed 19 December 2014).

2 These are the criteria for determining whether a person has the capacity to make decisions for themselves: Mental Capacity Act (MCA) 2005, s. 3(1).

3 *F v West Berkshire Area Health Authority* [1990] 2 AC 1, HL.

4 A. Grubb, 'Editorial: Who decides? Legislating for the incapacitated adult' (1998) 5 *European Journal of Health Law* 231, 232.

for the surgery. They found that nobody, including next of kin and the courts,[5] had the legal power to consent to medical treatment on behalf of another adult. Any doctor who operated would do so without consent and, hence, would prima facie be guilty of offences of battery and/or trespass against the person. Both F's mother and her professional carers wanted to protect F against pregnancy, which, according to psychiatric evidence, would be 'disastrous' for her mental health,[6] but F's access to the service they believed she needed was impeded by her inability to consent and the inability for anyone to consent on her behalf. The House of Lords held that unless some solution could be found, then not just sterilisation but *any* medical treatment and, indeed, any day-to-day care (for example, 'dressing, feeding and so on'[7]) that involved touching a patient without their capacitous consent risked liability for tortious or criminal offences.[8] The remedy fashioned in *F v West Berkshire* was that their Lordships, while acknowledging that they could not consent to treatment on F's behalf, nonetheless granted the declaration that surgery would not be unlawful. They did so by invoking the 'doctrine of necessity',[9] holding that surgery was 'necessary' because it was in the patient's 'best interests' as defined by the *Bolam* test.[10]

Although providing a stopgap solution for this particular case, *F v West Berkshire* exposed a serious lacuna in the common law and the lack of any comprehensive framework to deal with it. Consequently, the Lord Chancellor asked the Law Commission to carry out a consultation exercise on decision-making for incapacitous adults, resulting in a series of publications[11] that culminated in the final report (and draft Bill) in 1995 and eventually the Mental Capacity Act 2005. The Act provides the legislative framework in England and Wales for determining capacity, appointing decision-makers, and establishing the basis on which decisions regarding those

5 Despite common public belief to the contrary, family members have never had the right (qua family members) to consent to medical treatments on behalf of an adult relative (and still do not). The courts had jurisdiction to consent to surgery under the common law principle of *parens patriae*, the Crown's ancient duty to protect 'imbeciles, lunatics and idiots', but lost this, more by accident than design, in 1960 with the coming in to force of the Mental Health Act 1959, leaving the lacuna in the law to which the House of Lords was now responding.

6 *F* (n 3) 34, *per* Butler-Sloss LJ; 53, *per* Lord Brandon.

7 *F* (n 3) 72, *per* Goff LJ.

8 Emergency treatment was recognised as an exception (*Wilson v Pringle* [1986] 2 All ER 440, CA), as were mental health treatments delivered to patients detained under the Mental Health Act 1983.

9 This doctrine is traced back to *R v Dudley & Stephens* (1884) 14 QBD 273: see AWB Simpson, *Cannibalism and the Common Law* (University of Chicago Press, 1984).

10 This test is widely used in the law of medical negligence and requires doctors to act in accordance with a practice accepted as proper by a responsible and competent body of relevant professional opinion: *Bolam v Friern Hospital Management Committee* [1957] 1 WLR 582.

11 Law Commission, *Mentally Incapacitated Adults and Decision-Making: An Overview. Consultation Paper No. 119* (HMSO, 1991); Law Commission, *Mentally Incapacitated Adults and Decision-Making: A New Jurisdiction. Consultation Paper No. 128* (HMSO, 1993); Law Commission, *Mentally Incapacitated Adults and Decision-Making: Medical Treatment and Research, Consultation Paper No. 129* (HMSO, 1993); Law Commission, *Mentally Incapacitated Adults and other Vulnerable Adults: Public Law Protection, Consultation Paper No. 130* (HMSO, 1993); Law Commission, *Mental Incapacity, Consultation Paper No. 231* (HMSO, 1995).

who lack capacity should be made: 'best interests'. For people with disorders of consciousness then, best interests supplants consent as a key criterion on the basis of which an otherwise tortious or criminal act against the person becomes an appropriate and legitimate medical intervention.[12]

People with disorders of consciousness typically receive a wide range of different medical treatments from the moment of the injury onwards. The vast majority of these treatments are now commonplace and well-established treatments for patients generally (for example, ventilators and feeding tubes), rather than newer and more controversial treatments discussed elsewhere in this collection. The controversy, if there is one, lies only in the application of these life-prolonging medical treatments to this *particular* group of patients rather than involving a controversy about the treatments per se. The question that generates fierce debate is should we be prolonging, for years or even decades, the lives of people who have little or no consciousness and who are highly unlikely ever to regain it? This is a question that is addressed, and evaded, by law and social policy, by media coverage, by professional codes of practice, by practitioners, and by family members.

For treatment of an unconscious patient to be lawful (at least after the emergency stage), each treatment should be delivered only if a decision has been made (in accordance with the guidelines laid out in the 2005 Act and its associated Code of Practice) that it is in the patient's best interests to receive it. Best interests is not defined in the Act, but a non-exhaustive checklist (section 4) requires the decision-maker to 'consider all the relevant circumstances' (section 4(2)), including, in addition to clinical concerns, the person's past and present wishes, feelings, beliefs, values, and 'any other factors he would be likely to consider if he were able to do so' (section 4(6)). Alongside this, there is a requirement for the decision-maker to consult widely to discover what these wishes, feelings, beliefs, and so on are (section 4(7)), and the need for such consultation is also highlighted in professional guidelines.[13]

Consultation with those who knew the patient before they were rendered unable to speak for themselves is crucial for best interests decision-making as a route to try to access what the patient might have wanted, and recent case law has emphasised that:

> [I]nsofar as it is possible to ascertain the patient's wishes and feelings, his beliefs and values or the things which were important to him, it is those which should be taken into account because they are a component in making the choice which is right for him as an individual human being.[14]

12 The only exception is when the person has a valid and applicable advance decision to refuse treatment (under the MCA 2005, ss 24–26), in which case best interests gives way to the decisions made by the individual. As with a contemporaneous refusal by a person with capacity, these prospective decisions can be binding even if those caring for the person believe them to be counter to the person's current best interests: Department for Constitutional Affairs, *Mental Capacity Act Code of Practice* (TSO, 2007) paras 5.4, 5.34. Best interests also does not apply, in certain circumstances, to participation in research (para. 5.4).

13 RCP (n 1) para. 3.5.

14 *Aintree University Hospitals NHS Foundation Trust v James* [2013] UKSC 67, para. 45, *per* Lady Hale.

However, as the government acknowledges, the 2005 Act has 'suffered from a lack of awareness and a lack of understanding' and '[t]oo many people who may lack capacity may be missing out on the legal rights that the [Mental Capacity Act] gives them'.[15] Our research regarding people in chronic disorders of consciousness[16] suggests that they miss out on the legal right (under section 4(6) of the Act) to have their values, wishes, and beliefs represented in decision-making about their medical treatments because family members are frequently not consulted, as they normally should be (under section 4(7)) about what those values wishes and beliefs were. One reason for this is, undoubtedly, because the patient's own (presumed or reported) views are not determinative of treatment (as they are in some US jurisdictions which rely on 'substituted judgement'), but are subsumed by the broader category of best interests as a criterion for legitimate treatment.[17]

This chapter is based on interviews with 65 family members of people with chronic disorders of consciousness (such as in vegetative or minimally conscious states), and explores how people understand proper medical treatment in this context. In-depth narrative interviews (on average around three hours in duration) were carried out by one or the other of the two co-authors, and included questions about how medical decisions were made, who made them, the process of decision-making, and whether the interviewee considered particular treatments to be in the patient's best interests, as well as their view about whether or not the patient would have wanted them.[18] Here we present family accounts in relation to emergency treatments, life-prolonging but non-restorative treatments, and the special case

15 The Government's Response to the House of Lords Select Committee Report on the Mental Capacity Act 2005, *Valuing Every Voice: Making the Case for the Mental Capacity Act* (HM Government, 2014), Foreword by the Minister of State for Care Services and the Minister of State for Justice and Civil Liberties, available at www.gov.uk/government/publications (accessed 19 December 2014).

16 L. Clements, C. Kitzinger, J. Kitzinger, 'Serious medical decisions and the Mental Capacity Act: Giving and withholding treatment for patients in prolonged disorders of consciousness' (work in progress).

17 See *W Healthcare NHS Trust v KH and Others* [2004] EWCA Civ 1324, and *P (Statutory Will), Re* [2009] EWHC 163 (Ch), for judicial discussion of the distinction between best interests and substituted judgement. The distinction was also made in the Law Commission's 1991 consultation paper (n 11). By the second round of consultation in 1993, the Commission had arrived at the view that they 'doubt[ed] that the two tests need be mutually exclusive, and favour[ed] a compromise whereby a best interests test is modified by a requirement that the substitute decision-maker first goes through an exercise in substituted judgement', a position they confirmed in their final report on the grounds of the agreement of those they had consulted, Law Commission, *Consultation Paper No 128* (1993) (n 11) para. 2.14, leading to ss 4(6) and 4(7) of the 2005 Act.

18 For more information about families we interviewed, the interview questions, and our anonymising procedure see C. Kitzinger, J. Kitzinger, 'Withdrawing artificial nutrition and hydration from minimally conscious and vegetative patients: Family perspectives' (2015) 41 *Journal of Medical Ethics* 157; B. Saunders, J. Kitzinger, C. Kitzinger, 'Anonymising interview data: Challenges and compromise in practice' (2014) *Qualitative Research* (online advance access, DOI: 10.1177/1468794114550439), available at http://qrj.sagepub.com/content/early/2014/09/23/1468794114550439. refs (accessed 19 December 2014). Filmed extracts from many of our interviews can be viewed on our online module on 'Family experiences of the vegetative and minimally conscious states', available at http://www.healthtalk.org (accessed 19 December 2014).

of clinically assisted nutrition and hydration. We show that there was a diversity of views as to what constitutes appropriate or proper medical treatment for these profoundly brain-injured patients, but that, for most of them, the patients' own views (as families understood them) were crucially important. We set these family accounts in the context of contemporary law and medical practice relating to the treatment of people in chronic disorders of consciousness which (at least in theory) uses best interests, rather than the patient's reported views, as the criterion for determining treatment options.

Emergency treatments

Prolonged disorders of consciousness are caused by severe brain damage in combination with subsequent medical interventions that prevent the person from dying as a result of that damage. Brain damage is the result of traumatic injury (typically a road traffic accident, sporting injury, or assault), anoxic injury (loss of oxygen to the brain such as is caused by a stroke, cardiac arrest, or near-drowning), or brain disease (for example, viral encephalitis). In the emergency phase, the hours and days after the precipitating event when death is a likely outcome of non-treatment, patients are likely to receive at least some of the following treatments: cardio-pulmonary resuscitation (CPR), tracheotomy, mechanical ventilation, clinically-delivered nutrition and hydration, a brain shunt, and surgery to remove blood clots in the brain and/or a decompressive craniectomy (removal of part of the skull to relieve pressure on a swelling brain).

Legally, some emergency interventions without consent can be justified under the doctrine of necessity; that is, in the absence of any information that the patient would object to treatment, it is considered that doctors who carry out interventions in order to save life should not have criminal or civil liability imposed upon them because the good effect they are seeking to bring about 'outweighs the value of adhering strictly to the law'.[19] The extent and severity of a person's brain damage is very often not apparent at the point of emergency intervention, and when a patient ends up in a permanent disorder of consciousness this usually could not have been accurately predicted at the point of the initial medical intervention. Indeed, if a clinician had known this would be the outcome she might have deemed intervention futile in the first place. Intensivists and neurosurgeons intervening at this stage may have different clinical judgements about the likely outcome, and also different attitudes towards what risks should be taken of a poor outcome balanced against the chances of meaningful recovery. Some clinicians may judge intervention to be justified, while others are increasingly concerned at the future harm their interventions can cause, which leads them to become more conservative in their practice.[20]

19 J. K. Mason, G. T. Laurie, *Law and Medical Ethics* (8th edn, Oxford University Press, 2011) 66.

20 See H. Marsh, untitled video, available at http://www.healthtalk.org/peoples-experiences/nerves-brain/family-experiences-vegetative-and-minimally-conscious-states/professor-henry-marsh#ixzz3KdrZdq2p (accessed 19 December 2014).

How, then, against this background, do families talk about what is proper treatment? In our research, many family members accepted that, initially, medical treatments were justified, 'It's all about keeping someone alive . . . and you do whatever has to be done' (Kate). But, in retrospect, most expressed some concern about the decision to intervene to keep the patient alive, often based on the assumption that medical professionals must have known (or should have known) what the eventual outcome would be. Belinda, whose son was in a vegetative state eight months after being assaulted, describes her initial belief (reinforced by medical professionals) that her son 'was going to be okay'. It was this belief that, for her, justified doing surgeries:

> They took him right up for his first operation on his brain. The right side of his head was completely caved in and they haven't rebuilt it. Then he had to have another operation, swelling on the other side of the brain. They were very good there but they still assured us [he] was going to be okay. We knew he might have some disability like maybe a speech thing, or maybe not being able to walk straight off, you know the normal things that you'd think of . . . We really, really thought that he would come out of it.

Proper medical treatment in the early stages meant, for most family members, whatever doctors said it was. This is a position they have since re-evaluated. In retrospect, many thought they were too 'innocent', or that doctors 'never told us' important information:

> When we started this, I was such an innocent and if somebody had said to me 'Right, do we operate or don't we? Do we put him into intensive care or don't we?' . . . I wouldn't have actually known. I was very much in the hands of the professionals. (Dawn)

> *We* can't help him. We can't treat him. We can't look after him. So we're handing him over to somebody who has the skills, the knowledge, the experience, to take him through this stage and bring him out the other side and go, 'There we are. There's Patrick back!' They never told us they couldn't bring Patrick back. (Thomas)

Tania, interviewed jointly with her husband, Ian, describes how two different surgeons expressed contrasting views about the proper medical treatment of her son Charles:

> We were actually sitting up to the early hours, planning Charles's funeral. We went back the next day, we saw the *other* surgeon, with the optimistic air, and *he* didn't mention anything about us saying goodbye to Charles. It was a *completely* different track. He started talking about fitting a tracheostomy. And we were *absolutely staggered* . . . And so we'd got a complete *roller*coaster of you know, pretty much 'say goodbye to Charles, go home, come back the next

> day', and we came back the next day I suppose expecting to *be* asked about having the life machine turned off. But we *weren't*. It was this *other* man wasn't it, and he uhm (*Ian interjects*: gave us a bit of hope) Yeah! And he just said you know, 'he's *young*', and he just had this feeling . . . And you *want* everything to be okay. You want to believe the *good* things, and *we* didn't want to lose Charles, we were in total shock, so we agreed to the decision to have the trachy fitted . . . Would that I *hadn't* given permission to do the surgery. Would that they hadn't got to Charlie in time to resuscitate him – knowing *now* what I didn't know then.

Only a few families considered, at the time, that life-prolonging medical treatments in the early days or weeks might *not* be appropriate, and in every case family members said that this was because they knew that life with profound brain injuries (whatever the eventual diagnosis/prognosis) was not something the patient would have wanted, and that the patient would not have wanted to take the risk of such an outcome. For these family members the doctrine of necessity that would otherwise have justified emergency treatment to save life, was trumped by their belief that the patient herself would have refused treatment under these circumstances:

> They [other family members] said that this is a woman who loved country life, loved family, very, very active, don't operate on her if she is not going to have a quality of life that she – you know, if she's not going – if she's going to be very, very profoundly brain damaged . . . Exactly as she is now, we didn't want – because we knew that she wouldn't have wanted that at all. And they continued operating another two or three times to take blood clots. I think she had a massive swelling and they were taking blood clots out . . . I don't know why they went on operating on her, knowing how profound her brain damage was, why they didn't just let her go, why they didn't just stop. (Diana)

In sum, in the immediate aftermath of the emergency, life-prolonging treatment is often initiated and continued in order to keep people alive and prevent further damage occurring, so that once stabilized they can be properly assessed. For many people this is proper treatment, and many family members we interviewed believed that their relatives would have been willing to receive emergency treatments in such circumstances. But a few reported that their relative would never want to run even a small risk of ending up in such a condition and would want to refuse treatment early on.

It was also striking in our research that reporting on their *own* wishes, as opposed to what they believed their injured relatives' wishes would have been at the time of their injury, many interviewees had come to narrow their definition of proper medical treatment for themselves. Some family members, including those who supported or fought for treatments to keep their relative alive, had themselves made advance decisions refusing treatment in emergency situations like these,[21]

21 Advance decisions to refuse treatment now have statutory support: MCA 2005, ss 24–26.

'I don't want anything if my brain is damaged in any way. I'm really quite strict about it. I'm not that scared about death' (Daisy). For Daisy, and others like her, the only proper treatment after brain injury is palliative care permitting death.[22]

Life-prolonging but non-restorative treatments in 'continuing' and 'permanent' disorders of consciousness

Prognosis for patients in disorders of consciousness becomes more accurate over time. The longer a brain-injured patient remains unconscious, the less good their eventual recovery is likely to be. At four weeks post-injury, a patient who is still unconscious, or virtually so, is said to be in a 'prolonged' or 'continuing' disorder of consciousness.[23] This is not a 'permanent' diagnosis; recovery can and does continue for at least some months, and often for some years. A permanent vegetative state (PVS) cannot be diagnosed until several months after non-traumatic injury, three months in the US and six months in the UK.[24] It takes even longer for a PVS diagnosis if the injury is the result of a traumatic injury; in that case a permanent diagnosis is not appropriate until at least one year.[25] The time span is extended again if the patient is minimally conscious, rather than completely unconscious; only after five years can the 'minimally conscious state' (MCS) be formally diagnosed as permanent.[26] In practice, this means that many patients are maintained for years in vegetative or minimally conscious states in the hope of eventual recovery, and a few of the patients whose families we interviewed had, in fact, recovered full consciousness, albeit with profound multiple neurological (and physical) disabilities which meant that they still lacked capacity to make medical decisions for themselves.[27] However, as we have explored elsewhere, by the time that the patient's diagnosis (for example, as being in a PVS) is finally confirmed, the 'window of opportunity' for a relatively quick death (for example, by removing a ventilator) has usually long passed.[28]

Ongoing medical treatments and procedures provided to these patients can include, in addition to clinically assisted nutrition and hydration, some ongoing

22 See healthtalk.org, 'Reflections on own end of life wishes', available at http://www.healthtalk.org/peoples-experiences/nerves-brain/family-experiences-vegetative-and-minimally-conscious-states/reflections-own-end-life-wishes (accessed 19 December 2014).

23 RCP (n 1) section 1.5.

24 RCP (n 1) section 1.7.

25 RCP (n 1) section 1.7.

26 RCP (n 1) section 1.5: 'Permanent' means, in this context, that recovery 'may be regarded as highly improbable'.

27 See healthtalk.org, 'Recovery', available at http://www.healthtalk.org/peoples-experiences/nerves-brain/family-experiences-vegetative-and-minimally-conscious-states/recovery (accessed 19 December 2014).

28 J. Kitzinger, C. Kitzinger, 'The "window of opportunity" for death after severe brain injury: Family perspectives' (2013) 35 *Sociology of Health and Illness* 1095 (http://onlinelibrary.wiley.com/doi/10.1111/1467-9566.12020/pdf).

mechanical ventilation/breathing support (for example, oxygen at night, a tracheotomy, or regular suctioning), a range of medications including antibiotics (especially for pneumonia, which is common in this patient group), and physiotherapy. They may also receive other diagnostic procedures and interventions (such as routine cancer screening and testing for cholesterol, hypertension, or diabetes), plus any relevant treatments for these conditions and immunizations (for example, the 'flu jab'). For many family members these various treatments became less and less appropriate for their relative over time, as they came to believe that their relative would not want to be kept alive in their current state.

Many families were aware that CPR would not be available to their relative *and accepted this*. The single most common reason was that they came to believe that their relative would not want it. Mikaela's father had, some years prior to the injury which left him in a vegetative state, survived a stroke which left him impaired but still with a quality of life he considered worthwhile. Mikaela reported having had conversations with him about his wishes because of this earlier injury, 'I knew how he was. His views on this kind of thing before were so strong after his stroke that he didn't want to be alive if he couldn't do things for himself . . . So that [agreeing to no resuscitation] was easy for me'.[29] Mikaela was relieved that she knew her father's wishes, and it made it 'easy' for her to know that (for him) CPR was not an appropriate treatment. Jim, likewise, felt that the burden of deciding about proper treatment for his wife, Amber, was lifted by his knowledge that Amber did not want CPR. Asked how he knew, Jim said:

> From our discussion. I knew that Amber, if the only course of action was to resuscitate her, Amber didn't want it done. And it made – I mean, when the consultant told me, I turned round and said 'That is Amber's wishes'. I didn't have to make the decision.[30]

Another interviewee, Gordon, described how his family arrived at the decision that his wife should be given only limited CPR, and, again, this was based on the family understanding of what the views of the patient would have been:

> The three of us discussed it, and we told them what our view was . . . we said they should try and resuscitate her once and if it was a respiratory or if it was a cardiac, they should try and resuscitate her once and if she didn't respond forget it. And she pulled through. And that happened two – I think two other occasions. (*Interviewer: What did you take into account in trying to make that decision at that time?)* The life that she may have afterwards and also going back to her

29 Watch a video of Mikaela, available at http://www.healthtalk.org/peoples-experiences/nerves-brain/family-experiences-vegetative-and-minimally-conscious-states/resuscitation-and-dnr (accessed 19 December 2014).

30 Watch a video of Jim, available at http://www.healthtalk.org/peoples-experiences/nerves-brain/family-experiences-vegetative-and-minimally-conscious-states/resuscitation-and-dnr (accessed 19 December 2014).

> and my discussion, that she didn't want to be a burden on anybody. And if she wasn't going to have a reasonable life after it, if she was going to be more incapacitated than what she was – we didn't want that for her. We didn't want that for her and she wouldn't have wanted it either.

On the other hand, several families successfully challenged 'do not resuscitate' notices. For them, CPR *was* appropriate medical treatment because they did not want to 'give up on' the patient. They believed the patient 'deserved a chance', and would have wanted to take that chance themselves.[31] Fern, talking about her partner, said that she at first believed: 'He's got to have a fighter's chance, how dare you give him a DNR [Do Not Resuscitate order].' Shortly after the DNR had been removed, Fern's partner had a second cardiac arrest and was resuscitated. Reflecting on this some years later Fern commented:

> the brain damage he sustained the second time has been catastrophic. Absolutely catastrophic. . . . And I do regret that, you know, well no I don't, I don't regret it. At the time I made a choice for him that I felt was right at that time. But I now know I could never put another one on him and should I be in a situation with anybody else I care about, I probably wouldn't do it . . . I just couldn't do it to another human being what I feel like we've done to him . . . But having seen the damage of . . . removing the DNR . . . I think they were right to put it on him. I can't regret it. What can I do now – we did it. But I definitely – should I repeat this over again in some weird parallel universe I would not remove it. I would let him die on that second cardiac arrest.[32]

Like Fern, Daisy and the rest of her family also, at first, insisted that their relative should be resuscitated if necessary and receive all other possible treatments. However, the whole family subsequently came to believe that he would rather be dead than continue in his MCS. Looking back, Daisy (like Fern) still sees decisions made to demand treatments considered inappropriate by the medical professionals as right *at the time*. The decisions were right because they would have been what her brother would have wanted them to do, even though, like the rest of the family, he would later have changed his mind about wanting to be kept alive and might have made different decisions had he had more information:

> At the time we didn't know anything at all [about serious brain injury and its implications], and Nathan wouldn't have known anything at all. If Nathan

31 See *Aintree* (n 14), where there was a long disagreement between a family and a hospital as to whether particular medical treatments were appropriate. The patient, David James, died of a cardiac arrest after the Court of Appeal declared that it was lawful to withhold CPR, a decision subsequently upheld by the Supreme Court.

32 Watch a video of Fern, available at http://www.healthtalk.org/peoples-experiences/nerves-brain/family-experiences-vegetative-and-minimally-conscious-states/resuscitation-and-dnr (accessed 19 December 2014).

> had *me* in that situation, he would have fought for *me* to have everything possible . . . Because of what we've experienced we now know the consequences of everything. But not having known what the consequences were, we definitely, definitely, wanted to fight [for treatment] . . . I mean if all of us had been experts at the time in brain injury and Nathan had as well, then we would have all said, 'Oh no, don't worry about treatment. I know that he would prefer to die.' But the whole point is we *didn't*.

The importance placed on what the patient would have wanted extends, in some of these accounts, then, to recognising that the patient (like the family) would at first, albeit out of ignorance, have wanted all possible life-prolonging treatments and would (like the family) have only gradually come to realise that they were only extending a life which would never again be (for them) a life worth living.

Some family members reflected guiltily that the treatments they wanted for their relative, and were fighting for, might be ethically unjustifiable. The mother (Ann) and sister (Bea) of a long-term PVS patient (interviewed together) commented:

Bea: The other thing that . . . I had trouble with, was fighting for Fiona's care at the [financial] cost that we know it is and fighting for that above the care for possibly a cancer patient who's a parent of young children or something. And we find – I find that very difficult to deal with, to think about. I just try not to think about it.

Ann: Yeah, it gives you very much a guilt complex when you think how much money is involved and how that money could be used. Yes. But, you know, when it's your own, you have to fight for them. There's nothing else you can do. But, you know, common sense tells you that it could be used a lot better.

Once families accept a permanent diagnosis, they oppose many more treatments. When death is seen as what the patient would prefer, many treatments designed to keep the patient alive are seen as inappropriate. As Fern says, it is not a life her partner would want:

> You get to a point when there's no improvement and you stop being able to convince yourself there is. When they are constantly hooked up to IVs and having painful UTI infection . . . When they spend their entire life in a state of pain and discomfort . . . this isn't a life worth sustaining. It's not a life they would want and it's not a life I want for him. And no matter how much I would like to believe he would have a miracle and we would see him recover and how much joy that hope would give me, if you can't see that anymore and you realise that death would be better now, I think that's when the acceptance comes . . . There's better ways to show I love him than to prove I'm sustaining him. You know, he knows I loved him. I've done it. I've got my medals. I was there [laughs]. I supported him. I fought for him . . . Don't need to prove it to

> anyone, because I proved it to myself and I proved it to him. He knows it. He knows that I did everything I could.[33]

Phil was more ambivalent about whether antibiotics were appropriate treatment for his (minimally conscious) partner, setting his partner's previous views (that 'no one would ever want to be like this') against what he felt facing that situation, and holding open the 'horrible' possibility of non-treatment. Again, the touchstone for deciding on appropriate treatment was what the patient himself would have wanted and/or what he might plausibly want now:

> But I think if he did get really ill then I probably would look to see if he could just go quietly. And I talked to his – luckily he and I and his mum were always on the same page about no one would ever want to be like this. They say that if you *are* like this then your perspective changes, so you can't guarantee that he wouldn't want to have an existence where he could have pleasure from my daily visits, daily visits from other people and the dog and all those things. But if something serious happened to him health-wise again we might look to see if he would be able to go quietly instead of fighting so hard to help him live, and that's horrible.[34]

Withholding or withdrawing treatment is often described by families (and clinicians) as 'leaving nature to take its course' or 'letting fate decide', or even allowing the patient – or the patient's body – to decide. Ann and Bea, mother and sister of the patient, agreed with the hospital early on that mechanical ventilation was an inappropriate treatment for her pneumonia:

Ann: Yeah, but there was a question of her going back on a ventilator.
Bea: They suggested that we probably didn't want to do that.
Ann: And *we* decided we didn't want to do that because-
Bea: But it's interesting that they did suggest it.
Ann: Yes, because they said, 'Well, you know, she might get over it this time, but maybe two months down the line it'll happen again', and so on. And so we decided, no, we don't want to just see her weakened, weakened and weakened and, you know, go that way. So we decided that we'd leave it to fate at that point, you know.

Untreated illness without proper palliative care leads patients to behave in ways that family members interpret as evidence of pain; for example, the ragged

33 Watch a video of Fern, available at http://www.healthtalk.org/peoples-experiences/nerves-brain/family-experiences-vegetative-and-minimally-conscious-states/aggressive-treatment-infections#ixzz3KZize9Zt (accessed 19 December 2014).

34 Watch a video of Phil, available at http://www.healthtalk.org/peoples-experiences/nerves-brain/family-experiences-vegetative-and-minimally-conscious-states/aggressive-treatment-infections#ixzz3KZhTB9KA (accessed 19 December 2014).

breathing, choking, coughing, and gurgling phlegm of untreated pneumonia. When families experienced the patient as suffering they saw treatment such as ventilators and antibiotics as appropriate, even if they had previously believed that these treatments should be withheld to allow the patient to die. When life-prolonging treatments could also relieve suffering, they were actively requested for that reason. Ann and Bea (quoted above) subsequently reversed their agreement to non-treatment for their relative, with Bea actively involved in providing chest physiotherapy on one occasion when her sister became very unwell with pneumonia because she felt her sister was suffering. The wife of another patient similarly could not sustain her position that no treatment should be provided for her husband's chest infections. She said that, 'He had a lot of phlegm and was choking – and that's horrific, watching someone who's going through like that. And again you think, "Can I really be that cruel?" You can't'. (Shula)

Thus, distress about patient suffering during the dying process led families to request life-prolonging treatments, even when they considered them otherwise inappropriate and believed the patient would rather be dead.

When family members viewed treatment as possibly illegitimate they compared it to criminal acts like torture, Kathy said, 'I feel like I've sat watching her being tortured at times and I've tried to comfort her while that's happening to her. And that's a very morally ambiguous position'. Similarly, '[c]ontinuation of this painful, frustrating non-existence and not being able to do anything he was before is not in his best interests. Prolonging it is akin to torture' (Daisy). And Dee said:

> They kept saying, she'll still be PVS in a year. So just wait a year and then you go to court. And we were going, 'But she's suffering now. Why make her suffer 365 days before she can be put out of her suffering? And they just said, well, that's the law, you have to wait 365 days.' So as far as we saw it, she was being tortured for 365 days and then we would get a court to agree that she could be allowed to die.

Furthermore, the conduct of medicine/practitioners/medical institutions was sometimes presented as illogical, improper, and an abuse of power akin to hijacking and kidnapping:

> Just because you're in a uniform and you work for a big corporation, it does not give you the right to kidnap someone and force them. But evidently it does in the world we live in. Evidently, they can hide behind that . . . You love them. They don't . . . And if you don't have the right, which you don't, you know, and that goes all the way from the beginning all the way through. It's, well, disgusting. Disgraceful isn't the word for it. Again, it is just so wrong. They're hijacked and kidnapped throughout, yeah, because the kidnapping started for Bill there, and continued. (Rose)

In sum, families' beliefs as to what constitutes proper medical treatment for patients in long-term disorders of consciousness is a complex phenomenon generally rooted in their belief about what their relative would have wanted, with an understanding that this would have changed over time (as the outcome for the relative became clearer). Views are also informed by the desire to release the patient from a life not worth living, balanced by the desire to avoid the patient suffering repeated near-death experiences.

The special case of artificial nutrition and hydration

Severely brain-injured patients cannot swallow and can only be provided with the nutrition and hydration essential to sustain life by tube feeding. Usually, artificial nutrition and hydration (ANH) is delivered via a nasal-gastric tube within the first few days after injury, followed a few weeks or months later by surgery to insert a tube directly into the stomach (for example, percutaneous endoscopic gastrostomy (PEG) or other surgically inserted gastrostomy tube). Both inserting feeding tubes and delivering substances through them are legally defined as 'medical treatment',[35] and can be done without the patient's consent if (in the absence of a valid and applicable advance decision to refuse them) they are considered to be in the patient's best interests. What makes ANH a special case, and unlike all other medical treatments provided to patients in disorders of consciousness (and indeed, unlike all treatments for patients with any other diagnosis), is that, in England and Wales, it *cannot* be withheld or withdrawn without a declaration from the courts of the lawfulness of so doing.[36]

Inserting a feeding tube is an invasive procedure, and its use is associated with risks (for example bleeding, displacement, and infection) and burdens (discomfort caused by pulmonary edema and gastrointestinal disturbance). Feeding tubes can also become blocked, worn out, or require repositioning due to infection, all of which require further invasive procedures. It is widely recognised that ANH may not always be in a patient's best interests, especially near the end of life, and treatment is commonly withheld or withdrawn in these circumstances.[37] When a patient is not imminently dying, the General Medical Council's guidance requires that a second clinical opinion is sought before withholding or withdrawing ANH.[38] However, for PVS and MCS patients, and *only* for this group of patients, withdrawal of ANH requires legal review. An application *must* be made to the Court of Protection for a declaration that it would be lawful to withdraw ANH.[39] This requirement is a legacy of the *Bland* case, in which the House of Lords recommended that a court declaration should be required in such cases 'at least for the time being and until a body of experience and practice has been built up which might obviate the

35 *Airedale NHS Trust v Bland* [1993] AC 789, HL.

36 Court of Protection Practice Direction 9E, Applications relating to serious medical treatment, para. 5.

37 L. Ganzini, 'Artificial nutrition and hydration at the end of life: Ethics and evidence' (2006) 4 *Palliative & Supportive Care* 135.

38 General Medical Council (GMC), *Treatment and Care Towards the End of Life: Good Practice in Decision Making* (GMC, 2010) para. 106. Also, paras. 121–122.

39 Practice Direction (n 36).

need for application in every case'.[40] The requirement remains, despite the view of the British Medical Association and expressed more than a decade after the decision in *Bland*, that PVS cases should no longer inevitably require court review where consensus exists, as long as such withdrawal is in accordance with agreed guidelines.[41]

Following the decision of the Supreme Court in *Aintree University Hospitals NHS Foundation Trust v James*, the focus of the court is not supposed to be on whether it is in the patient's best interests to withhold treatment (of any kind) but on whether it is in their best interests to give or to continue treatment.[42] But the requirement to seek declaratory relief *specifically* in relation to withholding or withdrawing ANH from patients in a PVS or a MCS, and not for providing or continuing to provide this medical treatment, appears contradictory. It also places ANH in an anomalous position in relation to the concept of the medical exception. A procedure considered a tortious or criminal offence if it is not performed in the best interests of the patient is singled out for special scrutiny by the courts. But this special scrutiny is designed in order to establish the lawfulness of *non*-treatment rather than of treatment, and only for this particular group of patients. Following the decision in *Bland*, courts must be approached for declarations that it is lawful to *withdraw* feeding tubes from patients in a PVS, but not for permission to (re)insert them or to continue administration of nutrition and hydration through them after a PVS diagnosis is confirmed. Two recent Court of Protection cases addressed treatment provision for patients in a PVS for whom ANH had been provided for four years[43] and nine years,[44] respectively. Withdrawal was declared to be lawful in both cases, but neither judge conveyed any concern about the improper medical treatment meted out to these patients over such long periods of time. It is this focus on the lawfulness of *non*-treatment rather than of *treatment* that makes ANH a special case for patients with disorders of consciousness and for their families.

Every court case in England and Wales concerning the administration of ANH to a patient with a confirmed PVS diagnosis has resulted in the treatment being withdrawn or withheld. In the over 100 cases since *Bland*, ANH has never been found to be in the best interests of a patient in a PVS. There is, then, no legal justification for making a medical exception of ANH for PVS patients. However, ANH for PVS patients is routine practice, supported by families, treating clinicians, Clinical Commissioning Groups (CCG), insurance companies, and NHS continuing healthcare funding. Doctors do not seem to fear prosecution for offences against the person of the PVS patients to whom they *deliver* ANH, and the law seems tacitly to condone the widespread administration of ANH to PVS patients.

40 *Bland* (n 35) 859, *per* Lord Keith.

41 British Medical Association, *Withholding and Withdrawing Life-prolonging Medical Treatment: Guidance for Decision Making* (3rd edn, Blackwell Publishing, 2007) 61.

42 *Aintree* (n 14).

43 *NHS Trust v AW* [2013] EWHC 78 (COP).

44 *Gloucestershire Clinical Commissioning Group v AB* [2014] EWCOP 49.

For example, there has been no litigation against medical professionals who have authorised, permitted, or performed ANH-related treatments on their PVS patients, and public funds are used to support the practice.[45] Perhaps, then, we overstate the importance of the medical exception as providing protection for doctors who might otherwise face tortious or criminal charges, since it seems that a medical treatment that cannot claim this status is, nonetheless, widely practiced, commonly accepted, has never been prosecuted, and does not, even when treatment cessation is declared lawful, attract the censure of the courts.

One contributory factor that may help to account for this apparently contradictory situation is a widespread perception that ANH differs from other medical treatments in being an ordinary (as opposed to an extraordinary) part of basic care, and, perhaps, from some perspectives, not a medical treatment at all. Providing food and water has a powerful symbolic value, and the alternative is often described as starving someone to death. The legal requirement to apply for declaratory relief for withdrawing ANH, but not other treatments (such as antibiotics or mechanical ventilation), supports that perception. Most of the families we interviewed, even those who approved or initiated court applications for withdrawal of ANH, believed that ANH was, in fact, appropriate or proper treatment for their relative.[46] Those who accepted or advocated its withdrawal did so only because it was the 'least worst' option in a desperate situation; that, it was the only (lawful) way of bringing about the patient's death. For example, Jane responded angrily to a care home manager's advice about the possibility of ANH being withdrawn from her father, and expressed her baffled outrage to the interviewer:

> Have you heard of that? That's crazy to me. Because they can't tell you if they can feel anything, but they will let them die if they stop his feed. So you have to watch your family member starve to death. It's just – what – who would do – why? Why? Why would you want-? Why? That's the bit – *why*? It just doesn't make sense.

Similarly, Morag was completely opposed to withdrawing ANH from anyone, however badly brain-injured:

> We could have applied for a court order to remove his feeding, his tube feeding, but you wouldn't starve an animal to death, so you certainly wouldn't

45 See P. Lewis, 'The medical exception' (2012) 65 *Current Legal Problems* 355, for a cogent and incisive analysis of the ineffectiveness of the medical exception as a selection tool for new and controversial medical procedures.

46 Extending the torture analogy, a small number of interviewees described ANH as 'force-feeding' and drew comparisons with the force-feeding of political prisoners on hunger strike at Guantanamo Bay Detention Camp, or the force-feeding of imprisoned suffragettes in the early twentieth century. This view may be particularly likely for families whose relative is in a MCS rather than a PVS, and where the feeding tube is dislodged or pulled out by the patient. See *United Lincolnshire Hospitals NHS Trust v N* [2014] EWCOP 16 for one such case.

> starve your loved one to death because people can live for such a long time without food and just getting weaker and in more pain. And there was no way – you know, you wouldn't starve an animal to death, so there's no way that, you know – for me, that's not an option, you know. I just don't see how that could ever be an option.[47]

Families said they had come to see ANH as an *option* at the point at which they believed that the patient's suffering could no longer be justified and there seemed no other way out. For example, Helen initially believed that 'there's no way I would even consider that', but later changed her mind, and supported an application for ANH to be withdrawn so that her son could die:

> [A]bout twelve months later I'd seen him through several nightmare urinary tract infections. I'd watched him lose weight. I'd watched his skin start to break down. I'd seen him in pain. I'd seen the splints that he'd got on his hands start to cut into his wrists. And just the general wear and tear of intensive and invasive nursing practice began to tell on his overall physical health. And it was at that point I started to reassess.[48]

Another interviewee, Gunars, said that he had first realised that his sister was probably in a PVS after reading a newspaper story about the death of Helen's son from ANH-withdrawal. The family had never been given a diagnosis, but the journalist's description of PVS 'ticked every box'. His family then initiated the process whereby the CCG applied for a declaration from the courts that withdrawing the feeding tube from his sister would be lawful, and his sister died ten days after this declaration had been granted. Despite actively participating in this process, Gunars was, nonetheless, clear that the provision of nutrition and hydration to a PVS patient *is* appropriate treatment, and that withdrawing it in order to allow death is neither compassionate nor dignified:

> What we look for as human beings is to be treated compassionately and with dignity, and in many ways a prisoner on death row in America gets treated better because at the end of the day he will eventually find out that the day of reckoning's come and it's a simple injection. But what we discovered in the process we entered into was my sister was effectively going to be denied hydration and nutrition which basically means that you're starving somebody to death. Is that a humane way to treat a human being? My response to that is not . . . And fundamentally in this country we treat our pets, our farm

47 Watch a video of Morag, available at http://www.healthtalk.org/peoples-experiences/nerves-brain/family-experiences-vegetative-and-minimally-conscious-states/artificial-nutrition-and-hydration#ixzz3Kae439jJ (accessed 19 December 2014).

48 Watch a video of Helen, available at http://www.healthtalk.org/peoples-experiences/nerves-brain/family-experiences-vegetative-and-minimally-conscious-states/artificial-nutrition-and-hydration#ixzz3Kaek50Lm (accessed 19 December 2014).

animals, our equine friends, more sympathetically and with greater compassion and dignity than we do human beings.[49]

Gunars' partner, Margaret, pointed out that:

> [I]f we wished to bring this to a conclusion because we considered that it was in her best interests, then that was the only route that was available to us . . . We don't think it is the best option. We think there should be other options. But within the law at the moment it would appear that is the only option.[50]

There is a real disjuncture here between legal and family perspectives relating to ANH cessation. From the legal perspective, at least in theory (though as we have outlined above, the situation is more complicated in practice), ANH *is* medical treatment, and has never been considered appropriate for patients in a PVS. In addition, a person making a best interests decision regarding life-sustaining treatment 'must not, in considering whether the treatment is in the best interests of the person concerned, be motivated by a desire to bring about his death'.[51] From the family perspective, ANH is very often considered to be basic care, and, as such, *is* appropriate for PVS patients. They are often horrified and dismayed at the idea of ANH being withheld or withdrawn. The only reason family members are willing to support cessation of nutrition and hydration is because they believe their relative would rather be dead, and they understand that this is the only lawful method whereby this objective can be definitely accomplished,[52] most especially if, as most have, they have repeatedly witnessed the failure of other lawful methods of allowing death, for example, untreated pneumonia.

Conclusion

In this chapter we have explored family perspectives on proper treatment in relation to their vegetative and minimally conscious relatives. What is distinctive here, as compared to other treatments considered in this collection, is that the majority of the treatments provided to such patients are now commonplace and well-established treatments for patients generally, for example ventilators and feeding tubes, rather than being particularly new or controversial per se. Our analysis has shown that families' views about proper medical treatment for severely

49 Watch a video of Gunars, available at http://www.healthtalk.org/peoples-experiences/nerves-brain/family-experiences-vegetative-and-minimally-conscious-states/artificial-nutrition-and-hydration#ixzz3Kaf84oi3 (accessed 19 December 2014).

50 Watch a video of Margaret, available at http://www.healthtalk.org/peoples-experiences/nerves-brain/family-experiences-vegetative-and-minimally-conscious-states/artificial-nutrition-and-hydration#ixzz3Kfv1jcO1 (accessed 19 December 2014).

51 MCA 2005, s. 4(5).

52 Kitzinger and Kitzinger (n 18).

brain-injured patients generally include full emergency treatments and all possible life-prolonging measures in the acute period in order to stabilize the patient and buy time to consider diagnosis and prognosis. However, treatments seen as appropriate in the first year or so may be viewed as no longer appropriate two or three years later because if the patient remains in a vegetative or minimally conscious state, then the rationale for such interventions is no longer justified. The possibility that the suffering and indignity the patient is enduring might open the door to a future life that the patient would find worthwhile has receded. At this point families may agree with clinicians that certain treatments should not be given, in the full expectation that the patient may soon die (after all, the patient's life seemed to 'hang on a thread' in the emergency period). However, unlike patients with terminal cancer, or the very frail and elderly, these patients (often young and physically healthy) may continue to live for years or decades as long as ANH continues to be provided, despite decisions such as 'no aggressive treatment' of infections. This leaves some families retrospectively to view initial treatment decisions as misguided, questioning treatments that resulted in their relative being kept alive. On the other hand, some people retain a belief that decisions to deliver life-sustaining treatments early on were proper *at the time*, based on their own or their relative's ignorance, the clinician's lack of certainty of the outcome, and the need to give their relative the chance of a meaningful recovery (even if, as it turns out, that chance has not 'paid off').

The special place of ANH as a treatment that cannot be withdrawn without resort to the courts is highly significant in shaping family views of proper medical treatment. By requiring declarative relief for withdrawal of this particular treatment (and no other) from this patient group uniquely (while ANH can be withdrawn from all other patients without legal review), the law acts to deter ANH withdrawal from PVS and MCS patients, adding to the already hugely symbolic freight of ANH withdrawal the additional, often intimidating, obstacle of courtrooms with lawyers, expert witnesses, judges, and, potentially, the media. It leads to life-prolonging treatment by default, without reference to the best interests of the person who (in the opinion of many families) is 'trapped' in a 'fate worse than death'. Keith Andrews, a leading neuro-rehabilitation specialist, commented on the reasoning in *Bland* that 'the only reason that tube feeding has been identified as "treatment" has been so that it can be withdrawn'.[53] It is ironic, then, that two decades later, routine medical practice is to *deliver* ANH to PVS and MCS patients *as if* it were a proper and legitimate treatment, and that the law (in particular, Practice Direction 9E)[54] constitutes a barrier to any systematic consideration of whether or not continued delivery of this medical treatment is covered by the medical exception as being in the patient's best interests.

53 K. Andrews, 'Letter – Tortuous arguments evade the issue' (1995) 311 *British Medical Journal* 1347, 1347.

54 Practice Direction (n 36).

7 The medical exception and cosmetic surgery: Culpable doctors and harmful enhancement?

Danielle Griffiths and Alexandra Mullock

Introduction

Whether we are talking about ill-advised cosmetic surgery or essential life-saving surgery, consent alone is not sufficient to render such surgery lawful.[1] We know, however, that there is an obvious imperative to permit beneficial medical interventions, giving rise to a 'medical exception' to the criminal law. Thus, as Margaret Brazier and Sara Fovargue explain,[2] 'proper medical treatment' or 'reasonable surgical interference' can be performed without fear of prosecution.[3] For this medical exception to the criminal law to be applicable, there must be a public policy justification rooted in medicine.[4] In this chapter we examine how such public policy justifications relate to non-therapeutic cosmetic surgery. Cosmetic surgery initially developed as a therapeutic specialism in medicine, and in many instances it remains exactly that. We do not dispute the therapeutic importance of treating patients requiring surgery in order to address physical and/or psychological issues; however, a distinction can be made between therapeutic or plastic surgery, which is medically necessary, and non-therapeutic *cosmetic* surgery.[5] The former is available on the National Health Service (NHS), albeit that availability is variable and accessing such treatment may require patience, whereas the latter is purely a private sector option which is consumer driven, subject to evolving societal attitudes, and, as we highlight, has become a highly lucrative industry.

In this chapter we question whether the medical exception remains appropriate in relation to the non-therapeutic cosmetic surgery industry. We do not suggest that such surgery should be prohibited; rather, we question whether the cosmetic surgeon selling unnecessary and risky surgery, often to vulnerable people, should be regarded as performing proper *medical* treatment. After a brief overview of the

1 *R v Brown* [1994] 1 AC 212, HL.

2 See M. Brazier, S. Fovargue, 'Transforming wrong into right: What is "proper medical treatment"?' in this collection.

3 *Brown* (n 1) 226, *per* Lord Mustill.

4 *Airedale NHS Trust v Bland* [1993] 1 All ER 821, HL.

5 M. Latham, 'The shape of things to come: Feminism, regulation and cosmetic surgery' (2008) 16 *Medical Law Review* 437.

medical exception as it applies to cosmetic surgery, we consider the evolution of cosmetic surgery, assessing current problems and potential harms, before examining the social context and ethical implications of the growth and normalisation of such surgery. In a liberal, consumer-driven society, the autonomous choice to have non-therapeutic cosmetic treatment may be viewed as a natural, even positive development. Yet concerns associated with undergoing surgery for cosmetic rather than medical purposes lead us to question the assumption that such surgery is justified on the same legal basis as medically necessary surgery.

With the exception of feminist scholarship,[6] scant attention has been paid to cosmetic surgery from a bioethical or socio-legal perspective, and where it has the primacy of autonomy is often employed in debates on enhancement more generally.[7] Feminist perspectives have, in contrast, shown how the 'choice' to undergo cosmetic surgery is gendered, classed, raced, and (hetero)sexualised, and it is often the most vulnerable who 'choose' to undergo the more extreme and harmful forms of such surgery.[8] Such perspectives have also shown how surgeons come to use their powerful position to legitimise and normalise what is an ethically questionable sub-speciality of medicine. In this context, feminists advocate a more cautionary approach, recognising women's constrained autonomy and limited capacity for consent in a socio-cultural context which pressures women to conform to idealised versions of the female body. With this in mind, we argue that it is ethically unsound to include non-therapeutic cosmetic surgery within the medical exception as a means of justifying its performance. Instead, better regulated sufficiently informed consent for all non-therapeutic cosmetic surgery should be required in order to legitimise its performance.

The medical exception and cosmetic surgery

As a matter of public policy, the criminal law prohibits consensual harmful activities unless they can be justified because they are medically necessary or carried out in pursuit of legitimate sporting activity.[9] In the medical context, as Lord Mustill pointed out in *Bland*, 'bodily invasions in the course of proper medical treatment stand completely outside the criminal law'.[10] Penney Lewis has suggested that in addition to consent, or a decision to treat in the best interests of a person lacking capacity, the medical exception rests on one of three justifications in order to avoid possible criminal liability for harming others.[11] Provided the intervention is beneficial for the patient or is in the public interest (for example, live organ donation),

6 See e.g. K. Davis, *Reshaping the Female Body: The Dilemma of Cosmetic Surgery* (Routledge, 1995).

7 J. Harris, 'Reproductive liberty, disease and disability' (2005) 10 *Reproductive Medicine Online* 13.

8 J. Sanchez Taylor, 'The power of breasts: Gender, class and cosmetic surgery' (2012) 35 *Women's Studies International Forum* 458.

9 *R v Barnes* [2004] EWCA Crim 3246.

10 *Bland* (n 4) 889.

11 P. Lewis, 'The medical exception' (2012) 65 *Current Legal Problems* 355.

or is performed with the acceptance and approval of the medical profession, it is legitimately regarded as proper medical treatment. However, Dennis Baker has recently argued that following the decision in *Brown*,[12] English common law 'only provides an exception for *genuine medicine*',[13] and that non-therapeutic cosmetic surgery does not fall within this exception because it is not genuine medicine. He distinguishes between cosmetic surgery that causes only minor harm and no long term damage, and cosmetic surgery which causes more serious harm. The former is, he suggests, reasonable and should be legitimate according to the law allowing 'reasonable adornment' akin to a tattoo,[14] whereas the latter should be criminalised. We share Baker's concern regarding the assumption that non-therapeutic cosmetic surgery is genuine medicine, and support his assessment of the harmful consequences resulting from treating it as genuine medicine and proper medical treatment. However, his argument may lead to the criminalisation of all but extremely minor cosmetic procedures because all invasive cosmetic surgery carries the risk of serious harm. We therefore suggest that an examination of the medical exception and the question of what constitutes genuine medicine is necessary.

Returning to Lewis's categorisation of patient (private), public, or professional (medical policy) justifications and relating these to non-therapeutic cosmetic surgery, insofar as the patient wants the surgery in order to enhance herself, it can be viewed as being in her subjective broader interests but arguably not in her medical interests. From an objective medical perspective, unnecessary and potentially risky surgery does the opposite of improving the patient's physical health. But it could be argued that the psychological benefit justifies the physical risk, although this is debatable. Tracey Elliott has considered this, and the tension surrounding various forms of radical non-therapeutic cosmetic surgery, and suggested that the medical justification for it 'has come to look increasingly thin'.[15] Indeed, while the cosmetic surgery industry was born from medical advances originally developed in a therapeutic context, non-therapeutic cosmetic surgery has developed into a beauty enhancement industry that, arguably, should not be justified by reference to personal medical benefit given the risks involved. If personal medical benefit is, at best, a weak justification, does non-therapeutic cosmetic surgery serve any public interest at all? Aside from the wider state benefit to the economy from a lucrative industry, coupled with the employment opportunities for those engaged in this industry, any public policy (public) benefit also looks rather weak. Unlike other ethically questionable practices justified in the public interest, such as live organ donation or clinical research, which may be dangerous for the patient but clearly fulfils other important goals, there seems to be no such justification for non-therapeutic cosmetic surgery.

12 *Brown* (n 1).

13 D. J. Baker, 'Should unnecessary harmful non therapeutic cosmetic surgery be criminalized?' (2014) 17 *New Criminal Law Review* 587, 589, emphasis supplied.

14 For judicial support of this argument see *R v Wilson* [1997] QB 47.

15 T. Elliott, 'Body dysmorphic disorder, radical surgery and the limits of consent' (2009) 17 *Medical Law Review* 2, 149, 179.

One possibility remains: the participation and acceptance of the medical profession in such surgery transforms that which would otherwise be unlawful into proper medical treatment. This appears to be the only clear justification for permitting non-therapeutic cosmetic surgery under the medical exception. But this raises an important question about the role of doctors in perpetuating the growth of the cosmetic surgery industry. Are they complicit in encouraging the growth and normalisation of potentially harmful and socially damaging surgical procedures? And, as Baker contends, has an overly deferential approach to the medical profession *allowed* doctors to medicalise unnecessary and often harmful surgery?[16] Before considering these questions by exploring some of the medical, ethical, and social issues raised by cosmetic surgery, we reflect on the evolution of non-therapeutic cosmetic surgery and the influence of big business in order to explore how provision of such surgery has moved away from its traditional medical origins. We argue that this shift, from the medical to the commercial domain,[17] is an important reason why it is time to question whether non-therapeutic cosmetic surgery *is* proper medical treatment.

The evolution of non-therapeutic cosmetic surgery: from pioneering medicine to (harmful) big business

Undergoing surgery as a beauty-enhancing treatment has become a lifestyle choice for increasing numbers of people. Over the past few decades, societal attitudes to cosmetic surgery have evolved, and there has been an increase in people electing to undergo such procedures. According to the British Association of Aesthetic Plastic Surgeons, 50,122 cosmetic procedures were performed in 2013, a rise of 17 per cent from 2012. The cosmetic surgery industry was worth £750m in the UK in 2005, £2.3bn in 2010, and is forecast to reach £3.6bn by 2015.[18] As Sir Bruce Keogh's review of the industry recently reported, rising demand for cosmetic enhancement has been driven by a number of socio-economic and technological factors, leading to the normalisation of serious and potentially harmful cosmetic interventions.[19] Concern over the ethics of providing surgical enhancements on demand, and in exchange for payment, has led to cosmetic medicine undergoing what has been described as 'an unfortunate transformation' amounting to an 'identity crisis'.[20] In this context, the central aim of medicine, to heal

16 Baker (n 13). José Miola considers broader issues relating to judicial deference to the medical profession in his chapter in this collection: 'Moralising medicine: "Proper medical treatment" and the role of ethics and law in medical decision-making'.

17 Barry Lyons charts the contrary shift in the practice of medicine generally, from commercial enterprise to public provision, in his chapter in this collection: 'Papist potions and electric sex: A historical perspective on "proper medical treatment"'.

18 J. Gallager, 'Plastic surgery "booming" in the UK' (*BBC News*, 3 February 2014), available at http://www.bbc.co.uk/news/health-25986840 (accessed 17 December 2014).

19 Review Committee, *Review of the Regulation of Cosmetic Interventions: Final Report* (Department of Health, 2013).

20 B. S. Atiyeh, M. T. Rubeiz, S. N. Hayek, 'Aesthetic/cosmetic surgery and ethical challenges' (2008) 32 *Aesthetic Plastic Surgery* 829, 829.

and to serve the *medical* interests of the patient, seems to have been abandoned in favour of fulfilling desires fuelled by an ideology of youth and beauty.

Central to the increasingly consumerist approach to cosmetic surgery is the commercial nature of the industry. Non-therapeutic cosmetic surgery is largely provided by the private sector in response to an individual's request for cosmetic enhancement, rather than in response to disease or injury.[21] It is rarely available through the NHS because there must be overriding physical or psychological reasons for considering it as a treatment option.[22] A Clinical Commissioning Group may decide that cosmetic surgery is required for health reasons in rare cases, and examples may include breast implants to treat severe underdevelopment or asymmetry, breast reduction to treat back pain or shoulder pain, nose reshaping to treat breathing problems, or 'tummy tucks' to remove excess fat or skin after essential abdominal surgery.[23] In order to obtain cosmetic surgery on the NHS, a plastic surgeon and a psychiatrist or psychologist must determine whether there is enough social, psychological, or physical benefit to the patient.[24] However, the boundaries of these benefits are unclear, and there is no definition of what counts as enough physical or psychological benefit in this context, or severe underdevelopment of breasts, for example. In a society where larger breasts may be more aesthetically desirable, do smaller breasts cause some women social or psychological harm, and, if so, does this harm warrant therapeutic intervention? The lack of clarity here means that the availability of cosmetic surgery on the NHS may, in some cases, be controversial, such as where it is perceived as being provided for purely cosmetic reasons.[25] These cases may be rare because in most cases the NHS will only fund cosmetic surgery where there is a clear *clinical* need for it to improve a patient's health, including their psychological health. Thus, if we assume that most privately funded operations do not have a therapeutic basis, otherwise they would be provided and/or funded by the NHS, then non-therapeutic cosmetic surgery appears to be increasing.

We contend that non-therapeutic, consumer-orientated cosmetic surgery lies outside of the aims of medicine, and that the harmful practices inherent within this consumerist form of surgery means that its place in the medical exception should be questioned. While there is some accountability, through civil negligence claims and/or professional disciplinary actions,[26] do these provide sufficient means to hold

21 M. Latham 'A poor prognosis for autonomy: Self-regulated cosmetic surgery in the United Kingdom' (2010) 18 *Reproductive Health Matters* 47.

22 NHS Choices, 'Availability of Cosmetic Surgery' (16 May 2013), available at http://www.nhs.uk/Conditions/Cosmetic-surgery/Pages/Availability.aspx (accessed 17 December 2014).

23 NHS Choices (n 22).

24 Latham (n 21).

25 In June 2014 Jeremy Hunt, the then Health Secretary, voiced his concern about NHS funding of cosmetic surgery for purely aesthetic reasons: M. Tran, 'Jeremy Hunt calls for the end of cosmetic surgery on the NHS' (*The Guardian*, 18 June 2014), available at http://www.theguardian.com/politics/2014/jun/18/jeremy-hunt-end-cosmetic-surgery-nhs (accessed 05/01/2015).

26 The Medical Practitioners Tribunal Service within the General Medical Council is an example of such accountability.

the cosmetic surgery industry accountable when patients are harmed? Harms may arise from the nature of the surgery itself, and also the lack of specific regulation relating to this area of medicine. Data on harm in cosmetic procedures is scarce, but some is available from medical negligence claims. According to a report in *The Guardian* of an analysis of cosmetic surgery by the Medical Defence Union, increasing numbers of patients are suing cosmetic surgeons following mistakes during operations designed to improve their appearance.[27] Of negligence claims relating to cosmetic surgery, 80 per cent were concerned with breast surgery, facelifts, eyelid operations, nose reductions, and weight-loss procedures, and damages of more than £500,000 were paid out over a five-year (unstated) period. Furthermore, cosmetic surgery negligence claims were successful in 45 per cent of cases, compared with 30 per cent of medical negligence claims in general.[28] This suggests that cosmetic surgery is performed less carefully than medically necessary surgery. This might be due to the lack of regulation of cosmetic surgery, as highlighted in the Keogh Review and the PIP breast implants scandal,[29] and also the growing problem of harm caused by cosmetic interventions.[30] When surgery does go wrong and harm is caused, the NHS, rather than the responsible private clinic, is often left to make good the harm; thus, we may all bear the cost when this type of surgery causes harm. While this may be true for all surgery which goes wrong, for medically unnecessary cosmetic surgery, where harm is caused in pursuance of a contract exchanging cosmetic enhancement for profit, there should be an obligation upon those causing the harm to put right (or at least bear the cost of putting right) the damage. Other medically unnecessary and profit-driven procedures, such as in vitro fertilisation (IVF), could also result in harm that is then rectified by the NHS, and we discuss the similarities and differences in the next section.

People electing to undergo non-therapeutic cosmetic surgery run the risks normally associated with invasive surgery, but there may be additional risks associated with surgery provided by private clinics and surgeons. Initial consultations may be with a receptionist or a member of the sales team rather than a medical professional, and there are almost never waiting lists for treatment; thus, the patient may have less time to change their mind.[31] Furthermore, as cosmetic surgery is not a specialty of surgical practice, there is no individual professional organisation responsible for setting standards that could be used in training or revalidation.

27 D. Campbell, 'More patients sue plastic surgeons over faulty cosmetic surgery' (*The Guardian*, 8 January 2012), available at http://www.theguardian.com/society/2012/jan/08/patients-sue-plastic-surgeons-faulty (accessed 22 October 2014).

28 Campbell (n 27).

29 Press Association, 'Breast implant register for the UK in the wake of the PIP scandal' (*The Guardian*, 29 December 2013), available at http://www.theguardian.com/world/2013/dec/29/breast-implant-register-established-pip-scandal (accessed 5 January 2015). The PIP scandal arose after a French company manufactured breast implants using dangerous materials which proved harmful to many recipients.

30 Review Committee (n 19).

31 Latham (n 21) 47–48.

Indeed, a recent report of the Royal College of Surgeons concluded that 'the standards of practice are relatively unclear'[32]; therefore, there is also a risk to cosmetic surgery patients from unregistered or poorly qualified surgeons. Heeding to current trends and demands for certain types of non-therapeutic cosmetic surgery may also pose risks. For example, in 2013 the British Society for Paediatric and Adolescent Gynaecology stated that there was no scientific evidence to support labia reduction, and that health risks, particularly to girls under 18, included bleeding, infection, and a loss of sensitivity.[33] These further risks of harm associated with the cosmetic surgery industry lead us to question whether cosmetic surgery should be regarded as proper medical treatment. As Brazier and Fovargue discuss in this collection,[34] debating whether a contentious treatment is indeed proper and/or medical invites consideration of the influence of the medical professional upon such issues. Where non-therapeutic cosmetic surgery is concerned, it seems that the profession (or at least a sufficiently significant minority within the profession) has cast aside any misgivings regarding the growth, normalisation, and commercialisation of this branch of surgery in order to facilitate the evolution of the cosmetic surgery industry. In so doing, have such doctors abandoned important ethical principles that are essential to proper medical practice?

Complicit doctors, the goals of medicine, and cosmetic surgery

A number of professions are imbued with a certain moral identity associated with the main purpose of the work or vocation. The medical profession, in particular, might be viewed as having a distinctive internal morality associated with the ideal of medicine as a 'moral enterprise'[35] that seems to be directed towards the pursuit of health.[36] Despite some attempts to pin down a concept of health,[37] it remains, as Kenneth Boyd has argued,[38] an elusive concept, not easy to define. We do know, however, that significant moral value is placed upon the practice of medicine because of its importance in saving lives and promoting health, and that this justifies the special status afforded by the medical exception to the medical profession. This privileged status invites questions regarding the morality of medicine in general,[39] but in relation to ethically contentious or innovative medical activity

32 Report of the Surgical Working Party, *Professional Standards for Cosmetic Practice* (Royal College of Surgeons, 2013) 3.

33 Ethical Opinion Paper, *Ethical Considerations in Relation to Female Genital Cosmetic Surgery* (British Society for Paediatric and Adolescent Gynaecology, 2013).

34 Brazier and Fovargue (n 2).

35 M. Wicclair, 'Conscientious objection in medicine' (2000) 14 *Bioethics* 205, 215. See also L. Frith, 'What do we mean by "proper" medical treatment?' in this collection.

36 L. R. Kass, 'Regarding the end of medicine and the pursuit of health' (1975) 40 *Public Interest* 11.

37 Kass (n 36).

38 K. M. Boyd, 'Disease, illness, sickness, health, healing and wholeness: Exploring some elusive concepts' (2000) 26 *Medical Humanities* 9.

39 See e.g. J. Montgomery, 'Law and the demoralisation of medicine' (2006) 26 *Legal Studies* 185.

determining what should be regarded as legitimate invites particularly difficult and morally sensitive questions.[40] For example the question of which type of surgery should be permitted according to the illness or disorder requiring treatment is a thorny issue, inviting debates about what constitutes an illness or disorder, not to mention the meaning of 'treatment'.[41] Discerning proper medical treatment and the goals of health might, therefore, encourage only the acceptance of that which heals and promotes health, and, for incurable conditions, that which relieves suffering. On this conception, non-therapeutic cosmetic surgery neither heals nor relieves suffering; rather, in the immediate sense and at least in the short term, it (as with all surgery) is damaging to the patient's health. In addition to the risks of general anaesthetic, the surgery will cause extensive damage to soft tissue, and there are also risks of infection and the possibility of poor results and/or medical error causing harm to consider. However, if the surgery is ultimately successful and the patient becomes happier as a result, it might be viewed as having a beneficial impact on their health.

As Lucy Frith explores in this collection,[42] Franklin Miller and colleagues have considered the internal morality of medicine, and in relation to cosmetic surgery they suggest that '[i]nvasive surgical operations performed on healthy bodies for the sake of improving appearance lie far outside the core domain of medicine as a profession dedicated to saving lives, healing and promoting health'.[43] This, however, presents a narrow view of medicine and, as Miller and his colleagues observe, a number of accepted interventions, such as contraceptive sterilisation, do not directly promote health.[44] Consequently, they suggest that there is a 'peripheral' zone of medicine into which cosmetic surgery might fall, with the core domain of medicine being reserved for clinically necessary and beneficial interventions.[45] This is a compelling argument, but is it possible to distinguish other 'unnecessary' procedures as being medically (or perhaps socially) justified under the medical exception in a way that non-therapeutic cosmetic surgery is not?

For example, contraceptive sterilisation for an adult who has either completed their family or who has elected not to reproduce, will prevent an unwanted pregnancy and eradicate the physical, emotional, social, and financial burdens of pregnancy and childrearing, along with the risks of pregnancy to the woman's health. Sterilisation might thus be viewed as beneficial in avoiding the burdens of pregnancy and rearing an unwanted child. Yet, unless avoiding pregnancy is

40 Discussed by Lewis (n 11) and M. Neal, 'Locating lawful abortion on the spectrum of "proper medical treatment"' in this collection.

41 See e.g. Elliott (n 15); Brazier and Fovargue (n 2).

42 Frith (n 35).

43 F. G. Miller, H. Brody, K. C. Chung, 'Cosmetic surgery and the internal morality of medicine' (2000) 9 *Cambridge Quarterly of Healthcare Ethics* 353, 362.

44 Miller *et al.*, (n 43).

45 Miller *et al.*, (n 43). See also Neal (n 40), who argues that there is a spectrum of proper medical treatment.

related to a health need, many of the reasons for undergoing sterilisation are, like non-therapeutic cosmetic surgery, driven by socio-cultural factors such as the western preference for smaller families, or for women to pursue a career free from the burdens of childrearing. State funding for sterilisation, arguably, relates less to the degree of medical need and more to socially related needs which are beneficial to society. A key difference that might justify one being included within the medical exception and not the other, is that while there are some risks, contraceptive sterilisation does not have the harmful effects that non-therapeutic cosmetic surgery often does, both physically to the patient and socially in terms of perpetuating restrictive female body images. Thus, within this peripheral zone of treatments which do not directly benefit health, procedures that serve more important social goals and are less risky and harmful, than non-therapeutic cosmetic surgery, are less problematically included within the medical exception.

Other treatments also lie on the periphery of medicine and have harmful effects. Assisted reproductive technologies (ARTs) may seek to address, in some instances, a physical problem, but they have no direct benefit to health and may have some physically harmful effects.[46] The mental or physical need for ARTs is, in large part, socially driven rather than being related to the pursuit of health. Their use stems from the personal and socio-cultural desire to have children, and, in particular, genetically related children that the intending mother gestates herself. Many ARTs can harm patients and have a negative effect on health. For example, IVF and egg donation involve drugs which may have serious side effects, and there may be psychological effects if the ARTs are unsuccessful.[47] Future technologies, such as mitochondrial replacement techniques and womb transplants, may also contain known and unknown levels of harm to the users and children born from them.[48] Finally, as with non-therapeutic cosmetic surgery, ARTs are highly commercialised,[49] and may be subject to varied regulation and bad practice. Indeed, despite the regulation of IVF clinics by the Human Fertilisation and Embryology Authority, some clinics have been accused of putting money before safety by pursuing aggressive and risky high-dose stimulation of ovaries in women, in order to maximise pregnancy rates but at the expense of safety.[50]

46 See further Frith (n 35).

47 L. Putowskiemail, D. Darmochwal-Kolarz, J. Rolinski, J. Oleszczuk, J. Jakowicki, 'The immunological profile of infertile women after repeated IVF failure' (2004) 112 *European Journal of Obstetrics and Gynecology and Reproductive Biology* 192.

48 Human Fertilisation and Embryology Authority, *Mitochondria Replacement Consultation: Advice to Government* (2013), available at http://www.hfea.gov.uk/docs/Mitochondria_replacement_consultation_-_advice_for_Government.pdf (accessed 8 January 2015).

49 J. Laurance, 'IVF clinics accused of putting money before safety' (*The Independent*, 14 May 2012), available at http://www.independent.co.uk/life-style/health-and-families/health-news/ivf-clinics-accused-of-putting-money-before-safety-7743505.html (accessed 8 January 2015).

50 A. Stevens, 'IVF women prefer risky pregnancy to no pregnancy' (2007) 412 *Bionews*, available at http://www.bionews.org.uk/page_13157.asp (accessed 16 January 2015).

Nevertheless, the hoped-for result of ARTs, the birth of a healthy child, is arguably a more important, desirable, and worthwhile outcome than that of non-therapeutic cosmetic surgery to improve appearance. Indeed, (limited) state funding for some ARTs seems to support this argument, perhaps because children are usually seen as socially and economically beneficial for societies. Thus, ARTs may have more of a place within the medical exception than non-therapeutic cosmetic surgery because they have greater social value. However, and as with non-therapeutic cosmetic surgery, the desire to have children through ARTs might also lack a sufficiently socially valuable justification. As David Benatar contends, the desire to reproduce can even be argued to be selfish, based on self-interested and narcissistic motives,[51] and in an overpopulated world Cristina Richie has argued that we should restrict the use of ARTs and not use state funding to allow people to access them.[52] There is, then, some parity between non-therapeutic cosmetic surgery and ARTs in terms of their capacity to harm and their limited social value. They may both thus lack a justification to be included in the medical exception.

There are, of course, other medical procedures which fall into the peripheral zone of medicine and which are comparable to cosmetic surgery. Notable examples include gender reassignment surgery and circumcision. Gender identity disorder is currently listed in the World Health Organization's International Classification of Diseases as a mental illness.[53] However, Simona Giordano has argued that gender identity disorder should not be regarded as an illness because it stems from dominant social and cultural practices.[54] That is, it is a result of a world that tries to make gender and sex dimorphic when, in fact, there is evidence that this is an oversimplification of a more complex set of facts. Thus, if we accept that humankind is not made up of males and females but is populated by a variety of sexes and genders, then there are no sound reasons to continue to consider gender identity disorder as a mental illness or any other kind of illness. Rather, it is a desire to physically live as the sex(es) and the gender(s) which an individual identifies as. The compulsion for this may stem from a rejection of the imposition of external norms, whereas dominant forms of non-therapeutic cosmetic surgery (for example, breast augmentation or rhinoplasty) may stem from an acceptance of them. While there are differences between non-therapeutic cosmetic surgery and gender reassignment surgery in terms of the degree of psychological harm that may be suffered from *not* having the desired surgery, how significant are these differences? Both of these types of surgery can be harmful, but because gender reassignment surgery is currently listed as a mental illness it is generally treated on the

51 D. Benatar, *Better Never To Have Been: The Harm Of Coming Into Existence* (Oxford University Press, 2008).

52 C. Richie 'What would an environmentally sustainable reproductive technology industry look like?' (2014) 10 *Journal of Medical Ethics* 1136.

53 World Health Organization, ICD-10 Version:2015 (2015), available at http://apps.who.int/classifications/icd10/browse/2015/en (accessed 23 January 2015).

54 S. Giordano 'ICD-11 reforms: Where should gender identity disorder go?' in B. Miller (ed.), *Gender Identity: Disorders, Developmental Perspectives and Social Implications* (Nova Publishers, 2014).

NHS along with other medically necessary surgery. Yet gender reassignment surgery may also stand in a similarly problematic relationship to the medical exception as non-therapeutic cosmetic surgery because it is, according to Giordano,[55] not based on a medical need and it can be risky. So, should it too be excluded, along with non-therapeutic cosmetic surgery, from being deemed to be proper medical treatment? Or does the fact that it is not commonly performed within a commercial context mark a difference, and mean that there is more of a public policy justification for it?

Circumcision is also a procedure with uncertain health benefits that is regularly performed for cultural and religious reasons. It is risky and sometimes fatal, particularly in infants.[56] As Sally Sheldon and Stephen Wilkinson have observed,[57] the justifications for banning female genital mutilation (FGM), the harmful physical and associated psychological consequences and the impact on vulnerable people, might equally be used to justify banning cosmetic surgery. If we exclude FGM, we can see that there are a number of risky, socially driven procedures which *are* lawful and enjoy the backing and involvement of the medical profession. So should, as we suggest, non-therapeutic cosmetic surgery be singled out and be excluded from the ambit of the medical exception as not being proper medical treatment? It seems sensible to accept non-therapeutic cosmetic surgery and, relatedly, contraceptive sterilisation, ARTs, gender reassignment surgery, and circumcision within a peripheral zone of medicine which might be viewed as providing a medical service that meets the broader interests of the patient as a user of those services. Indeed, Giordano suggests that medical treatment should be deemed necessary not according to whether a condition is classified as pathological but on need and likelihood of minimisation of suffering.[58] And Robert Veatch has argued that medicine should reflect societal values rather than internally generated codes of conduct.[59] We know that societal values are diverse, pluralistic, and may be consumer-driven; thus, the acceptance of non-therapeutic cosmetic surgery as a peripheral medical treatment seems essential. However, distinctions can be made between treatments. Unlike core medical treatment or even other peripheral treatments, the dubious social value and social consequences, which we discuss further below, of non-therapeutic cosmetic surgery are good reasons for questioning the ethics of providing such 'treatment' within a poorly regulated

55 Giordano (n 54).

56 H. Weiss, 'Complications of circumcision in male neonates, infants and children: A systematic review' (2010) 10 *BMC Urology* 1186. See also 'Boy bled to death after home circumcision by nurse who was paid £100 to use scissors, forceps and no anaesthetic' (*Mail Online*, 14 December 2012), available at http://www.dailymail.co.uk/news/article-2248333/Nigerian-nurse-Grace-Adeleye-guilty-manslaughter-after.html (accessed 9 January 2015).

57 S. Sheldon, S. Wilkinson, 'Female genital mutilation and cosmetic surgery: Regulating non-therapeutic body modification' (1998) 12 *Bioethics* 263.

58 Giordano (n 54).

59 R. M. Veatch, 'The impossibility of a morality internal to medicine' (2001) 26 *Journal of Medicine and Philosophy* 621.

commercial industry that is subject to minimal regulation and is characterised by a laissez-faire approach to patient/consumer protection. The growth of the industry, coupled with the capacity to harm patients due to the dearth of effective regulation in non-therapeutic cosmetic surgery, are further reasons why we should question whether it, in particular, should fall within the medical exception.

Returning to the issue of the involvement of the medical profession in perpetuating the growth of non-therapeutic cosmetic surgery, we can make a further distinction between it and other peripheral treatments because of the visibility of the effects of the surgery. Rather than being instrumental to the traditional aims of medicine, cosmetic surgeons are instrumental to the beauty industry, and this has damaging implications for both individuals and society at large. As more people with surgically enhanced bodies are present in society, such bodies may be perceived as normal and/or desirable and this could have negative implications for those whose age or natural attributes place them far from this perceived ideal. And this, in turn, fuels the demand for cosmetic surgery. Moreover, the norms that have developed via the growth of non-therapeutic cosmetic surgery are often suspect, particularly for women.[60] For example, we see the 'Barbie-fication' of women, portraying the ideal physical specimen as a large-breasted, slender child/woman.[61] This can have a particularly damaging effect on very young or vulnerable women. We consider in more detail in the following section how some women can resist and reject such images but others cannot or do not, and are particularly susceptible to wanting to emulate the (false) ideals of femininity.

Margaret Little argues that the complicity of the doctor in creating such suspect norms is ethically problematic.[62] As a highly regarded profession, the involvement of doctors in non-therapeutic cosmetic surgery may provide a stamp of approval for these socially damaging norms,[63] and, as Miller and his colleagues argue in relation to advertisements for cosmetic surgery:

> the willingness of physicians to provide treatments may operate as a legitimation in the minds of patients. That professionally qualified physicians are prepared to offer invasive procedures may encourage ambivalent patients to submit to medical intervention.[64]

Cosmetic surgeons are aware of the negative meanings associated with their field, and empirical research suggests that they might try to legitimise and normalise

60 See e.g. Latham (n 5); Davis (n 6).

61 See e.g. H. Freeman, 'Can a woman shave her armpits and still call herself a feminist?' (*The Guardian*, 15 July, 2013), available at http://www.theguardian.com/fashion/2013/jul/15/woman-shave-armpits-still-feminist (accessed 16 January 2015).

62 M. O. Little, 'Suspect Norms of Appearance and the Ethics of Complicity' in I. De Beaufort, M. Hilhorst, S. Holm (eds), *In The Eye if the Beholder: Ethics and Medical Change of Appearance* (Scandinavian University Press, 1997).

63 Miller *et al.*, (n 43).

64 Miller *et al.*, (n 43) 355.

their work by using a number of strategies.[65] For example, some construct notions of 'surgical otherness', defined as surgery that is extreme and which sacrifices a 'natural' or authentic look in favour of an obviously enhanced 'artificial' one.[66] In encounters with patients, surgeons may employ references to the surgical other as part of their presentation of a professional identity, their ethical stance, and their competence.[67] They may also refer to their willingness to resist the demands of patients who display unreasonable expectations or have excessive demands; for example, asking for disproportionately large breast implants or excessive fat removal. Bishara Atiyeh and colleagues suggest that by employing these approaches, surgeons are trying to legitimise the image of an ethically suspect sub-specialty of medicine, supporting its expansion and profit making by displacing its negatives onto certain patient psyches.[68]

In considering whether non-therapeutic cosmetic surgery should be excluded from the public policy justification of the medical exception because of the risk of harm, the lack of medical benefit, and the ethical concerns regarding professional medical involvement in perpetuating suspect norms, two further issues are relevant. First, the evidence and feminist perspectives relating to *who* is opting for cosmetic surgery and why they are doing so in the light of the risks and harm at stake, and, second, how consent is currently negotiated and the implications for vulnerable consumers.

The 'vulnerable'[69] cosmetic surgery consumer

Autonomy is often given precedence in debates about whether certain medical treatments are ethically permissible. In relation to human reproduction, for example, Ronald Dworkin has argued for a right to 'procreative autonomy' which he characterised as 'a right [of people] to control their own role in procreation unless the state has a compelling reason for denying them that control'.[70] Liberal democracies have to justify limitations on freedom. Purported restrictions cannot simply invoke unease about unnaturalness or transgression of certain traditional boundaries, there must be evidence and adequate argument to show that such considerations point to serious and real dangers to others and/or society itself. Absent such evidence and argument, there is scant justification to constrain liberty.[71] We have outlined how cosmetic surgery may harm patients, either as a result of accidents, bad and reckless practices, or as a direct result of the procedures themselves. We have also noted that the extent and visibility of non-therapeutic cosmetic surgery

65 D. Gimlin, 'Imagining the "other" in cosmetic surgery' (2010) 16 *Body and Society* 57.

66 Gimlin (n 65).

67 Gimlin (n 65).

68 Atiyeh *et al.* (n 20).

69 For a detailed exploration of the concept of vulnerability in legal thought see M. Fineman, A. Grear (eds), *Vulnerability: Reflections on a New Ethical Foundation for Law and Politics* (Ashgate, 2013).

70 R. Dworkin, *Life's Dominion* (Harper Collins, 1993) 148.

71 Harris (n 7).

may be harmful to society for promoting an unrealistic version of aesthetic beauty. Thus, there may be reasons for constraining the use of such surgery. However, restricting access to surgery would be an affront to patient autonomy, and, so long as they are informed of risks, we could argue that patients have the right to access such treatments just as they have the right to make other potentially unwise lifestyle decisions. Given this, perhaps constraint should come from excluding cosmetic surgery from the medical exception. If excluded, then patient consent alone could provide justification for non-therapeutic cosmetic surgery. In order to determine the impact and effect of this suggestion, the characteristics and motivations of those seeking to undergo such (harmful) surgery need to be considered so as to ensure that processes of gaining consent are robust.

The early feminists' position on women's reasons for undergoing non-therapeutic cosmetic surgery was that they were victims of a patriarchal culture and beauty industry that pressurised them into making themselves more sexually desirable to men.[72] They were passive victims of a patriarchal system who were capitulating to their own sexual objectification. Non-therapeutic cosmetic surgery was, thus, another form of cultural oppression, perpetuating idealistic representations of women's bodies and encouraging women to undergo risky surgery in order to conform to these representations. Women, in this account, needed protection from their exploited and duped status.[73] Consent was not enough to protect them. The patriarchal nature of medicine was also emphasised, and the power of clinicians meant that women could not make autonomous choices in this context.[74] But this view was challenged by other feminists who emphasised choice and autonomy. For example, Kathy Davis has emphasised women as active agents, carefully negotiating and controlling their surgeries, rather than being mere puppets of patriarchy.[75] Decisions about non-therapeutic cosmetic surgery *can* be made autonomously by women, because women are aware of the objectification of their bodies and having to live up to unrealistic ideals of femininity. Nevertheless, women use non-therapeutic cosmetic surgery as a means to control their own bodies and identities.[76] Similarly, Susan Bordo has argued that women are prepared to undertake the risks inherent in non-therapeutic cosmetic procedures in order to gain some power that they may not be able to gain elsewhere.[77] Women thus use their agency to improve their appearance in a culture that rewards them for their looks. These accounts too have been critiqued for overemphasising women's agency. How far can women be said to choose non-therapeutic cosmetic surgery when that choice is constrained by larger patriarchal structures?[78]

72 S. Dodds, 'Choice and control in feminist bioethics' in C. Mackenzie, N. Stoljar (eds), *Relational Autonomy: Feminist Perspectives on Autonomy, Agency and the Social Self* (Oxford University Press, 2000).

73 V. Blum, *Flesh Wounds: The Culture of Cosmetic Surgery* (University of California Press, 2003).

74 E. Haiken, *Venus Envy: A History of Cosmetic Surgery* (John Hopkins University Press, 1997).

75 Davis (n 6).

76 Davis (n 6).

77 S. Bordo, *Unbearable Weight: Feminism, Western Culture and the Body* (University of California Press, 1993/2003).

78 K. Pauly Morgan, 'Women and the knife: Cosmetic surgery and the colonisation of women's bodies' in S. Sherwin, B. Parish (eds), *Women, Medicine, Ethics and the Law* (Ashgate, 2002).

A third position has evolved which views the motivation for those undergoing non-therapeutic cosmetic surgery as neither fully internal nor external, but as an intersubjective process that takes place in a consumerist environment.[79] Placing non-therapeutic surgery in a consumer context shifts the focus away from the disembodied individual patient who has dominated much of the previous research, and allows us to take into account agency and choice within a constrained cultural context. Such surgery is thus approached as 'a purchase, characterised by the rhetoric of fashion, consumption and self-presentation rather than medical or psychological necessity'.[80] Yet, women do not make the same kinds of 'choice' in this context. Consumers of non-therapeutic surgery raise not only gender but also class and race issues, and evidence suggests that some women are more likely to undergo risky and extreme surgery. Jacqueline Sanchez Taylor has argued that we are not all the same kind of makeover citizens, nor do we all experience the same pressure to conform to the same patriarchal ideals of feminine beauty.[81] White middle class feminist academics, for example, can (usually) 'do' their gender without undergoing invasive procedures. They will not be dishonoured by their lack of attention to the kind of beauty and fashion regimes some other women are attached to. In fact, the reverse is true; low key performances of gender are typically more highly valued and respected.[82] In Sanchez Taylor's study, for (some) working class women, buying fake breasts was a way to perform a particular gendered and classed feminine identity that has value. More extreme breast augmentation may be linked to a form of economic capital for some women who, because of structural inequality, lack the means to gather such capital elsewhere.[83] Thus, extremely augmented breasts are a source of economic capital. These women *wanted* their breasts to be visibly the result of surgery; they did not want to come out of surgery looking like a naturally big breasted woman. Visibly 'fake' breasts were a way of displaying this form of capital. Sanchez Taylor's interviews showed that these women were using cosmetic surgery as a consumer purchase to increase their value in ways they could not find elsewhere.[84] She suggested that the desire of these women to position themselves within the hierarchies of class and gender was exploited by cosmetic surgery companies who market a means to achieve this. Furthermore, they often use a (working class) woman who has successfully used augmented breasts to succeed in the beauty and glamour industry in their advertisements, for example.[85]

Taking into account the differential positioning of consent in relation to gender, class, and race, autonomy can be emphasised in the context of non-therapeutic

79 D. Gimlin, 'Cosmetic surgery: Beauty as commodity' (2000) 23 *Qualitative Sociology* 1.

80 V. Pitts-Taylor 'Becoming-being a cosmetic surgery patient: Semantic instability and the intersubjective self' (2009) 122 *Studies in Gender and Sexuality* 3.

81 Sanchez Taylor (n 8).

82 Sanchez Taylor (n 8) 450.

83 Sanchez Taylor (n 8) 451.

84 Sanchez Taylor (n 8) 451.

85 See e.g. Make Yourself Amazing – Cosmetic Surgery, 'Patient Stories', available at http://www.mya.co.uk/patient-stories/ (accessed 9 January 2015).

cosmetic surgery, but only in a way which recognises that, in relation to women, certain conditions need to be tackled in order to make the realisation of autonomy possible.[86] Not only do the standard procedures and processes for obtaining consent need to be improved, but more is required to ameliorate the dangers inherent in a situation where people are making choices to undergo risky surgery in a highly constrained socio-cultural context where appearance may be a form of economic and social capital which cannot be obtained elsewhere.[87] Thus, those seeking cosmetic surgery must receive counselling from trained and objective professionals before they consent to a particular procedure. This will assist them to choose the treatment that is most appropriate to their circumstances, understand the risks involved, and give them the opportunity to decide not to have the treatment at all.[88] This would mirror, to some extent, the position in France where a cosmetic surgery patient must be informed by the surgeon of all risks, no matter how unlikely or insignificant, future consequences and complications, and 'all the inconveniences' associated with a procedure.[89] As long as regulation is accompanied by other resources such as 'a strong social support and constructive networks of relationships', Emily Jackson has argued that autonomy can be a guiding principle of regulation.[90] Thus, rather than including non-therapeutic cosmetic surgery in the medical exception, where the justifications for causing harm are weak, or advocating a near ban on cosmetic procedures along the lines of Baker's argument,[91] should we amend the requirements of and processes for obtaining consent instead?

Consent

Concerns have been raised that the usual approach to obtaining consent for medical treatment is unsuited to commercial transactions for non-therapeutic cosmetic surgery where deals and finance packages can tempt the vulnerable to sign-up without appreciating the serious risks. But Sally Taber, for example, has argued that advertisements for cosmetic surgery should be allowed in the same way that other consumer goods are advertised; adverts are a public good which give information and allow choice.[92] In the context of non-therapeutic cosmetic surgery this is questionable, and Fazel Fatah suggests that there should be a ban, as in France, on encouraging people to undergo non-therapeutic surgery.[93] Advertising

86 Latham (n 5).

87 Sanchez Taylor (n 8). For an analysis of gender, social class, and forms of capital women have access to, see B. Skeggs, *Formations of Class and Gender: Becoming Respectable* (Sage, 1997).

88 Latham (n 5) 447.

89 C. Durrieu-Diebolt, 'Chirurgie esthetique' *Droit pour tous* ('Plastic surgery' Law for All), available at http://sos-net.eu.org/medical/chirgurg.htm (accessed 9 January 2015).

90 E. Jackson, *Regulating Reproduction: Law, Technology and Autonomy* (Hart, 2001) 9.

91 Baker (n 13).

92 S. Taber, 'Should all advertising of cosmetic surgery be banned? No' (2012) 345 *British Medical Journal* 7508.

93 F. Fatah, 'Should all advertising of cosmetic surgery be banned? Yes' (2012) 345 *British Medical Journal* 7489.

cosmetic surgery has traditionally been avoided by physicians for ethical reasons,[94] and Fatah argues that 'the doctor-patient relationship and the professional duty of care a physician has for patients is not similar to business relationships, where advertising plays an important role in bringing customers and providers together'.[95] Advertising preys on vulnerabilities surrounding body image and stimulates demand for high-risk, invasive surgery. For example, 'bikini body transformation packages' that are targeted at recently divorced women and new mothers are clearly not designed to inform.[96] These sales pitches may not even include details of the risks and side effects of the procedure(s). And consent may only be obtained once the patient has signed up for the surgery and already contracted to pay for the procedure, and so might fear losing their money if they decide not to proceed.

The current approach to gaining consent to non-therapeutic cosmetic surgery in England and Wales is, we suggest, problematic. Concerns surrounding consent are amplified when we consider feminist literature on 'informed consent as a mechanism for ensuring patient autonomy'.[97] Some have argued that medicine is essentially patriarchal, and that there is a power imbalance between the clinician and the patient, particularly the female patient.[98] The law does little to address this. Provided the patient is 'informed in broad terms of the nature of the procedure which is intended', consent will be legally valid and an action for battery avoided.[99] A negligence claim may be possible if there has been an inadequate form of consent, such as if the doctor fails to warn of a significant risk which subsequently transpires, so that the patient is unable to make an adequately informed decision.[100] There is, however, no obligation on medical professionals to ensure that the patient understands the information regarding risks and side effects.[101] Nevertheless, the General Medical Council (GMC) urges doctors to take a patient-centred approach to information disclosure, and tailor information according to the needs, wishes, and concerns of each patient.[102] In spite of some developments regarding the standard of care for information disclosure,[103] the law sets the standard low for valid consent and for ensuring that a patient has understood the information so disclosed. Furthermore, the GMC's vague guidance means that doctors are able to interpret their obligations to suit their own agenda.[104] We suggest that

94 Fatah (n 93).
95 Fatah (n 93).
96 Fatah (n 93).
97 Jackson (n 90).
98 Bordo (n 77).
99 *Chatterton v Gerson* [1981] 1 All ER 257, 265, *per* Bristow J.
100 *Chester v Afshar* [2004] UKHL 41.
101 *Al Hamwi v Johnson* [2005] EWHC 206.
102 General Medical Council (GMC), *Patients and Doctors Making Decisions Together* (GMC, 2008).
103 See e.g. *Pearce v United Bristol Healthcare NHS Trust* [1999] PIQR P53, CA; *Birch v University College London Hospital NHS Foundation Trust* [2008] EWHC 2237; and now the Supreme Court decision in *Montgomery v Lanarkshire Health Board* [2015] UKSC 11.
104 S. Fovargue, J. Miola, 'One step forward, two steps back? The GMC, the common law and "informed" consent' (2010) 36 *Journal of Medical Ethics* 494.

the law and the professional ethical guidance concerning consent reflect the fact that a doctor who is engaged in saving lives and healing patients may be forgiven if she cannot always be sure that a patient understands all the implications of a necessary and medically beneficial surgical procedure. If we consider the challenges of ensuring that all patients in need of medical treatment fully understand the relevant information within an under-resourced NHS hospital, we accept that while 'fully informed consent' is desirable and important it may not always be possible. While this might be an imperfect yet pragmatic approach to consent for medically necessary surgery, it is inadequate for non-therapeutic cosmetic surgery because the risks are not justified by the medical benefit.

Comparisons can be drawn here with clinical research involving healthy participants where, similarly, the medical benefit is absent although other benefits (financial or altruistic) may be present for participants. It is, therefore, interesting to consider the more robust approach to obtaining consent from adults with capacity who want to participate in clinical trials. The Medicines for Human Use (Clinical Trials) Regulations 2004 state that consent must be 'informed' in respect of the nature, significance, implications, and risks of the trial, and must be given in writing.[105] Notwithstanding the ethical concerns surrounding consent for such human trials,[106] we suggest that this should be a starting point for considering a contextually appropriate and more robust approach to obtaining consent for non-therapeutic cosmetic surgery.

We began this chapter by reflecting on the fact that consent is a necessary but not sufficient requirement before any surgery can take place. The other necessary element is the public interest justification embodied by the medical exception. Without this, according to the decision in *Brown*, consensual harmful activity is unlawful *regardless* of whether the victim/patient/participant consents.[107] However, as some of the feminist literature we have discussed contends,[108] with further support from some bioethical literature,[109] there is a powerful argument for allowing people to improve and enhance themselves if they so choose. For this reason, and despite identifying numerous concerns relating to the provision of non-therapeutic cosmetic surgery, we disagree with Baker that invasive non-therapeutic cosmetic surgery should be criminalised.[110] His argument that cosmetic surgery causing serious harm should be regarded as criminal would be sound except for the fact that without the medical exception, which we agree should not apply to non-therapeutic cosmetic surgery, *all* cosmetic surgery would potentially become a serious criminal offence. Thus, some other legitimising principle is necessary. This, we argue, should be legally robust and sufficiently informed consent. Such consent should be sufficient to legitimise non-therapeutic cosmetic surgery *without* recourse to the medical exception and a public policy justification for its performance.

105 Part 3, Schedule 1.

106 See e.g. R. Dresser, 'First-in-human trial participants: Not a vulnerable population, but vulnerable nonetheless' (2009) 37 *The Journal of Law, Medicine & Ethics* 38.

107 *Brown* (n 1).

108 E.g. Davis (n 6) and Bordo (n 77).

109 See e.g. J. Harris, 'Moral enhancement and freedom' (2011) 25 *Bioethics* 102.

110 Baker (n 13).

Conclusion

In the light of the evolution of non-therapeutic cosmetic surgery, the risks of harm, and the social and ethical concerns associated with commercial cosmetic surgery, we suggest that there is no public policy justification for the medical exception to apply. We have argued that there are a number of ethical concerns associated with providing non-therapeutic cosmetic surgery on demand in a commercial context. Even if the surgery goes well, the professional ethics of the surgeon in normalising such invasive interventions for cosmetic purposes will look dubious to some. Yet there are other treatments which lie on the periphery of medicine, and which also normalise and perpetuate certain ethically suspect norms. Nevertheless, we contend that there is something particularly harmful about non-therapeutic cosmetic surgery which justifies re-appraising the applicability of the medical exception in this area of medicine, questioning whether it is, in reality, proper medical treatment.

We have also argued that the standard approach to obtaining consent is inadequate for commercial non-therapeutic cosmetic surgery. Consent should be sufficiently detailed and informed so that the patient understands the risks and implications in order to reflect the fact that the surgery is both risky and not medically beneficial, as research has shown that, in practice, this is not routinely done.[111] We can see from the French reforms that a different approach to consent is possible,[112] and we argue that this would provide better protection for those seeking non-therapeutic cosmetic surgery while still allowing that type of surgery to be performed. We recognise that changing the approach to consensual harmful activity in this context might mean that continued legal moralism in other comparable issues where people clearly derive personal benefit from potentially (or even actually) harmful activity, such as sadomasochism in *Brown*,[113] should also be addressed.[114] But that is beyond the scope of this chapter.

111 Fatah (n 93).

112 Durrieu-Diebolt (n 89).

113 *Brown* (n 1).

114 For interesting discussions on this see R. A. Duff, 'Towards a modest legal moralism' (2014) 8 *Criminal Law and Philosophy* 217; D. Gurnham, 'Legal authority and savagery in judicial rhetoric: Sexual violence and the criminal courts' (2011) 7 *International Journal of Law in Context* 117.

8 Locating lawful abortion on the spectrum of 'proper medical treatment'

Mary Neal

Introduction

As every undergraduate medical law student knows, when a patient is capable of giving her consent, the least touching *without* consent may amount to a tort and a crime.[1] But, as Lord Mustill remarked in *R v Brown*,[2] more invasive medical treatments (those intrusions which outside the medical context might amount to assaults causing actual or grievous bodily harm, or maim) may be 'well above any point at which consent could even arguably be regarded as furnishing a defence'.[3] According to his Lordship, where such treatments are concerned, it is not the existence of consent but the fact that the intervention counts *as* proper medical treatment, which prevents criminal liability from attaching to those treatments. In these more invasive cases, as Margaret Brazier and Sara Fovargue suggest, proper medical treatment works 'magic'[4] and 'transform[s] something wrong into something 'right''.[5]

Where abortion is concerned, the concept of proper medical treatment *never* works to transform wrongs into rights. That magic is worked, instead, by the Abortion Act 1967, as amended by the Human Fertilisation and Embryology Act 1990. The practice of abortion, otherwise a statutory crime in England and Wales under sections 58 and 59 of the Offences Against the Person Act 1861 (and a common law crime in Scotland), is transformed, provided that certain conditions are met, into lawful medical treatment by section 1 of the amended 1967 Act. Why consider the concept of proper medical treatment in this context at all, then? I suggest that there are at least two reasons to regard the concept as being relevant to abortion law, notwithstanding that the current lawfulness of abortion is not attributable to it. The first is that the concept of proper medical treatment is

1 See e.g. *Sidaway v Board of Governors of the Bethlem Royal Hospital* [1985] 1 All ER 643, HL, *per* Lord Scarman.

2 [1994] 1 AC 212, HL.

3 *Brown* (n 2) 266.

4 M. Brazier, S. Fovargue, 'Transforming wrong into right: What is "proper medical treatment"?' 12 in this collection at page 12.

5 Brazier and Fovargue (n 4) 13.

wider than just the medical exception. Whether an intrusion is minor enough that consent alone can render it non-criminal (as is the case with superficial examinations and treatments involving only minor touching of the body), or is sufficiently severe to require the 'magic' power of the medical exception, the idea of proper medical treatment is busy in the background. It defines the nature and contours of the practitioner–patient relationship and sketches out the landscape of health care law.

The second reason why we need to be clear about whether, and to what extent, the practice of abortion conforms to the notion of proper medical treatment is that although the lawfulness of abortion does not *currently* depend upon such conformity, an emerging strand of pro-choice activism is focused on the demand that abortion be completely decriminalised.[6] It is unclear at the time of writing precisely how the fulfilment of that demand would be cashed out in terms of detailed law reform, but it is likely that the legislative apparatus that currently marks out the (admittedly somewhat byzantine) boundary between lawful and unlawful abortion would need to be repealed or amended, at least in part. Depending on how and to what extent the current legislative framework is disturbed, surgical abortion, like other invasive treatments, may come to depend for its lawfulness upon the transformative power of proper medical treatment. Medical abortion, as a less invasive form of treatment, may remain within the category of treatments for which consent alone is enough to remove criminality. If so, proper medical treatment would retain the same kind of background role in relation to *medical* abortion, post-decriminalisation, that (I will argue) it currently has in relation to *all* cases of abortion.

Understanding proper medical treatment

In their chapter, Brazier and Fovargue subject the concept of proper medical treatment to forensic analysis, exploring each of its component parts in order to build up a picture of what counts as proper medical treatment and why. They begin by noting what appear to be 'two elements to the medical exception' (over and above the presence of consent, where consent is possible), namely 'the reasonableness of the activity under consideration' and the fact that 'that activity is in the public interest'.[7] Of these two, reasonableness seems to have a particularly fundamental role, '[t]he *reason* for the treatment (. . .) appears central to the medical exception'.[8] In highlighting reasonableness, Brazier and Fovargue join a tradition

6 See e.g. British Pregnancy Advisory Service (bpas), 'Four good reasons for Britain to decriminalise abortion altogether', *BPAS Reproductive Review: Issues in Abortion, Pregnancy, and Birth* (12 June 2014), available at http://www.reproductivereview.org/index.php/rr/article/1592/ (accessed 1 December 2014); S. Sheldon, 'Why We Should Take Abortion out of the Criminal Law', Centre for Law and Society seminar, University of Edinburgh, 6 November 2014.

7 Brazier and Fovargue (n 4) 14.

8 Brazier and Fovargue (n 4) 15, emphasis in original.

which was, arguably, begun by Denning LJ in *Bravery v Bravery*[9] when he implied that operations must be carried out with 'just cause or excuse',[10] and continued by Lord Lane CJ in *Attorney-General's Reference (No. 6 of 1980)*,[11] who referred to the undesirability of bodily harm 'for no good reason'.[12] From the initial insight that proper medical treatment is somehow connected with reasonableness of purpose, Brazier and Fovargue embark upon a detailed inquiry into the various factors that seem capable either of rendering a practice 'proper' in themselves, or at least of contributing to a determination of properness. From their analysis, several factors seem to emerge as having justificatory potential, notably that the activity is beneficial to (or has the potential to benefit) the patient,[13] that the activity is in the public interest (or 'public good'),[14] that the activity is in accordance with the norms of the health care profession(s),[15] and that it is performed by 'trusted' health care professionals.[16] The idea of 'reasonableness' seems immanent in all of these, so that it has the air of an overarching or background element in the process of justification.

To a significant extent, Brazier and Fovargue's analysis reflects (although it does not replicate) Penney Lewis's evaluation of the medical exception in her seminal paper.[17] The factors they identify as relevant to assessments of properness largely map on to Lewis's discussion of public policy justifications. Lewis argues that the medical exception operates only where two conditions are met: consent (where that is possible), and the existence of a public policy justification. She distinguishes between 'patient-focused', 'public-focused' and 'professionally focused' public policy justifications,[18] and the main factors identified by Brazier and Fovargue seem broadly to mirror these categories.[19]

Since Lewis is concerned with the line between criminality and non-criminality, it is unsurprising that her discussion focuses exclusively on tracing that boundary. Brazier and Fovargue's examination of proper treatment likewise concentrates on what might be required, over and above consent, in order to prevent actions from attracting criminal liability. They focus on the medical exception and do not explicitly distinguish this from proper medical treatment; nevertheless, the two terms are not synonymous. Whereas the medical exception has a limited role insofar as it applies only to those interventions which are intrusive enough to amount to serious offences against the person, the concept of proper medical treatment as described by Brazier and Fovargue encompasses *all* lawful medical treatment,

9 [1954] 1 WLR 1169, CA.
10 *Bravery* (n 9) 1179.
11 [1981] 1 QB 715, CA.
12 *Attorney-General's Reference* (n 11) 719.
13 Brazier and Fovargue (n 4) 18–19.
14 Brazier and Fovargue (n 4) 20.
15 Brazier and Fovargue (n 4) 21.
16 Brazier and Fovargue (n 4) 16–17.
17 P. Lewis, 'The medical exception' (2012) 65 *Current Legal Problems* 355.
18 Lewis (n 17) 357–364.
19 Brazier and Fovargue (n 4) 19–21.

and not only those treatments which involve the kind of significant intrusions authorised by the medical exception. The medical exception performs a specific function (the exclusion of criminal liability) and, in so doing, it ushers new and controversial practices into the fold of proper medical treatment. Thus, we begin to build a picture of the relationship between the two concepts. The medical exception appears to serve to police and extend the boundaries of the wider and more general category of proper medical treatment.

The spectrum of proper medical treatment: paradigm, clear, and liminal

If one feature of the existing literature is that it has not yet begun to tease out the distinction between the medical exception on the one hand, and the wide concept of proper medical treatment on the other, another feature is that little attention seems to have been paid so far to gradations of properness *within* the landscape of the lawful. Because so much attention has been trained on the medical exception, it is the line between the lawful and the unlawful which has drawn the academic eye. But further distinctions are possible. In the context of a recent discussion of conscience rights,[20] Sara Fovargue and I have argued that within the category of 'proper medical treatment', a given treatment can be either 'clearly proper' or 'liminally proper':

> A treatment may occupy liminal status because, despite being lawful, it is 'morally controversial and contentious'. Practices which involve the ending of human life, such as abortion, IVF, and withholding or withdrawing treatment from unconscious patients or severely disabled newborns may be liminally proper for this reason; assisted dying will be too, if it becomes lawful to provide it within the healthcare context . . . A treatment may also have liminal status if it is extremely risky or experimental, or if it is more concerned with the satisfaction of preferences than with healing or treating disease.[21]

We distinguished between clear and liminal cases of proper medical treatment in order to identify liminal treatment as the zone within which conscience-based exemptions can be appropriate. The existence of a conscience clause may be a clue that the status of the treatment in question is liminal; hence, the existence of conscience-based exemptions in relation to (non-emergency) abortion,[22] the activities governed by the Human Fertilisation and Embryology Act 1990,[23] and the

20 S. Fovargue, M. Neal, '"In good conscience": Conscience-based exemptions and proper medical treatment' (2015) 23 *Medical Law Review* 221, 229, reference removed.

21 Fovargue and Neal (n 20).

22 S. 4(1) of the Abortion Act 1967 provides that 'no person shall be under any duty, whether by contract or by any statutory or other legal requirement, to participate in any treatment authorised by this Act to which he has a conscientious objection'.

conscience clauses in Bills aimed at decriminalising assisted suicide.[24] Indeed, the existence of a permitting statute (whether or not it contains a conscience clause) may be a clue in itself, since the need for clear statutory authority may indicate that a practice exists at the margins of what can be accepted as proper. Practices currently permitted by statute include living organ donation,[25] abortion, and embryo research, and assisted suicide seems also to be regarded as a matter for the legislature.[26]

The distinction between clear and liminal proper treatment is, in a sense, the subject-matter of the present volume, and many of the chapters herein can be read as mapping out areas of liminality *within* the category of proper medical treatment, as much as charting the border between the proper and the improper.[27] In the passage quoted above, Fovargue and I focused on specific contexts and examples where treatments might be regarded as liminal as a (non-exhaustive) way of describing the realm of liminality. But another approach to describing the distinction between clearly and liminally proper treatments might be to identify what the features of a 'paradigm case' of proper medical treatment are, and to regard a treatment as proper in a stronger or weaker sense depending on how closely it models that paradigm.

In *Bravery* Denning LJ described 'ordinary' surgery as being 'done for the sake of a man's health, with his consent'.[28] Borrowing this formulation and adapting it slightly, I propose that we regard the *paradigm case* of proper medical treatment as being treatment carried out with the consent of the patient and for the patient's therapeutic benefit. The first element of this formulation, consent, is indicated by the centrality of the principle of autonomy in contemporary health care law and the resulting requirement that where consent is possible, it *must* be obtained on pain of criminal and civil sanction. The second element, therapeutic benefit,[29] is indicated by the widespread perception that one of the central purposes of

23 S. 38(1) of the 1990 Act provides that 'No person who has a conscientious objection to participating in any activity governed by this Act shall be under any duty, however arising, to do so'.

24 Provision for conscience was included in the various Assisted Dying for the Terminally Ill Bills tabled by Lord Joffe, and there was a conscience clause in the Assisted Dying Bill [HL] 2014–15 (the 'Falconer Bill'). The version of the Assisted Suicide (Scotland) Bill before the Scottish Parliament in 2014–15 does not include a conscience provision because although health (including assisted dying) is devolved, regulation of the professions is reserved to Westminster.

25 Under the Human Tissue Act 2004 and the Human Tissue (Scotland) Act 2006.

26 *R (Nicklinson) v Ministry of Justice* [2014] UKSC 38.

27 D. Griffiths, A. Mullock, 'The medical exception and cosmetic surgery: Culpable doctors and harmful enhancement?'; R. Huxtable, 'Death on demand: "Proper medical treatment"?', C. Kitzinger, J. Kitzinger, 'Family perspectives on "proper medical treatment" for people in prolonged vegetative and minimally conscious states'; J. Laing, 'Doctors' orders?: Analysing appropriate medical treatment in mental health law', in this collection.

28 *Bravery* (n 9) 1180.

29 I adopt the phrase therapeutic benefit from Brazier and Fovargue because it reflects the idea of a therapeutic relationship and captures the sense in which 'benefit' in the context of health care law and ethics goes wider than narrow *clinical* benefit, but not so wide as to encompass the mere satisfaction of patients' personal preferences.

health care is to provide health-related benefit to patients (only a minority of practices permitted in the health care context have *no* potential therapeutic benefit for the patient), and the resulting mainstream characterisation of the relationship between the health care professional and patient as a therapeutic relationship. The British Medical Association characterises the doctor patient relationship as 'a "therapeutic relationship"',[30] and the encounter between doctor and patient as 'a "therapeutic encounter"'.[31] It contrasts the 'usual model of a therapeutic partnership'[32] and the 'normal therapeutic role'[33] of the doctor with other situations where doctors act in a dual capacity (for example, doctors who work in prisons have duties to their employers as well as to their patients), or where there is no therapeutic aspect to the relationship at all (for example, where a doctor completes a report for an insurance company as an independent assessor).[34]

Space does not permit a discussion of the 'ends of medicine debate' here, except to note that while there is disagreement among scholars regarding what the proper ends of medicine are, plausible suggestions invariably seem to cite beneficence/best interests.[35] This is clearly so where the doctor patient relationship is regarded, in the traditional way, explicitly as a 'healing relationship'.[36] However, a set of revised goals identified by an international panel of experts which set out specifically to challenge traditional views of the goals of medicine and identify new goals more reflective of the realities of modern medicine seems to rely just as heavily on notions of beneficence/best interests.[37] The new goals are (i) the prevention of disease and injury and promotion and maintenance of health, (ii) the relief of pain and suffering caused by maladies, (iii) the care and cure of those with a malady, and the care of those who cannot be cured, and (iv) the avoidance of premature death and the pursuit of a peaceful death.[38] Each of these seems obviously to be focused on producing benefit for patients. While Mark Wicclair regards the traditional claim that medicine is oriented towards 'healing' as overly essentialist, he concludes, nevertheless, that 'it is plausible to maintain that healing is associated with the concept of medicine (or any credible conception of it), and it is arguable that an individual who is not committed to that end fails to qualify as a physician, let alone a virtuous one'.[39]

30 British Medical Association (BMA) Ethics Department, *Medical Ethics Today: The BMA's Handbook of Ethics and Law* (Wiley, 2012), 27, 208, 702.
31 BMA (n 30) 6.
32 BMA (n 30) 649.
33 BMA (n 30) 690.
34 BMA (n 30) 27–28.
35 See L. Frith, 'What do we mean by "proper" medical treatment?'; R. Huxtable, 'Death on demand: "Proper medical treatment"?', in this collection.
36 E. D. Pellegrino, 'Toward a reconstruction of medical morality' (2006) 6 *The American Journal of Bioethics* 651, 67.
37 An International Project of the Hastings Center, 'The goals of medicine: Setting new priorities' (1996) 25 *Hastings Center Report* S1.
38 Hastings Center (n 37) S10-S14.
39 M. Wicclair, 'Is conscientious objection incompatible with a physician's professional obligations?' (2008) 29 *Theoretical Medicine and Bioethics* 171, 174.

Clearly, there are health care interventions which do not model the paradigm case outlined above, but which are, nevertheless, well-accepted. Treatment without consent is possible where a patient lacks the capacity to consent, either temporarily (in which case any proposed intervention must be justified on the grounds of necessity) or permanently (in which case any proposed intervention must satisfy a best interests test). However, I suggest that the *paradigm case* of proper treatment is one where consent is present; the justification for intervention in other cases, although still patient-centred, takes an alternative form. The therapeutic benefit element can also be absent in certain cases without this meaning that the intervention is impermissible. Cases of living organ donation are an example. The bodily intrusion involved in retrieving an organ from a living donor is significant, and it is not performed for the direct therapeutic benefit of the patient being intruded upon. Arguably, the retrieval of the organ provides a psychological or emotional benefit to the donor. This argument is perhaps strongest where the recipient of the organ is a loved one of the donor but may also be present where the donation is impersonally altruistic. Usually, however, the permissibility of such interventions is discussed in terms of 'public interest' or 'public good' justifications, perhaps implying that the benefit to the donor is regarded as being too weak, or too indirect, to provide a convincing justification in itself. That the permissibility of living organ donation is established by statute in the UK may hint at the exceptional nature of this kind of intervention. The need for a statute to put its lawfulness beyond doubt is surely connected to the lack of a therapeutic benefit to the donor and could be regarded as implying that, in the absence of clear statutory authorisation, the lack of such a benefit would render the practice questionable and locate it at (or possibly beyond) the periphery of proper medical treatment.

The two key elements of the paradigm case, consent and therapeutic benefit, have different roles in determining the properness of treatment. Consent operates in an all-or-nothing way. If it is possible, it must be present, and if it is present and the intervention is also clearly therapeutic, we have a paradigm case of proper medical treatment. If the capacity to consent is absent, then providing that the relevant patient-centred test is met (necessity or best interests, depending on the patient's condition), and providing that the intervention is clearly therapeutic, the absence of consent does not preclude proper medical treatment. Although we are not dealing in such circumstances with a paradigm case, the properness of the treatment is not in doubt. This is because treatment in cases where patients cannot consent is both necessary and desirable, and also because the portion of the overall justification which consent represents in the paradigm case can be satisfied by necessity or best interests in other cases. Therapeutic treatment without consent which is justified by necessity in the case of an unconscious patient or in the best interests of a patient who lacks capacity on a longer term basis, is thus clearly proper, albeit not paradigmatic.

If consent is possible, but is not obtained, then any intervention on the patient is *improper*. The absence of consent cannot, therefore, be what locates an intervention within the liminal zone of proper medical treatment. If consent is absent because the patient lacks capacity, then provided that the appropriate alternative mechanism for justification is satisfied, treatment (if clearly therapeutic) is clearly proper. On the other hand, if consent is absent because the consent of a patient with capacity has not been given for a particular intervention, this is not liminal but *improper*. Liminal proper medical treatment is still lawful and, indeed, still proper. It occurs at the margins or peripheries of what is proper. By contrast, any treatment of a patient with capacity *without* her consent stands completely outside of the realm of what is proper. As such, the consent element of the paradigm can never be the basis for a determination of liminality.

What *could* point to liminally proper treatment, then? Determinations regarding whether an intervention is clearly or only liminally proper will focus on the *therapeutic value* or potential of the intervention (the second element of the paradigm case). If it can be shown, or if a strong consensus emerges, that a whole practice or a particular intervention is positively *harmful*, either exclusively harmful or so harmful that any supposed countervailing benefit(s) cannot render it therapeutic on balance, then whether it is liminally proper or improper will depend on the circumstances. Notwithstanding the practitioner's ethical duty to do no harm (non-maleficence), living organ donation, which represents a net harm to the donor, can be lawful. For a harmful intervention to be liminally proper, consent must be present, and so must a strong public interest justification. Statutory authorisation may also be necessary, as discussed above, and it is present in the case of living organ donation. Even with all of this in place, I suggest that a harmful intervention can only ever be *liminally* proper at best, never clearly or paradigmatically proper. Harmful interventions where consent and/or public interest are absent cannot even be liminally proper. Whole practices that fall into this category might include female genital mutilation, extreme or multiple cosmetic procedures, and, perhaps less clearly, the amputation of healthy limbs as treatment for body integrity disorder. Individual interventions that belong in this category might include burdensome interventions upon dying patients (for example, the resuscitation of a patient who is terminally ill and close to death, or the aggressive treatment of an infection in a dying patient with antibiotics which cause unpleasant side effects). Insofar as such interventions cause suffering which is not outweighed by any meaningful gain in comfort or enhanced life expectancy, they too may be outside the boundaries of proper treatment.

In other cases therapeutic benefit is speculative or uncertain, but the intention in providing the treatment is clearly to *try* to benefit the patient. The provision of a risky or experimental new cancer treatment might be one example. Alternatively, although therapeutic potential for the patient is absent, there may be an overwhelming public interest in permitting the practice, which may be sufficient to compensate for the absence of the therapeutic element. Penney Lewis discusses what she terms 'new or controversial medical procedures', such as: 'cosmetic surgery; circumcision and genital mutilation; contraceptive sterilization; organ donation; non-therapeutic research; gender reassignment surgery; and amputation for body integrity disorder'.[40] These practices exist at the boundaries of proper medical treatment, and Lewis has explored how the medical exception might operate to bring them within it. My claim here is that the potential for recognising them as proper will depend on the extent to which *either* the therapeutic element can be made out, *or* its absence can be compensated by overwhelming public interest.

Much more could be said about all of this and, in particular, about which categories particular practices and interventions belong in. For example, is living organ donation positively harmful to the donor or just not therapeutic? Different commentators will come to different conclusions about this and similar questions, but I want to sidestep such questions for the moment, since it is not necessary for present purposes to resolve the content of each of the categories which is entailed by my analysis so far. It will be necessary, however, before I can proceed to apply that analysis in the context of abortion, to summarise my argument and to sketch the (necessarily basic) typology of proper medical treatment that emerges from it.

A basic typology of proper medical treatment

The essence of my argument so far has been threefold. First, proper medical treatment is wider than the medical exception. Second, as Sara Fovargue and I have argued elsewhere, within the category of proper medical treatment we can distinguish between clear and liminal cases of proper treatment. Finally, developing the second point, I want to understand proper medical treatment as a spectrum. At one end of this spectrum are paradigm cases of proper treatment, treatment (i) where consent is both possible and clearly present, *and* (ii) which has clear therapeutic benefit for the patient being intervened upon. Further along the spectrum there are other cases where interventions 'clearly' constitute proper treatment because two criteria are satisfied: (i) they are justified not by consent, because consent is impossible, but by some other patient-centred test such as necessity or best interests, *and* (ii) there is clear therapeutic benefit to the patients concerned. Further along still, interventions which are consensual may be proper notwithstanding that their potential for therapeutic benefit is either contested or non-existent, providing *either* that the intervention is not a clear harm which is not outweighed by (potential for) benefit (risky/experimental cancer treatment, for example), *or* that there are public interest considerations which weigh in favour of allowing the intervention to take place (if we construe live organ donation as a net harm to the donor, we may decide, nonetheless, as UK law has done, that it ought to be permitted as a public good). *This* is the liminal zone of proper medical treatment; still proper but less *clearly* proper than the first two categories of treatment. If therapeutic potential is absent or contested, a treatment is either liminally proper or even improper, depending on the circumstances; but it is liminally proper *at best*.

40 Lewis (n 17) 355.

Perhaps the most controversial category of liminal treatment is treatment where the patient lacks capacity and a procedure with no therapeutic value is performed. Infant male circumcision might be one example of this. Academic opinion is divided regarding whether this practice ought to be permitted. Margot Brazier has taken the view that '[a]lthough medical opinion may not necessarily regard [infant circumcision] as positively beneficial, it is in no way medically harmful if properly performed'.[41] Michael Thomson and Marie Fox, on the other hand, have criticised 'continued professional willingness to tolerate the non-therapeutic, non-consensual excision of healthy tissue'.[42] Another example is the non-therapeutic sterilisation of a patient who lacks capacity. This is permissible if it is authorised by a court; on the other hand, *therapeutic* sterilisation of a patient without capacity, for example to deal with a medical condition such as excessive menstruation or cancer, does not require such authorisation.[43]

When we pass the liminal area of the spectrum we reach the realm of *improper* activity, which includes non-consensual treatment of patients with capacity, treatment of patients who lack capacity which is not in their best interests, and activity carried out by non-qualified persons.[44]

The largest category is likely to be that containing paradigm cases of proper medical treatment, where consent and therapeutic benefit are both clearly established. The next largest category is probably clearly proper treatment, where therapeutic benefit is not contested but consent is substituted by another patient-centred justification. The liminal zone of proper treatment where therapeutic benefit is absent or contested will be a smaller category, followed by 'improper activity'. As we travel along the spectrum from the paradigm case to the improper, therapeutic benefit tends to decrease. The only exception to that general trend is that at the 'improper' end of the spectrum, interventions will be improper regardless of clear therapeutic benefit if they are performed in the absence of a patient-centred justification, which must be consent in the case of a patient with capacity.

Abortion and proper medical treatment

What light, if any, can the foregoing analysis of proper medical treatment shed on the status of abortion? I claimed in the introductory section of this chapter that it is useful to consider abortion in the light of the emerging discussion about proper medical treatment for two reasons. First, because pro-choice activists have recently put the decriminalisation of the practice of abortion on the political agenda, and decriminalisation would be likely to involve the removal of any *statutory* justification

41 M. Brazier, *Medicine, Patients and the Law* (2nd edn, Penguin, 1992) 350.

42 M. Fox, M. Thomson, 'A covenant with the status quo? Male circumcision and the new BMA guidance to doctors' (2005) 31 *Journal of Medical Ethics* 463.

43 J. Herring, *Medical Law and Ethics* (5th edn, Oxford University Press, 2014) 281.

44 Note that interventions performed negligently, or performed where consent is insufficiently informed, occupy a subcategory of *proper* treatment, albeit that they are not 'properly' carried out.

for the practice so that surgical abortion would require to be justified in the same way as any other intrusive intervention. Second, because the concept of proper medical treatment is wider than just the medical exception. It is, I have claimed, a graduated concept, so that all treatment can be located somewhere on the spectrum of the proper. The issues at stake in lawful abortion have, of course, been considered thoroughly from a range of angles, but the lens of proper medical treatment offers yet another perspective from which to consider the practice.

One key measure in determining where practices ought to be located along the spectrum will be their potential therapeutic value, or, in other words, the extent to which we regard a practice as capable of serving patients' best interests or offering them benefit. In the context of abortion, the state of modern medical science is such that '[lawful] abortion is almost always safer than . . . a full term birth'.[45] One recent US study found that '[t]he risk of death associated with childbirth is approximately 14 times higher than that with abortion', and that 'the overall morbidity associated with childbirth exceeds that with abortion'.[46] The implication of this is that in almost all cases, performing a safe, lawful abortion prevents a greater risk to maternal health, and on this basis it could be argued that where abortion is performed non-negligently and lawfully, it is *always* clearly therapeutic. Providing that clear consent is also present, then, on this view all safe and lawful abortion would always fall within the *paradigm* zone of proper medical treatment. Alternatively, recalling the passage above in which Fovargue and I discuss the factors that might render a practice liminal, it could be concluded that lawful abortion will always fall within the *liminal* zone of proper medical treatment, because it always involves the destruction of human life. Abortion always ends the life of an individual human entity, *regardless* of the reason for performing it. This is so even where it is performed in an emergency to save the life of the pregnant woman. We could choose to regard abortion as always liminal for this reason.

A discussion of abortion and proper medical treatment could end in either of these ways, and some may decide that it should. Others may be unsatisfied with an account which fails to take recognise the diversity of abortion, however, and may consider that the fact that abortion is almost always safer than carrying a pregnancy to term fails to get to the heart of what is under discussion here. When we speak of an intervention being therapeutic, it could be argued that there is implicit in this description the idea of a link between the therapeutic *purpose* and the therapeutic *benefit*.[47] In other words, the intervention is performed *in order to produce*, or

45 A. Furedi, 'Abortion is safe, and it should be as available as easily as contraception: the time has come to decriminalise it altogether' (*The Independent*, 21 October 2014), available at http://www.independent.co.uk/voices/comment/abortion-is-safe-and-it-should-be-as-available-as-easily-as-contraception-9808803.html (accessed 1 December 2014).

46 See e.g. E. G. Raymond, D. A. Grimes, 'The comparative safety of legal induced abortion and childbirth in the United States' (2012) 119 *Obstetrics & Gynecology* 215, 215.

47 See e.g. S. Fovargue, *Xenotransplantation and Risk: Regulating a Developing Biotechnology* (Cambridge University Press, 2012) 63.

in the hope of producing) the contemplated benefit. And it is the potential for *that* benefit that contributes to the justification of the intervention, although, as I have noted already, some manner of patient-centred justification (consent, best interests, or necessity) must also be present. Abortion is permitted by the law in Scotland, England and Wales on any one or more of the following grounds:[48]

A that the continuance of the pregnancy would involve risk to the life of the pregnant woman, greater than if the pregnancy were terminated;[49]
B that the termination is necessary to prevent grave permanent injury to the physical or mental health of the pregnant woman;[50]
C that the pregnancy has not exceeded its twenty-fourth week and that the continuance of the pregnancy would involve risk, greater than if the pregnancy were terminated, of injury to the physical and mental health of the pregnant woman;[51]
D that the pregnancy has not exceeded its twenty-fourth week and that the continuance of the pregnancy would involve risk, greater than if the pregnancy were terminated, of injury to the physical and mental health of any existing children of the family of the pregnant woman;[52]
E that there is substantial risk that if the child were born it would suffer from such physical or mental abnormalities as to be seriously handicapped;[53]
F that the termination is immediately necessary to save the life of the pregnant woman;[54] and
G that the termination is immediately necessary to prevent grave permanent injury to the physical or mental health of the pregnant woman.[55]

Officially, all terminations of pregnancy are performed on one or more of the above grounds. While it is not impossible that fear of childbirth or of the risks associated with carrying a pregnancy to full term may be the reason why some women seek to terminate their pregnancies, there is no way of estimating how

48 The convention of lettering the statutory grounds A-G is used by the Department of Health in England and Wales and the equivalent reporting body in Scotland when reporting the abortion statistics annually. See e.g. Department of Health (DH), *Abortion Statistics, England and Wales: 2012* (DH, 2014). Sched. 1 of the Abortion Regulations 1991 No.499 uses the letters A-E, and Sched. 1 of the Abortion (Scotland) Regulations 1991 No. 460 (S41) uses A-G. Grounds A-E inclusive must be certified by two registered medical practitioners, whereas grounds F and G (the emergency grounds) require certification only by a single practitioner.
49 Abortion Act 1967, s. 1(1)(c).
50 Abortion Act 1967, s. 1(1)(b).
51 Abortion Act 1967, s. 1(1)(a).
52 Abortion Act 1967, s. 1(1)(a).
53 Abortion Act 1967, s. 1(1)(d).
54 Abortion Act 1967, s. 1(4).
55 Abortion Act 1967, s. 1(4).

many abortions, if any, are carried out for that reason. Given that childbirth and abortion are *both* very low risk,[56] and that narratives about fear of childbirth do not seem to feature in explanations about why women require access to safe, lawful abortion, it makes sense to assume that the vast majority of abortions are carried out for other reasons. In any case, if we accept the argument above that 'therapeutic' implies a link between therapeutic *purpose* and therapeutic *benefit*, the fact that abortion always removes the greater (but still slight) risk to health associated with childbirth establishes the procedure's therapeutic nature *only where it is carried out for this purpose*. In all other cases, whether abortion is therapeutic must be established and cannot simply be presumed.

Abortion will clearly satisfy the 'therapeutic' test where it is performed on one of the emergency grounds listed above (F or G). The rubrics of grounds A, B, and C also presuppose that where an abortion is performed this is in order to avoid a risk to the pregnant woman's life (A), to prevent grave permanent physical or mental harm (B), or otherwise to protect her physical or mental health (C). Where an abortion is performed in order to avoid risks like these, its therapeutic value seems straightforward. Whether such a risk is genuinely present in a given case is, of course, an empirical question, and, as such, whether an abortion in a particular case is *in fact* therapeutic will depend on whether there is genuinely a reasonable perception of the relevant risk (specified in the statutory ground being utilised) on the part of the certifying practitioner(s). In this regard, there is a particular issue around the interpretation and use of ground C to allow practitioners to provide abortions which are not genuinely therapeutic in the medical sense, discussed further below. Abortions provided only under grounds D and E are also explicitly *not therapeutic for the woman*. D refers to the risk to the existing children of the pregnant woman's family, and E to foetal abnormality. Where an abortion is performed to avoid risk to existing children or to terminate a pregnancy due to foetal abnormality, this *cannot* be construed as therapeutic for the pregnant woman herself, unless her own mental or physical health is jeopardised by these circumstances. If the latter is the case, the abortion will be justifiable not *only* under grounds D or E but also under one of the other grounds, and can be regarded as therapeutic on *that* basis. Grounds D and E do not refer to the woman's health and so do not, by themselves, set out any therapeutic basis for abortion.

Focusing on the straightforwardly therapeutic grounds A, B, F, and G, what proportion of all abortions are being represented as 'therapeutic' on one of these grounds? In Scotland, the numbers and percentages of abortions carried out

56 See e.g. Raymond and Grimes (n 46), whose study 'estimated mortality rates associated with live births and legal induced abortions in the United States in 1998–2005 by combining published data from several national data sets' including 'the Centers for Disease Control and Prevention's Pregnancy Mortality Surveillance System, birth certificates, and Guttmacher Institute surveys' and found that '[t]he pregnancy-associated mortality rate among women who delivered live neonates was 8.8 deaths per 100,000 live births' and '[t]he mortality rate related to induced abortion was 0.6 deaths per 100,000 abortions', 215.

under these grounds are almost invariably suppressed 'due to the potential risk of disclosure'.[57] In other words, the numbers in these categories are so small that their publication may result in a reader being able to identify an individual from the statistics.[58] It is impossible to know with any certainty the numbers and/or percentages of abortions carried out in Scotland under grounds A, B, F, and G, not only because the direct data on those grounds is suppressed, but also because certifications of abortion may cite more than one statutory ground. It is thus not possible simply to calculate the total numbers/percentages of abortions performed under grounds C, D, and E and deduct that total from the overall total in order to arrive at the combined figure for grounds A, B, F, and G. Nevertheless, this method can tell us the combined percentage of abortions carried out under A, B, F, and/or G *only* (that is, abortions which cite one or more of those grounds but do not also cite C, D, and/or E). It reveals that the percentage of abortions carried out in 2012 and 2013 which cite *only* grounds A, B, F, and/or G is under 1 per cent (because the combined percentages for C, D, and E in those two years total 100 per cent), and that the percentage of abortions carried out in 2010 and 2011 which cite *only* A, B, F, and/or G was 0.1 per cent at most in each of those years.

Because England and Wales has a much larger population than Scotland, the risk of identification is lower; accordingly, the figures for England and Wales are reported, and reveal that in 2010 '[g]rounds A and B together accounted for *less than a quarter of one per cent* of abortions',[59] and that in each of 2011, 2012, and 2013 '[g]rounds A and B together accounted for *about a tenth of one per cent* of abortions', approximately 0.1 per cent.[60] In relation to F and G, the most recently reported statistics note that '[a]bortions are rarely performed under grounds F or G. In the past 10 years, 4 such abortions have been performed, 1 in each of years 2006, 2011, 2012 and 2013'.[61]

57 This is the form of words used in the published statistics.

58 The reporting of abortion statistics for Scotland follows the guidance on disclosure of information in relation to 'sensitive topics' contained in the Information Services Division (ISD) Scotland, *Statistical Disclosure Control Protocol Version 2.3* (ISD, 2012), available at http://www.isdscotland.org/About-ISD/Confidentiality/DISCLOSURE-PROTOCOL-VERSION-2-3_FULLVERSION.PDF (accessed 1 December 2014).

59 DH, *Abortion Statistics, England and Wales: 2010* (DH, 2011) 8, emphasis supplied, available at https://www.gov.uk/government/uploads/system/uploads/attachment_data/file/215584/dh_127202.pdf (accessed 1 December 2014). Hereafter, e.g. DH, *ASEW: 2010*.

60 DH, *Abortion Statistics, England and Wales: 2011* (DH, 2012) 8, available at https://www.gov.uk/government/uploads/system/uploads/attachment_data/file/213386/Commentary1.pdf (accessed 1 December 2014); DH, *Abortion Statistics, England and Wales: 2012* (DH, 2013) 12, available at https://www.gov.uk/government/uploads/system/uploads/attachment_data/file/307650/Abortion_statistics__England_and_Wales.pdf (accessed 1 December 2014); DH, *Abortion Statistics, England and Wales: 2013* (DH, 2014) 12, emphasis supplied, available at https://www.gov.uk/government/uploads/system/uploads/attachment_data/file/319460/Abortion_Statistics__England_and_Wales_2013.pdf (accessed 1 December 2014).

61 DH, *ASEW: 2013* (n 60) 12.

The vast majority of lawful abortions in the UK are performed under ground C. In England and Wales, 98 per cent of all abortions in 2011,[62] 97 per cent in 2012,[63] and 97 per cent in 2013[64] were carried out under ground C, almost always under its 'risk to mental health' aspect (99.96 per cent,[65] 99.94 per cent,[66] and 99.84 per cent[67] in 2011, 2012, and 2013, respectively). The picture in Scotland is similar. 94 per cent,[68] 93 per cent,[69] and 94.5 per cent[70] of all abortions were carried out under ground C in 2010, 2011, and 2012, respectively, with the figure increasing to 98.6 per cent in 2013.[71] Ground C is sometimes referred to as the 'social ground' because it is acknowledged to be interpreted liberally so as to effectively allow 'abortion on demand'. Ann Furedi, Chief Executive of the British Pregnancy Advisory Service (bpas), a private abortion provider, has claimed that '[w]e all know, if we are honest, that ground C is a kind of code for "it's an unwanted pregnancy"'.[72] Furthermore:

> at the moment . . . women have to pretend they will have a nervous breakdown if they continue the pregnancy, and doctors pretend to believe them. The current situation makes actors of both women and doctors; it would be far better if the law was explicit and if women were able to obtain an abortion because the pregnancy is unwanted.[73]

Furedi's organisation is actively campaigning for the complete decriminalisation of abortion and the removal of the current statutory requirements, and

62 DH, *ASEW: 2011* (n 60) 8.
63 DH, *ASEW: 2012* (n 60) 12.
64 DH, *ASEW: 2013* (n 60) 12.
65 DH, *ASEW: 2011* (n 60) 8–9.
66 DH, *ASEW: 2012* (n 60) 12.
67 DH, *ASEW: 2013* (n 60) 12.
68 ISD Scotland, *Abortion Statistics: Year ending 31 December 2010* (ISD Scotland/ National Statistics, 31 May 2011) 12, available at http://www.isdscotland.org/Health-Topics/Sexual-Health/Publications/2011-05-31/2011-05-31-Abortions-Report.pdf (accessed 1 December 2014).
69 ISD Scotland, *Abortion Statistics: Year ending 31 December 2011* (ISD Scotland/ National Statistics, 29 May 2012) 13, available at http://www.isdscotland.org/Health-Topics/Sexual-Health/Publications/2012-05-29/2012-05-29-Abortions-Report-2011.pdf (accessed 1 December 2014).
70 ISD Scotland, *Abortion Statistics: Year ending 31 December 2012* (ISD Scotland/ National Statistics, 28 May 2013) 13, available at http://www.isdscotland.org/Health-Topics/Sexual-Health/Publications/2013-05-28/2013-05-28-Abortions-Report.pdf (accessed 1 December 2014).
71 ISD Scotland, *Abortion Statistics: Year ending 31 December 2013* (ISD Scotland/ National Statistics, 27 May 2014) 14, available at https://isdscotland.scot.nhs.uk/Health-Topics/Sexual-Health/Publications/2014-05-27/2014-05-27-Abortions2013-Report.pdf?14501589537 (accessed 1 December 2014).
72 A. Furedi, 'Are there too many abortions?' (Winter 2008/9) Special Edition 2 *Abortion Review Special Edition: Abortion and Women's Lives (Papers from the BPAS conference, London 25–26 June 2008)* 3, available at http://www.abortionreview.org/images/uploads/AR_SpecialEdition_2.pdf (accessed 1 December 2014).
73 Furedi (n 72) 3–4.

for abortion to be treated by the law as a women's rights issue rather than as a criminal/medical matter.[74] In the context of that campaign, it makes strategic sense to acknowledge that the decision to terminate a pregnancy often has no medical basis, and that, except in cases where a woman's health is genuinely at risk from the continuation of her pregnancy, abortion is more accurately regarded as a matter of personal choice with no therapeutic imperative. Furedi highlights the pretence of women and their doctors around the mental health aspect of ground C in order to demonstrate that the 1967 Act fails to reflect modern social reality. Nowadays, the argument goes, abortion is 'widely accepted as "part of life"',[75] and understood as a matter of personal choice and a right. As such, the decision to terminate or continue with a pregnancy is properly a decision for the pregnant woman herself. If *she* decides that she needs an abortion, she should have access to it regardless of her reasons. It is highly undesirable that women and their doctors are forced to pretend that the reason for the termination is a ground C reason, and the law should change so that such pretence is no longer necessary.

It is not my concern here to approve or disapprove of this as a campaigning narrative. It is relevant to the present discussion, however, insofar as it implies that many ground C abortions may not be therapeutic in the sense envisaged by the 1967 Act. As Sally Sheldon has observed, 'in the vast majority of cases . . . the request for abortion is not grounded primarily in medical factors'.[76] Claiming that a procedure is non-therapeutic (in the medical sense) is not the same as claiming that it is undertaken in a 'frivolous or unconsidered' manner.[77] Nevertheless, according to my analysis here, if a significant number of ground C terminations have no potential for therapeutic value (unless we take refuge in the 'abortion is almost always safer than childbirth' formulation, which, I have argued, is of no assistance in this context), the status of these interventions as proper medical treatment must be liminal at best.

So far as ground C is concerned, each individual intervention would need to be judged on its merits. The above-quoted statements by Furedi and Sheldon certainly suggest that many ground C abortions may not be therapeutic, but the wording of the ground itself permits abortion *only* for therapeutic reasons. In contrast with this, any reference to therapeutic value *for the patient* is missing from the wordings of grounds D and E. Applying the basic typology of proper medical treatment that I set out in the first part of this chapter, where therapeutic value is absent (as it is on a literal reading of grounds D and E, and de facto in an unknown number of ground C cases), an intervention may still have the status of proper treatment if it is clearly in the public interest to permit it. I suggested earlier that living organ

74 bpas (n 6).

75 bpas (n 6).

76 S. Sheldon, 'The Abortion Act's paternalism belongs to the 1960s' (*The Guardian*, 22 March 2012), available at http://www.theguardian.com/law/2012/mar/22/abortion-act-needs-reform (accessed 1 December 2014).

77 Sheldon (n 76).

donation is an example of treatment which is proper *and* permitted despite lacking therapeutic benefit for the patient who is the subject of the intervention. In that case, the overriding public interest consideration could be framed as an interest in encouraging altruism, or in addressing the chronic shortfall in donor organs, or both. In the abortion context, public interest considerations would need to be framed carefully, particularly where ground E is concerned. Any public interest consideration would presumably need to be constructed so as to avoid creating norms that discriminate against people with disabilities or devalue their lives. The most likely public interest justifications in the abortion context would be ones formulated in terms of child welfare (grounds D and E), or in terms of respecting autonomy and choice. It will be for others to identify and frame the relevant justifications. My purpose here is only to point out that public interest or public good type justifications will be necessary. If a sufficient public interest justification *can* be made out, then even a non-therapeutic abortion can be proper, just as living organ donation can; although, according to my typology, it will be liminally so.

In the absence of a compelling public interest justification, non-therapeutic interventions *cannot*, I argue, be proper medical treatment. What might the implications be of some abortions *not* qualifying as proper medical treatment? First, were existing laws governing abortion to be repealed, *surgical* abortions would require the benefit of the medical exception, not because abortion per se is criminal, but because surgical intrusions in general involve a greater level of intrusion than consent alone can mitigate. One consequence of my argument is that if the existing statutory justification were to be removed, surgical abortions could only benefit from the medical exception if they could be regarded as proper medical treatment. Where abortion is clearly therapeutic, and the appropriate patient-centred justification is present, its status as proper medical treatment is unproblematic. If the patient-centred justification takes the form of *consent*, a paradigm case of proper medical treatment is constituted. If the patient is unconscious or lacks capacity and the abortion is performed on grounds of necessity or best interests, it will, so long as it is therapeutic, be a clear case of proper medical treatment. A *non*-therapeutic intervention upon a patient who lacks capacity would be *im*proper. Where there is no potential for therapeutic benefit, however, an intervention can only qualify as proper medical treatment if consent *and* an overriding public interest can be established, as in the case of living organ donation. Even then, the status of the treatment will be liminal at best.

My suggestion here, and I acknowledge that this will be controversial, is that abortions carried out *only* under grounds D and E, and those where ground C has been deployed in the way described by Furedi and Sheldon, can qualify as *liminally* proper treatment if an overriding public interest justification can be identified. If no such justification can be made out, they cannot count as proper medical treatment at all. The latter possibility might be viewed as an opportunity to demedicalise abortion, wresting control of the process away from doctors and the state, and giving it to women for the first time.[78] In addition, it could offer a solution to the

78 Sheldon (n 76).

issue of conscientious objection.[79] But it also raises the possibility that if the existing statutory framework were to be removed, surgical abortions, lacking the benefit of the medical exception, would become vulnerable under the criminal law.

Conclusion

The medical exception demarcates the boundary between the proper and the improper. I have argued that on the 'proper' side of that boundary there exists a *spectrum* of proper medical treatment, within which some treatments are more *clearly* proper than others. Furthermore, the *therapeutic value or potential* of treatments plays a key role in determining where we ought to locate them on that spectrum. Treatment that lacks therapeutic value *may* be proper if consent is clearly present *and* an overwhelming public interest justification exists (as in the case of living organ donation), but it can only ever be *liminally* proper. It is certainly not paradigmatic of proper treatment, since the paradigm case of such treatment involves *both* consent *and* a reasonable expectation of therapeutic value. It is also too far away from the paradigm case to count as clearly proper. Treatment without therapeutic value or potential is either liminally proper (at best) or improper, depending upon the other circumstances of the case.

Having rejected *both* the suggestion that all abortion is automatically therapeutic because birth is riskier, *and* the possibility that abortion can only ever be liminally proper at best because it always involves the destruction of human life, I have argued that whether abortion counts as proper medical treatment (and if so, how *clearly* proper it is) is something that can be determined only on a case-by-case basis. Nevertheless, proposals for completely decriminalising abortion ought to bear in mind that, at least so far as surgical interventions are concerned, the complete exclusion of the criminal law is impossible (given that *all* surgery depends upon a medical exception to the criminal law), and interference with the current statutory framework may, in fact, leave the practice more, rather than less, vulnerable. Accordingly, law reform proposals should be cognisant of the need for a governing statute which provides explicit authorisation for abortion.

79 See e.g. J. K. Mason, R. A. McCall Smith, G. T. Laurie, *Law and Medical Ethics* (6th edn, Butterworths, 2002), 175: 'a logical case can be made, and a major ground for confrontation thereby removed, for delegating abortions which have no immediate therapeutic dimension to trained abortionists'.

9 Death on demand: 'Proper medical treatment'?

Richard Huxtable

Introduction

Although the message is sometimes lost in translation,[1] English law proclaims death on demand to be unlawful.[2] Various parliamentarians have pled the merits of a different message, that the unlawful should be rendered lawful.[3] Their efforts have (yet?) to prove successful. Equally unsuccessful (again, so far) have been numerous attempts to petition the courts to lift the ban.[4] Despite the Houses' ongoing resistance, the courts continue to insist that only Parliament can pull apart the prevailing prohibition.[5] So constrained, the judiciary is left to restate the basic message; assisted dying is not lawful.

According to Lord Mustill, the principled basis for resisting assisted dying is that 'the interest of the state in preserving life overrides the otherwise all-powerful interest of patient autonomy'.[6] Mustill is not alone in pointing to the state interest in upholding the sanctity of human life.[7] John Keown suggests that the principle, which opposes the intentional ending of innocent human life, has long been a feature of English law and, on his account, rightly so.[8] This is no mere theistic and anachronistic hangover; Article 2 of the European Convention (given domestic effect by the Human Rights Act 1998), the right to life, expresses the same essential idea in a secular tongue.

The sanctity of life may dominate whenever death on demand enters the courtroom, but it is occasionally united with suggestions that 'vulnerable' citizens must

1 See R. Huxtable, *Euthanasia, Ethics and the Law: From Conflict to Compromise* (Routledge-Cavendish, 2007).

2 'Death on demand' refers to requests for (active) voluntary forms of assistance in dying (i.e. voluntary euthanasia and assisted suicide), which are motivated by a desire to avoid current or anticipated suffering.

3 E.g. Lord Joffe's Assisted Dying for the Terminally Ill Bill and, more recently, Lord Falconer's Assisted Dying Bill.

4 E.g. *R (on the application of Nicklinson and another) v Ministry of Justice; R (on the application of AM) v The Director of Public Prosecutions* [2014] UKSC 38.

5 E.g. *Nicklinson* (n 4) para. 116, *per* Lord Neuberger, paras 343–344, *per* Lord Kerr.

6 *Airedale NHS Trust v Bland* [1993] AC 789, 892–893, HL, *per* Lord Mustill.

7 See Huxtable (n 1) 131–133.

8 J. Keown, *The Law and Ethics of Medicine: Essays on the Inviolability of Life* (OUP, 2013) 3.

be protected and dangerously slippery slopes avoided.[9] The public interest seems, therefore, to comprise various (potentially overlapping)[10] interests. Yet, these are not always spelt out. In this chapter, I outline those indications we have from the lawmakers, focusing specifically on the proclaimed integrity of medicine and what the claim could, or should, mean in relation to death on demand.

It becomes apparent that medicine is protected in and by the law; 'proper medical treatment' is exempted from some of the rules that might otherwise inhibit its practitioners. Should medically assisted dying also be exempt? I suggest that medicine's 'internal morality' appears not to provide a necessary answer to this question,[11] and, indeed, that any such answer would be insufficient since we need also to look to the wider public interest. But we will see that this too is a contested concept. Ultimately, we cannot escape a values choice, such as that between autonomy and the sanctity of human life. I do not here seek to specify the right choice of values which should guide our laws or even the right combinations thereof (whatever these might be). I do, however, hope to show why appeals to the integrity of medicine, proper medical treatment, and the public interest cannot do the necessary moral work. This remains work for us to do, collectively, as members of a society which is contemplating, and may be edging nearer towards, the legalisation of assisted dying.

Proper medical treatment and the public interest

When the demand before the court is 'help me to die', the sanctity of life tends to dominate. Yet, other state interests evidently occupy the judges' minds, although these are rarely spelt out. In *Robb*, however, the demand was 'allow me to die'.[12] Thorpe J ruled that hunger-striking Mr Robb could not be forcibly fed as his decision had been competently reached. Thorpe J was refreshingly open about the state interests in issue in the case: '(1) preserving life; (2) preventing suicide; (3) maintaining the integrity of the medical profession; and (4) protecting innocent third parties'.[13] In this particular case, autonomy triumphed since it was judged to outweigh the obligation to protect life. Furthermore, the refusal of food was not considered equivalent to suicide, the integrity of the medical profession was not found to be directly engaged, and there were no (pertinent) third parties judged to be in need of protection.

Thorpe J is not alone in citing these particular state interests. In *Brady*,[14] Kay J referred to the same list, albeit reaching the opposite conclusion about the legitimacy of force-feeding this particular (notorious) prisoner.[15] He hoped that the law

9 E.g. *Nicklinson* (n 4) paras 228–232 *per* Lord Sumption.

10 E.g. protecting the vulnerable might be connected with upholding the sanctity of life.

11 See also L. Frith, 'What do we mean by "proper" medical treatment?'; M. Neal, 'Locating lawful abortion on the spectrum of "proper medical treatment"', in this collection.

12 *Secretary of State for the Home Department v Robb* [1995] Fam 127.

13 *Robb* (n 12) 131.

14 *R v Collins and Ashworth Hospital Authority ex p Brady* [2000] Lloyds Rep Med 355.

15 See M. Brazier, 'Do no harm: Do patients have responsibilities too?' (2006) 65 *Cambridge Law Journal* 397.

had not reached the point 'where the rights of a patient count for everything and other ethical values and institutional integrity count for nothing'.[16] Both judges had acquired their lists from a US authority, *Thor*,[17] in which, as in *Robb*, the patient's right to refuse even life-sustaining intervention had been upheld. In such cases, provided that the patient is indeed autonomous, autonomy will outweigh any state interests in protecting people or protecting a particular profession. Of course, the possibility remains that the order of priority will be reversed in other cases, which is precisely what happens when the patient seeks active assistance in dying.

Given the apparent role that they play in denying death on demand, these different state interests invite further investigation, not least the idea that the integrity of the medical profession merits protection, including from the autonomous claims of some patients. Medicine, it seems, is special, and it deserves special protection. The law has accordingly created a special exception by which doctors can avoid the taint of criminality that might otherwise impede their practices. As, again, Lord Mustill famously put it:

> Many of the acts done by surgeons would be very serious crimes if done by anyone else, and yet the surgeons incur no liability. Actual consent . . . is an essential element in this immunity; but it cannot be a direct explanation for it, since much of the bodily invasion involved in surgery lies well above any point at which consent could even arguably be regarded as furnishing a defence. Why is this so? The answer must in my opinion be that proper medical treatment, for which actual or deemed consent is a prerequisite, is in a category of its own.[18]

His Lordship had made similar comments in *Bland*,[19] while earlier, in *Attorney-General's Reference (No 6 of 1980)*, Lord Lane had referred to 'the accepted legality of . . . reasonable surgical interference', which he judged to be 'needed in the public interest'.[20]

The law, therefore, suggests that proper medical treatment should be afforded the (legal) space to thrive. Notice in the above passages that respect for patient autonomy (and thus consent) does not wholly determine the propriety of medical treatment. Autonomy is a component of proper medical treatment but it does not do all of the heavy lifting; quite what does, and, therefore, what is to count as proper medical treatment, and who is to say so, are nevertheless open to interpretation. To a significant extent, the law seems content to leave the identification

16 *Brady* (n 14) 367.

17 *Thor v Superior Court* 5 Cal 4th 725 (1993). See M. Stauch, K. Wheat, with J. Tingle, *Text, Cases and Materials on Medical Law and Ethics* (4th edn, Routledge, 2012) 86–92.

18 *R v Brown* [1993] 2 All ER 75, 109–110, HL, *per* Lord Mustill.

19 *Bland* (n 6) 891, *per* Lord Mustill.

20 (1981) 73 Cr App R 63, 66, HL. For further discussion see M.Brazier, S. Fovargue, 'Transforming wrong into right: What is 'proper medical treatment'?' in this collection.

of the precise parameters and their policing to the profession itself. The medical profession accordingly has the freedom to self-govern, with the General Medical Council (GMC) setting the relevant standards and overseeing doctors' compliance therewith.[21] Doctors who fail to satisfy the GMC's standards of good medical practice can be disciplined and removed from the profession where necessary.[22] Notably, these standards themselves refer to the importance of integrity; individual professionals are instructed to behave with integrity so that public trust can be maintained, in order to sustain the integrity of the profession itself.

The scope afforded to doctors' views of good doctoring in the quasi-law of the GMC is further replicated in the law itself, not least in the all-conquering *Bolam* standard.[23] According to this standard, which originated in the civil law of clinical negligence, a doctor will satisfy the standard of care expected of her if she acts in accordance with a practice accepted as proper by a responsible body of professionals skilled in that particular art. So far, so good, perhaps, at least insofar as this phrase appears simply to translate the 'reasonable person' standard into the 'reasonable doctor' standard. *Bolam*'s reach, indeed, the *Bolam*isation of medical law has, nevertheless, caused alarm.[24] Doctors' views about what doctors (should) do has certainly proven determinative of all manner of medico-legal dilemmas, from the provision of information in the consent process,[25] to judging the best interests of patients who lack capacity,[26] to the withdrawal of life-sustaining treatment therefrom.[27]

But it is not merely the case that the law allows doctors to determine how they should do what they do; it is also apparent that doctors are legally entitled to do that which the rest of us cannot. The suspension of otherwise general rules does not only empower surgeons.[28] In life-and-death situations exceptions are also made,[29] such that doctors (but not non-doctors) can refrain from providing the necessities for life,[30] and can run the (admittedly, small) risk of shortening patients' lives when relieving their symptoms.[31] The freedom also extends to decisions *not* to do certain things. The courts appear resistant to prescribing for doctors; they will not *order* doctors to act contrary to their clinical judgement.[32] The judges will declare the law; they will not prescribe the course.

21 Medical Act 1983, s. 35.
22 General Medical Council (GMC), *Good Medical Practice* (GMC, 2013), updated 29 April 2014.
23 *Bolam v Friern Hospital Management Committee* [1957] 1 WLR 582.
24 E.g. J. Miola, *Medical Ethics and Medical Law: A Symbiotic Relationship* (Hart, 2007) 14.
25 *Sidaway v Board of Governors of the Bethlem Royal Hospital and the Maudsley Hospital* [1985] AC 871, HL.
26 *Re F (Mental Patient: Sterilisation)* [1990] 2 AC 1, HL.
27 *Bland* (n 6).
28 E.g. Female Genital Mutilation Act 2003, s. 1(2).
29 Including for surgeons, *Re A (Children) (Conjoined Twins: Surgical Separation)* [2000] 4 All ER 961, CA.
30 E.g. *Bland* (n 6); *Re J (A Minor) (Wardship: Medical Treatment)* [1991] 1 FLR 366, CA. See further Huxtable (n 1) 123–128. Regarding other health care professionals see G. Birchley, 'Angels of mercy? The legal and professional implications of withdrawal of life-sustaining treatment by nurses in England and Wales' (2012) 20 *Medical Law Review* 337.
31 *R v Adams* [1965] *Crim LR* 365.
32 E.g. *Re J* (n 30).

Doctors are, therefore, protected and empowered, but they are not entirely free from oversight or constraint; the courts will still peer over the shoulders of the doctors and those of the GMC too.[33] Thus, the propriety of proper medical treatment is not wholly determined by the profession itself. This should not be surprising because, as Thorpe J and Kay J indicated, the state's interests encompass more than the integrity of the medical profession. As agents of the state, the judges (and, of course, Parliament) will erect boundaries around what even doctors can do, presumably by reference to other important state interests. There will sometimes be external, and critical, scrutiny of doctors' practices; for example, *Bolitho*[34] issued a reminder that the courts ultimately assess the defensibility of doctors' chosen standards.[35] The law has also moved on from a *Bolam*ised view of information disclosure and the best interests of patients.[36] Sometimes accepted practices must be modified in the wake of court rulings,[37] and, occasionally, medical personnel might be at greater risk of liability or culpability than the rest of us. For example, prosecution guidance on complicity in suicide appears to render doctors particularly vulnerable.[38] As such, even if doctors are willing in principle to offer this (or any other) form of assisted dying, the law currently instructs them not to do so in practice, unless they are willing to accept the adverse consequences.[39]

The continued illegality of death on demand might rest, albeit partially, on doctors' own views of the demerits thereof. Many such professional organisations oppose a permissive repositioning of the law, and research reveals a strong palliative care ethos in this jurisdiction (doctors in this specialty, at least in this country,[40] appear resistant to such a development).[41] More often, however, the courts explicitly refer to protectionist norms, and particularly to the need to uphold the sanctity of life, when they rule against assisted dying. In *Bland*, Lord Keith opined that the sanctity of life 'is the concern of the state, and the judiciary as one of the arms of the state, to maintain'.[42] These sentiments echo those of the judge in

33 E.g. Medical Act 1983, s. 40.
34 *Bolitho v City and Hackney Health Authority* [1998] AC 232, HL.
35 But see M. Brazier, J. Miola, 'Bye-bye *Bolam*: A medical litigation revolution?' (2000) 8 *Medical Law Review* 85.
36 See e.g. *Chester v Afshar* [2004] UKHL 41; *Re A (Medical Treatment: Male Sterilisation)* [2000] 1 FLR 549, CA; and Mental Capacity Act 2005, s. 4.
37 See e.g. Miola (n 24) 173–185.
38 Director of Public Prosecutions, *Policy for Prosecutors in Respect of Cases of Encouraging or Assisting Suicide* (Crown Prosecution Service, February 2010, updated October 2014); GMC, *When a Patient Seeks Advice or Information about Assistance to Die* (GMC, January 2013). The guidance to prosecutors was updated in October 2014: para. 43.14 states that '[a] prosecution is more likely to be required if . . . the suspect was acting in his or her capacity as a medical doctor, nurse, other healthcare professional, a professional carer (whether for payment or not), or as a person in authority, such as a prison officer, and the victim was in his or her care'.
39 Although, for whatever reason, prosecutions and convictions are, in fact, scarce: Huxtable (n 1).
40 See A. V. Campbell, R. Huxtable, 'The position statement and its commentators: Consensus, compromise or confusion?' (2003) 17 *Palliative Medicine* 180.
41 C. Seale, 'National survey of end-of-life decisions made by UK medical practitioners' (2006) 20 *Palliative Medicine* 3.
42 *Bland* (n 6) 859, *per* Lord Keith.

Thor, who usefully identified 'two separate but related aspects' to this 'paramount concern', 'an interest in preserving the life of the particular patient and an interest in preserving the sanctity of all life.'[43]

So much for what the law *happens* to say, but what *should* be said? In order to assess the appropriateness of the legal prohibition, we need to take a more critical look at the apparently prohibitive principles and, particularly, the integrity of medicine.

Death on demand and the integrity of medicine

Permissive proposals for assisted dying typically empower doctors as providers,[44] so surely their professional integrity, and any impact thereon, is a crucial concern? However, integrity is a complex concept.[45] Personal integrity can be characterised in terms of an individual's deep desires or her identity-conferring values. It can also be tethered to general moral constraints. Maybe a person only has integrity if she stands for something that is objectively morally worthwhile. Martin Benjamin tries to unite the accounts; a person of integrity will strive for *consistency*, in the sense that she honours her own values, and also *wholeness*, since she will be responsive to other external values and will, where appropriate, yield to these.[46] Balancing these competing commitments might prove difficult on occasion, but the individual must somehow seek to preserve her integrity if she is to maintain her self-respect.[47]

These same concepts, and challenges, can be encountered among groups. Any group with a particular identity can be said to possess (or judged to lack) integrity. For example, Franklin Miller and Howard Brody suggest that:

> Professional integrity in medicine represents what it means normatively to be a physician; it encompasses the values, norms, and virtues that are distinctive and characteristic of physicians. Accordingly, the identity to which professional integrity corresponds is tied to a specific social role.[48]

So what, then, is the distinctive identity of medicine, and what are the moral considerations to which it gives rise, as well as those with which it should engage?

43 *Thor* (n 17) para. 8.

44 Contrast e.g. S. Ost, 'The de-medicalisation of assisted dying: Is a less medicalised model the way forward?' (2010) 18 *Medical Law Review* 497.

45 D. Cox, M. Le Caze, M. Levine, 'Integrity' in E. N. Zalta (ed.), *The Stanford Encyclopedia of Philosophy* (2013), available at http://plato.stanford.edu/archives/fall2013/entries/integrity/ (accessed 8 May 2014).

46 M. Benjamin, *Splitting the Difference: Compromise and Integrity in Ethics and Politics* (University Press of Kansas, 1990).

47 See e.g. D. P. Sulmasy 'What is conscience and why is respect for it so important?' (2008) 29 *Theoretical Medicine and Bioethics* 135, 136.

48 F. G. Miller, H. Brody, 'Professional integrity and physician-assisted death' (1995) 25 *Hastings Center Report* 8, 9.

In seeking to answer these questions, various commentators have contemplated the internal morality of medicine,[49] along the lines first explored by Lon Fuller in his examination of the internal morality of law.[50] Fuller sought to identify the *nature* of the particular practice and the *norms* its practitioners should observe if the practice is to succeed (or even be labelled) as such a practice. This was a conceptual quest, not an empirical enquiry,[51] and we too are interested here in what medicine involves and entails *by definition*, irrespective of the values its practitioners happen in fact to espouse.[52]

The basic structure of Fuller's account is as follows. For Fuller, law (making) is the enterprise of guiding people's behaviour via rules.[53] From here arises an overarching obligation, implicit in the nature of the enterprise; there must be rules which are capable of guiding the relevant subjects. From this end, there then arise more specific instrumental obligations. The lawmaker should issue rules (as opposed to specific edicts), which should be clear, constant, non-contradictory, promulgated, prospective, possible of performance, and administered in a manner that is congruent with their official articulation.

Accounts of the internal morality of medicine can be reconstructed along Fullerian lines.[54] First, consider Edmund Pellegrino's account,[55] which builds on work by Alisdair MacIntyre[56] and, especially, Leon Kass.[57] For Pellegrino, (clinical) medicine appears to be the enterprise of promoting and protecting the good of the whole person of the patient, with particular reference to her health. From here arises an overarching obligation; to serve the patient's good the clinician should promote and protect the medical good (which requires technical competence), the good as perceived by the patient (which requires respect for their autonomous wishes), the good for the patient as a human being, and the spiritual good. From this end, there then arise more specific instrumental obligations which Pellegrino depicts as virtues that should be exhibited by the medical practitioner if she is to serve the end of the person's (overall) good: fidelity to trust, suppression of self-interest, intellectual honesty, compassion, courage, and prudence (so that the best means are chosen).

49 See e.g. R. M. Veatch, 'The impossibility of a morality internal to medicine' (2001) 26 *Journal of Medicine and Philosophy* 621. Also, L. Frith, 'What do we mean by 'proper' medical treatment' in this collection.

50 L. L. Fuller, *The Morality of Law* (revised edn, Yale University Press, 1969).

51 Similar distinctions between what *is* and *should be* the case feature in analyses of the *Bolam* (n 23) standard, see e.g. Miola (n 24) 11–12.

52 Veatch (n 49) 623–625, 627. Of course, these elements can be difficult to disentangle. As an autonomous individual, I can presumably choose my values, and, perhaps, so can a profession if we link integrity to identity or desires. Big shifts in the values might mean that I, or the profession, become something other. I will leave such disentanglement to others.

53 Fuller (n 50) 106.

54 Although particular theorists might disagree, Veatch suspects that such accounts commonly look to an 'end' or 'goal' for medicine: (n 49) 627.

55 E. D. Pellegrino, 'The internal morality of clinical medicine: A paradigm for the ethics of the helping and healing professions' (2001) 26 *Journal of Medicine and Philosophy* 559.

56 A. MacIntyre, *After Virtue* (3rd edn, University of Notre Dame Press, 2007).

57 L. R. Kass, 'Regarding the end of medicine and the pursuit of health' (1975) 40 *Public Interest* 11.

Miller and Brody offer an alternative account, according to which (clinical) medicine is a multifaceted enterprise, which encompasses healing, promoting health, and helping patients to achieve dignified and peaceful deaths. From here arise the overarching obligations on medicine's practitioners: to heal, promote health, and help patients to achieve dignified and peaceful deaths. From these ends arise instrumental obligations on the practitioners: to be competent, to avoid harms when conferring benefits, to avoid fraudulent misrepresentation (and departure from accepted standards), and to maintain fidelity to the therapeutic relationship (thus maintaining patients' trust).

There are striking differences between these accounts. First, there is a significant difference between, on the one hand, Fuller's internal morality of law and, on the other, both of the attempts to specify the internal morality of medicine. Fuller had positioned himself among jurisprudence's natural lawyers, rather than its legal positivists. As such, he believed there to be a necessary connection between law and morality. For example, Fuller suggested that his *desiderata* provided the ground rules for social co-existence, and that their observance 'affects and limits the substantive aims that can be achieved through law', which thereby made them moral.[58] Critics like Herbert Hart disputed the 'morality' of Fuller's internal principles.[59] Certainly, Fuller seemed to stop short of supplying any substance to the ends of law; his account has a degree of moral content and orientation,[60] but it is less substantive than other natural law theories.[61] Of course, neither Pellegrino nor Miller and Brody are so reticent about stipulating the substantive ends of medicine. Fuller's definition of law, and his ensuing norms, appeared to leave open important questions about the appropriate moral content that the rules should capture. The theorists of the internal morality of medicine, however, appear to beg such questions; they seem to insist that there are particular moral messages that medicine should be imparting about particular activities. These accounts, therefore, beg the specific question about the moral permissibility of doctors offering death on demand.

But, here, a second difference emerges. Pellegrino insists that assisted dying is written out of medicine, as unacceptable by definition, while Miller and Brody take the opposite view. Pellegrino's prohibitive position is initially apparent from his alignment with Kass. According to Kass, medicine is an inherently ethical practice which is orientated towards the end of health. Its internal values are explicitly said to encompass the injunction 'do not kill'.[62] Pellegrino follows Kass's Aristotelian approach, explicitly adopting an essentialist, teleological, and realist position.[63] His promotion of a transcendent and spiritual account of the good,

58 Fuller (n 50) 184.

59 H.L.A. Hart, 'Review: Fuller, the morality of law' (1965) 78 *Harvard Law Review* 1281.

60 See Huxtable (n 1) 18–20.

61 E.g. J. Finnis, *Natural Law and Natural Rights* (Clarendon Press, 1986); D. Beyleveld, R. Brownsword, *Law as a Moral Judgment* (2nd edn, Sheffield Academic Press, 1994).

62 Kass (n 57).

63 Pellegrino (n 55) 560.

rather than one autonomously chosen by the individual, ultimately reveals his fundamental allegiance to Roman Catholic values: '[w]hat the patient describes as good for himself – cloning, let us say, or self-mutilation, human embryo research, euthanasia – may violate the good for humans or the spiritual good. The good perceived as good by the patient is not to be a moral law in itself.'[64] Since medicine is aimed at the good, which on this definition excludes assistance in dying, doctors' provision of assistance in dying would violate the integrity of medicine.

While Pellegrino and Kass evince Hippocratic beneficence,[65] and postulate a prohibitive position on assisted dying, Miller and Brody point to a permissive position. They anticipate an allegation of question-begging for including in medicine's goals the provision of a dignified death.[66] They, quite reasonably, note that some advocates of this goal nevertheless resist the allure of assisted dying,[67] so they see no necessary connection between this goal and that activity. But they still happen to think that the activity *can* be considered compatible with the medical enterprise; so, presumably, they perceive some sort of necessary connection. Admittedly, they do not place any doctor under a *duty* to assist in dying; instead, they leave this to the doctor's *discretion*, suggesting at most that it can be 'justifiable only as a last resort'.[68]

As such, Miller and Brody critique the prohibitionists, specifically Kass, and argue that medicine's core concern with respect for the person need not rule out assisted dying.[69] The willing doctor will still need to be competent; for example, she should not offer assistance in dying when palliative care 'is capable of relieving patients' suffering to a satisfactory degree'.[70] But such care should not be imposed on patients.[71] Nor should death always be regarded as more harmful than beneficial. However, the doctor is no mere technician or tool of the patient; professional integrity 'excludes physician assistance on demand',[72] so the doctor must still 'be convinced that this course is the best option for the dire situation of this particular patient'.[73] Miller and Brody admit that assistance in dying will lie outside mainstream practice, so willing professionals might plausibly be charged with fraudulent misrepresentation, as they conceive this. Despite this, they suggest that departures from accepted standards can be justified (as is the case with research), provided that there are suitably robust qualifying criteria which encompass medical indications, such as the patient's suffering and their mental capacity, as well as the patient's subjective appraisal of their situation. Finally, they submit that

64 Pellegrino (n 55) 572.
65 See B. Freedman, 'A meta-ethics for professional morality' (1978) 89 *Ethics* 1.
66 Miller and Brody (n 48) 11.
67 E.g. D. Callahan, *The Troubled Dream of Life* (Simon and Schuster, 1993).
68 Miller and Brody (n 48) 12.
69 Miller and Brody (n 48) 12–13.
70 Miller and Brody (n 48) 13.
71 Miller and Brody (n 48) 13.
72 Miller and Brody (n 48) 14.
73 Miller and Brody (n 48) 14.

trust need not be abused, nor patients abandoned, if a policy that permits assisted dying is formulated along such careful lines.[74]

Richard Momeyer works towards similar conclusions and finds Kass's promotion of Hippocratic ideals to be too vague, general, and selective. For example robust adherence to a Hippocratic ethic would also require doctors to honour a panoply of ancient gods.[75] Momeyer does, however, join Kass in suggesting that medicine's end includes healing, but, unlike Kass, he believes the end to be stipulated by humans rather than by nature.[76] He also thinks that there are other important values also to be served in and by medicine, such as 'respect for patient values, or preservation of patient dignity'.[77] For underplaying such values, Momeyer charges Kass with favouring an illiberal, paternalistic prioritisation of the doctor's view of the patient's good.[78] He admits that respect for autonomy is sometimes taken too far and, like Miller and Brody, accepts that external arguments will have a bearing on the legitimacy of assisted dying.[79] Ultimately, however, Momeyer rejects the idea that assistance in dying 'is incompatible with the very nature of medicine or the essential identity of physicians as healers'.[80]

The integrity of medicine: neither necessary nor sufficient?

Traditionalists, therefore, claim that assisted dying is incompatible with the integrity of medicine, but others maintain that, while not mandatory, neither is it incompatible. Both sides appear to reach these conclusions by writing assisted dying into or out of the essence of medicine from the outset. In so doing, each side begs the question as to whether assisted dying can be compatible with the integrity of medicine. Maybe this is not entirely problematic, if one or other of these accounts captures the essence (and internal morality) of medicine. As it is, however, we can dispute the *necessity* of each account and, correspondingly, each of the different answers given about medicine's compatibility with assisted dying. Indeed, the fundamental question about the permissibility of assisted dying will still remain open even if a necessary account can be settled upon. We cannot hope to arrive at a *sufficient* answer to that question merely by reflecting on the nature and internal morality of medicine. Let us consider each of these problems in turn.

We cannot establish which, if either, of the rival accounts is superior, in the sense that it offers a necessary view of the nature of medicine. Robert Veatch identifies three problems with the entire enterprise of identifying an internal

74 Miller and Brody (n 48) 15.

75 R. Momeyer, 'Does physician assisted suicide violate the integrity of medicine?' (1995) 20 *Journal of Medicine and Philosophy* 13, 18.

76 Momeyer (n 75) 17, 19.

77 Momeyer (n 75) 20.

78 Momeyer (n 75) 21.

79 Momeyer (n 75) 22–23.

80 Momeyer (n 75) 23.

morality. First, medicine encompasses many roles and many ends; second, even within a single medical role, there may be more than one end being served; and, finally, even if we could determine a single end for medicine, an outside view will still be needed on the appropriateness of that end.[81] Veatch's first two allegations initially undermine Miller and Brody's position. Miller and Brody saw medicine as encompassing different goals and its core values as susceptible to evolution. Their openness to the fact of change suggests that they are not directly concerned with the essential nature of medicine, unlike Pellegrino and, importantly, Fuller. Fuller wanted to capture the essence of law, whatever its rules happen to say and wherever they happen to be said. Like Miller and Brody, Veatch appears troubled by the complexity, and apparent impossibility, of the task of *describing* the goals of medicine. For example, he says that '[t]he awful truth is that different cultures seem to shape the terrain of medicine very differently'.[82] Mapping medicine, and its morals, seems, on this view, to be too vast a task, so we cannot hope to specify a single secure answer as to the rightness or wrongness of a particular activity like assisted dying.

Veatch has a point, but perhaps he, like Miller and Brody, is wrong to embark down this empirical avenue. The mere fact that, *in practice*, medicine has many goals and can accordingly encompass many means, arguably tells us nothing about whether medicine, *by definition*, has any particular goal or goals, such that it should encompass only particular means. However, Veatch does appear to recognise that the alternative to the empirical avenue is a contestable conceptual cul-de-sac. As such, even if we seek to glean the essence of medicine, like Pellegrino, we still encounter difficulty. A more charitable reading of Veatch's position would suggest that he disputes the feasibility of arriving at a suitably agreeable concept of medicine.[83] Pellegrino, of course, offered a particular take on the essence of medicine. Perhaps if we extend our charity to Miller and Brody, they too were seeking some sort of conceptual essence, albeit one that would be open to evolution. Both accounts do at least converge, albeit partially, on medicine's concern with health and healing. The problem with even this essence is that it is still difficult to see what medicine, by definition, should therefore say about the legitimacy of assisted dying.

'Medicine', says Tom Beauchamp, 'is a vague and inherently contestable concept'.[84] 'Health' seems no less elusive,[85] since it can align with very different versions of value theory. Perhaps health is about quality of life; perhaps it should be considered as, or in the light of, an objective good (like life itself); or perhaps it requires reference to people's own preferences.[86] Pellegrino favours an objective

81 Veatch (n 49) 628.

82 Veatch (n 49) 631.

83 We might, similarly, ask whether Fuller provides a defensible definition of the essence of law.

84 T. L. Beauchamp, 'Internal and external standards for medical morality' (2001) 26 *Journal of Medicine and Philosophy* 601, 604.

85 K. M. Boyd, 'Disease, illness, sickness, health, healing and wholeness: Exploring some elusive concepts' (2000) 26 *Medical Humanities* 9.

86 D. DeGrazia, 'Value theory and the best interests standard' (1995) 9 *Bioethics* 50.

account of health, which forbids the intentional ending of life; autonomy matters, but it is not the fundamental value.[87] Miller and Brody, meanwhile, allow more room for preferences, although, in doing so, they skirt a very fine line between defending values internal to and external from medicine.[88] Although they depict autonomy as a value *outside* the internal morality of medicine,[89] they also suggest not only that it would be contrary to the endeavour to impose unwanted treatment on patients,[90] but also that trust, which is essential to the endeavour, requires reference to patients' considered judgements.[91] In making these points, Miller and Brody either smuggle in values from outside medicine or implicitly allow that the goals of medicine do include due regard for the patient's autonomy. Certainly, their enthusiasm for autonomy is not unbridled. For example they do not support death on demand as such.[92] Yet, whatever role autonomy is playing in their particular argument, it still seems plausible that health and healing might require recourse to the patient's own preferences. But, at the same time, we might also think that Pellegrino has a point about medicine's concern with health as a more objective end.

If medicine has an essence, we might suppose that one of these rival readings must be superior. Of course, determining the victor has proven, and will likely long prove, difficult.[93] But maybe we do not need a single victor; perhaps, indeed, a dose of agnosticism can salvage the very enterprise of specifying the internal morality of medicine. Fuller, you will recall, restricted the concept of law to guiding action via rules, from which end particular norms then arose. He left open the question of the substantive content of the rules themselves. Perhaps we can do the same for medicine; for example, by saying that medicine is all about health (from which particular norms will flow), but then declining to give any particular content to the concept of health. Leaving ourselves open to variation, somewhat akin to Miller and Brody, would allow us to focus on form as opposed to substance. Then, however, we would confront a new problem. We would be left with little (perhaps no) idea about what medicine should involve or require and, accordingly, about the legitimacy of assisted dying as judged from within medicine. And there is a bigger problem here; resolving the rightness of the different views thereon, and, more specifically, the right answer to the question of death on demand is not something we can achieve merely by looking to, and in, medicine.

It appears that even if we could resolve the end or essence of medicine, and thereby its means, this *alone* cannot tell us whether the end, essence, or means are *good*. As Nicholas Dixon comments, '[w]hether a doctor's participation in active

87 Pellegrino (n 55).

88 Miller and Brody (n 48). Beauchamp suspects that they ultimately prioritise external values: (n 84) 605–607.

89 Miller and Brody (n 48) 12.

90 Miller and Brody (n 48) 13.

91 Miller and Brody (n 48) 15.

92 Miller and Brody (n 48) 14.

93 DeGrazia (n 86) and Beauchamp (n 84) make similar points about the varieties of value theory and moral theory, respectively.

euthanasia is a violation of her integrity depends on whether the act is wrong, so we cannot without circularity use the concept of integrity to prove that it is wrong'.[94] Dixon appears to adopt an external view on integrity, in which integrity is not merely about one's identity or deep desires, but is instead about standing for the (objectively) right things. Since, on this view, rightness is prior to (and constitutive of) integrity, we cannot reverse the order of priority and use integrity to establish rightness or wrongness. Of course, we might depart from Dixon and prefer to see integrity as tied to identity or desires. But even the individual (and, by extension, the group) that is integrated on such a basis cannot avoid external appraisal. I may sincerely cleave to certain values and ways of being, but I can still legitimately be subject to moral censure.[95]

Here we reach Veatch's third criticism, that even if we could determine an end for medicine, we will need an outside view on the appropriateness of that end. He states that '[t]he ends of promotion of health and healing are themselves meaningless unless one turns outside medicine to know whether the ends are worth pursuing'.[96] Beauchamp joins him in suggesting that an internal 'morality is not self-justifying by its own internal norms'.[97] Medicine's ends are 'inevitably derived from the ends of the human as seen – imperfectly – by the broader society'.[98] We, therefore, need to look beyond medicine in order to judge its practitioners' activities. Implicit in the indications of judges such as Thorpe J and Kay J[99] is the idea that medicine is protected *because* it provides something of social value. Freedman would seem to endorse this interpretation, as he suggests that a profession, and therefore its internal morality, is granted a privileged position in, and by, society:

> The internal morality of law . . . as the internal morality of medicine, rests ultimately on society's commitment to preserving and ensuring continuation to a value through allocating it to be especially safeguarded by concerned professionals in society. By adopting a profession with its central value, society has given warrant to corollaries of that value to be pursued irrespective (sometimes) of, for example, simple considerations of utility.[100]

On this account, society wants medicine to protect its core values, whatever these happen to be. Here, then, we return to where we began. Perhaps the judges had it right; the integrity of medicine, as a component of the public interest, deserves protection. Veatch, of course, would not want the purported integrity of medicine to do any heavy moral lifting. However, we should remain mindful of

94 N. Dixon, 'On the difference between physician-assisted suicide and active euthanasia' (1998) 28 *Hastings Center Report* 25, 29.

95 To think otherwise would mean that anything goes, which would allow a particularly impoverished account of autonomy (and/or liberty) to triumph.

96 Veatch (n 49) 635.

97 Veatch (n 49) 607.

98 Beauchamp (n 84) 639.

99 *Robb* (n 12) and *Brady* (n 14), respectively.

100 Freedman (n 65) 17.

the aforementioned problem of (self-) disrespect.[101] Maybe some room *should* be allowed for the profession's self-conception. But now our familiar problems also return. We cannot resolve what the internal morality of medicine requires, allows, or prohibits, as the *necessary* core is too amorphous, and, even if we could, a view from within will be *insufficient* to resolve the general moral questions about what *should* be required, allowed, or prohibited. If, then, we are seeking to resolve a general question about the legitimacy of assisted dying, we must look to the source of medicine's purported legitimacy, that is to morality, and to the society in question. In short, we must turn to the public interest.

Death on demand and the public interest

Unfortunately, the public interest is another amorphous concept. The sorts of claims that are usually advanced in law in the name of the public interest can be distinguished according to whose interests are in issue: *my* interests, *your* interests, or *our* interests.[102] Sometimes, as we see in mental health law, my liberty will be limited in order to protect my welfare. Alternatively, there might be a public interest in protecting you from me; this is certainly a theme of the rulings denying death on demand. Finally, the public interest will sometimes be said to protect us collectively, such as when a purportedly objective ethical principle, like the sanctity of human life, operates to prevent contrary demands from being met.

Yet, the law appears to lack a consistent or clear approach to the public interest. Although life sometimes trumps choice, inroads have been made into the sanctity of life,[103] and sometimes choice does trump life, specifically if the claim is 'allow me to die'. Neither is it clear how the particular interests in autonomy, say, or welfare, are being conceptualised or even the level at which they operate. For example, some judges depict autonomy as a private interest,[104] while others see respect for autonomy as part of the public interest:

> There are some moral values, of which the state is the proper guardian, with no rational or utilitarian justification, but which are nevertheless accepted because they are fundamental to our humanity and to our respect for our own kind. The principle of autonomy is one of these values.[105]

On this account, autonomy stands shoulder to shoulder with the sanctity of life. The problem, of course, is that each happens *in fact* to compete with the other, with neither emerging *wholly* victorious in law. Can a victor be found *in principle*?

101 Furthermore, identity might consequently alter, such that the entity becomes something other.

102 R. Huxtable, 'Autonomy, best interests and the public interest: Treatment, non-treatment and the values of medical law' (2014) 22 *Medical Law Review* 459; R. E. Ashcroft, 'From public interest to political justice' (2004) 13 *Cambridge Quarterly Healthcare Ethics* 20.

103 E.g. Huxtable (n 1).

104 *Nicklinson* (n 4) para. 267, *per* Lord Hughes.

105 *Nicklinson* (n 4) para. 208, *per* Lord Sumption.

In order to determine a victor, we need an account of what the public interest *should* encompass, and how it should resolve the different claims that are advanced by different individuals and groups. According to Held, accounts of the public interest tend to fall into three categories: *preponderance* (or aggregative) theories, *unitary* theories, and *common interest* theories.[106] Each deploys a different concept of 'interest', and each differs in its conception of the relationship between the public interest and the interests of individuals.

Preponderance theories adopt a subjective account of interests in which individuals determine their interests according to their preferences.[107] The public interest, therefore, aggregates these preferences, in a utilitarian fashion, and the general will dictates matters of social policy. According to such an approach, the public interest requires respect for autonomy, or, at least, respect for the autonomous choices of the majority. This leaves the account susceptible to the charge that no practicable mechanism exists 'for determining what is in the interest of a preponderance of individuals'.[108] Furthermore, the minority, whoever these are, seems doomed to lose out. We see these sorts of difficulties arise in relation to assisted dying. Do a majority of people genuinely want the option of death on demand?[109] And, even if they did, can the interests of the minority be sufficiently protected if such a policy is adopted? *Unitary* theories take a different approach. Here, the public interest is an overriding interest, which is tied to objective accounts of the good and thus to what people *should* want or *should* receive.[110] The problem with this approach is that it will be difficult to determine that which serves, or pleases, everyone. Specifying the objective good is notoriously difficult. For example, life might generally be worth protecting, but not everyone will want such protection at all times. There are echoes, here, of the problems that Momeyer detected with Kass's position on the internal morality of medicine, since we run the risk of affording too little room to autonomous choice.

Perhaps *common interest* theories can fare better. Here, the interests in question are those that all individuals have in common. For example, Brian Barry combines subjective and objective positions. Individuals should be free to pursue their own conceptions of the good life, and it is in the public interest to ensure that they have the opportunities to do so.[111] People will advance quite different claims, but Barry recommends looking to the elements that are common and universalisable; these make up the distinctive public interest. For Barry, the public interest refers to the promotion of collective welfare (broadly defined), but it is not the only

106 V. Held, *The Public Interest and Individual Interests* (Basic Books, 1970).

107 This aligns with one version of value theory: see DeGrazia (n 86).

108 A. McHarg, 'Reconciling human rights and the public interest: Conceptual problems and doctrinal uncertainty in the jurisprudence of the European Court of Human Rights' (1999) 62 *Modern Law Review* 671, 675.

109 See P. Saunders, 'Support for UK assisted dying bill plummets to 43% after hearing opposing arguments' (*Life Site*, July 18 2014), available at http://www.lifesitenews.com/pulse/support-for-uk-assisted-dying-bill-plummets-to-43-after-hearing-opposing-ar? (accessed 18 December 2014).

110 This aligns with another version of value theory: see DeGrazia (n 86).

111 B. Barry, *Political Argument* (Humanities Press, 1965).

consideration when designing public policy. Sometimes the public interest will conflict with other considerations. So, for example, there might be a public interest in ensuring public safety. If one individual is to benefit from such an interest, then so must everyone else. Certainly, some will fall foul of a rule designed to ensure public safety; for example, they might feel that they should not be imprisoned.[112] Such concerns can be addressed in the ways in which the rules are designed or applied. As such, there might be other goals which the public will occasionally choose to prioritise over the collective good; equally, sometimes, subjective preferences will give way to other important goals. As Aileen McHarg clarifies, '[t]he balance struck between competing interests and goals in any situation will inevitably reflect a value choice, but not one which purports to eradicate the initial conflict'.[113] McHarg admits, however, that a common interest theory might still be of limited application, since people will not agree about the goals that society should adopt or the best means of achieving these goals. Identifying the group's goals will also be complex, although democratic processes seem to offer the best chances.

How might a common interest theory apply to the case of assisted dying? If we follow McHarg, we might see a prima facie case for allowing the practice, if this reflects the public will.[114] Yet, the question will remain about whether the practice contributes in some way to the collective good. As McHarg notes, a value choice must ultimately be made. So which values should dictate our appraisals of, and policy responses to, assisted dying?

Conclusion

Determining the proper content of, and role to be played by, the public interest will, therefore, involve a value choice, about the interests in issue and also about the proper balance to be struck between protecting individuals and protecting others (including society at large). We well know that the values associated with death and dying remain hotly contested. Determining the legitimacy of assistance in dying involves a genuine moral dilemma in which it is difficult to know which way to jump. The integrity of medicine seems not to offer a secure answer.[115] Resolving the question by reference to what doctors happen to think seems to be an insufficient basis for determining policy, given the wider interests at stake.[116] At the same time, no single answer appears (necessarily) to emerge from the concept of medicine; but, even if one did, this too would be insufficient. The integrity of medicine is, therefore, part of, but by no means exhausts, the public interest. Unfortunately, when we widen the pool of interests, we find that we are still required to make a value choice.

112 See McHarg (n 108) 677.

113 McHarg (n 108) 677.

114 But see Saunders (n 109).

115 See J. D. Arras, 'A method in search of a purpose: The internal morality of medicine' (2001) 26 *Journal of Medicine and Philosophy* 643.

116 S. H. Miles, 'Physician-assisted suicide and the profession's gyrocompass' (1995) 25 *Hastings Center Report* 17, 18.

Perhaps the right choice will one day be revealed, and a principled answer will be found to the enduring question of whether society should permit death on demand. But, perhaps, that is a pipe dream, given that the different answers, which alternately emphasise choice, suffering, and the intrinsic value of life, continue to be both commended and condemned.[117] Maybe, as Hoffmann LJ once indicated, the law can live with the conflicts:

> A conflict between the principles of the sanctity of life and the individual's right of self-determination may . . . require a painful compromise to be made . . . There must be an accommodation between principles, both of which seem rational and good, but which have come into conflict with each other.[118]

The law achieves this accommodation in a variety of ways; in some situations autonomy triumphs, and on other occasions the sanctity of life wins out. And although the law purports to prohibit assistance in dying, ways are usually found to secure humane disposals for those who do so.[119] In such endeavours, the law reveals itself to be open to different accounts of the good life. Indeed, the judges admit that they will have regard for the different values present in society, and that they will adapt the law as society evolves:

> The determination of the public interest is a matter for the courts, applying, subject to any statutory provisions which may be relevant, the common law . . . [T]he common law is capable of moving with the times to meet changing conditions so that as far as possible it reflects the acceptable standards of the day.[120]

Maybe there is a case for such value pluralism or 'value agnosticism' in the law.[121] Maybe, too, there is a principled case for the adoption of middle ground positions, given the considerable complexity and uncertainty which cloud practices like assistance in dying.[122] Indeed, even if the law does edge towards embracing death on demand,[123] it must remain not only appropriately 'moralised'[124] but also alert to the need to secure an 'appropriate pay-off between allowing so much liberty that an excess of harm results, and such restricted liberty that people have too little control of their lives to make them worthwhile'.[125] At the same time, the

117 Huxtable (n 1).
118 *Bland* (n 6) 827, *per* Hoffmann LJ.
119 Huxtable (n 1).
120 *Re F* (n 26) 29, *per* Neill LJ.
121 J. Coggon, J. Miola, 'Autonomy, liberty, and medical decision-making' (2011) 70 *Cambridge Law Journal* 523, 528.
122 Huxtable (n 1).
123 Notice the gradual judicial inclination towards allowing death on demand, evident in some speeches in *Nicklinson* (n 4).
124 J. Montgomery, 'Law and the demoralisation of medicine' (2006) 26 *Legal Studies* 185.
125 Coggon and Miola (n 121) 531.

law must also work *as* law. It must be clear and consistent, and, thus, observant of criteria like those of Fuller's 'internal morality', if its rules are to guide people as they should. These are matters for elsewhere.[126] For now, I hope to have shown that appeals to the integrity of medicine, proper medical treatment, and even the public interest cannot resolve the values choices we must make whenever death on demand is in issue.

126 See Huxtable (n 1).

10 Doctors' orders? Analysing appropriate medical treatment in mental health law

Judy Laing

Introduction

In this chapter I explore what is meant by proper medical treatment in mental health law by focusing on the concept of 'appropriate' medical treatment in the Mental Health Act 1983, as amended by the Mental Health Act 2007 (the Act). The Act provides a framework for compulsory admission and treatment in hospital and, in some circumstances, coercive treatment in the community. It introduced an 'availability' of appropriate treatment test in the admission criteria. This test has proved controversial, particularly in its application to patients with a personality disorder. I examine what these terms mean, how they have been interpreted by the judiciary, and the breadth of the concept of medical treatment in section 63 of the Act. In the context of mental health, the courts have moved well beyond core treatment, such as medication or psychotherapy. As a consequence, the concept of medical treatment for mental disorder is extremely broad and highly subjective. There is also a lack of clarity about the appropriateness of such treatment. This raises important questions about the primary function of mental health law, and about what is 'appropriate' or 'proper' medical treatment. My discussion will lead on to exploring the changing nature of the professional roles and expanding expertise in diagnosis and treatment. This latter shift lies in contrast to other areas of medical practice, where there has, perhaps, been greater reluctance to dilute the traditional dominance of the medical profession. I consider the implications of this shift.

The function of mental health law

The use of compulsion in mental health care tends to be the exception rather than the rule, although there are approximately 18,000 compulsory admissions to psychiatric facilities under the Act every year.[1] The majority of patients with a mental illness will seek treatment on a voluntary basis through primary

1 Health and Social Care Information Centre (HSCIC), *In Patients Formally Detained in Hospitals Under the Mental Health Act 1983, and Patients Subject to Supervised Community Treatment* (HSCIC, 2014) 12.

care services by visiting their GP. This is preferable to compulsory admission, and more beneficial to patients, because evidence suggests that recovery rates are higher when patients work in partnership with their doctor and engage directly with treatment.[2] Mutual collaboration fosters greater patient satisfaction, reduces the risks of non-compliance, and improves patients' healthcare outcomes. But there may be situations where patients are reluctant to seek help or refuse treatment. Consequently, there is a risk of a significant deterioration in their mental and/or physical health, which could lead to harm to the patient or, in exceptional cases, to others. In such circumstances, the Act permits mental health professionals to *compel* patients for appropriate treatment (for example, medication) for their mental disorder, *irrespective* of their individual capacity or consent. Patient autonomy can thus be overridden here, and this contrasts with other areas of medical practice where patient autonomy has been accorded more respect in treatment decisions, provided that the patient has the requisite mental capacity.[3] Paternalism trumps autonomy in the Act on the basis of the potential harm the patient may cause to herself if left untreated, as well as the potential health benefits to the patient. Statistics suggest that people with mental health problems are more likely to self-harm and are at greater risk of suicide.[4] However, this paternalistic approach runs counter to current government mental health policy, as patient choice and empowerment should be at the forefront of treatment decisions.[5]

Yet, in extreme cases, patients may be at risk of causing harm to others, in which case the law provides an alternative protectionist (the protection of others) justification for compulsion. The consequences of not taking any action can be detrimental in a number of ways to the patient's family, friends, or broader community. But this intervention has implications from a European Convention on Human Rights (ECHR) perspective, as it encroaches on personal liberty. Article 8 rights to respect for family and private life extend to physical integrity and the imposition of medical treatment without consent. In *X v Austria*, it was stated that compulsory medical treatment, even if it is of minor importance,

2 L. Martin, S. L. Williams, K. B. Haskard, M. R. Dimatteo, 'The challenge of patient adherence' (2005) 1 *Therapeutics and Clinical Risk Management* 189.

3 E.g. in *Re C (Adult: Refusal of Medical Treatment)* [1994] 1 WLR 290, a 68-year-old paranoid schizophrenic prisoner was entitled to refuse amputation of his gangrenous leg even though the prognosis was that he was likely to die without the amputation. His right to self-determination had not been displaced, as he was competent to make the decision. Also, see *Ms B v An NHS Hospital Trust* [2002] EWHC 429 (Fam), where an adult patient was deemed competent to refuse life sustaining treatment. Capacity is now determined by the Mental Capacity Act 2005.

4 Mental Health Foundation (MHF), *The Fundamental Facts: The Latest Facts and Figures on Mental Health* (MHF, 2007). In a national study, 42 per cent of those who took their own lives in England and Wales were diagnosed with either a depressive illness or bipolar disorder (at 10). People with mental health problems were 20 times more likely than others to report having harmed themselves (at 12).

5 Department of Health (DH), *Closing the Gap: Priorities for Essential Change in Mental Health* (DH, 2014) 16.

constitutes an interference with this right.[6] As the *Code of Practice* which accompanies the Act recognises:

> compulsory administration of treatment which would otherwise require consent is invariably an infringement of article 8 . . . However, it may be justified where it is in accordance with law (in this case the procedures in the Act) and where it is proportionate to a legitimate aim (in this case, the reduction of the risk posed by a person's mental disorder and the improvement of their health).[7]

The recent case of *Atudorei v Romania*[8] demonstrates that the European Court of Human Rights (ECtHR) will look at the circumstances in which treatment has been provided to psychiatric patients to assess whether the treatment does comply with Article 8. On the facts of this case, the court found that there had been an interference with the applicant's right to respect for her private life under Article 8, as she had been unlawfully deprived of her liberty (under Article 5) in a State-run psychiatric hospital and forced to take treatment in the absence of her valid consent. The ECtHR was not, however, willing to find a breach of Article 3, protection from inhuman or degrading treatment, as the treatment imposed was in line with accepted practice and did not appear to have had any long-lasting psychological or physical effects. Thus, it did not attain the level of severity required by Article 3. So, the court implicitly endorsed the imposition of drug therapy here, despite its potentially harmful and adverse side effects on the patient.[9]

It is against this backdrop that the Act sits, focusing, as it does, on compulsory admission and coercive hospital care. It is thus important to examine in more detail who is making these decisions about the use of compulsion, and to explore what forms of coercive treatment are available and when they may be imposed. My focus is on exploring what proper or appropriate medical treatment means in mental health law.

The origins of the current framework: medicalism v legalism

Before considering these issues in more depth, it is worth highlighting the recent history of mental health legislation, to shed some light on the primary functions of

6 (1979) 18 DR 154.

7 DH, *Mental Health Act 1983 Code of Practice* (TSO, 2015) para. 24.43.

8 [2014] ECHR 947.

9 See also *Stanev v Bulgaria* (2012) 55 EHRR 22, ECtHR, where, for the first time, the Court found a violation of Article 3 due to the appalling conditions that Stanev had experienced over seven years in a Bulgarian care home. The food was insufficient, the building was inadequately heated, and he was only able to shower once a week in a dilapidated bathroom. There was no suggestion that the Bulgarian authorities deliberately intended to treat Stanev in this way, but, taken as a whole, his living conditions throughout this period were severe enough to amount to degrading treatment. However, note that the breaches here related to the conditions in which Stanev was detained, rather than the imposition of any compulsory medical treatment.

the current framework and the central role of the medical (psychiatric) profession within it. As Phil Fennell has described:

> The history of mental health law charts the development of an increasingly complex codification of clinical authority whereby mental health professionals are given the authority to detain and treat mentally disordered people without consent where necessary to prevent harm to the patient or to others.[10]

The history of mental health law has been described by Kathleen Jones as a pendulum swinging between two schools of thought.[11] On the one hand lies a response rooted in the legal paradigm. This approach places the emphasis on due process and minimising psychiatric power in the interests of civil liberty; '[t]he legal position is one of concern to protect liberty unless there is good justification for its suppression'.[12] The Lunacy Act 1890 represented the so-called triumph of legalism,[13] as it created an elaborate system of judicial certification and procedures before patients could be admitted to lunatic asylums for treatment. At the other end of the pendulum is the medical model, medicalism, where the emphasis is on clinical discretion, early treatment, and alleviating the suffering caused by the illness. Within this approach, the medical profession is given prominence in decisions about detention and treatment unhindered by legal formalities. This approach stems from the biomedical model, and the 'central contention that psychiatric patients are afflicted by an illness which has the special character of depriving them of the ability to calculate their own best interests'.[14] The Mental Health Act 1959 typified this approach, as it promoted clinical discretion in securing prompt and early treatment, and diluted legal formalities in the admission and treatment process.

Neither of these approaches is without difficulty, and both have been subject to critique. Some argue that medicalism is wrong as it represents:

> the professionalization and medicalization of social control . . . modern societies tend to allocate procedures of control of deviant and troublesome groups and individuals to 'experts'. These experts rationalize and legitimize such control by appeal to a specialized body of esoteric scientific knowledge – medical or psychological – which provides the basis and justification for their social role and power.[15]

10 P. Fennell, 'Mental health law: History, policy and regulation' in L. Gostin, P. Bartlett, P. Fennell, J. McHale, R. Mackay (eds), *Principles of Mental Health Law and Policy* (Oxford University Press, 2010) para. 1.01

11 K. Jones, *A History of Mental Health Services* (Routledge, Keegan and Paul, 1972).

12 C. Unsworth, *The Politics of Mental Health Legislation* (Clarendon Press, 1987) 7.

13 Jones (n. 11).

14 Unsworth (n 12) 7.

15 N. Rose, 'Unreasonable rights: Mental illness and the limits of the law' (1985) 12 *Journal of Law and Society* 199, 202.

Those who support medicalism maintain that this control is justified as it is an 'enlightened' approach which is 'motivated by humanitarian concern for the good of the sick individual rather than social and political concern for the maintenance of a docile population'.[16] In contrast, legalism is criticised for being too rigid or prescriptive and because the formalities can impede prompt and timely treatment.[17]

The current legislative framework is, essentially, found within the Mental Health Act 1983. When introduced, this Act was described as representing a 'new' rights-based legalism because it attempted to strike a balance between clinical discretion and legalism.[18] Clinicians were central to the admission and treatment process, but the 1983 Act also bolstered formal legal safeguards with procedural and professional checks and balances,[19] independent monitoring in the form of an inspection watchdog,[20] and automatic rights to a tribunal to review the grounds for continued detention.[21] The 1983 Act was subject to piecemeal amendments by the Mental Health Act 2007, but the amended Act continues to seek a balance between legalism and medicalism. The amendments sought to strengthen some of the external patient safeguards such as tribunal review, and introduced independent advocacy for detained patients,[22] but also expanded the criteria for compulsion. In many respects, it bolstered the discretion of the medical profession in the process, as there are still limited restrictions on the compulsory treatment of detained patients, as I explore below.

The role of psychiatry in diagnosis and treatment

Medical professionals, normally psychiatrists, have a key role in the compulsory admission process in terms of making a diagnosis of mental disorder and providing supporting medical recommendations. But providing an answer to the question of what is a mental disorder is not straightforward. The ECtHR recognised, in *Winterwerp v The Netherlands*,[23] that the definition should be fluid in order to accommodate changing social and professional attitudes. Thus, the term 'unsound mind' in Article 5(1) is not one that can be given a definitive interpretation; 'it is a

16 Rose (n 15) 202.

17 Rose (n 15) 202.

18 L. Gostin, 'The ideology of entitlement: The application of contemporary legal approaches to psychiatry' in P. Bean (ed.), *Mental Illness: Changes and Trends* (Wiley, 1983).

19 The presence of an independent Approved Social Worker in the admissions process is intended to counterbalance the medical opinion, Mental Health Act (MHA) 1983, ss 13 and 114.

20 MHA 1983, s. 121. Initially this was the Mental Health Act Commission (MHAC), but its functions have now been taken over by the Care Quality Commission (CQC).

21 MHA 1983, ss 65–66.

22 There are concerns about the adequacy of some of these patient safeguards, however, as the tribunal system is still subject to delays, the advocacy service is under-resourced, and the CQC has struggled to discharge aspects of its monitoring function. See further J. M. Laing, 'Perspectives on monitoring mental health legislation in England: A view from the front line' *Medical Law Review* (online advance access, DOI: 10.1093/medlaw/fwu029).

23 (1979) 2 EHRR 387, ECtHR.

term whose meaning is continually evolving as research in psychiatry progresses, an increasing flexibility in treatment is developing and society's attitude to mental illness changes'.[24]

Part of the problem is the fact that there has been considerable dissonance at times within the psychiatric profession about the causes and symptoms of mental ill health and associated behaviour. As legal academics have commented, the relationship between mental illness and medicine is a 'complex' and uncertain one.[25] The psychiatric profession traditionally developed specialist expertise based on the biomedical model of medicine which focuses on biological factors in the diagnosis and treatment of disease. Accordingly, treatments focused on targeting physical processes in the brain. This approach was assisted during the 1950s by the pharmacological revolution and the development of a range of psychotropic drugs, such as anti-depressants, to treat a broad range of mental disorders. As Barry Lyons charts, more generally, in this collection,[26] this enabled the medical profession to gain significant power and control over the diagnosis and treatment of mental disorders.

But the 1960s and 1970s witnessed the emergence of the anti-psychiatry movement. Some eminent psychiatrists, such as Ronald Laing and Thomas Szasz, questioned these traditional biomedical conceptions and treatments. For example, Szasz, essentially argued that mental illness was a myth and that individuals who exhibited signs of mental illness were 'malingerers' who experienced problems in living and/or displayed deviant behaviours.[27] Medical professionals mistakenly interpreted this behaviour as the signs or symptoms of real illness, and while diagnoses of mental illness or mental disorder were described by psychiatrists as 'scientific categories', they were, in fact, subjective judgements to support the use of power and imposition of harmful treatments.[28] Consequently, psychiatry was an agent of social control, and the medicalisation of government in this way produced a powerful and dangerous therapeutic state.[29] Laing also rejected the biomedical approach in its application to schizophrenia, as it ignored the cultural and/or social factors of the illness.[30]

Indeed, a common criticism of the biomedical approach is that it medicalises social problems. By focusing on the symptoms and prescribing drugs to control them, psychiatrists may overlook important environmental or cultural causes of behaviour or illness. The challenges presented by the anti-psychiatry movement led to the development of a range of alternative approaches to mental ill health,

24 *Winterwerp* (n 23) para. 37.

25 P. Bartlett, R. Sandland, *Mental Health Law, Policy and Practice* (Oxford University Press, 2014) para. 1.3.

26 B. Lyons, 'Papist potions and electric sex: A historical perspective on "proper medical treatment"' in this collection.

27 T. Szasz, *The Myth of Mental Illness: Foundations of a Theory of Personal Conduct* (Harper and Row, 1961).

28 Szasz (n 27).

29 Szasz (n 27).

30 R. D. Laing, *The Divided Self: An Existential Study in Sanity and Madness* (Penguin, 1960).

and to greater focus on other causes of it such as genetic and social factors, as well as the involvement of other professionals, such as social workers, in the care and treatment of mental disorders. Other professions have different approaches; for example, social workers are trained to adopt a more holistic approach, and psychologists will focus on other methods, such as talking therapy, to modify mental processes and human behaviour. There is now a range of treatments, such as counselling, group or talking therapies, and educational and exercise programmes which complement the traditional reliance on the biomedical approach of drug therapy. Indeed, current guidelines from the National Institute for Health and Care Excellence (NICE) suggest that 'a variety of psychological therapies *in addition to, or instead of* medication' can be helpful for managing anxiety, depression, bipolar disease, and schizophrenia.[31] However, the guidelines also state that:

> [t]he most common method of treatment for common mental health disorders in primary care is psychotropic medication [i.e. drugs which alter mood, behaviour, or perception]. This is due to the limited availability of psychological interventions, despite the fact that these treatments are generally preferred by patients.[32]

A Mental Health Foundation (MHF) online survey in 2007 found that 60 per cent of patients who visited their GP with depression were prescribed anti-depressant drugs, 42 per cent were offered counselling, and 2 per cent were offered exercise therapy.[33] For some, medication *is* a helpful short-term solution, but for others drugs may be an ongoing longer-term treatment that enables them to live with a severe and persistent mental health problem. Medication is easier, quicker, and cheaper to administer than exercise or talking therapies; however, some people are reluctant to take medication, as most drugs have adverse side effects and some people experience difficulties when they stop taking them. One study suggests that 22 per cent of the 69 patients surveyed experienced side effects which they considered intolerable,[34] and the detrimental side effects of psychotropic and antipsychotic medication are well documented.[35] This is significant when we consider that mental health law *enables* clinicians to *force* patients to take this type of medication against their will.

31 National Institute for Health and Care Excellence (NICE), *Common Mental Health Disorders: Identification and Pathways to Care*, NICE Guideline CG123 (May 2011), emphasis supplied.

32 NICE (n 31) Introduction.

33 MHF (n 4) 50. Data on the total number of respondents in the survey is not available.

34 R. Grey, D. Rofail, J. Allen, T. Newey, 'A survey of patient satisfaction with and subjective experiences of treatment with anti-psychotic medication' (2005) 52 *Journal of Advanced Nursing* 31.

35 See e.g. M. De Hert, J. Detraux, R. van Winkel, W. Yu, C. U. Correll, 'Metabolic and cardiovascular adverse effects associated with antipsychotic drugs' (2012) 8 *Nature Reviews Endocrinology* 114; R. S. McIntyre, 'Psychotropic drugs and adverse events in the treatment of bipolar disorders revisited' (2002) 63 *Journal of Clinical Psychiatry* 15.

When patients do receive treatment, research indicates that recovery rates can be high, particularly for psychological/talking therapies. One study suggests that success rates for mental health interventions are higher than with many physical illnesses.[36] Of course, not all patients will make a permanent recovery, and serious mental illness is often a chronic condition which can be controlled but may recur if the patient suffers from a relapse or refuses to comply with the medication. Indeed, statistics highlight that more than half of the people who suffer from one episode of depression will have another at some stage in their life.[37] This has implications for the use of compulsory treatment, especially if some patients are likely to need to continue to take the medication for a considerable period of time, possibly for the rest of their lives. So, what is the scope of the mental health legislation, and what is the role of psychiatry in compulsory admission and treatment?

'Medical treatment' for a 'mental disorder'

For compulsory admission, an Approved Clinician (AC), normally a psychiatrist, must be satisfied that the patient satisfies the legal definition of mental disorder in section 1 of the Act. Mental disorder is broadly defined as 'any disorder or disability of the mind', and this expansive definition embraces a diverse range of conditions and behaviours. It replaces the more explicit definition that existed prior to 2007, which included distinct subcategories such as mental illness, mental impairment, and psychopathic disorder, and specific exclusions, such as promiscuity and sexual deviancy. The only remaining exclusion in the Act now relates to sole dependency on alcohol or drugs. This broad definition is, nevertheless, compatible with Article 5 of the ECHR.[38] In *Winterwerp v the Netherlands* the ECtHR interpreted the requirements of Article 5(1)(e) in relation to patients of 'unsound mind' and stated that:

> The very nature of what has to be established before the competent national authority – that is, a true mental disorder – calls for *objective medical expertise.* Further, the mental disorder must be of a *kind or degree* warranting compulsory confinement. What is more, the validity of continued confinement depends upon the *persistence of such a disorder.*[39]

This gives latitude to the medical professionals involved in the process, as their diagnosis of a true mental disorder which meets the threshold is a crucial element

36 Centre for Economic Performance Mental Health Policy Group, *How Mental Health Loses Out in the NHS* (LSE, 2012) 13–15.

37 MHF (n 4) 10–13.

38 The minimum condition in Article 5 is that everyone has the right to liberty and security of person. No one shall be deprived of his liberty save in the following cases and in accordance with a procedure prescribed by law: the lawful detention of persons for the prevention of the spreading of infectious diseases, of persons of unsound mind, or of alcoholics, drug addicts, or vagrants.

39 *Winterwerp* (n 23) para. 39, emphasis supplied.

in the legality of the decision to detain. But the terminology in section 1 of the Act is incredibly loose. As John Dawson has pointed out, broad and/or undefined terms, such as those now found in that section, have the advantage of flexibility and are 'capable of adaptation to continuing trends within the professions . . . No particular philosophy or clinical approach is endorsed or rejected'.[40] However, the danger with this approach is that 'an undefined term has no clear content or boundaries. Application that is flexible may be unreliable or arbitrary. Marked regional or personal variations may occur. There is no common standard stated against which interpretations can be tested or reviewed'.[41]

And when there is such scope for subjective interpretation, there are corresponding concerns about potential abuse and misuse of the legislation. The Mental Health Act *Code of Practice* seeks to promote consistency by advising professionals to determine mental disorder 'in accordance with good clinical practice and accepted standards of what constitutes such a disorder or disability'.[42] Given the tensions within psychiatry (and allied professions) about the nature of certain disorders or disabilities, this advice is not particularly constructive. Accepted standards are found in psychiatric diagnostic manuals such as the World Health Organization's International Classification of Diseases (ICD-10),[43] but, as Fennell has observed, while manuals such as this are keen to emphasise the distinction between mental disorders and socially deviant behaviour, they 'offer only imprecise boundaries between the two'.[44] The lack of precision is exacerbated by the fact that psychiatric diagnoses have been criticised for not being as reliable or 'scientific' as other areas of medical practice, due to their lack of objectivity.[45] However, many others would maintain that there is no difference in principle between diagnosis in psychiatry and the rest of medicine.[46]

Consequently, there are legitimate concerns about the breadth and application of this definition of mental disorder, especially when statistics on the rates of compulsory admission are considered. There has been a steady increase in the use of compulsion since the amendments introduced by the 2007 Act came into force, and annual hospital detentions rose from 15,181 in 2008 to 18,166 in 2014.[47] The precise reasons for this are not known, but the expanded definition of mental disorder may be a contributing factor. Indeed, the Richardson Committee, which

40 J. Dawson, 'Psychopathology and civil commitment criteria' (1996) 4 *Medical Law Review* 62, 66.

41 Dawson (n 40) 66.

42 *Code of Practice* (n 7) para. 2.4. The *Code* now includes some examples of clinically recognised conditions which could fall within the Act's definitions, including affective disorders such as depression, and organic disorders such as dementia.

43 World Health Organization, ICD-10 Version:2015, available at http://apps.who.int/classifications/icd10/browse/2015/en (accessed 23 January 2015).

44 Fennell (n 10) para. 2.23.

45 See e.g. S. Morse, 'Crazy behaviour, morals and science: An analysis of mental health law' (1978) 51 *California Law Review* 527; L. Gostin, 'Contemporary social historical perspectives on mental health reform' (1983) 10 *Journal of Law and Society* 47; A. Aboraya, 'The reliability of psychiatric diagnosis revisited' (2006) 3 *Psychiatry* 41.

46 Rose (n 15) 205.

47 HSCIC (n 1) Table 1.

was appointed to advise the government about reform in the 1990s, was worried that a broad concept of mental disorder could lead to this 'net widening' effect.[48] These sorts of concerns are reinforced when the interpretation of other criteria in compulsory admission and treatment are examined.

Compulsory admission: is 'appropriate' treatment available?

For longer-term admission to hospital the statutory criteria require that 'appropriate' medical treatment must be available to the patient, taking into account the nature and degree of the mental disorder.[49] The definition of 'medical treatment' in section 145 of the Act is expansive, and includes 'nursing, psychological intervention and specialist mental health habilitation and rehabilitation'. Examples of the type of treatments which fall within the broad headings are provided, such as psychological treatments like cognitive therapy and counselling, and interventions designed to modify patients' physical or mental abilities and social functioning, and help them to learn or relearn skills or abilities.[50] This is clearly very wide, and while it is intended only to cover *medical treatment for the mental disorder*, and not any unconnected physical illness, that is not always an easy line to draw.

The appropriate treatment test replaced a test of 'treatability', which applied to certain groups of patients (with psychopathy or mental impairment) prior to the 2007 amendments. The treatability test required the treatment to provide some therapeutic benefit to the patient,[51] and it was regarded as problematic for patients with a personality disorder ('psychopaths'), who may not respond to conventional treatments, such as medication. Some mental health diagnoses, including personality disorders, are controversial, and there is a lack of consensus within the psychiatric profession about these disorders and suitable interventions for them. Indeed, the MHF suggests that '[m]any people believe [personality disorder] is used in cases where symptoms do not obviously fit any other diagnosis'.[52]

The government's rationale for the change from treatability to an appropriate treatment test was to counteract a 'culture in which certain groups of patients are labelled untreatable and thereby denied services'.[53] The new test means that:

> The treatment must be not only available and appropriate to the medical condition but appropriate to the circumstances. For instance, factors such as how far the services are from the patient's home or whether those services are culturally appropriate will need to be considered. That is very much in line with

48 *Report of the Expert Committee, Review of the Mental Health Act 1983* (London, 1999) para. 4.4.

49 MHA 1983, s. 3(2)(a). For discussion of appropriate treatment in a different context see K Syrett, 'Rationing, resource allocation, and appropriate medical treatment' in this collection.

50 *Mental Health Act 2007 Explanatory Notes* (TSO, 2007) para. 39.

51 The MHA 2007 amended the admission criteria to include that 'appropriate treatment must be available' to the patient (s. 3(2)(d)) rather than 'such treatment is likely to alleviate or prevent a deterioration of his condition', as in the original 1983 Act.

52 MHF (n 4) 19.

53 HL Debs 28 November 2006, cols 654–659.

> the move across the NHS towards more tailored, individual patient-focused services. It is a change that links mental health very much to the mainstream of NHS reform and improvement.[54]

While this new appropriate treatment provision may appear more straightforward and pragmatic, it is still problematic. For example, how effective must the treatment be for it to be deemed to be appropriate? As Peter Bartlett has observed, there is no requirement that 'optimal' treatment must be available.[55] There is no statutory definition of 'available' either, and the *Code of Practice* states that it must 'actually' be available 'for the time being', and 'it is not sufficient that appropriate treatment could theoretically be provided'.[56] Some treatments are in short supply and subject to long waiting lists, particularly psychological therapies, and will not necessarily be available at that time. There is also concern that this provision is still flexible or ambiguous enough to be employed as a reason *not* to admit certain types of 'problematic' patients. Clinicians must act in the best interests of their patients, and if the clinician decides that there is no clinical benefit to the patient from the treatment, then it is unlikely to be appropriate.[57]

What little case law there is on this provision suggests that the appropriate treatment which is available can be minimal in nature. For example, in *MD v Nottinghamshire Healthcare NHS Trust*, MD had a personality disorder and was unable to engage with psychological therapy.[58] The Tribunal found that there was appropriate and available treatment for him, as he had the potential to benefit from 'the milieu of the ward both for its short-term effects and for the possibility that it would break through the defence mechanisms and allow him later to engage in therapy'.[59] The broad definition of treatment in section 145(1) enabled the Tribunal to conclude that the ward environment *itself* was capable of providing appropriate medical treatment. However, as Peter Bartlett and Ralph Sandland have pointed out, this 'comes perilously close to finding that detention is, itself, appropriate treatment', as the notion of any therapeutic benefit is so widely construed.[60]

The decision in *MD* can be contrasted with the approach adopted in *DL-H v Devon Partnership NHS Trust and Secretary of State for Justice*.[61] This case also involved questions about the availability of appropriate treatment for DL-H, who was diagnosed with a personality disorder and detained under the Act. The Upper Tier Tribunal took a more interventionist approach than in *MD*, and expressed concern that the broad language relating to medical treatment should not create the

54 HL Debs (n 53) cols 654–659.

55 P. Bartlett, 'Civil Confinement' in L Gostin *et al.* (n 10) para. 12.43.

56 *Code of Practice* (n 7) paras. 23.14, 23.21.

57 Bartlett (n 55) paras. 12.38. The *Code of Practice* appears to endorse this view, as it states that the treatment must be appropriate for the individual mental health condition. This is a matter of professional judgement in accordance with 'a strong evidence base', compliant with professional standards and NICE/DH guidance: Code of Practice (n 7) paras. 24.6–24.7.

58 [2010] UKUT 59 (AAC).

59 *MD* (n 58) para. 39.

60 Bartlett and Sandland (n 25) 255.

61 [2010] UKUT 102 (AAC).

illusion that appropriate treatment *was* available, masking detentions solely based on risk/dangerousness. The Tribunal also emphasised that treatment refusals by patients should not be equated with unavailability of treatment. This is significant from the point of view of psychological or talking therapies which require a degree of engagement by the patient.

But there is still some ambiguity about the new terminology employed in the Act, coupled with the broad discretion accorded to the clinician making the diagnosis. The *Code of Practice* contains limited guidance on the construction of these terms, and suggests that the test 'requires a balanced and holistic judgement'.[62] It is noteworthy that in the Health Committee's report on post-legislative scrutiny of the Act, it was said that:

> Although the [Health] Committee was told that the introduction of the appropriate treatment test had not resulted in a change of clinical practice, it is striking that the development of the test has coincided with a substantial increase in the total population of patients detained under section.[63]

The Health Committee heard no convincing evidence that there was 'an increased cohort of people in England suffering from psychotic illnesses' and expressed concerns that compulsory admission had become the 'ticket to getting a hospital bed', due to shortages in acute mental health services, and difficulties faced by professionals in accessing in-patient beds.[64] I argue that this is both unacceptable and unethical, and it suggests that psychiatrists and other mental health professionals may be taking advantage of the breadth of discretion afforded by vague and expansive criteria to secure a hospital bed; or, as the College of Social Work has suggested, that a person's liberty may be restricted for reasons other than those provided in the criteria for formal detention (for the patient's own health/safety or the protection of others).[65] That was clearly not the intention behind the legislation, which includes a least restriction principle so that compulsory admission is a last resort.[66] In its response to the Committee, the government accepted

62 *Code of Practice* (n 7) para. 23.11. Ch. 23 of the *Code* now includes some additional factors for decision-makers under the Act, suggesting that appropriateness will depend on the individual patient. It must be clinically suitable for that patient, as well as appropriate more generally. The treatment must be available at that time, and a patient's willingness to co-operate with a treatment does not make it inappropriate.

63 Health Committee, *First Report Post-Legislative Scrutiny of the Mental Health Act 1983*, Session 2013–14, HC 584 (House of Commons, 2013) para. 18.

64 Health Committee (n 63) para. 20.

65 Health Committee (n 63) para. 25. A postal survey of Approved Mental Health Professional (AMHP) leads in all Local Social Services Authorities (LSSA) in 2013 by the College of Social Work confirms this perception, as 16.5 per cent of respondents (out of a total of 102 responses from all LSSAs) stated that in one or more cases, a person has been detained under the MHA because an informal admission to psychiatric inpatient care was not available: The College of Social Work, *AMHP Community of Interest: AMHP Practice Survey 2013* (The College of Social Work, 2013) 5, available at www.tcsw.org.uk/uploadedFiles/TheCollege/_CollegeLibrary/ (accessed 26 January 2015).

66 *Code of Practice* (n 7) para. 1.2 and p. 22.

that this may be an issue, and stated that the Care Quality Commission (CQC) would explore this further in the future.[67] The fact that clinicians and other mental health professionals may feel they have been forced into this situation brings into focus the perennial problem of under-resourcing, and the urgent need for the government to invest in the provision of mental health care and inpatient beds.[68]

Compulsory treatment: is the proposed treatment 'appropriate'?

Once the patient had been compulsorily admitted to hospital, the breadth of medical discretion is amplified by some of the provisions regulating the imposition of compulsory medical treatment. The patient's treatment will be approved and overseen by a Responsible Clinician (RC).[69] RCs are approved clinicians, ordinarily psychiatrists, with appropriate competence in the diagnosis and treatment of mental disorders. The RC has a powerful role, taking 'overall responsibility for the patient's case', including powers to administer medical treatment for mental disorder without consent.[70] But she must also act as an 'advocate' and make sure that patients are fully aware of their rights when they are admitted to hospital.[71] Nevertheless, there is evidence to suggest that many patients do not have their rights adequately explained to them. The CQC commented in its annual Mental Health Act monitoring report in 2012/13, that '[i]n the last two years we have not seen adequate evidence of discussions with patients about their rights in at least 1 in 10 wards'.[72]

Section 63 of the Act regulates the administration of general medical treatment for a mental disorder, for example psychotherapy, rehabilitation programmes, medication, or drug therapy, as well as care on the ward. It permits the exercise of unfettered medical discretion, as the general rule is that detained patients can be treated for their mental disorder under section 63 without their consent, subject to a few exceptions,[73] and without specific safeguards. The scope of this section is as broad as the definition of medical treatment is expansive; clinicians are thus able to offer a wide range of therapies or interventions. The *Code of Practice* provides that section 63:

> includes treatment of physical health problems only to the extent that such treatment is *part of, or ancillary to, treatment for mental disorder* (e.g. treating wounds

67 Department of Health, *Post-legislative scrutiny of the Mental Health Act 2007: Response to the report of the Health Committee of the House of Commons*, Cmnd 8735 (TSO, 2013) R1.2.

68 The then Deputy PM, Nick Clegg, recognised this in October 2014 in his annual LibDem Conference address: P. Wintour, 'Nick Clegg promises £120m boost for mental health care waiting time targets' (*The Guardian*, 8 October 2014), available at http://www.theguardian.com/society/2014/oct/08/mental-health-care-120m-funding-waiting-time-targets-nick-clegg (accessed 15 January 2015).

69 MHA 1983, s. 34.

70 MHA 2007, ss 9–12.

71 Health Committee (n 63) para. 8.

72 CQC, *Monitoring the Mental Health Act 1983 in 2012/13* (TSO, 2014) 26.

73 Under ss 57, 58, and 58A, Electro-Convulsive Therapy, neurosurgery and the imposition of medication beyond three months are subject to a patient consent and/or a second medical opinion system.

self-inflicted as a result of mental disorder). Otherwise, the Act does not regulate medical treatment for physical health problems.[74]

Treatments for a mental or physical disorder?

Treatment may be authorised for a period of up to three months under section 63 if it alleviates the symptoms and external manifestations of the mental disorder, but it is not always clear when such physical intervention may be linked to an underlying mental disorder. Indeed, this section has been interpreted broadly by the domestic courts to allow physical treatments if they are ancillary to treatment for the mental disorder, thereby moving beyond core treatments, such as medication and psychotherapy. But the dividing line between mental and physical treatment is not always an easy one to draw. For example, in *B v Croydon Health Authority*, B suffered from a psychopathic disorder, and one of her symptoms was a compulsion to harm herself.[75] During her detention in hospital she stopped eating and her weight fell to a dangerous level. She was threatened with feeding by nasogastric tube and applied to the High Court for an injunction to restrain Croydon Health Authority from tube-feeding her without her consent. The court considered whether force-feeding was within the scope of medical treatment in section 63, and adopted an expansive approach to the definition of medical treatment. Hoffmann LJ held that:

> a range of acts ancillary to the core treatment fall within the definition [of medical treatment under section 145(1)] . . . Nursing and care concurrent with the core treatment or as a necessary prerequisite to such treatment or to prevent the patient from causing harm to himself or to alleviate the consequences of the disorder are in my view all capable of being ancillary to a treatment calculated to alleviate or prevent a deterioration of the psychopathic disorder. It would seem to me strange if a hospital could, without the patient's consent, give him treatment directed to alleviating a psychopathic disorder showing itself in suicidal tendencies, but not without such consent be able to treat the consequences of a suicide attempt. In my judgment the term 'medical treatment . . . for the mental disorder' in section 63 includes such ancillary acts.[76]

Ewbank J came to a similar conclusion about tube-feeding an anorexic patient in *Re KB (Adult) (Mental Patient: Medical Treatment)*; 'relieving symptoms is just as much a part of treatment as relieving the underlying cause'.[77] It would be difficult for clinicians to draw a clear distinction between procedures or parts of

74 *Code of Practice* (n 7) para. 24.5, emphasis supplied.
75 [1995] 2 WLR 294.
76 *B v Croydon* (n 75) paras. 138–139.
77 (1994) 19 BMLR 144, para. 146.

procedures which were designed to treat the disorder itself, and those procedures or parts which were designed to treat its symptoms. Not surprisingly, this reasoning has been criticised because it encroaches on patient autonomy and dignity, as forcible tube-feeding is invasive, painful, and distressing for patients.[78] It could also breach Articles 3 and 8 of the ECHR.[79] Furthermore, section 63 was not originally designed to cover such controversial treatments as force-feeding,[80] and the Joint Committee on Human Rights, reporting on the Draft Mental Health Bill in 2007, suggested that the government should consider including additional safeguards for nasogastric tube-feeding.[81] The government did not respond to this recommendation.

This broad interpretation of treatment was taken further in *Reid v Secretary of State for Scotland*.[82] Reid was detained in a high-security facility suffering from a personality disorder. His doctor believed that his anger management improved in the structured ward environment, and that this satisfied the wide definition of medical treatment in section 63. Reid challenged this, but the court agreed with his doctor, and the *Code of Practice* permits this:

> There may be patients whose particular circumstances mean that treatment may be appropriate even though it consists only of nursing and specialist day to day care under the clinical supervision of an approved clinician, in a safe and secure therapeutic environment with a structured regime.[83]

As Bartlett and Sandland have pointed out,[84] the *Code of Practice* appears contradictory on this, because the next paragraph emphasises that 'simply detaining someone, even in a hospital, does not constitute medical treatment'.[85] In the light of the government's risk agenda during the 1990s and the controversy about diagnoses such as personality disorder/psychopathy, it is difficult not to conclude that mental health law is being used as a mechanism of social control.

78 See e.g. P. Lewis, 'Feeding anorexic patients who refuse food' (1999) 7 *Medical Law Review* 21.

79 See *Nevmerzhitsky v Ukraine* (2006) 43 EHRR 32, ECtHR. Some legal commentators argue that section 63 is now vulnerable to a challenge under Article 8 in the wake of the ECtHR decision in *X v Finland* (Application no. 34806/04; 3 July 2012), as the administration of compulsory treatment was incidental to the compulsion and was not subject to further procedural/substantive safeguards, in the same way as treatment without consent under section 63 can be when it is interpreted in this expansive way.

80 See also *Tameside and Glossop Acute Services Trust v CH* [1996] 1 FLR 762, where section 63 was extended to cover the use of force to deliver a baby by caesarean section as treatment for a mental disorder when the mother was detained under section 3 of the original 1983 Act. In *St George's Healthcare NHS Trust v S* [1998] 3 All ER 673, CA, however, the Court disapproved of the use of the original MHA 1983 in this context.

81 House of Lords/House of Commons Joint Committee on Human Rights, *Legislative Scrutiny: Mental Health Bill Fourth Report of Session 2006–07* (HL Paper 40, HC Paper 288; 4 February 2007) para. 80.

82 [1999] 2 AC 512, HL.

83 *Code of Practice* (n 7) para. 23.17.

84 Bartlett and Sandland (n 25) para. 6.3.1.2.

85 *Code of Practice* (n 7) para. 23.18.

In some cases, it looks suspiciously like containment, albeit with an illusion of 'therapy'. Undoubtedly the dividing line between the two is blurred, but this approach has been endorsed at the ECtHR level in *Hutchinson Reid v UK*, in the interests of public safety.[86] But, as there are no additional procedural safeguards in section 63, patients can be contained in this way or treated against their will with powerful drugs and other controversial treatments, for up to three months, solely on the basis of medical opinion. This highlights the social control function of the legislation and the propriety of this loose interpretation of medical treatment.

Restraint and seclusion

This therapeutic illusion is also visible in the context of two other controversial treatments which have come to be regarded as acceptable practice and are imposed on detained patients, often too frequently. Chapter 26 of the *Code of Practice* contains detailed guidance on how to manage disturbed behaviour by patients who may present a particular risk to themselves or others. For example, it may be necessary to control dangerous, threatening or abusive behaviour, a physical assault by the patient, or self-harm or risk of physical injury by accident.[87] In these circumstances, specific methods of intervention or control might be needed, such as restraint[88] and/or seclusion. Both interventions fall within the broad legal definition of medical treatment in section 145,[89] and the courts have sanctioned their use.[90] These practices involve using physical force, segregation, and confinement to manage a particular risk posed by the patient. In England and Wales, restraint techniques will include the use of chemicals (such as sedatives or rapid tranquilisation) or physical force. The use of mechanical restraints are not common in the UK and should only be used 'exceptionally', as the *Code of Practice* recognises. However, they are used in some parts of the US and Europe. The *Code of Practice* advises that restrictive interventions such as this 'should only be used in a way that respects human rights', and mental health providers should have in place programmes or policies to reduce the use of such interventions.[91] Seclusion is defined in the *Code* as 'the supervised confinement and isolation of a patient, away from other patients, in an area from which the patient is prevented

86 (2003) 37 EHRR 211, ECtHR. See further P. Fennell, 'Convention compliance, public safety, and the social inclusion of mentally disordered people' (2005) 32 *Journal of Law and Society* 90.

87 *Code of Practice* (n 7) para. 26.40.

88 The legal basis for the use of restraint can be found in *Pountney v Griffiths* [1976] AC 314, HL. The House stated that some control, over and above that necessary to prevent harm, is implicit in the hospital's power to compulsorily detain patients.

89 In *S v Airedale NHS Trust* [2002] All ER (D) 79 the court found that decisions on the use of seclusion are decisions about care and treatment under the MHA 1983, and fall within the definition of treatment under the Act.

90 *R v Ashworth Hospital Authority, ex p Munjaz* [2003] EWCA Civ 1036; *Tameside and Glossop* (n 80).

91 *Code of Practice* (n 7) paras. 26.2, 26.4–26.6, 26.45.

from leaving, where it is of immediate necessity for the purpose of containment of severe behavioural disturbance which is likely to cause harm to others'.[92]

This is solitary confinement and can be extremely distressing and undignified for patients.[93] In *R v Ashworth Hospital, ex parte Munjaz*,[94] three primary reasons for the use of seclusion were suggested: therapeutic, containing, and punitive. The fact that solitary confinement may still be viewed as a form of punishment within an essentially therapeutic framework is a cause for concern. Indeed, Fennell has described seclusion as occupying a 'twilight zone',[95] and there is even some doubt within the psychiatric profession about its therapeutic value.[96]

Article 3 of the ECHR is relevant here. The prohibition on inhuman and degrading treatment within that Article is absolute, and it applies to the imposition of all medical treatment under the Act. But, again, the primacy of medical expertise and opinion is further reinforced. Failure to provide adequate medical treatment may be contrary to this provision,[97] as stated in the *Code of Practice*:

> compulsory treatment *is* capable of being inhuman treatment (or in extreme cases even torture) contrary to Article 3 of the Convention, if its effect on the person concerned reaches a sufficient level of severity. But the European Court of Human Rights has said that a measure which is convincingly shown to be of *therapeutic necessity* from the point of view of established principles of medicine cannot in principle be regarded as inhuman and degrading.[98]

The use of restraint and seclusion must be judged by reference to the ECtHR jurisprudence in *Herczegfalvy v Austria*.[99] Here, the applicant was detained in an institution for mentally ill offenders in Austria. He alleged brutal treatment and breaches of Articles 3 and 8 as he had been forcibly administered food and neuroleptics, isolated, and attached with handcuffs to a security bed without his consent. The ECtHR recognised that patients in psychiatric hospitals are in a 'position of inferiority and powerlessness', which 'calls for increased vigilance in reviewing whether the Convention has been complied with'.[100] Yet, it held that:

> the established principles of medicine are admittedly decisive in such cases . . . While it is for the medical authorities to decide, on the basis of the recognized rules of medical science, on the therapeutic methods to be used,

92 *Code of Practice* (n 7) para. 26.103.
93 T. Wynn, 'Psychiatric inpatients experiences with restraint' (2004) 15 *Journal of Forensic Psychiatry* 124.
94 [2005] UKHL 58.
95 P. Fennell, *Treatment without Consent* (Routledge, 1996) 225.
96 T. Exworthy, D. Mohan, N. Hindley, J. Basson, 'Seclusion: Punitive or protective' (2001) 12 *Journal of Forensic Psychiatry* 423.
97 *Kotälla v. the Netherlands* (1978) 14 D & R 238.
98 *Code of Practice* (n 7) para. 24.43, emphasis supplied.
99 (1993) 15 EHRR 437, para. 82.
100 *Herczegfalvy* (n 99) para. 82.

> if necessary by force, to preserve the physical and mental health of patients who are entirely incapable of deciding for themselves and for whom they are therefore responsible, such patients nevertheless remain under the protection of Article 3, the requirements of which permit of no derogation . . . *as a general rule, a measure which is a therapeutic necessity cannot be regarded as inhuman or degrading.* The Court must nevertheless satisfy itself that the medical necessity has been convincingly shown to exist.[101]

On the facts, there was no violation of Article 3 because there was insufficient evidence to substantiate the applicant's claims. The treatment at issue was deemed to be necessary, according to the psychiatric principles generally accepted at the time. As discussed earlier, a similar conclusion was reached in *Atudorei v Romania*.[102] Bartlett has described the ECtHR jurisprudence here as 'unconvincing',[103] as the courts are slow to challenge accepted medical practice, even when it is of a contentious or questionable nature. The potential for judicial scrutiny of appropriate medical treatment in this context would appear to be extremely limited.

Furthermore, accepted medical practice in England can be judged by reference to professional standards and guidelines. The *Code of Practice* contains detailed guidance on the use of restraint techniques and advises all providers to have written policies or programmes on reducing the use of such interventions, as well as ensuring that all staff receive appropriate training.[104] NICE has also published guidance for National Health Service (NHS) staff which states that '[c]ontrol and restraint, and compulsory treatment including rapid tranquillisation, should be used as a last resort . . . and only by healthcare professionals trained and competent to do this'.[105] Furthermore, '[t]hese interventions are management strategies and are not regarded as primary treatment techniques'.[106] But there is little detail in either document about the nature and type of restraint methods which can be employed, and much is devolved to local policies and practice. This creates the risk of inconsistency and points to the need for greater clarity, and stricter audit and regulation of the use of restraint.

The CQC (and its predecessor, the Mental Health Act Commission) which monitors the use of the Act, has commented regularly in its reports on the excessive use of restraint and expressed concerns about some inappropriate practices; for example, the use of straitjackets, wristlocks, and Taser guns while transporting

101 *Herczegfalvy* (n 99) para. 82, emphasis supplied.

102 *Atudorei v Romania* (n 8).

103 P. Bartlett, 'The necessity must be convincingly shown to exist: Standards for the compulsory treatment for mental disorder under the Mental Health Act 1983' (2011) 19 *Medical Law Review* 514, 524.

104 *Code of Practice* (n 7) para. 26.175.

105 NICE, *Service User Experience in Adult Mental Health: Improving the Experience of Care for People Using Adult NHS Mental Health Services* (NICE Guideline CG136, December 2011) para. 1.8.10.

106 NICE, *Violence: The Short-Term Management of Disturbed/Violent Behaviour in In-Patient Psychiatric Settings and Emergency Departments* (NICE Guideline CG25, February 2005) para. 1.8.1.1.

patients to wards.[107] Evidence suggests that a high number of detained patients have experienced restraint methods. For example, a report by Mind, based on freedom of information data obtained from NHS mental health trusts, indicated that there were nearly 40,000 restraint episodes in 2011/12.[108] Prone or face down restraint, described by Mind as 'pinning and holding someone face down on the floor for a period of time', was used more than 3,000 times in NHS Trusts in 2011/12.[109] Undoubtedly, some aggressive and violently disturbed patients may need to be restrained by staff who have been trained in the use of restraint techniques, and the CQC has observed that most staff do now receive some degree of training on this.[110] But there is still considerable ambiguity about the boundary between treatment and restraint, and further research is needed on the efficacy of restraint techniques in order to justify its proper use *as* a form of medical treatment.

The CQC reports also highlight several instances of the misuse of seclusion, including inadequate lighting, heating, and ventilation in seclusion rooms, patients detained in padded rooms with no access to toilet facilities, and reviews not always conducted within the required time.[111] In a CQC patient census in 2010, 4 per cent of patients had experienced at least one episode of seclusion in the previous year,[112] and there is huge disparity in the use of seclusion by race; white British patients have a relatively low seclusion rate of 9 per cent, but it rises to 90 per cent for mixed white/black patients.[113] Again, it must be questioned whether these methods are proper and appropriate medical treatments for a mental disorder. As Kirsty Keywood has commented:

> [t]he presumed therapeutic rationale of behaviour management, underscored by the court's willingness to consider the management of symptoms as an acceptable therapeutic strategy even when there is little or no gain for the patient, offers scant hope that adults with mental health problems will not be subject to unwanted interventions.[114]

Diluting medical dominance? The expansion of professional roles and responsibilities

I have highlighted the extent to which medical discretion is permitted under the Act, but this could be countered by the recent expansion of professional roles. In

107 See e.g. CQC (n 72) 47–52; CQC, *Monitoring the Mental Health Act 1983 in 2011/12* (TSO, 2013) 44–51; MHAC, *Risk, Rights, Recovery Twelfth Biennial Report 2005–2007* (TSO, 2008) 93–98.

108 Mind, *Mental Health Crisis Care: Physical Restraint in Crisis. A Report on Physical Restraint in Hospital Settings in England* (Mind, 2013) 13.

109 Mind (n 108) 12, 15.

110 CQC (n 107) 46.

111 CQC (n 107) 44–45.

112 CQC, *Count Me In 2010* (TSO, 2011) 24.

113 CQC (n 112) 24–25.

114 K. Keywood, 'Psychiatric injustice? The therapeutic presumption of behaviour management in mental health law' (2005) 7 *The Journal of Adult Protection* 25.

contrast to other areas of medical practice discussed in this collection,[115] the traditional dominance of the psychiatric profession was diluted (at least in theory) by some of the amendments introduced by the 2007 Act. Professional involvement in the diagnosis and treatment of mental disorder has been diversified, so that other mental health professionals (nurses, social workers, psychologists, and occupational therapists) can now also be involved in the admissions decision-making process, and take responsibility for the provision of patient care and treatment. Given that the *Code of Practice* advises that the assessment of what is appropriate medical treatment is a 'holistic' judgement, which includes a range of social as well as clinical factors,[116] this professional shift is significant. It represents a move away from the medical model of mental illness, and it could also be viewed as having potentially negative implications for the rights of mental health patients. This is because now they may be treated against their will in hospital on the basis of even more divergent and imprecise views of what is appropriate treatment.

The government's rationale for this professional change was, essentially, pragmatic; to reflect the modernisation of careers within the NHS and ensure that professional skills were best matched with the treatment needs of patients. This amendment has, thus, significantly expanded the professional skills base of decision-makers under the Act, reflecting a more holistic and multidimensional approach to mental disorder and an increasing focus on social influences and psychosocial treatments. This expansion has occurred in two key ways. First, the Approved Mental Health Professional (AMHP) role has expanded beyond the traditional social work sphere to include registered nurses, psychologists, and occupational therapists. The AMHP role is key in making applications for compulsory admission, supported by the medical diagnosis and recommendations. The *Code of Practice* emphasises that AMHPs have a professional responsibility to 'exercise their own judgement, based on social and medical evidence' in deciding whether an application for compulsory admission should be made.[117] Indeed, '[t]he role of the AMHPs is to provide an independent decision about whether or not there are alternatives to detention under the Act, bringing a social perspective to bear on the decision'.[118]

In that sense, the AMHP role is intended to provide a social counterbalance to the medical opinion, and an independent professional check on the exercise of medical discretion. Research carried out by Jill Peay into joint decision-making under the 1983 Act suggests that this approach can be effective and reduces the use of compulsory powers.[119] In her study, there was evidence that social workers tended to 'act as a brake on making decisions to invoke the Act', which was the preferred approach by the medical professionals in the study.[120]

115 See e.g. D. Griffiths, A. Mullock, 'The medical exception and cosmetic surgery: Culpable doctors and harmful enhancement?' in this collection.

116 *Code of Practice* (n 7) para. 23.12.

117 *Code of Practice* (n 7) para. 14.52.

118 *Code of Practice* (n 7) para. 14.52.

119 J. Peay, *Decisions and Dilemmas: Working with Mental Health Law* (Hart, 2003).

120 Peay (n 119) 47.

In its evidence to the parliamentary Joint Committee on the Draft Mental Health Bill in 2004–5, the British Association of Social Workers (BASW) was concerned that this expansion could be detrimental to patients, resulting in a dilution in expertise and less focus on the social or non-medical factors. BASW stressed that the social work role was crucial in ensuring:

> that the legal requirements are met and that a proper balance is struck between the interests of the patient and other parties . . . Since they view the situation from a social care perspective, they provide a counterbalance to any tendency to over-medicalise what are often multi-dimensional problems.[121]

But there is a suggestion that mental health nurses may be unable to provide this counterbalance because, like doctors, they come from the medical tradition and may not be as aware of the social dimensions of mental health care. Furthermore, the traditional professional hierarchy within the NHS could make it difficult for nurses to feel able to challenge the opinion of more senior medical colleagues, such as consultant psychiatrists. Nevertheless, the Joint Committee believed that this change was desirable, as long as the additional professions received appropriate training and competencies to carry out the role.[122] That, of course, is the key to success.

The expansion of professional roles and responsibilities has also spread to another central role, that of AC.[123] Approval enables a practitioner to take on the role of RC to oversee the patient's care and treatment, as noted above. In the same way that the 2007 amendments expanded the AMHP role, approval here is no longer restricted to medical practitioners (normally psychiatrists) but now also encompasses occupational therapists, psychologists, social workers, and registered mental health nurses. The AC must be able to demonstrate competency in terms of having the ability to carry out a mental health assessment, lead a multidisciplinary team, and formulate and review a treatment plan for the patient.[124] Again, the provision of appropriate training and support will be crucial to enable professionals from other backgrounds to effectively fulfil this role. The Joint Committee stated that this expansion was not a retrograde step because:

> within a modern multi-disciplinary team approach to mental health care and treatment there is scope for broadening professional roles such as that of clinical supervisor to encompass suitable professionals with non-medical qualifications. We agree with the British Psychological Society that the fundamental role of the clinical supervisor is to assess and coordinate the

121 House of Commons/ House of Lords Joint Committee on the Draft Mental Health Bill, *Draft Mental Health Bill Session 2004–05: Volume I Report, together with formal minutes and annexes* (HL Paper 79; HC Paper 95; March 2005) para. 441.

122 House of Commons/House of Lords (n 121) para. 445.

123 Mental Health (Approved Clinicians) Directions 2008.

124 Mental Health (Approved Clinician) Directions 2008, Sched. 2.

> patient's care and treatment needs rather than the prescription of medication. Psychologists possess the competencies and it is true to say that 'the clinical actions of psychologists cover the breadth of mental health problems, and certainly all of the so-called categories of people that fall under the Mental Health Act'.[125]

In many ways, it is a positive development that approval is no longer confined to medical professionals because other perspectives can be brought to the diagnosis and treatment of mental disorder, and the medical model will, thereby, be diluted. This could improve the quality of patient care and help to target some of the social or environmental dimensions of mental ill health. Yet, at the same time, it could be a retrograde step leading to more disagreement about diagnoses, and an inconsistency of approach at both the inter- and intra-professional level. Nicola Glover-Thomas and I have argued elsewhere that these changes have not been primarily driven by patient needs but by cost-cutting and staff shortages in the NHS.[126] They also could be viewed negatively by those who argue that the government has simply substituted one form of agency of social control with another.[127] Nevertheless, this shift has the potential to be progressive and bolster professional safeguards. It also may go some way towards ensuring that key professional roles, such as the AC or the AMHP, do not remain unfilled. This can only benefit patients, as there is evidence of a recent decline in recruitment and retention in psychiatry, as well as high levels of burnout within the social work profession.[128]

Conclusion

Developments in mental health law reveal the tensions and shifts between medicalism and legalism. The current framework is intended to strike a balance between the two, but I suggest that the process is still weighted in favour of medical discretion. In the context of compulsory mental health care and treatment, psychiatry continues to occupy a privileged position to diagnose and determine what is proper or appropriate medical treatment for mental disorder. This has persisted despite the divisions within the discipline about the nature and aetiology of some disorders, question marks about the reliability of psychiatric diagnosis, and conflicting evidence about the therapeutic basis and efficacy of some of the available treatments. Medical dominance has been reinforced by recent changes in the legislation, as the government introduced

125 House of Commons/House of Lords, (n 121) para. 448, reference removed.

126 J. Laing, N. Glover-Thomas, 'Mental Health Professionals' in L. Gostin *et al.* (n 10) para. 8.131.

127 Rose (n 15) 202.

128 See R. Kendell, A. Pearce, 'Consultant psychiatrists who retired prematurely 1995 and 1996' (1997) 21 *Psychiatric Bulletin* 741; M. J. Goldacre, S. Fazel, F. Smith, T. W. Lambert, 'Choice and rejection of psychiatry as a career: Surveys of UK medical graduates from 1974–2009' (2013) 202 *British Journal of Psychiatry* 228.

what have been described as 'feeble' standards and 'fuzzy' terminology.[129] As Fennell has remarked:

> The combined effect of the changes to the definition [of mental disorder], the removal of all exclusions save those for addiction, and the replacement of the treatability test with the availability of appropriate treatment, is to remove areas of clinical discretion *not to use* compulsory powers.[130]

Little wonder, therefore, that we have witnessed such an increase in the detained mentally disordered population.[131]

The role of the courts in providing effective oversight of medical practice in this area has been questioned,[132] and there is continued deference to psychiatric expertise in relation to medical treatment at both the domestic and ECtHR level.[133] This contrasts to the courts' somewhat less deferential attitude in other areas of medical practice, as José Miola considers in this collection,[134] where there is evidence of greater judicial challenge and enquiry.[135] This medical authority in the sphere of mental health may, however, be tempered by the expansion in professional roles to include social work and allied professions, who bring a more holistic perspective to the diagnosis and treatment of mental disorder, and, thus, may be better placed to respond to the diverse needs of patients. However, what little available evidence there is to date suggests that the uptake to fill the AC role from those with non-clinical backgrounds is low, so the traditional medical hegemony persists.[136] The professional expansion may also merely heighten the variability in diagnosis and treatment methods, creating conflict and yet more uncertainty about the limits of proper medical treatment for a mental disorder. This, in turn, could lead to inconsistent approches and poor decision-making and by practitioners about what is 'appropiate' and proper medical treatment.

129 Bartlett (n 55) para. 12.23.

130 Fennell (n 10) para. 2.105, emphasis supplied.

131 HSCIC (n 1) Table 1.

132 Fennell (n 10) para. 13.94.

133 P. Fennell, 'Doctor knows best? Therapeutic detention under common law, the Mental Health Act, and the European Convention' (1998) 6 *Medical Law Review* 322, 323.

134 J. Miola, 'Moralising medicine: "Proper medical treatment" and the role of ethics and law in medical decision-making' in this collection.

135 See e.g. Lord Woolf's comments in 'Are the courts excessively deferential to the medical profession?' (2001) 9 *Medical Law Review* 1. In *Bolitho v City and Hackney Health Authority* [1998] AC 232, HL, the House suggested that, in the context of diagnosis and treatment in medical negligence, the court must be satisfied that a particular body of medical opinion is 'responsible' or 'reasonable' (243, *per* Lord Browne-Wilkinson).

136 See e.g. 'London's first non-medical approved clinician' (23 May 2013), available at www.oxleas.nhs.uk/news/2013/5/londons-first-non-medical-appr/ (accessed 15 January 2015); A. McNicol, 'The pilot scheme that could shatter the glass ceiling for mental health social workers' (*Community Care*, 27 November 2013), available at www.communitycare.co.uk/2013/11/27 (accessed 15 January 2015).

11 The economics of 'proper medical treatment'

*Cam Donaldson, Rachel Baker, and Neil McHugh**

Introduction

There are places where health economics and health economists should not go, and the topics discussed in this collection would, on the face of it, appear to be prime candidates for us to avoid. However, a health economics perspective can prove particularly useful in addressing the question of what is proper when resources are at stake and when all possible claims on such resources are competing with each other. That perspective allows us to assess competing claims in relation to one another rather than looking at each in isolation. Such relative assessment is particularly important in the context of most advanced economies, almost all of which operate publicly funded health care systems, resourced through the allocation of fixed funding envelopes, and such systems form the context of our suggested approach. Given this, the term 'proper', from an economics perspective, can be equated to achieving the most benefit from limited resources, and two theoretical principles from economics can usefully be brought to bear in deciding on the appropriateness of health interventions: opportunity cost and marginal analysis. In this chapter, these will be described using a well-known example from the medical literature, though it is unrelated in terms of clinical context to those examples appearing elsewhere in this collection.

Opportunity cost and marginal analysis may appear to be 'value-free' concepts, even as initially portrayed in this chapter, but they are not. In what follows, the value-laden nature of (health) economic evaluation will be illustrated by considering the implications of opportunity cost and marginal analysis for (a) what counts in economic evaluations and (b) how economic evaluations can used by clinicians and health care managers (the main 'resource-influencers' in health care systems). Finally, further challenges to health economists, with respect to how to deal with the potential limitations of efficiency-based frameworks based on opportunity cost and marginal analysis, will be addressed. These limitations, along with potential

* This chapter was presented as a paper at the Wellcome Trust funded seminar on 'Transforming wrongs into right(s): The power of "proper medical treatment"', organised by the Universities of Lancaster and Manchester on 12 September 2013. We are grateful to the workshop participants, particularly John Coggon, for their comments on the version of this chapter presented at the seminar.

clashes with rights-based and legal approaches, will be discussed, particularly in the light of the issues raised in other chapters in this collection, but also in a way that (hopefully) does not lead to the perceived relevance of economic approaches being reduced.

Opportunity cost and marginal analysis: the case of colon cancer screening

An often-cited illustration of opportunity cost is provided in the case of the sixth stool guaiac.[1] In the mid-1970s, the American Cancer Society recommended that when attempting to detect cancer of the colon, each stool sample should be tested six times. The first part of a sample would be tested and, if positive, the subject would go on to have a further confirmatory test and, if necessary, treatment. If negative, the second part of the sample would be tested. If positive, the subject would have further confirmatory testing and, if negative, the third part of their sample would be tested, and so on. A screened person would be confirmed as negative only after all six parts had tested so. This policy was analysed on the basis that (i) out of a population of 10,000, it is known (from epidemiological studies) that there are 72 cases of cancer, and (ii) each test detects 91.67 per cent of cases undetected by the previous test. Therefore, the first test will detect 91.67 per cent of cases, the second test will detect 91.67 per cent of the 8.33 per cent of cases left undetected by the first test, and so on.[1] Thus, as is shown in Table 1, 66 of the 72 cases are detected after the first round of testing, and the cost of this was $1,175 per case detected, where costs include resources used in initial and confirmatory tests. The second round of testing ensures that almost all cases are detected at an average cost of $1,507 per case detected, and six rounds of testing capture all cases at a cost of $2,451 per case detected.

This seems, on the face of it, like a good buy for detecting what is otherwise a life-threatening condition. However, a more revealing way to look at the data is in

Table 1 Cases detected and costs of screening with six sequential tests

No. of tests	*Total cases detected*	*Total costs ($)*	*Average costs ($)*
1	65.0465	77,511	1,175
2	71.4424	107,690	1,507
3	71.9003	130,199	1,811
4	71.9385	148,116	2,059
5	71.9417	163,141	2,268
6	71.9420	176,331	2,451

1 D. Neuhauser, A. M. Lewicki, 'What do we gain from the sixth stool guaiac?' (1975) 293 *New England Journal of Medicine* 226.

Table 2 Incremental cases detected and incremental (and marginal) costs of screening with six sequential tests

No. of tests	*Incremental cases detected*	*Incremental costs ($)*	*Marginal costs ($)*
1	65.0465	77,511	1,175
2	5.4956	30,179	5,492
3	0.4580	22,509	49,150
4	0.0382	17,917	469,534
5	0.0032	15,024	4,724,695
6	0.0003	13,190	47,107,214

terms of the extra costs incurred and the extra cases detected by each successive round of testing, as set out in Table 2. Two rounds of testing add an extra 5.5 cases detected compared with one round of testing, at an extra cost of $30,179, or $5,492 per extra case detected. Having six rounds of testing rather than five adds very little in terms of cases detected, at an extra cost per extra case detected of over $47 million. And it is this figure of $47 million which is the reason why Duncan Neuhauser and Ann Lewicki's article is so often cited. But, in opportunity cost terms, it merely indicates that the opportunity cost of spending $13,190 on having six rounds of testing rather than five is too great in that these resources could be better spent (that is produce more benefit in terms of health gain or some other maximand) on addressing another need elsewhere. The opportunity cost of having five rounds of testing rather than four is probably also too great. Using marginal analysis in this way to examine the optimal size of a programme rather than whether the programme should exist does not give 'the right answer'. It is still up to decision-makers to judge how much it is worth spending to detect another case of cancer of the colon. Using the economics framework does, however, result in a better decision than if this policy had been implemented in its absence. Thus, these concepts can, perhaps uncontroversially, be accepted as relevant to deciding what is proper in publicly funded health care.[2]

Implications of opportunity cost and marginal analysis

More generally, the implications of the concepts of opportunity cost and marginal analysis are that to have more of something, in a fixed-budget health care system, we have to have less of other things. This can be achieved in two ways. First, by delivering the same of level of service at less cost, which economists would label as being more technically efficient, or, second, if we are as technically efficient as we can be, then by reducing the level of a service which, despite being effective, is

2 See also K. Syrett, 'Rationing, resource allocation, and appropriate medical treatment' in this collection.

only marginally beneficial relative to whatever new use of resources is being proposed, leading to greater allocative efficiency. We have thus introduced two more concepts, technical and allocative efficiency, as well as our original concepts of opportunity cost and the margin, the last of which means we are rarely talking about using economic valuation to consider wiping out whole services, but rather aiding decisions on the appropriate balance of care.

Our case study illustrates all of these points well. Allocative efficiency judgements might appear, on the face of it, difficult to implement. What is often unsaid, even by health economists, is that such judgements involve the difficult reality of taking resources from one group of patients or clients to give to another. Nevertheless, most people would agree that however well-resourced a health care system is, six rounds of testing, despite being effective, is likely too much, and the resources are likely better used elsewhere. This 'thinking at the margin' is, we suggest, useful in deciding what is proper in health care.

Although fairly uncontroversial up to now, one final point by way of introducing basic economic concepts raises our first potential flash point. One interpretation of the above arguments is that economics-based frameworks might struggle with rights-based arguments if the latter implies that any claimed right to treatment should be met *regardless* of resource implications. Strictly, an economist might say that meeting such rights must be compared with the opportunity cost of doing so. This highlights rights as a relative concept. Perhaps a more conciliatory way of dealing with this potential conflict could be to say that some forms of treatment (or, strictly, the potential beneficiaries of such treatment) have as much of a right as others *to be considered* for resources. Of course, this does not get rid of resource scarcity and the associated need to evaluate publicly funded treatments in terms of their costs and benefits. Indeed, it may even exacerbate these issues. But, it might lead to more neutral questions, such as whether health economics currently has the methods in its toolbox to adequately evaluate the kinds of treatments discussed elsewhere in this collection, relative to others to which it is more conventionally applied. Nevertheless, questions that are explicitly value-laden remain, such as whose preferences should count when claims on resources for particular interventions compete with all other possible uses of such resources, or, indeed, where society insists on spending resources against the prior stated wishes of the individual concerned.

Health economics controversies with respect to what is 'proper'

We might agree that, generally, governments and health care systems are not good at recognising or managing scarcity. The usual response of governments to resource crises is to reform the health care system. However, it could be argued that all such reforms (continually) do is create new entities that still have to manage scarcity without facing up to the need to develop people and processes for doing this. Also, reform, in and of itself, is costly. We might also agree, then, that the processes required should facilitate decision-making which matches resources to needs, accepting that resource availability will be outstripped by the claims made. If agreed, then one question and two challenges present themselves with respect to operationalising the principles of opportunity cost and marginal analysis. And this is where controversies may begin to arise with respect to the issue of what is proper, such as what should be counted in economic evaluations, and how we operationalise economic evaluation in clinical and management settings.

What counts in economic evaluation?

A very general classification of what economists mean by costs and benefits is given in Table 3. Usually, a broad (societal) perspective is taken rather than just focusing on health resources or on resource use which is publicly funded. Resources used are measured in money and usually referred to as costs. However, it is important to remember that this 'money' is not the sort that can be accrued in a bank; it provides a measure of different packages of resources in a common unit through which the health (and other) benefits associated with these alternative packages can be compared. Only by having information on costs and benefits can that combination of health care activities be chosen which maximises benefit to the community from our limited budget.

For our purposes here, the more controversial part of Table 3 likely relates to the measurement of the Benefits/Outcomes column. More often than not, outcomes of health interventions are multidimensional. Health economists have developed methods for calculating quality adjusted life years (QALYs),[3] and even monetary values of health. Although disputed, even within health economics, it is important to note that one main reason for their development has been to aid decision-making with respect to resource allocation by capturing multidimensional and apparently intangible benefits of health programmes in a single unit of account. This can then be compared with the resource impacts which, as we have said, are usually more readily expressed in monetary terms. Estimating QALYs gained from treatments, or monetary valuations of health, are methodologically challenging even within the realms of standard medical interventions, but issues of gender reassignment, cosmetic surgery, abortion, and assisted dying would, no doubt, challenge them even more. Furthermore, it is not clear if even the disaggregated list of benefits/outcomes as listed in Table 3 would cover what people see as

3 The QALY approach involves measurement of gains in health according to years of life lived (whether these would be years lived anyway or extra years gained through enhanced survival), but adjusting for the quality of those years. 'Quality', here, refers to degrees of impairment or health-related quality of life. So, one year in a significant degree of impairment would not be valued as much, in QALY terms, as one year in full health. Conventionally, death might be equated to 0, and full health to 1, with various degrees of impairment ('health states') in between being allocated a score on a 0–1 scale. QALY gains would then be calculated by observing movements through health states over time, both in the presence and in the absence of the treatment being evaluated, and calculating the QALYs gained (or lost) as implied by the differential trajectories. States worse than death are allowable within this framework.

Table 3 Costs and outcomes considered for inclusion in an economic evaluation

Costs	*Benefits/Outcomes*
Costs to health care system (including cost savings): Staffing Consumables Overheads Capital	Health gains (in terms of life expectancy, quality of life or both) Health deterioration (e.g. side effects, anxiety)
Other public and third sector costs (including cost savings): Primary care Social and residential care Community services	Non-health-related effects on well-being (e.g. pregnant women may have preferences over the location for delivery of their baby)
Costs incurred by clients and family: Inputs to treatment Out of pocket expenses Time lost from work	Contributions to the economy (e.g. changes in production due to illness and treatment, welfare payments) [could be either gains or losses]

the benefits of procedures in these broad areas. Here the controversy over health economics aiding judgements about what is proper is more to do with what is left out of the above rubric. New economic metrics might be required.

For completeness, it is also worth mentioning the Costs column of Table 3. Aspects left out there, but relevant to the issues discussed elsewhere in this collection, might be resource impacts on the criminal justice system, and wider forms of social support required in various contexts. This is seen as less challenging, however, because, once identified, their measurement might be more straightforward; amounts of resource inputs tend to be measured and then multiplied by respective prices or wage rates. But some aspects can still be controversial; measuring things like productivity and welfare payments could make the 'unproductive' appear less cost-effective to treat. If time lost from work in order to be treated (on the cost side) and contributions to the economy in the form of enhanced productivity as a result of treatment (on the benefit side) are to be counted, this might mean that more vulnerable groups (older people and the unemployed) might be valued less, simply because they are not participating in the labour market. This is controversial, and practice varies around the world on whether to include such costs and benefits in economic evaluations. This is further complicated by the notion of 'friction costs'. If we count lost productivity from a societal perspective, and if an employee can be replaced, then only productivity lost during the gap between one employee leaving and another starting (the friction period) would count. Likewise with welfare costs, which essentially amount to 'transfer payments', a transfer of cash as a result of redistributive policies, (are thought to) have no impact on resources, and thus should not be counted in economic evaluations.

Operationalising opportunity cost and marginal analysis: the clinical challenge

Despite potential controversies, our economic principles present a very simple framework that can get clinicians a long way in the management of scarcity. Basically, in making service delivery choices and setting health care priorities, we want to maximise benefits and minimise opportunity costs. To achieve efficiency, we need to be able to link inputs to outputs, or costs to benefits, for the different courses of action making claims on scarce resources. The 'evidence-based medicine' movement has promoted the use of randomised trials, other controlled comparisons, and systematic reviews of effectiveness as methods to compare what works (what improves health) when examining alternative ways to treat similar groups of patients. However, though useful, 'what works' is not enough. If value for money is the goal, this means combining information on what works (or 'effectiveness') with costs. More often than not, a new proposal for treatment is compared with current practice. Linking effectiveness to costs will then allow us to determine whether a new procedure is less costly and at least as effective as its comparator (the status quo), or whether it is more costly, and more effective, than the comparator. If it is the former, then the new procedure would be judged, unequivocally, to be a better use of health care resources, or in economics language, 'dominant' and, as discussed above, 'more technically efficient'. And if it is the latter, then a judgement would have to be made about whether the extra cost of the new procedure is worth incurring given the gains in health achieved (an 'allocative efficiency' question).

The allocative efficiency question also brings us back to the notion of opportunity cost. Given that a new procedure is more beneficial but is going to cost more than current practice, should more resources be allocated to that area of care given the alternative uses of the resources available? Data on effectiveness and costs can be brought together in a matrix format (Figure 1) to aid judgements about whether a new procedure is preferable to the status quo. In Figure 1, it can be seen that, relative to the status quo, the new procedure could achieve (1) greater effectiveness, (2) the same level of effectiveness, or (3) less effectiveness. Of course, a fourth option (4) is possible whereby, after reviewing the literature, there is not enough evidence to make a judgement on whether the new procedure is more or less effective. What economics most obviously adds to the evaluation is consideration of the resource consequences of any proposed changes in the way health care is delivered. Thus, in terms of cost, a new procedure could (A) save costs, (B) result in no difference in costs, or (C) increase costs. Again, there is the possibility of there being not enough evidence to judge, as represented by row (D).

We have adapted Figure 1 from that which appeared in early editions of the Cochrane Collaboration Handbook,[4] and in a book on evidence-based health economics which one of us co-edited with Miranda Mugford and Luke

4 The Cochrane Collaboration, *Cochrane Handbook for Systematic Reviews of Interventions* (version 5.1.0, updated March 2011), available at http://www.cochrane-handbook.org/ (accessed 11 December 2014).

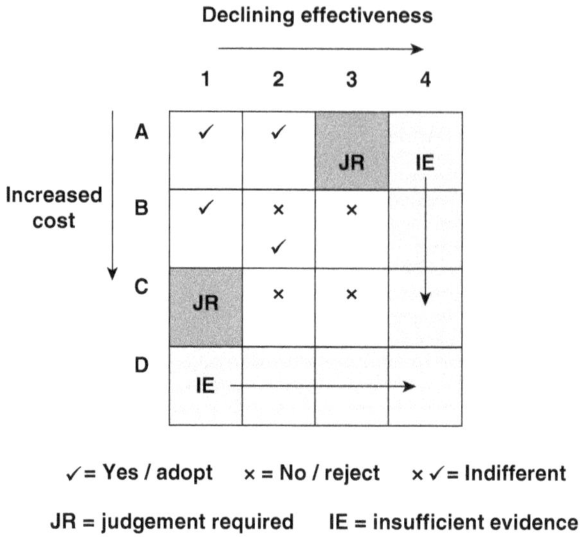

Figure 1 Matrix linking effectiveness with cost

Vale.[5] For any procedure, the optimum position on the matrix (Figure 1) is square A1, where an experimental treatment would both save costs *and* have greater effectiveness relative to current treatment. In squares A1, A2, and B1 the new procedure is more efficient and is assigned a ✓ response to the question of whether it is to be preferred to current practice. In squares B3, C2, and C3 the new procedure is less efficient, and thus receives a × response. In squares A3 and C1 a judgement would be required as to whether the more costly procedure is worthwhile in terms of the additional effectiveness gained; this is the allocative efficiency question again. All the light grey areas in the matrix represent situations in which there is not enough evidence on effectiveness, costs, or both to judge whether the new procedure is to be preferred.

Figure 1 shows that the economic approach adds the consideration of resource use to effectiveness evidence. By highlighting issues of technical efficiency and opportunity cost, this alone should make evidence-based medicine more relevant for decision-making. Indeed, this was also the view of Archie Cochrane, after whom the Cochrane Collaboration was named, and who, in his famous Rock Carling lectures in the early 1970s, made several references to the importance of health economics, from which the following quote is taken:

> Allocation of funds and facilities are nearly always based on the opinion of consultants but, more and more, requests for additional facilities will have to be

5 C. Donaldson, M. Mugford, L. Vale (eds), *Evidence-based Health Economics: From Effectiveness to Efficiency in Systematic Review* (BMJ Books, 2002).

based on detailed arguments with 'hard evidence' as to the gain to be expected from the patient's angle and the cost. Few could possibly object to this.[6]

What of the challenge to clinicians? In our view, one of the most important things clinicians can do is to categorise all interventions within their specialty according to the matrix in Figure 1. They can then ask themselves why they are not doing more of procedures in cells A1, A2, and B1, and, if they are doing them, why are they continuing with procedures in cells B3, C2, and C3. But judgements about cells A3 and C1 are trickier. They require decisions about absolutes (for example, how much is health worth?), or at least more disparate, relative comparisons (for example, hip replacements versus heart procedures). Some of the discussions elsewhere in this collection consider issues of what 'health' or 'benefit' is, and, thus, what counts on the effectiveness dimension of the above matrix.[7]

The management challenge

Turning to managers, at any level of the system at which budget constraints (scarcity) bites, five questions about resources apply. These can be portrayed as an economics approach to needs assessment, and the questions are (1) What *resources* are available in total? (2) In what ways are these *resources* currently spent? (3) What are the main candidates for more *resources*, and what would be their effectiveness and cost? (This might be characterised as a 'wish list', often of service developments.) (4) Are there any areas of care which could be provided to the same level of effectiveness but with less *resources*, so releasing those resources to fund candidates from (3)? (This is the technical efficiency question again.) (5) Are there areas of care which, despite being effective, should have less *resources* devoted to them, because a proposal (or set of proposals) from (3) is more effective (for pounds spent)? (This is the allocative efficiency question again.)

This set of questions can be applied at micro or programmatic levels, or, in principle, across programmes. One of us has argued (with Craig Mitton) in 2004,[8] and in various published papers written with senior health care managers,[9] that project management schemes have been developed for implementing these questions in ways that take account of planning cycles in health authorities, and there are now various examples of the successful development and sustained use of schemes based on answering such questions in over 150 health

6 A. L. Cochrane, *Effectiveness and Efficiency: Random Reflections on Health Services* (Nuffield Provincial Hospitals Trust, 1972) 82.

7 See M. Brazier, S. Fovargue, 'Transforming wrong into right: What is "proper medical treatment?"' and L. Frith, 'What do we mean by "proper" medical treatment?', in this collection.

8 C. Mitton and C. Donaldson, *The Priority Setting Toolkit: A Practical Guide to the Use of Economics in Health Care Decision Making* (BMJ Books, 2004)

9 C. Mitton, S. Patten, H. Waldner, C. Donaldson, 'Priority setting in health authorities: A novel approach to a historical activity' (2003) 57 *Social Science and Medicine* 1653.

organisations worldwide.[10] The essential feature of such schemes is that through extensive qualitative research, the framework has been formulated as a process that can be embedded into management systems. This research has turned the adoption process for health economics on its head. Here, we are trying to understand management systems and cycles and make the economics fit them, so opportunity cost becomes central and is the currency through which important attributes of service delivery are traded. This framework is so generic as to be able to accommodate any aspect of outcome or benefit deemed relevant by those using the framework to aid their decision-making. However, once again, it is rare for such frameworks to go beyond the outcomes and benefits listed in Table 3 above. Where they do, it is not to consider a wider set of benefits to patients, clients, or the population, but, rather, to consider whether the health organisation concerned is meeting some political objectives or targets (for example, with respect to reducing inequalities) which may have been stated recently by government.

Challenging health economics

Health economics approaches to managing scarcity can, of course, be challenged, and these challenges will relate not only to what *is* and what *should be* counted in economic evaluations but also to issues of equity. We consider such challenges in this final section, and, as far as possible, do so in relation to the examples discussed elsewhere in this collection. Before doing so, the potential conflict between legal and economic arguments must be addressed, because legal arguments are key in assessing what is proper. On the face of it, conflicts might arise between legal and economic arguments because the law often operates at the level of individual cases, whereas economic arguments are more about issues of resource allocation *across* programmes of care (that is, *groups* of people). Nevertheless, this difference might not result in as many conflicts as may be presumed. For example, many legal cases arise precisely because small or minority groups feel unjustly excluded. Although the implications of a decision in their favour may be costly at the level of any given individual, this can often be accommodated within budget because the total (opportunity) cost implications remain small (because the number of people treated is small). However, this may raise equity arguments about whether more pounds per unit of benefit *should* be spent on groups just because they are small, and we return to this below. Additionally, while the cost implications need to be addressed, it is the opportunity costs that really count. This was eloquently illustrated when media-based arguments supporting the availability of Herceptin for early breast cancer were supported by a favourable judgement from (what was

10 See e.g. C. Donaldson, G. Mooney, 'Needs assessment, priority setting and contracts for health care: An economic view' (1991) 303 *British Medical Journal* 1529; S. Peacock, D. Ruta, C. Mitton, C. Donaldson, A. Bate, M. Murtagh, 'Using economics for pragmatic and ethical priority setting: Two checklists for doctors and managers' (2006) 332 *British Medical Journal* 482.

then) the National Institute for Clinical Excellence (NICE).[11] Research showed that, at a local level of decision-making, other more cost-effective cancer therapies would have to be given up to support the NICE judgement.[12] And, more often than not, when a health authority states that its exclusion of individual cases is not to do with cost it will lose the case; whereas, those authorities that invoke the opportunity cost argument ('we had other uses of resources to consider') will tend to find themselves on stronger ground, especially if they can show they followed a defensible process to deal with difficult decisions.[13] So the economic and the legal are often more in congruence than might first be thought.

In terms of what is counted in economic evaluations, the areas discussed in this collection are, indeed, challenging. Without going into the minute details of how QALYs are constructed, an interesting question is whether this commonly used measure of health outcome would be able to capture all that is relevant in gender reassignment, cosmetic surgery, assisted dying ('death on demand'), and abortion, for example.[14] Economic studies of these interventions are limited, but there are some examples. With regard to gender reassignment and cosmetic surgery, studies have examined the impact of decisions to provide certain treatments by outlining the financial implications of elective surgery versus self-castration,[15] and the hospital admission costs associated with cosmetic surgery patients with a mental health or substance abuse diagnosis.[16] In the area of assisted dying, typically the debate centres on the ethical implications of reforming the law in order to legalise some form of it. However, economic arguments regarding possible health care savings from, for example, cases of physician-assisted suicide,[17] could augment such discussions, particularly if the economic argument is in line with the preferences of the individual. And in relation to abortion the evidence is perhaps even more detailed. During 2004 and 2005, one of us (Cam Donaldson) was Chair of the fpa (formerly the Family Planning Association) Expert Panel on the Economics of Sexual Health in England, and a researcher was employed to review

11 National Institute for Health and Clinical Excellence, *Trastuzumab for the Treatment of Early Stage HER-2 Positive Breast Cancer*, Technology Appraisal 107 (NICE, 2006).

12 R. T. Barrett, M. Small, R. D. Smith, 'How much will Herceptin really cost?' (2006) 333 *British Medical Journal* 1110.

13 For example, in 2006, Swindon Primary Care Trust lost a case in the Court of Appeal after withholding Herceptin on the grounds of exceptionality when money had, nevertheless, been set aside to provide it: *Rogers v Swindon NHS PCT* [2006] Lloyd's Rep Med 364. For discussion of the arguments used by health authorities, and their success in court, see Syrett (n 2).

14 As discussed by D. Griffiths, A. Mullock, 'The medical exception and cosmetic surgery: Culpable doctors and harmful enhancement?'; R. Huxtable, 'Death on demand: "Proper medical treatment"?'; M. Neal, 'Locating lawful abortion on the spectrum of "proper medical treatment"', in this collection.

15 M. St. Peter, A. Trinidad, M. S. Irwig, 'Self-castration by a transsexual woman: Financial and psychological costs: A case report' (2012) 9 *Journal of Sexual Medicine* 1216.

16 S. M. Wimalawansa, J. P. Fox, R. M. Johnson, 'The measurable cost of complications for outpatient cosmetic surgery in patients with mental health diagnoses' (2014) 34 *Aesthetic Surgery Journal* 306.

17 E. J. Emanuel, M. P. Battin, 'What are the potential cost savings from legalizing physician-assisted suicide?' (1998) 339 *New England Journal of Medicine* 167.

the economics of contraception and abortion, and evaluate a UK-specific policy change for each.[18] Studies have shown that the public provision of abortion *is* cost saving as well as beneficial, if unwanted births prevented is an acceptable measure of benefit (which would, indeed, seem reasonable if it is a genuine reflection of women's preferences). The UK-specific recommended policy change was for reduced delay in the provision of abortion, which was shown to be cost saving in most scenarios. The question, however, arises as to what might happen if such evaluations had shown that abortion services resulted in a net overall cost increase; how would the value of the abortions provided be measured? Studies have been undertaken of the willingness to pay for different (medical as opposed to surgical) methods of abortion,[19] but not for abortion provision in and of itself. We highlight this literature to show that economic studies of these difficult issues can (at least partially) be done. A key issue for further research is, thus, to determine the nature of preferences of such groups, before examining whether and how best to measure and value such preferences.

Finally, health economists are often accused of being too concerned with maximising output with respect to input (for example, maximising health from available resources) without paying due concern to issues of equity. However, it should be remembered that concerns for equity also arise from scarcity of resources, otherwise it would be considered fair for people to claim as much of any resource (including health care) as they wish. This means that costs and benefits still need to be measured. A concern for equity requires us to provide data on *who* accrues the benefits and incurs the costs of resource allocation decisions, in addition to *the magnitude* of such costs and benefits. It is only by estimating the costs and benefits of proposed changes of action that decisions can be made to produce a more equitable and efficient use of resources. The equity question has been debated in the health economics literature, particularly focusing on the possibility of attaching equity weights to health gains (QALYs) for different beneficiaries of care. To put this in another way, and using age as an example, a common argument in relation to elderly people who are major beneficiaries of many health services is that they should receive less priority for high-technology (high-cost, life-extending) interventions, because they have already had a 'fair innings' in terms of years of life lived.[20] But it is also argued that if they are older they will likely present for treatment with more severe conditions and, therefore, are more deserving of intervention. At the other end of the age spectrum, should health gains to children be weighted higher than for other members of the population, and, if so, where should lines be drawn? Should the same weights be applied to children of,

18 N. Armstrong, C. Donaldson, *The Economics of Sexual Health* (Family Planning Association, 2005).

19 S. Gibb, C. Donaldson, R. Henshaw, 'Assessing strength of preference for abortion method using willingness to pay' (1998) 27 *Journal of Advance Nursing* 30.

20 A. Williams, 'Intergenerational equity: An exploration of the 'fair innings' argument' (1997) 6 *Health Economics* 117.

say, ages 5 to 10 as to newborns? Should culpability count, whereby past lifestyle might weigh for or against patients when being considered for treatment? Or is it the case that one's past lifestyle is more socially determined, in which case there is less blame to be attached to people in ill health? Equally, many desirable or worthy lifestyle choices, such as sport, may cause illness or injury to participants; how are these to be handled in the light of the culpability argument?

These questions have spawned much research in recent years, among health economists and others.[21] Unfortunately, these issues are, as yet, unresolved in policy circles. Evidence shows that people will say things like 'gains to children are worth more', 'people in more severe health states should be given priority', but, as yet, it has been rare for governments to explicitly adopt a position on such issues. Likewise, members of the public may support such a principle on the face of it, but react negatively when such issues are made explicit in policy. The most famous example of this, reported by the US economist John Graham, is the abandoned attempt by the US Environmental Protection Agency to instigate a 'senior health discount' on older lives saved from environmental regulation, whereby such lives would be valued at two-thirds the rate of others.[22] When trying to sell such a notion on a road trip around the US, members of the public objected so much that the idea was dropped. This is despite the fact that the idea came from results of surveys of members of the public in the first place. Nevertheless, issues of severity and age are now entering the discourse of decision-making, even if not going as far as using explicit weights for such attributes of potential beneficiaries.[23]

Conclusion

Unless one denies scarcity of resources, the logic of economics is undeniable. Following the principles of opportunity cost and marginal analysis, it is important to measure the costs and benefits of activities which seek to enhance well-being. Only by doing this can we choose the combination of activities that maximises such well-being. However, despite such logic, this approach then raises all sorts of

21 R. Baker, I. Bateman, C. Donaldson, M. Jones-Lee, E. Lancsar, G. Loomes, H. Mason, M. Odejar, J. L. Pinto Prades, A. Robinson, M. Ryan, P. Shackley, R. Smith, R. Sugden, J. Wildman, 'Weighting and valuing quality-adjusted life-years using stated preference methods: Preliminary results from the Social Value of a QALY project' (2010) 14 *Health Technology Assessment*, available at http://www.journalslibrary.nihr.ac.uk/__data/assets/pdf_file/0011/64748/FullReport-hta14270.pdf (accessed 11 December 2014); E. Lancsar, J. Wildman, C. Donaldson, M. Ryan, R. Baker, 'Deriving distributional weights for QALYs through discrete choice experiments' (2011) 30 *Journal of Health Economics* 466.

22 J. D. Graham, *Memorandum to the President's Management Council, Benefit-Cost Methods and Life-Saving Rules* (Office of Information and Regulatory Affairs, Office of Management and Budget, Executive Office of the President, 2003).

23 M. Rawlins, D. Barnett, A. Stevens, 'Pharmacoeconomics: NICE's approach to decision making' (2010) 70 *British Journal of Clinical Pharmacology* 346.

issues with respect to equity and fairness. What counts as a cost, and what counts as a 'benefit'? In making choices, do we need to recognise that some will lose out while others gain? All of these issues place health economists on a very slippery slope. We hope that we can at least agree that the economics of proper medical treatment cannot be ignored, and, indeed, would represent a fascinating area of academic endeavour. This may require, however, more open-mindedness from non-economists about what economics can do, and from health economists about what they do do!

12 Rationing, resource allocation, and appropriate medical treatment

Keith Syrett

Introduction

The appropriateness of medical treatment has been an important talking point in the health policy arena for more than three decades. For those concerned to address the seemingly insoluble mismatch between a highly elastic demand for, and a highly inelastic supply of, health care services and treatments, the concept held much promise insofar as it was believed that it might assist in identifying and eliminating waste and inefficiency, thereby enabling scarce resources to be redeployed to more beneficial areas of health care. Indeed, there was initial optimism that development of techniques to evaluate effectiveness might provide a means of *avoiding altogether* the rationing of health care, in contradistinction to the commonly held belief that such rationing is inevitable. Thus, researchers for the RAND Corporation in the United States, who drew up the first widely accepted appropriateness methodology,[1] expressed the hope that elimination of 'ineffective' or 'unproductive' care could trim expenditure by one-third with the consequence that 'explicit rationing or stringent economic measures would not be necessary'.[2]

While subsequent developments have, perhaps, not matched up to this early ambition, appropriateness continues to occupy a high profile in the debate upon rationing in health systems, and it therefore remains important to subject the principle to detailed scrutiny. Moreover, since it is in the context of decisions upon whether a particular technology or intervention is appropriate for the treatment of a patient that the inherently contested nature of resource allocation in health care is most vividly revealed, consideration of appropriateness enables the observer of a health system to better understand the nature of opposing claims to resources and the criteria upon which they are based. In turn, this allows for critical analysis of the institutional processes and mechanisms used to manage such contestation, and, perhaps optimistically, the identification of means by which conflict may be resolved or, at least, minimised.

1 R. Brook, M. Chassin, A. Fink, D. H. Solomon, J. Kosecoff, R. E. Park, 'A method for the detailed assessment of the appropriateness of medical technologies' (1986) 2 *International Journal of Technology Assessment in Health Care* 53.

2 R. Brook, K. Lohr, 'Will we need to ration effective health care?' (1986) 3 *Issues in Science and Technology* 68, 75.

In this chapter I aim to contribute to these goals by offering an account of the manner in which appropriateness has been understood and applied to resource allocation in health care. The focus is upon the National Health Service (NHS) in the UK, although it is intended that the discussion should have broader relevance given that similar issues have arisen in health systems across the globe, notably in developed nations.[3] An additional objective is to analyse how the various readings of appropriateness translate into claims or counterclaims which can be articulated before, and, at least potentially, be resolved by a court in instances where the legal process is activated by stakeholders who contest a health care resource allocation decision. I argue that insights from systems theory may prove of value in understanding the evolution of the judicial response to such questions.

Appropriateness, demand, and need

Notwithstanding the long-standing interest in evaluation of the appropriateness of medical care, the meaning of the term remains elusive. Indeed, it has been claimed that 'most users of this concept make no attempt to define it and presumably intend to convey no more than [a] sense of "rightness" for the circumstances'.[4] However, many widely accepted definitions express the need to weigh utility against disutility; for example, the RAND Corporation methodology defined care as being appropriate when:

> for an average group of patients presenting to an average US physician . . . the expected health benefit exceeds the expected negative consequences by a sufficiently wide margin that the procedure is worth doing . . . excluding considerations of monetary cost.[5]

3 A further dimension of appropriateness is *cultural* appropriateness or acceptability, defined in respect of the right to health under the International Convention on Economic, Social and Cultural Rights (1966) as being 'respectful of the culture of individuals, minorities, peoples and communities, sensitive to gender and life-cycle requirements': Committee on Economic, Social and Cultural Rights, General Comment No. 14, E/C.12/2000/4. This dimension of appropriateness may, clearly, carry implications for the allocation of resources, but it is not the focus of the present discussion. For an account of the practical aspects of this form of appropriateness, see W. S. Tseng, J. Streltzer, *Cultural Competence in Health Care: A Guide for Professionals* (Springer, 2008), and for application in resource allocation in a particular situation, see G. Mooney, S. Jan, V. Wiseman, 'Staking a case for claims: A case study of resource allocation in Australian Aboriginal health care' (2002) 54 *Social Science and Medicine* 1657.

4 S. Buetow, B. Sibbald, J. Cantrill, S. Halliwell, 'Appropriateness in health care: Application to prescribing' (1997) 45 *Social Science and Medicine* 261, 262. For discussion of the meaning of 'proper' (which can be seen as analogous to 'appropriate') from the perspectives of health economists see C. Donaldson, R. Baker, N. McHugh, 'The economics of "proper medical treatment"', and for 'appropriate' as it relates to mental health law see J. Laing, 'Doctors' orders?: Analysing appropriate medical treatment in mental health law', in this collection.

5 Brook *et al.* (n 1). See also R. Harvey, *Making it Better: Strategies for Improving the Effectiveness and Quality of Health Services in Australia* (National Health Strategy Unit, 1991) 79, defining appropriate care as 'that strategy of action which maximises the potential health benefits valued by informed individuals or populations after considering the likely outcomes, their probabilities and their costs'.

This is important because it signifies that the *appropriateness* of care must be distinguished from the *demand* for care. A patient may desire to receive a certain health care service or treatment because they consider themselves to be ill, but it does not follow from the existence of such demand that provision of care is appropriate, notwithstanding the potency of contemporary rhetoric and policy initiatives concerning patient choice. To cite a straightforward (if crass) example, expensive cancer treatments would not be an appropriate form of care for an otherwise healthy hypochondriac who is convinced that they are suffering from the disease (although some other, undemanded, form of treatment, such as cognitive behavioural therapy, might instead be appropriate).

Before returning to the task of unpacking the meaning of appropriateness, it would be helpful to consider a further concept which is integral to decision-making on access to health care treatments, services, and technologies, and consequent expenditure upon these. 'Need' occupies a prominent position as a foundational principle of health systems and their organisation. Nye Bevan stated in 1948, at the establishment of the NHS, that 'healthcare will be provided free of charge based on clinical need and not on ability to pay',[6] and this pledge has been repeated more recently as one of the NHS's seven key 'principles'. These are described as 'enduring high-level "rules" that govern the way that the NHS operates, and defines how it seeks to achieve its purpose',[7] and are contained in the *NHS Constitution for England*, first published in 2010. But need can be distinguished from demand, with the former 'exist[ing] when an individual has an illness or a disability for which there is an effective and acceptable treatment or cure', whereas the latter 'exists when an individual considers that he has a need and wishes to receive care'.[8] It is thus evident that demand is purely patient-driven, in other words it is a matter of preference, while need is objectively determined by someone other than the patient, based upon criteria of effectiveness and acceptability. Since it is common to speak, as Bevan did, of *clinical* need as a determining factor, the most obvious gatekeeper is a clinical professional, applying her expert judgment.

However, before we reach the conclusion that clinical need and appropriateness are synonymous in the resource allocation context, two further issues warrant discussion. First, as Anthony Culyer observes, expertise in identifying both the needs of the patient and the potential for various treatments to address those needs does not necessarily connote expertise in evaluating the *worth* of the health outcome, whether this is assessed either on the basis of the individual patient (for example, the number of extra years of life which a particular treatment may be expected to yield, and in what state of health), or in terms of the health outcomes which might have to be foregone elsewhere in the population as a consequence of allocating the

6 A. Bevan, Speech in Preston, 5 July 1948.

7 Department of Health (DH), *Handbook to the NHS Constitution* (DH, 2013).

8 G. Matthew, 'Measuring need and evaluating services' in G. McLachlan (ed.), *Portfolio for Health* (Oxford University Press, 1971) 27.

treatment to the patient.[9] This leads to the second point. While it is clear that clinical need must be *present* where health care resources are allocated, as Culyer notes, 'having a need remains a necessary condition for receiving anything at all', but it is 'insufficient on its own as a distributional principle'.[10] This is so because first, need is not a monolithic concept; it may be understood in terms of present degree of ill health, or degree of ill health assessed over a lifetime, or as capacity to benefit from the treatment provided.[11] Hence, if need alone were to determine allocation, it would be necessary to establish which of these meanings is preferred. Second, allocation according to need may conflict with other goals which are considered important when distributing health care resources. For example, if we understand need in terms of capacity to benefit, the socially disadvantaged or the aged, both of whom are more likely to suffer from unrelated pre-existing health conditions which may lessen the beneficial consequences of receiving treatment, may lose out to the socially advantaged and the young, exacerbating health inequalities. Alternatively, if we construe need as related to degree of ill health, we might prioritise some whose conditions have been caused by lifestyle choices for which they might be seen to bear responsibility (such as alcoholics needing liver transplants, or smokers requiring treatment for lung cancer) over those whose conditions cannot be viewed as self-induced, but which do not present as serious and immediate a threat to health.[12] Consequently, the concept of clinical need does not (or, at least, *should* not) determine how priorities for the use of health care resources are established, but it does operate as a prerequisite to any such distribution.

It might be objected that the RAND Corporation definition of appropriateness explicitly omits considerations of cost, thus diminishing the distinction between the two concepts. However, limiting the principle in this way has been seen as unsatisfactory. Stephen Buetow and colleagues argue that 'the exclusion of financial costs is problematic because tensions arise in real life between societal resources (including money and the social and cultural values of society as a whole), the needs of the individual and the effectiveness of the intervention'.[13] Similarly, the report of a World Health Organization workshop on appropriateness noted that 'as no healthcare system can afford to provide access to all effective care, the effectiveness per unit of cost is an important dimension of appropriate care', albeit also observing that the extent to which this criterion is accorded priority over other

9 T. Culyer, 'Need – the idea won't do, but we still need it' in R. Cookson, K. Claxton (eds), *The Humble Economist: Tony Culyer on Health, Health Care and Social Decision-Making* (Office of Health Economics/University of York, 2012) 138.

10 Culyer (n 9) 152.

11 For discussion see R. Cookson, P. Dolan, 'Principles of justice in health care rationing' (2000) 26 *Journal of Medical Ethics* 323.

12 The legitimacy of merit/desert and individual responsibility as distributional principles in health care is highly contested, see R. Klein, J. Maybin, *Thinking About Rationing* (King's Fund, 2012) 7. For a recent discussion of the latter principle, see G. Bognar, I. Hirowse, *The Ethics of Health Care Rationing: An Introduction* (Routledge, 2014) ch. 6.

13 Buetow *et al.* (n 4) 263.

objectives for health services is an 'extremely contentious' matter.[14] A clear line of analysis, therefore, regards the marginalisation of resource considerations as unsuited to the realities of health systems.

Aside from underscoring the fuzziness of the concept, disagreement as to the relation of appropriateness to resources prompts two further lines of inquiry. First, how has appropriateness been understood and applied in the 'real-life' environment of policy-making in health care, particularly in respect of the distributive dimension of those policies? Second, if (as seems probable) distinctive readings of appropriateness signify differing perspectives on the concept, what are those perspectives, who holds them, and can they be reconciled? In the subsequent discussion I will seek to address these issues.

Appropriateness in health policy: the NHS

Interest in utilisation of the concept of appropriateness as a tool of health policy in the UK can arguably be traced back to the establishment of an NHS Research and Development Directorate in 1990.[15] The Directorate commissioned a Working Group to investigate the topic, and its report in 1993 sought specifically to connect appropriateness to the rational and equitable distribution of resources (which it labelled 'rationing'), stating that 'the appropriateness of healthcare interventions must also be considered . . . with regard to the justice of resource allocation'.[16] However, it stopped short of making specific policy recommendations in respect of connecting the two aspects, calling instead for 'a wider public and professional debate about the meaning of appropriate care . . . [upon which] allocation of resources will depend in part'.[17] This 'proceduralist' proposition appears to have been rooted in the Working Group's perception that differing perspectives on appropriateness (examined in greater detail below) would generate conflict, management of which should be seen as a 'political rather than a professional responsibility'.[18] As such, it accords with a growing emphasis upon processes of decision-making, rather than the substantive criteria upon which such decisions might be based, in contested fields of public policy in general[19] and in health care resource allocation in particular.[20]

14 WHO Regional Office for Europe, *Appropriateness in Health Care Services: Report on a WHO Workshop* (Copenhagen, WHO EUR/00/5022388, 2000) 5.

15 See M. Peckham, 'Research and development for the National Health Service' (1991) 338 *Lancet* 367.

16 Report of a Working Group prepared for the Director of Research and Development of the NHS Management Executive, 'What do we mean by appropriate health care?' (1993) 2 *Quality In Health Care* 117, 117.

17 Report of a Working Group (n 16) 122.

18 Report of a Working Group (n 16) 120.

19 See e.g. J. Black, 'Proceduralising regulation: Part I' (2000) 20 *Oxford Journal of Legal Studies* 597; J. Black, 'Proceduralising regulation: Part II' (2001) 21 *Oxford Journal of Legal Studies* 33.

20 Notably the model of 'accountability for reasonableness' developed by Norman Daniels and James Sabin, see *Setting Limits Fairly: Learning to Share Resources for Health* (2nd edn, Oxford University Press, 2008).

The attention given to appropriateness can best be understood as a dimension of the wider evidence-based medicine (EBM) movement, which burgeoned from the 1980s onward, and of which the research carried out by the RAND Corporation formed a part. EBM has been defined as:

> the conscientious, explicit, and judicious use of current best evidence in making decisions about the care of individual patients. The practice of EBM means integrating individual clinical expertise with the best available external clinical evidence from systematic research . . . External clinical evidence both invalidates previously accepted diagnostic tests and treatments and replaces them with new ones that are more powerful, more accurate, more efficacious, and safer.[21]

The connection between EBM and appropriateness, which is readily apparent within this passage, was explored further in the Working Group report. Illustrative of this was its reference to research revealing variation in coronary artery bypass surgery between the US and the UK.[22] The Working Group commented that the:

> differences may reflect not only the different cultural values of the societies of the United States and United Kingdom and the values of the panellists but also the fact that the reviews of the published literature submitted to the panels have not used scientific methods to generate the summarised evidence. Original but basically statistically unsound papers may have been given equal or near equal weight as more valid work, and unpublished but sound work resulting in negative observations may not be available for review.[23]

Accordingly, the Working Group believed that it was important to 'develop measures of professional appropriateness based upon scientific evidence of appropriateness'.[24] While the nature of such evidence remained unspecified, techniques such as the randomised controlled trial, the 'gold standard' for evaluation of therapeutic interventions,[25] and the meta-analysis of such trials,[26] became widely used during the latter part of the twentieth century and afforded the 'underlying basis' for EBM.[27]

21 D. L. Sackett, W.M.C. Rosenberg, J. A. Muir Gray, R. B. Haynes, W. S. Richardson, 'Evidence based medicine: What it is and what it isn't' (1996) 312 *British Medical Journal* 71, 71.

22 R. H. Brook, R. E. Park, J. B. Kosecof, M. R. Chassin, C. M. Winslow, J. R. Hampton, 'Diagnosis and treatment of coronary disease: Comparison of doctors' attitudes in the USA and UK' (1988) 331 *Lancet* 750.

23 Report of a Working Group (n 16) 118.

24 Report of a Working Group (n 16) 122.

25 See D. McGovern, 'Randomized controlled trials' in D. McGovern, R. Valori, W. Summerskill, M. Levi, *Key Topics in Evidence-Based Medicine* (BIOS Scientific Publishers, 2001) 27.

26 See e.g. R. DerSimonian, N. Laird, 'Meta-analysis in clinical trials' (1986) 7 *Controlled Clinical Trials* 177.

27 H. Stolberg, G. Norman, I. Trop, 'Randomized controlled trials' (2004) 183 *American Journal of Roentgenology* 1539, 1539.

Of course, as noted by the Working Group, gathering evidence which might inform decisions on appropriateness is insufficient on its own.[28] Such evidence requires dissemination if more appropriate care is to be delivered. A key tool in this regard, indeed the 'main vehicle for implementing EBM', has been the clinical guideline, defined as a 'systematically developed statement to assist practitioner and patient decisions about appropriate health care for specific clinical circumstances'.[29] Guidelines seek to foster best practice and thus enhance quality of care, in addition to reducing variation in clinical practice. Their value to medical practitioners has been explained as follows:

> They offer explicit recommendations for clinicians who are uncertain how to proceed, overturn the beliefs of doctors accustomed to outdated practices, improve the consistency of care, and provide authoritative recommendations that reassure practitioners about the appropriateness of their treatment policies. Guidelines based on a critical appraisal of scientific evidence (evidence based guidelines) clarify which interventions are of proved benefit and document the quality of the supporting data. They alert clinicians to interventions unsupported by good science, reinforce the importance and methods of critical appraisal, and call attention to ineffective, dangerous and wasteful practices.[30]

Thus far, the discussion has centred on notions of *clinical effectiveness* as a dimension of appropriateness, but the reference to wastefulness provides an insight into the connection between EBM, appropriateness, and resource allocation in the 'monument to institutionalised scarcity' that is the NHS.[31] Notwithstanding claims that 'doctors practising evidence based medicine will identify and apply the most efficacious interventions to maximise the quality and quantity of life for individual patients; this may raise rather than lower the cost of their care',[32] evidence derived from methods such as randomised controlled trials could easily be utilised in support of rationing because it not only assisted in the determination of what was appropriate but also of that which was *inappropriate*.

The association between provision of evidence and reduction in the costs of health care was recognised at an early stage, as the work of the RAND Corporation makes clear.[33] In the UK, the first Director of Research and Development in the NHS and Department of Health, Sir Michael Peckham, estimated that

28 Report of a Working Group (n 16) 121. See also J. Grimshaw, A. Hutchinson, 'Clinical practice guidelines: Do they enhance value for money in health care?' (1995) 51 *British Medical Bulletin* 927, 929.

29 M. Field, K. Lohr (eds), *Clinical Practice Guidelines: from Development to Use* (National Academy Press, 1992) 2.

30 S. Woolf, R. Grol, A. Hutchinson, M. P. Eccles, J. M. Grimshaw, 'Potential benefits, limitations and harms of clinical guidelines' (1999) 318 *British Medical Journal* 527, 528.

31 R. Klein, P. Day, S. Redmayne, *Managing Scarcity* (Open University Press, 1996) 37.

32 Sackett *et al.* (n 21) 72.

33 Brook and Lohr (n 2). See also Grimshaw and Hutchinson (n 28).

£1 billion could be saved every year by eliminating 'ineffective' treatments.[34] To this end, health authorities in the NHS were requested in 1993 to take clinical effectiveness and clinical guidelines into account when purchasing services for their local populations.[35] Subsequently, national planning guidance expressed the objective that the NHS should invest 'an increasing proportion of resources in interventions known to be effective and reduce investment in interventions shown to be less effective', entailing reduction in investment in at least two interventions which evidence had shown to be ineffective.[36]

Clinical guidelines played an important role in this regard. Klein, Day, and Redmayne note that the creation of the 'internal market' in the NHS by the Health and Community Care Act 1990 exposed the fact that a number of health authorities were explicitly excluding certain treatments at the margins of health care, including tattoo removal, breast augmentation, and reversal of sterilisation or vasectomy, from the 'menu' of services available to their populations.[37] In these instances, the question of appropriateness rested upon conceptions of the nature of ill health or, to put matters differently, whether *any* patient could be said to exhibit a clinical need for such interventions *in any circumstances*. However, this form of rationing was controversial because it both limited clinical discretion and because it suggested a 'weakening of the NHS's commitment to a comprehensive service'.[38] By contrast, guidelines served to 'remedicalise' decisions up on which treatments and services it was appropriate for health authorities to provide,[39] grounding these in objective, clinically oriented evidence as distinct from value judgments as to the proper scope and goals of a health system. Moreover, since they took a non-mandatory form, they did not override the judgment of individual physicians. In principle, therefore, they offered a more legitimate means to 'promote distributive justice, advocating better delivery of services to those in need . . . [functioning to] improve the efficiency of healthcare [by] free[ing] up resources needed for other (more equitably distributed) healthcare services'.[40] Yet this is arguably to understate the political dimension of guidelines, and, by extension, EBM in general, which may be used 'to modify the behaviour of practitioners to steer their decisions toward actions that the policy-makers consider desirable'.[41] In particular, the inclusion

34 N. Timmins, 'NHS wastes £1 billion on ineffective treatments' (*The Independent*, 2 January 1996).

35 NHS Management Executive, *Improving Clinical Effectiveness* (NHS Management Executive, 1993, (EL(93)115)).

36 NHS Executive, *Priorities and Planning Guidance for the NHS: 1995/96* (NHS Executive, 1994 (EL(94)55)).

37 Klein *et al.* (n 31) 68–70.

38 B. New, J. LeGrand, *Rationing in the NHS: Principles and Pragmatism* (King's Fund, 1996) 16.

39 Klein *et al.* (n 31) 71–72.

40 Woolf *et al.* (n 30) 527.

41 D. Eddy, 'Clinical decision-making: From theory into practice: Guidelines for policy statements: The explicit approach' (1990) 263 *Journal of the American Medical Association* 2239, 2243. See also O. Norheim, 'Healthcare rationing – Are additional criteria needed for assessing evidence based clinical practice guidelines?' (1999) 319 *British Medical Journal* 1426.

of *cost-effectiveness*, which is regarded as a principal desirable attribute of clinical guidelines,[42] as an additional criterion of appropriateness 'complicates the definition of evidence'.[43]

Cost-effectiveness analysis enables the relative costs and outcomes of medical interventions to be compared. The most widely deployed measure of outcomes is the Quality Adjusted Life Year (QALY), this being the arithmetic product of life expectancy and the quality of the remaining life-years (the latter being measured on a scale where 1 is a state of perfect health and 0 is death). This 'common currency' can be combined with monetary data to enable comparisons to be made between interventions as to the cost of generating a year of perfect health.[44] In this manner, priorities can be established, most obviously in respect of different forms of treatment for the same condition but, potentially, also between different conditions; for example, the cost of treating coronary heart disease compared with the cost of treating prostate cancer.

Evaluation of cost-effectiveness began to emerge as a dimension of clinical guidelines in the UK in the mid-1990s,[45] but unquestionably the most significant development in this regard was the establishment of what was then called the National Institute for Clinical Excellence (NICE) in April 1999.[46] NICE was mandated to 'provide the NHS . . . in England and Wales with authoritative, robust and reliable guidance on current "best practice"',[47] with secondary legislation specifying that its functions included promotion of 'the effective use of available resources'.[48] A particular objective was to reduce geographical inequity in access to treatment, so-called postcode prescribing.[49] To this end, NICE issued clinical guidelines which provided health professionals with information on best practice in the management of specified conditions, and technology appraisals in which NICE assessed whether new medical technologies should be made available on the NHS, based upon clinical evidence of effectiveness and deploying the QALY as a means of evaluating cost-effectiveness. Although non-mandatory in form, and, in particular, not intended to override clinical judgment, the NICE clinical guideline could be regarded as constituting an authoritative, evidence-based statement of appropriate modes of care, while the Institute's appraisal recommendations functioned, in effect, to determine which new (and often costly)

42 Field and Lohr (n 29) 141.

43 S. Saarni, H. Gylling, 'Evidence based medicine guidelines: A solution to rationing or politics disguised as science?' (2004) 30 *Journal of Medical Ethics* 171, 172.

44 See C. Phillips, *What is a QALY?* (Hayward Publishing, 2009).

45 See C. Ham, 'Health care rationing' (1995) 310 *British Medical Journal* 1483.

46 Now renamed the National Institute for Health and Care Excellence: Health and Social Care Act 2012, s. 232.

47 National Institute for Clinical Excellence (NICE), *A Guide to Our Work* (NICE, 1999), Introduction.

48 National Institute for Clinical Excellence (Establishment and Constitution) Order, SI 1999/220, Art. 3.

49 For discussion see K. Syrett, 'NICE and the problem of "postcode prescribing" in the English National Health Service' in A. den Exter, M. Buijsen (eds), *Rationing Health Care: Hard Choices and Unavoidable Trade-Offs* (Maklu, 2012).

technologies it was appropriate for the NHS to provide given limitations on its available resources.[50]

With NICE now established as a central feature of the health policy landscape, appropriateness continues to constitute a significant dimension of efforts to limit health care expenditure in the NHS. Indeed, the concept has arguably acquired additional weight as a consequence of austerity measures being applied to this health system, as well as others, in response to the global financial crisis that commenced in 2007. For example, the publication of an *NHS Atlas of Variation in Healthcare* in 2010 was designed to demonstrate to those commissioning health care in England that there was a 'need to focus on appropriateness of the clinical service, and to investigate the possibilities that there is overuse of some technologies, with some lower value activities being undertaken'.[51] This would, in turn, help to increase value from the resources allocated to the NHS. A subsequent briefing issued by the Audit Commission was even more explicit as to the connection between appropriateness and financial stringency, noting that identification and elimination of 'low clinical value treatments' would assist in meeting the 'Nicholson Challenge' to the NHS, that it should achieve £15–£20 billion of efficiency savings between 2011 and 2014.[52]

Appropriateness and resources in the English courts

It should be readily apparent from the preceding discussion that the concept of appropriateness is multidimensional. As the Working Group of the NHS Directorate of Research and Development noted in 1993, differing stakeholders will possess differing perspectives as to the meaning of the term, and the aspects which they consider to be most significant. Those which were identified included the professional perspective, defined as focusing upon 'those interventions that most contribute to health gain'; the perspective of the individual patient, or 'effectiveness modified by patient characteristics and patient preference'; and the societal perspective, in which effectiveness is 'constrained by societal judgments of the value of different interventions and by available resources'.[53] The concept, therefore, offers ample scope for contestation between those who would seek to claim, and those who would seek to restrict, access to health care resources, and one forum in which such disagreements may be played out is the courtroom. This is

50 NICE's crucial role in establishing the scope of NHS coverage is underlined by an obligation upon those commissioning care to fund its technology appraisal recommendations: see National Institute for Health and Social Care Excellence (Constitution and Functions) and the Health and Social Care Information Centre (Functions) Regulations 2013, SI 2013/259, Regs. 7 and 8; *NHS Constitution* (n 7), s. 3a.

51 NHS, *The NHS Atlas of Variation in Healthcare* (NHS, 2010) 9.

52 Audit Commission, *Reducing Spending on Low Clinical Value Treatments* (Audit Commission, 2011) 3. The Nicholson Challenge is named after the former Chief Executive of NHS England. It was first articulated in May 2009: D. Nicholson, *The Year: NHS Chief Executive's Annual Report 2008/09* (DH, 2009) 47.

53 Report of a Working Group (n 16) 117, 118.

especially likely given that the shift to explicit modes of rationing, of which the developments described herein form an important part, are now well known to have engendered a degree of systemic instability, one symptom of which is resort to litigation.[54]

It might be contended that all legal challenges to decisions to restrict access to health care technologies and services on grounds of resources hinge, to some degree, on questions of appropriateness. Simple *demand* is, undoubtedly, insufficient. Any patient who cannot at least demonstrate a clinical need for treatment will not meet the threshold test of arguability, which is a precursor to exercise of the judicial review jurisdiction.[55] Instead, the crux of the case is likely to be a dispute between a patient with a clinical need, defined as such by a health professional, who argues that a particular treatment will effectively produce health gain given her individual circumstances, and a body undertaking the commissioning of health care which contends that the treatment in question is not clinically effective and/or cost-effective, particularly in the light of its obligations to the wider population for which it is responsible. However, within these admittedly broad parameters, it is possible to identify two categories of litigation in which the aspects of appropriateness discussed above are especially closely engaged, and which therefore best illuminate the judicial attitude on this matter. First, there are cases involving appropriateness *strictu sensu*, those involving treatments or services at the margins of health care for which the very notion of the existence of any clinical need is in some question. Second, there are cases in which allocative decisions are premised on application of the guidelines which, as noted in the preceding section, might be viewed as constituting definitive contemporary statements of appropriateness from the perspective of clinical effectiveness and cost-effectiveness.

Within the first group fall two cases relating to transsexualism. In *R v North West Lancashire Health Authority, ex parte A, D and G*,[56] the health authority refused funding for gender reassignment surgery as a treatment for gender identity dysphoria. It did so in accordance with two policies which allocated low priority to procedures considered to be of no beneficial health gain or proven benefit, and which sought to ensure that resources were used appropriately. Evidence presented to the court indicated that the authority regarded the effectiveness of surgery as unproven and considered the condition to be one in respect of which it was 'difficult to imagine what an exceptional clinical need for services might be', given that it did not view gender dysphoria as having the status of a disease, but rather as being 'related to a desire to achieve an ideal body image or a bodily function that cannot currently be achieved'.[57] Its decision to refuse funding was quashed both at first instance and on appeal. In the Court of Appeal, Auld LJ conceded that it was for the authority to judge what might be effective treatment for transsexualism, but held that a

54 For discussion see K. Syrett, *Law, Legitimacy and the Rationing of Health Care: A Contextual and Comparative Perspective* (Cambridge University Press, 2007).

55 See *Sharma v Brown-Antoine* [2006] UKPC 57.

56 [2000] 1 WLR 977, CA.

57 *A, D and G* (n 56) 986–987.

policy which, in practice, acted as a 'blanket ban' on this form of treatment was an unlawful fetter on discretion given that the authority had, in fact, acknowledged before the court that transsexualism *was* an illness.[58] Buxton LJ also took the view that the authority had failed to demonstrate that it had accorded a sufficient degree of rational consideration to a 'substantial literature' that indicated that the treatment was clinically effective, because it had provided no explanation of its position on this matter.[59]

In contrast, in *R (AC) v Berkshire West Primary Care Trust*,[60] a refusal to fund breast augmentation surgery for a patient who had undergone gender reassignment was upheld in court. In this case, the Trust had also allocated low priority to gender reassignment surgery on the basis of limited evidence of clinical effectiveness, coupled with the absence of any evidence of cost-effectiveness. It did provide funding for certain core surgical procedures for reassignment patients (even though no professional consensus existed as to the classification of core and non-core procedures) but breast augmentation was not classified as core, being bracketed with procedures of a cosmetic character. Some judicial criticism of the use of the latter adjective was expressed by Bean J at first instance, since such use suggested a perception on the part of the Trust that treatment was not appropriate, that is, the patient was seeking it 'in order to look more attractive', when it had accepted that the patient had a psychological illness.[61] However, the decisive question was the classification of treatment as non-core. In this regard, the Trust had acted lawfully. The clinical evidence of effectiveness was contested, and the Trust had explained its position in respect of such evidence;[62] it was obliged to make 'very difficult choices' on funding in the light of its statutory responsibilities,[63] and, unlike the North West Lancashire Health Authority, it had provided adequately for exceptions to the policy not to fund the treatment.

To turn to the second of the categories of cases, *R v North Derbyshire Health Authority, ex parte Fisher* is notable as the first judicial review challenge to be lost by a health authority; it concerned the issuing of national guidance by the NHS Executive on the use of beta-interferon for treatment of multiple sclerosis.[64] Given the authorship of the document in this case,[65] it cannot be considered a true clinical guideline, but, insofar as it contained clinical advice on the drug and its goal was expressed to be intended to 'target the drug appropriately at patients who

58 *A, D and G* (n 56) 994.

59 *A, D and G* (n 56) 999.

60 [2010] EWHC 1162 (Admin); [2011] EWCA Civ 247.

61 *AC* [2010] (n 60) para. 16.

62 Thus, the Trust's Priorities Committee had noted the 'poor quality' of evidence on clinical effectiveness of gender reassignment surgery 'due to lack of standardised criteria for assessment and management', evidence of varying degrees of complications and patient satisfaction, and the absence of any evidence on cost-effectiveness: *AC* [2010] (n 60) para. 13.

63 *AC* [2011] (n 60) para. 35, *per* Hooper LJ.

64 (1997) 38 BMLR 76.

65 The NHS Executive, part of the DH, advised ministers on the development of NHS policy and was responsible for effective management of the service. It was wound up in 2002.

are most likely to benefit from treatment',[66] it performed a similar function. The authority, which was unconvinced of the clinical effectiveness of beta-interferon and which believed it was not cost-effective, refused to follow the guidance, which provided that patients with multiple sclerosis should be referred to a hospital neurologist for consideration as to whether treatment with the drug was appropriate. Instead, it sought to restrict funding to those patients who were participating in a randomised controlled trial, although the NHS Executive had indicated that any such trial would take several years to produce results and that purchasers should make funding decisions based upon the existing state of knowledge of the drug's clinical effectiveness and cost effectiveness. This position was held to be unlawful, the court holding that the authority had failed to take account of the essential requirements of the guidance in adopting its policy, not because it considered that there were special circumstances which exceptionally justified departure, but 'principally because they disagreed with it altogether'.[67]

Fisher predated the establishment of NICE as an authoritative source of clinical guidelines, but it was followed in *R (Rose) v Thanet Clinical Commissioning Group*.[68] Here, Thanet Clinical Commissioning Group refused a sufferer of Crohn's disease funding for oocyte cryopreservation, notwithstanding that NICE had issued a clinical guideline strongly recommending that patients in this position should be offered the treatment on the basis that it would be clinically effective and beneficial in the majority of cases, as well as cost-effective.[69] Once again, scepticism as to the clinical effectiveness of the treatment underpinned the policy not to fund the intervention, and, again, this position was deemed unlawful, albeit *obiter*. The claimant lost the case on the basis that the challenge was to the 'legally unobjectionable' decision not to reopen her individual funding request on grounds of exceptionality, given that she had presented no new clinical information to justify such reopening.[70] But, applying the decision in *Fisher*, Jay J held that while there was no obligation on the Clinical Commissioning Group (CCG) to comply with the guideline (which has a non-mandatory status under the regulatory scheme),[71] it could not simply disagree with it in the absence of some special factor which exceptionally justified doing so, and, in the alternative, it had failed to put forward any clear, lawful reasons for departing from the NICE recommendation.[72] The judge noted that the effect of the ruling was 'that in reality the CCG could not lawfully disagree with the medical or scientific rationale for NICE's recommendation in relation to oocyte cryopreservation'.[73] The outcome of the case would thus have been different had the challenge focused on the general funding policy.

66 NHS Executive, *New Drugs for Multiple Sclerosis*, EL (95)97 (DH, 1995) para. 6.

67 *Fisher* (n 64) 89, *per* Dyson J.

68 [2014] EWHC 1182 (Admin).

69 NICE, *Fertility: Assessment and Treatment for people with fertility problems* (NICE, 2013, CG156).

70 *Rose* (n 68) para. 102.

71 National Institute for Health and Social Care Excellence (Constitution and Functions) and the Health and Social Care Information Centre (Functions) Regulations 2013, SI 2013/259, Reg. 5.

72 *Rose* (n 68) paras. 116, 131.

73 *Rose* (n 68) para. 131.

What conclusions can be drawn from these cases? First, it is apparent that the English courts do not routinely privilege the 'patient perspective' on appropriateness (as outlined in the Working Group report)[74] over other approaches. Patients succeeded in their challenges in *A, D and G* and *Fisher* but failed in the other two cases; albeit that in *Rose* the judge expressed sympathy for much of the claimant's argument in respect of the general policy on funding. However, it should be noted that *A, D and G* establishes the principle, later encapsulated in statutory Directions,[75] that those making decisions on access to treatments and services are obliged to give proper consideration to those particular circumstances of the patient's case which might warrant departure from a general policy not to fund. In this respect, courts might be seen to be especially attentive towards the patient perspective while not regarding this as decisive, as the decision in *Rose* demonstrates. In so acting, they are also according weight to an aspect of the 'professional perspective', since the mechanism through which such exceptional criteria must now be assessed by the body commissioning health care, the individual funding request, will in practice be activated by a clinician making a request for treatment on the patient's behalf based upon evaluation of the health gain likely to eventuate in view of the patient's clinical status.[76] This was the process used in both *AC* and *Rose*, while the treating doctors in *Fisher* and *A, D and G* also supported the arguments of the patients for access to treatment. As I have already noted, a reviewing court would surely not entertain a claim of this type if it was simply based upon mere patient preference in the absence of professionally determined clinical need; so the coincidence of these two perspectives in judicial determinations is perhaps unsurprising.

A second observation relates to the important role played by evidence in shaping the responses of the judiciary to the conflicting perspectives on appropriateness. In all four of these cases, the courts accorded considerable weight to evidence on effectiveness, the allocative decision-maker's engagement (or lack of it) with *clinical* evidence being a decisive factor in the ultimate outcome. In two of the cases, *Fisher* and *Rose*, the evidence was contained in guidelines disseminated on a national basis by an authorised body (respectively, the NHS Executive and NICE). While the former case differed from the latter insofar as the guidelines were not purely clinical in nature, they had been formulated in an effort to realise specific clinical objectives as recommended by the Standing Medical Advisory Committee, a body whose scientific advisory role was later assumed by NICE, albeit that NICE engages more closely with the principles and methodologies of EBM than did the Committee. By contrast, there were no national guidelines at play in *A, D and G* or *AC*, but the courts, nonetheless, took note of professional consensus on

74 Report of a Working Group (n 16).

75 Directions to Primary Care Trusts and NHS Trusts concerning decisions about drugs and other treatments 2009, Dir. 2(3)(b).

76 For critical discussion of this process see A. Ford, 'The concept of exceptionality: A legal farce?' (2012) 20 *Medical Law Review* 304.

effectiveness in each case, there being a 'strong and respectable body of medical opinion' that treatment was clinically effective in the former case,[77] while there was 'no agreement' as to clinical effectiveness in the latter.[78] Significantly, it was only in the last of these cases, where the evidence of effectiveness was limited, that departure from it was regarded as permissible by the court, although the decision of the CCG in *Rose* was deemed lawful in other respects.

Two deductions are possible from this. First, one might surmise that the evidence-based evolution of the professional perspective on appropriateness called for by the Working Group in 1993 has found its place in the courtroom.[79] It is now necessary to distinguish the perspective of the treating physician from that of others with clinical expertise who are not engaged in providing care to the patient, but rather in the production of evidence, via clinical guidelines or a more informal consensus, for their fellow professionals to utilise in specific treatment scenarios. While the goal of both groups of professionals is to bring about health gain, the concern of the former is for the health gain of the *individual patient*, whereas the latter necessarily take a more detached standpoint to assess *average gain across a range of patients suffering from the condition in question.* The latter perspective may well connect more closely to the societal perspective identified by the Working Group insofar as it is likely to entail consideration of the relative value of different interventions to treat the same condition, although it should be noted that there remains a degree of resistance to the utilisation of evidence of clinical effectiveness for purposes of husbandry of scarce health care resources.[80] Second, it appears that this professional societal perspective on appropriateness is regarded by the English courts as possessing the greatest potency, given that where such evidence clearly points to provision of access to a particular treatment, the courts expect compliance or, at the very least, reasoned explanation of the failure to comply (as stated in *A, D and G*) or special factors which might justify so doing (as stated in *Rose*).

As regards evidence of cost-effectiveness, it was only the treatment at issue in *Rose* which was evaluated (to positive effect) using the full range of contemporary methodologies and metrics of health economics. In *AC*, no evidence on cost-effectiveness was available. This also appears to have been the case in *A, D and G*, although the matter receives no specific mention in the judgments of either court. The guidelines in *Fisher* did make reference to 'further consideration . . . being given to the funding consequences on hospital and community health services of the introduction of beta-interferon for 1996/7 and beyond';[81] however, the purpose of the guidelines was, in large part, precisely to enable both clinical

77 *A, D and G* (n 56) 997, *per* Buxton LJ.
78 *AC* [2010] (n 60) para. 22.
79 See (n 24) and accompanying text.
80 See e.g. R. Broughton, B. Rathbone, *What Makes A Good Clinical Guideline?* (Hayward Publishing, 2001) 2: 'Guidelines that have cost reduction as their main rationale may not always be an appropriate basis on which to make a clinical decision'.
81 NHS Executive (n 66) para. 9.

and cost outcomes to be monitored and evaluated prior to licensing of the drug, indicating that evidence on cost-effectiveness was, at that stage, limited.[82]

Given the relative scarcity of evidence of cost-effectiveness in these cases, one might suppose that the courts would not regard this as a decisive factor in determining the lawfulness of the position adopted by the various decision-makers. Certainly, this assessment appears accurate in respect of *A, D and G* and *AC*, where the courts indicated that scarcity of resources necessitated making 'very difficult choices as what procedures to fund'[83] in order to 'provide the most benefit with the most significant impact for [the local] population',[84] this being a choice which should be left to the authority concerned. However, the position is somewhat different in the two guidelines cases. Clinical considerations were more prevalent than those of cost in *Rose*, but it seems plausible to assume that the determination by NICE that oocyte cryopreservation was effective in respect of cost as well as clinical aspects strengthened the obligation to comply, or to offer evidence of special factors which justified departure, notwithstanding that no mandatory funding obligation attaches to this form of clinical guideline. As for *Fisher*, there was a clear difference of opinion between the NHS Executive, which wished to measure the cost implications of the introduction of beta-interferon, and the health authority, which had already formed a view that the treatment was not cost-effective. Dyson J accepted the proposition that the authority was under a duty not to overspend and that its decisions needed to be taken against a backdrop of scarce resources, but rejected its argument that a small sum which had notionally been allocated to fund the drug could not equitably be utilised because it was insufficient to meet all clinical needs for it.[85] In so doing, the judge effectively privileged the approach to cost considerations taken in the national guideline over the view taken by the health authority as to how limited resources might most appropriately be spent on its local population. One might accordingly posit a further modification of the categories identified by the Working Group, albeit one which fuses with that previously identified, namely, a professional perspective which evaluates the appropriateness of treatments utilising objective cost-effectiveness criteria (latterly, the QALY) applicable across the patient population as a whole against a backdrop of scarce resources, thus taking account of a societal perspective. This is to be distinguished from the purely managerial perspective of the health authority, which is also constrained by limited resources but which is driven by solely local factors. The obligations to utilise scarce resources to meet the health needs of the local population and not to overspend the annual budget appear not to be so

82 The drug was subsequently appraised by NICE, which recommended against general availability on the NHS on cost-effectiveness grounds: *Beta Interferon and glatiramer acetate for the treatment of multiple sclerosis* (NICE, 2002, TA32). However, a 'risk-sharing scheme' agreed between the four UK governments and pharmaceutical manufacturers, underpinned by a statutory funding obligation in respect of eligible patients, enabled access.

83 *AC* [2011] (n 60) para. 35, *per* Hooper LJ.

84 *AC* [2010] (n 60) para. 24, *per* Bean J. See also *A, D and G* (n 56) 991, *per* Auld LJ.

85 *Fisher* (n 64) 91.

open-ended that they entitle the decision-maker to disregard the professional perspective on what can appropriately be afforded, albeit that considerable discretion is retained in situations where evidence of cost-effectiveness is limited, or absent.

Finally, an interesting comparison can be drawn between these cases and those heard in the US. It has been claimed that US courts are relatively unreceptive to arguments advanced by insurers that specific forms of care should not be covered on health plans because they are deemed to be inappropriate. This is so whether the basis for the insurers' decision on (in)appropriateness is a professional consensus statement or more scientifically grounded criteria, and whoever is the source of the evaluation (for example, federal agency, professional association, or the insurer itself).[86] This might suggest that there exists a tendency among American judges to favour the patient perspective on appropriateness, an approach which may well be rooted in the more individualistic character of health provision in the US.[87] The preceding analysis indicates that the attitude of the English judiciary to the question of appropriateness is more equivocal and nuanced than that of their American brethren. Certainly, the acknowledgment of the imperative to set priorities for expenditure of scarce resources so as to meet the needs of the wider population for whose health needs the body has responsibility, which was most overt in *A, D and G* and *AC*,[88] suggests some judicial recognition of the value of social solidarity on which the NHS is founded.

Conclusion

The four cases analysed in the preceding section demonstrate the multifaceted nature of the concept of appropriateness as it relates to scarcity of health care resources. These cases are characterised by multiple readings of the factual scenario: the emotive claims of the patient; the individualised experiential judgment of the treating physician who acts as advocate for that patient; the objective, aggregative scientific and social scientific evidence of clinical effectiveness and cost-effectiveness; and the managerial political prioritisation choices of the allocative decision-maker.

The first wave of English judicial review challenges to rationing decisions, culminating in the decision of the Court of Appeal in *R v Cambridge Health Authority, ex parte B*,[89] was marked by judicial reluctance to accord preference to any one of these readings over others. Dicta such as '[t]hey are questions to be raised, answered and dealt with outside the court',[90] '[t]he court by this application is being asked

86 G. Anderson, M. Hall, T. Rust Smith, 'When courts review medical appropriateness' (1998) 36 *Medical Care* 1295. Note, however, that the research covered cases from 1960 to 1994, many of which, therefore, preceded the emergence of the EBM movement.

87 For discussion see e.g. J. Sabin, 'Individualism, solidarity and US health care' (2012) 14 *Virtual Mentor* 415; M. Crowley (ed.), *Connecting American Values with Health Reform* (Hastings Center, 2009).

88 See (n 83) and (n 84) and accompanying text.

89 [1995] 1 WLR 898.

90 *R v Central Birmingham Health Authority, ex parte Walker* (1987) 3 BMLR 32, *per* Macpherson J.

to conduct an investigation which it has no power to conduct',[91] and '[t]hat is not a judgment which the court can make',[92] reflect the courts' unwillingness to engage with the competing perspectives, although the practical consequence of this extreme judicial deference was that the priority-setting choice of the health authority remained intact. By contrast, the four cases discussed here, which range from the first judicial review case decided after *ex parte B* to the most recent in the field, show that English judges are now prepared to mediate in a more thorough fashion between the varying perspectives on appropriateness in order to determine whether access to treatments and services can lawfully be restricted or denied. The catalyst for so doing appears to be the availability of objective evidence on effectiveness, the normal expectation being that such evidence will be respected, absent special factors, when it points clearly to a particular outcome. EBM and cost-effectiveness analysis have thus afforded the judiciary 'purchase' in these cases, such that arguments of non-justiciability, as articulated in the early judicial review cases,[93] no longer appear germane in this context.

It is interesting to speculate why this shift in judicial attitudes has occurred, and I suggest that some understanding of this can be gained by application of insights derived from systems theory. Following Niklas Luhmann, it might be posited that medicine, politics (here, taking the form of priority-setting by the allocative decision-maker), and law constitute autonomous functional subsystems. Functional differentiation of this type means that 'the highly specialised types of communication developed within the subsystems of society are no[t] . . . interconnected or interchangeable, and attempts to artificially impose one type of systemic communication on another fail'.[94] Hence, as seen in the early judicial review cases, law as an operationally closed subsystem (one which 'recognises everything that may be understood as lawful or unlawful as belonging to the legal system and to no other system, while at the same time it alone is capable of determining the difference between lawful and unlawful')[95] must necessarily fail to communicate with and intervene in the operations of the other closed subsystems (medicine and politics) because it 'see[s] things differently and there is no possibility of one system being able to internalise the world-view of another'.[96]

However, Gunther Teubner argues that it is a mistake to see law as a system which is wholly independent from changes in the environment. Rather, it is both closed and open: possessing the latter characteristic not because it interacts *directly* with other functional subsystems, but by 'selectively filtering' external changes

91 *R v Central Birmingham Health Authority, ex parte Collier* (1988, unreported), per Ralph Gibson LJ.

92 *ex parte B* (n 89) 906, *per* Bingham MR.

93 Most overtly in *ex parte Walker* (n 90), where Macpherson J stated that he was 'wholly convinced that this decision of the health authority is not justiciable, that is to say that it is not a matter in which the court should intervene'.

94 H. G. Moeller, *Luhmann Explained: From Souls to Systems* (Open Court, 2006) 33.

95 M. King, C. Thornhill, *Niklas Luhmann's Theory of Politics and Law* (Palgrave Macmillan, 2005) 24.

96 King and Thornhill (n 95) 27.

into legal structures and adapting them,[97] 'constructing internal models of the outside world with which [it is] able to interact internally'.[98] Thus, 'legal and social changes are . . . related but distinct processes. Legal change reflects an internal dynamic which, nevertheless, is affected by external stimuli and, in turn, influences the external environment'.[99] Understood in this manner, the epistemological and methodological shift to EBM and cost-effectiveness analysis as key determinants of appropriateness has been filtered by the judiciary into a model consonant with its world view, namely, as a form of *legal* evidence (such filtering being relatively straightforward given that judges are, of course, already highly familiar with evidence as the basis of their own decision making).[100] This adaptation, thus, enables courts to understand lawfulness/unlawfulness in this context in a manner which was not previously possible, thus shaking off the shackles of non-justiciability. In Luhmann's terms, scientific/social scientific evidence on effectiveness effects a form of 'structural coupling' between the subsystems of medicine, politics, and law.[101] But each of these subsystems continues to interpret the output of the others in its own terms. Thus, for the courts, judgments are framed in terms of rationality or irrationality (such as lawfulness/unlawfulness); for medicine, the output of the legal case will be construed as denial of care or approval of treatment; and for the allocative decision-maker, the judgment is viewed either as an interference with or approval of the priorities which have been established.

Many who are wary of judicial involvement in health care priority-setting will be troubled by the conclusions reached here. If the preceding analysis is correct, a return to the extreme judicial deference of early cases appears unlikely since EBM and cost-effectiveness analysis seem certain to constitute central features of the health policy landscape for the foreseeable future. The courtroom is thus likely to continue to function as a forum in which conflicting readings of the appropriateness of medical services and treatments will be played out against a backdrop of scarce resources. To secure legitimacy in this highly contentious area of health policy, judges must remain attentive to the need to mediate carefully between the differing perspectives on this complex but significant concept. I am cautiously optimistic as to their capacity to act in such a manner, but the future development of this field will certainly warrant close observation.

97 G. Teubner, 'Substantive and reflexive elements in modern law' (1983) 17 *Law and Society Review* 239, 249.

98 G. Teubner, 'Autopoiesis in law and society: A rejoinder to Blakenburg' (1984) 18 *Law and Society Review* 291, 297.

99 Teubner (n 97) 249.

100 For further discussion of this point, see K. Syrett, 'Courts, expertise and resource allocation: Is there a judicial "legitimacy problem"?' (2014) 7 *Public Health Ethics* 112.

101 See N. Luhmann, 'Operational closure and structural coupling: The differentiation of the legal system' (1992) 13 *Cardozo Law Review* 1419.

13 Comments and reflections on 'proper medical treatment'

A case for coherent inconsistency

John Coggon

Introduction

In this collection, Sara Fovargue and Alexandra Mullock have provided an important forum for the contributors to explain what it means to say that a treatment, practice, or procedure is 'proper medical treatment'. This exploration looks both to affirming how something receives legitimacy within the medical context and to how it receives a wider, legal legitimacy. The chapters offer substantive conclusions on how we ought to understand different practices, and insightful ideas about the means that we might use in order to approach this area. In this concluding chapter, I outline four particularly strong themes that emerge from this book. I then develop some ideas about how we might approach our conceptual and analytical study of the idea of proper medical treatment, and assess our modes of understanding. In so doing, I hope to assist further scholarly endeavour in this important area of health care law. I will also situate the concerns explored within this book in a wider context of theoretical health care law and legal theory more broadly. My further goal in this chapter is to present an argument against seeking to find, or indeed establish, a single, universally applicable legal concept of proper medical treatment that could feature as fitting in all practical and legal circumstances. I will build this case by reference to distinct areas of law and practice, and distinct means of establishing their legitimacy.

Four themes in the study of proper medical treatment

Different readers will undoubtedly take many different things from each of the chapters in this collection, but I have identified four themes reflected across the contributions. First, how authors have considered the concept of medical treatment as relating to something that is both medical *and* something else. Second, how the collection as a whole looks not just to proper medical treatment as a narrow, technical criminal law concept, but aims at general medico-legal analysis of different measures for assessing when an intervention is (not) legitimate. Third, how contributors have developed approaches to studying the questions raised. And finally, how the purposes of different modes of legal governance are understood and explained.

On the first point, it is useful to begin looking at the conceptualisation of medical treatment by reference to Mary Neal's idea of the paradigm case of proper medical treatment, which she categorises as 'treatment carried out with the consent of the patient and for the patient's therapeutic benefit'.[1] In this neat encapsulation of the paradigm example, the patient's consent addresses concerns about wrongs in terms of uninvited invasions of bodily integrity, while the therapeutic benefit affords a legitimacy to the intervention that is rooted soundly in public policy concerns (here serving the patient's interests in a way that is recognised according to a standard beyond the patient's own wishes). As Richard Huxtable explains, the concept of proper medical treatment is not rooted simply in what the patient may want, but also by reference to 'the public interest'.[2]

There seems to be a consensus throughout the collection that we should recognise both medical and non-medical components of treatment decisions, and that the medical and other components are conceptually separable. Influenced particularly by Ian Kennedy, José Miola frames this by reference to the technical *versus* the ethical components of a decision,[3] and Danielle Griffiths and Alexandra Mullock are among those who urge separation of medical from broader interests.[4] Perhaps most strikingly in Celia Kitzinger and Jenny Kitzinger's analysis, which firmly grounds concerns about the introduction of patients' values within medical decision-making (here for patients who lack capacity, through section 4(6) of the Mental Capacity Act 2005), we see a critique of the (il)legitimacy of practices where the medical decision is not adequately infused with the non-medical values that ought to inform it.[5]

Lucy Frith lends further subtlety still to the analysis by considering how values come into the concept of the proper medical decision.[6] Her arguments demonstrate well that we need to assess both the internal morality of medicine and wider social moralities. In parallel with scholars who have moved from the study of medical law to health care law,[7] Frith encourages analysis that accounts for the impact of a range of actors, including doctors, the pharmaceutical industry, and patient interests groups. Returning to Neal's framing of the paradigm, we have the clear concept but we now can see how it is infused with controversies. So while all might agree on the definition of proper medical treatment, there is much to be done to explain what the therapeutic (the technical, health expertise) component is and should be informed by. Equally, analysts will arrive at different views on the wider assessment of propriety, the public interest or ethical

1 M. Neal, 'Locating lawful abortion on the spectrum of "proper medical treatment"' in this collection.
2 R. Huxtable, 'Death on demand: "Proper medical treatment"?' in this collection.
3 J. Miola, 'Moralising medicine: "Proper medical treatment" and the role of ethics and law in medical decision-making' in this collection.
4 D. Griffiths, A. Mullock, 'The medical exception and cosmetic surgery: Culpable doctors and harmful enhancement?' in this collection.
5 C. Kitzinger, J. Kitzinger, 'Family perspectives on "proper medical treatment" for people in prolonged vegetative and minimally conscious states' in this collection.
6 L. Frith, 'What do we mean by "proper" medical treatment?' in this collection.
7 J. Montgomery, *Health Care Law* (2nd edn, Oxford University Press, 2002).

component. And, as Neal notes, as we move from the paradigm to non-paradigm examples, in her case considering non-therapeutic abortions, the concept of proper medical treatment, and thus the means of establishing these matters, becomes fuzzier still.

The second theme can be stated more briefly but is, I think, no less fundamental to the project of this collection. It is a general point but one that may be made with reference to the chapters written by Judy Laing and Keith Syrett. Laing's practical focus is on mental health law,[8] while Syrett looks at resource allocation.[9] In each case, the authors are looking to *how* we assess the legitimacy of decision-making. In neither case is the focus on proper medical treatment taken as a narrow term of legal art. Rather, and each in different senses, the concern is with 'appropriate' treatment. Laing critiques the means of establishing what may be considered appropriate treatment in mental health law; for example, should detention be considered appropriate treatment? Syrett looks at how public decision-makers establish which treatments it is appropriate (or not) to fund. We should not underestimate the importance of extending analysis, as happens in chapters throughout this collection, to assess health care law's varying means of assessing the legitimacy of treatments. While we may take as *part* of our focus the idea of proper medical treatment in regard to the 'medical exception' in criminal law, this is better addressed as an aspect of a wider analysis of modes of assessing legitimacy in medical decision-making.

The third theme that presents itself on my reading of the chapters, concerns analytical approaches. I cannot here speak to each chapter, but wish to highlight the great service the contributors do in offering different means of coming to a view on whether an intervention should be considered appropriate. Reflective of the separation of issues presented in Neal's definition of proper medical treatment, the chapters offer arguments about how and why we should account for the patient's view, and how and why we give importance to some external (for example scientific) means of finding that an intervention serves an interest. As a matter of recent history, Miola tracks the developments in medical law from deference to medical discretion to a patient-focused means of achieving legitimacy. For Miola, the approach is right where it entails both reference to professional agreement and to a role for external (potentially judicial) scrutiny to ensure that a logical basis for the intervention exists. Barry Lyons takes a much longer historical view.[10] His approach allows us to recognise the power struggles between the groups that would wish to claim the expert part of the decision-making while casting others as quacks. Lyons's analysis raises and addresses important questions about whom we should allow to give treatment and how we assess what they do. Despite the widespread focus on patient autonomy and respecting the patient's wishes, he raises

8 J. Laing, 'Doctors' orders? Analysing appropriate medical treatment in mental health law' in this collection.

9 K. Syrett, 'Rationing, resource allocation, and appropriate medical treatment' in this collection.

10 B. Lyons, 'Papist potions and electric sex: A historical perspective on "proper medical treatment"' in this collection.

questions about how much we should be guided by the patient's (or 'client's' or 'consumer's') perspective. This historical approach is interestingly reinforced, for example in Syrett's administrative law analysis, which distinguishes what people may want and what is appropriate. Syrett argues that people do not always know what is good for them, and in an assessment of appropriateness we should distinguish an objective concept of need from a subjective concept of demand.

A further consensus seems to exist in the collection that while 'doctor knows best' is not on its own a good measure of proper treatment, equally we should not simply bow to patients' wishes and demands. For example, Griffiths and Mullock, looking at non-therapeutic cosmetic interventions, are clear in considering why consent, as generally negotiated in the medical context, might not be a sufficient justification for performing such procedures. Huxtable's discussion of the public interest is again relevant too. And finally, here I would highlight the fascinating contribution from Cam Donaldson, Rachel Baker, and Neil McHugh, who bring insights from health economics that will be less familiar to many medical lawyers.[11] As often happens in interdisciplinary discussions, important questions are raised that will test the guiding presumptions and presuppositions of medico-legal scholars. Contrast Neal's analysis, for example, with Donaldson, Baker, and McHugh's invitation that we test the propriety of, say, abortion through an economic analysis. In short, there is much to think about in developing a method to substantiate the idea of 'proper' in proper medical treatment.

The final theme that I wish to raise, before exploring and developing these ideas in my own analysis, looks to the purposes of different sorts of legal approaches. Huxtable in particular makes forceful arguments about assessing legitimacy by reference to purposes in different spheres. But to make this point here, I will refer to Margaret Brazier and Sara Fovargue's opening analysis.[12] Their chapter speaks to all of the points made above. For example, its contribution to the conceptual understanding is impressive. With regard to the theme of different purposes for different spheres of activity, they focus on criminal liability and how and why immunity should be granted in the medical context. Brazier and Fovargue suggest that criminal law protects patients' interests, while civil standards ensure responsible medical practice. That is, we find different roles given the function of different areas of law. I propose in what follows, among other things, to break these ideas down further still. I will suggest that it is right that this project should have opened up a whole range of approaches to understanding what is proper in different medico-legal contexts, and I will advance an argument that the result is that we may rightly and coherently allow for different measures of appropriateness in different settings. Both of my goals in this chapter form important bases of analysis of proper medical treatment.

With regard to the first goal, concepts are fundamentally important both in practice and in theoretical approaches. In the context of health care law, it is through

11 C. Donaldson, R. Baker, N. McHugh, 'The economics of "proper medical treatment"' in this collection.

12 M. Brazier, S. Fovargue, 'Transforming wrong into right: What is "proper medical treatment"?' in this collection.

concepts and categories that we are able to understand, explain, and, indeed, criticise the law. It is for this reason that scholars, judges, and policy-makers work so hard to establish, for example, what is and what should be meant by autonomous decisions, expertise, best interests, patients, persons, and so on. Take the phrase 'the patient had capacity'. To the health care lawyer, this short statement carries several messages, each of which has received sustained attention over the years and could be developed at some length with reference to various sources of legal authority.

We know, for example, on reading this claim that there is a person who is usefully and meaningfully identified as being within a health care context. She is a patient, and thus stands in a particular relationship to the health care system and to health care practitioners. This means that a particular set of rights and responsibilities is at play and may be critiqued by reference to how the law (or ethics) tells us they should operate. We know too that she has particular decision-making rights, that the presumption of capacity as enshrined in the Mental Capacity Act 2005 will be upheld, and that she does not fall foul of the test for incapacity in that statute. We know that capacity in this context refers to her standing in relation to a specific decision. All of this is so even while we might acknowledge that many of us, scholars and judges, talk of the concept of competent patients, a category that strictly is not part of English health care law! We know too that her capacity to decide is circumscribed by a distinction between choosing between or refusing interventions, as opposed to demanding any intervention that she might want.[13] We also know, given recent judicial activism, that her decision-making may still be interfered with in her 'best interests', through the High Court's inherent jurisdiction.[14]

With regard to the second focus of inquiry, this collection exposes part of a wider landscape of academic, professional, and political interest in the legitimacy of medical practice itself, and of how it should be regulated. In that sense, the concerns go to the heart of health care law as a discipline; they are at the core of the very rationales for engaging in study in this area. As such, there are clear links and symbioses between this chapter's two goals. In short, there is value in understanding the rationales for, as well as the meanings of, proper medical treatment, and I hope here to contribute to that understanding.

Approaching the concept of proper medical treatment

It is apposite to introduce this section with reference to the analytical framing in two works that are seminal in the very conception of medical law: Ian Kennedy's examination of the idea of medical treatment, initially presented in 1979,[15] and Penney Lewis's critical and conceptual treatment of the medical exception,

13 *R (On the Application of Oliver Leslie Burke) v The General Medical Council* [2005] EWCA Civ 1003.

14 See e.g. *Re G (An Adult) (Mental Capacity: Court's Jurisdiction)* [2004] EWHC 2222 (Fam); *Re SA (Vulnerable Adult with Capacity: Marriage)* [2005] EWHC 2942 (Fam); *A Local Authority* v. *DL & Ors* [2010] EWHC 2675 (Fam).

15 I. Kennedy, 'What is a medical decision?' in I. Kennedy, *Treat Me Right: Ethics in Medical Law and Ethics* (Clarendon Press, 1988).

published almost 35 years later.[16] These scholars have shown their influence in the chapters included in this collection, and their work will form the springboard for my discussion in the remainder of this chapter.

What is medical law about?

This collection invites reflections on, and critiques of, conceptual and analytical points that may be reduced to two questions that are central to the very rationale for medical law's (and more recently health care law's) existence as a discrete field of study. The first is how the law should have us conceive of 'medical' in the first place. The second, is whether, and if so how, 'the medical' should be regulated. As he was one of the most notable influences on the establishment of the field of medical law, it is useful to begin with Kennedy's examination of the foundational question, 'what is a medical decision?' In his 1979 Astor Lecture on this topic, reproduced in his influential book *Treat Me Right*, Kennedy explains:

> The title I have chosen, 'What is a medical decision?' is in the form of a question. The question may better be framed: what decisions are within the specific competence of a doctor to make? Put another way, what is appropriate for a doctor to decide (and thereafter do)? Still further, it can be turned around to the question: are there decisions which should be made by doctors alone? . . . [I]t may be that we do have to begin our enquiry far away from what is thought to be traditional doctoring, at the outer edges of what may be the sphere of their decision making, and then work inwards until we reach the point at which we can begin to hear the answer, yes, that is a medical decision.[17]

Kennedy's concern, which has come to characterise much medico-legal scholarship, focused on the dominion afforded to doctors and the propriety of their practice going unscrutinised externally (a matter, as noted, that is also examined in Miola's chapter). Kennedy was, of course, writing at a time when the great part of medical practice was subject to what he perceived as jealously protected self-regulation. The medical domain was, as is clear from developments in Kennedy's writings over time, becoming subject to increasing critique through the developing subject of medical ethics, and works such as Ivan Illich's *Medical Nemesis*,[18] which Kennedy found in many regards to provide a persuasive critique. But there was, in 1979, clear salience and novelty in a lawyer examining the concept of a medical decision. The implication was that doctors' exclusive competences might be more limited than was widely supposed at the time, and that the guiding norms and

16 P. Lewis, 'The medical exception' (2012) 65 *Current Legal Problems* 355.

17 Kennedy (n 15) 20.

18 I. Illich, *Limits to Medicine – Medical Nemesis: The Expropriation of Health* (Marion Boyars, 1976).

rules in health care should be defined in part by (what, on Kennedy's argument, were wrongly considered to be) external standards.[19]

So in exploring the concept of the medical decision, Kennedy sought to find the matters on which doctors *could* claim exclusive jurisdiction. And in examining their expertise, he sought to discover the legitimate scope of their rightful position in establishing what decisions and interventions could be made by them, what decisions they might contribute to, and what decisions they might have no business in making. Thinking about the aims of this chapter, and the wider project of this collection, it is instructive to refer to Kennedy's argument not simply because of its conclusions, but also because of the salience of his approach to understanding the essence of a medical decision. His approach is developed through reference to the following reasoning:

> [W]e could say that a medical decision is a decision made by a doctor in a medical context. But this is obviously circuitous. It merely says that what is medical is what is medical. So, let us approach it from a different angle and say that doctors are competent to decide upon issues of health and ill health.[20]

In Kennedy's words, this 'brings us a little closer' to understanding what a medical decision is.[21] But he notes that it does not finally answer the question. Rather, it shifts the burden of analytical inquiry from needing to know what medical means towards a need to understand exactly what health means. And this is something to which various contributors to the current collection have paid attention; for example, how we understand, in Neal's terms, the therapeutic aspect of a medical decision.

Kennedy argues that if we find that the unique competence of physicians is coterminous with the boundaries of our concept of health, doctors' dominion logically extends as far as that concept permits. As such, it is crucial to determine what we mean by health. I will demonstrate in the next section how an examination of the legitimacy of medical interventions benefits from a study of the philosophy of health. But prior to doing so, it should be clear that a narrow concept of health, such as a biomedical definition, would afford doctors a relatively limited expert competence. A broad definition, by contrast, such as the World Health Organization's concept of total well-being,[22] would afford doctors a vast jurisdiction.

19 It might be noted that critics of Kennedy, such as Petr Skrabanek, a disciple of Illich, argue that Kennedy's attack on one dominant profession, medicine, was itself subject to critique as he sought to dominate with another one, law. See e.g. P. Skrabanek, *The Death of Humane Medicine and the Rise of Coercive Healthism* (St Edmundsbury Press, 1994).

20 Kennedy (n 15) 20.

21 Kennedy (n 15) 20.

22 The World Health Organization's constitution states that 'Health is a state of complete physical, mental and social well-being and not merely the absence of disease or infirmity': Constitution of the World Health Organization, available at www.who.int/governance/eb/who_constitution_en.pdf (accessed 19 February 2015).

The normative conclusions of our analysis are necessarily tied to the upshot of our conceptual claims; therefore, the latter demand careful and precise attention.

Suffice to say, for Kennedy it was not acceptable that doctors should enjoy too large a dominion or too great a range of exclusive decision-making power. Rather:

> a doctor's special competence lies in, first, the knowledge which allows him to make a diagnosis and prognosis of what is generally accepted as being ill health; second, the knowledge of what therapies, if any, are available in the context of a particular condition of ill health; third, the judgment of which therapy or response to adopt so as to produce, to the best of his ability, an end result deemed appropriate not by him but by the patient, one approved by society at large. No more, no less.[23]

We may or may not be persuaded by Kennedy's conclusions or his assertions about general acceptance and deeming appropriate as marking the touchstones of legitimacy. But his approach to tackling the question of the legitimacy and scope of understanding a medical decision is useful. Before outlining the application of works from the philosophy of health to our analysis of proper medical treatment, I will introduce a more recent, equally important paper, which helps us uncover further the shared nature of competences in medical decision-making.

Penney Lewis's paper 'The medical exception' has rightly featured as a framing device for various chapters in this book.[24] She is interested there in criminal law and regulation, and her focus is on the bands of harms that only escape criminal sanction because they are deemed to be justified by virtue of their being medical interventions. To fall within the medical exception, Lewis notes that two criteria must be met. First, consent must be given by the person on whom an intervention will take place, or if it cannot be (because the patient lacks decision-making capacity), some other form of lawful authorisation must be provided. And second, in Lewis's words, 'some form of public policy justification is required'.[25] She then presents and explains three means of establishing this justification. As these have featured elsewhere in this collection, I will not re-present them in depth, but will offer a short outline.

Briefly, within Lewis's framing we first find 'patient-focused public policy justifications'.[26] This means justifications whose reference point is the impact of the intervention on the individual patient. What is notable here is that, for Lewis, the focus is on interventions that find justification in benefit to the patient. The point bears emphasis as the focus is on the patient's *interests*. We may contrast this with a concern for the will of the patient, or a basis founded on patient autonomy (not forgetting that consent, treated separately, is a criterion that Lewis already places as necessary). It is salient, therefore, to note that an estimation of what serves a patient's interests may not rest

23 Kennedy (n 15) 30.
24 Lewis (n 16).
25 Lewis (n 16) 357.
26 Lewis (n 16) 357–359.

entirely with the patient's views on this. This is a point that, as I noted above, seems to find agreement with various contributors to this collection. It is reflected, furthermore, as a general principle of health care law,[27] and is well-explored, as I argue below, through the philosophy of health and the lens of rights theory.

Second, Lewis looks to 'public-focused public policy justifications'.[28] Under this form of justification, a therapeutic benefit may not accrue for a given patient, but some general benefit arises and is sufficient to found a claim for legitimacy. Examples given by Lewis include non-therapeutic research and organ donation. Finally, there are 'professionally focused public policy interventions'.[29] Here we find a legitimiser in the idea that something is *good*, or *proper* medical treatment, or, perhaps less stringently, that something is *accepted* practice within the profession. And provided such an endorsement is available, the fact of medical treatment may be sufficient to render the intervention lawful.

In fleshing out her analysis, Lewis refers both to formal and informal means of recognising legality. These obtain most clearly in legislation and judicial opinions, but also, more commonly, through governmental decisions to allow funding for a particular treatment. National and international regulations may also serve as an indication of legality.[30] More informal legal changes come as professional practices develop and gain acceptance.[31] With regard to these ideas, the role of law is arguably more useful in establishing medical practices that are not *proper* medical practices, those that should be prohibited.[32] The conceptual tools that Lewis provides assist in attempts to consider these questions, and, as I will argue shortly, these are bolstered if we also bring tools from rights theory to our analysis.

Advancing the analysis

Having presented Kennedy's and Lewis's approaches and situated them in the context of the work presented in this collection, in the following two sections I will advance the lessons already learned. Complementing the above ideas with insights from literatures on the philosophy of health and from rights theory, I will demonstrate how we might enhance our capacity for understanding the idea of proper medical treatment.

Drawing from the philosophy of health

There are interesting, and well-explored, questions to ask about why we conceive of health care law as a field of study in the first place. Answers differ greatly, and include those from colleagues who do not even recognise health care law as a

27 *Burke* (n 13).
28 Lewis (n 16) 359–362.
29 Lewis (n 16) 362–364.
30 Lewis (n 16) 364–366.
31 Lewis (n 16) 366–370.
32 Lewis (n 16) 372–373.

'real' subject of legal study.[33] For current purposes, two potential rationales for sustaining the field are pertinent. First, health care is a particular area of law and policy of particular social value, and, as such, there is a significant benefit in subjecting the way it is administered to particular scrutiny. Second, health itself is considered to be such an important value that it alone presents a sufficiently strong central theme for a whole area of study. In other words, even if they are wrong to do so, enough people consider health and health care to be a sufficiently important social concern that it warrants sustained critical engagement. And recognising concerns beyond those that might be addressed directly by doctors, we have naturally found expansions to the field from *medical* law, at the time when Kennedy was writing, to *health care* law and now *health* law more generally.[34]

Regarding each of these rationales for the field, there is clear importance, as highlighted by Kennedy, in understanding what health itself means. The focus of inquiry in this collection, questions about legitimacy in relation to medical (health-based) interventions, is assisted by understanding the concept. I will point here to a particular aspect of the wider literature on the philosophy of health.[35] This will help us to understand both in what senses health is important and who can claim to hold a specialist understanding and expertise in health. Through performing this conceptual analysis, we can explain what rights, freedoms, and duties ought to exist concerning health interventions, and what role the law and other institutions should have in health governance.

Kennedy's question was 'what is a medical decision?' It may be rephrased, albeit crudely, in order to tease out some of its complexities. We might ask 'who owns the judgement of what constitutes proper medical treatment?' And, 'who decides what your health is, and what serves it?' I alluded above to the distinction between narrow definitions of health, which look to the absence of disease, as opposed to broader definitions, which look to a positive, complete state of well-being. Coming to a conclusion on which conception should predominate is important, and it is clear that the more holistic a concept of health, the less reason there is to suppose that expertise and insights into the concept are limited to those who understand medicine. In the opening section, I highlighted how chapters in this collection have explained the importance of understanding who has expertise and precisely in what. We need here to dissect different approaches to understanding what is, and what benefits, a person's health. Here, I suggest, we do well to point to Amartya Sen's presentation of 'internal' *versus* 'external' definitions of health, which may also be cast, as per Syrett's analysis, as subjective *versus* objective concepts.[36]

33 For sustained analysis of these questions I find T. W. Ruger, 'Health law's coherence anxiety' (2008) 96 *Georgetown Law Journal* 625 and K. Veitch, *The Jurisdiction of Medical Law* (Ashgate, 2007) particularly useful.

34 See further J. Coggon, *What Makes Health Public? A Critical Evaluation of Moral, Legal, and Political Claims in Public Health* (Cambridge University Press, 2012), ch. 5.

35 For a more detailed survey of the wider debates, see Coggon (n 34) ch. 1.

36 A. Sen, 'Health achievement and equity: External and internal perspectives' in S. Anand, F. Peter, A. Sen (eds.), *Public Health, Ethics, and Equity* (Oxford University Press, 2004).

If we follow an internal definition of health, we simply rely on the individual's estimation of what health means and what serves her health. With regard to proper medical treatment, an exclusive commitment to an internal perspective would mean deferring entirely to the wishes and demands of the patient. If, for example, a person claims that her health is served by removal of a healthy limb or by administration of a performance-enhancing drug, we respect that view. Equally, if she fails to recognise what appears to others to be ill health, we might think here, for example, of psychiatric conditions, then there is no legitimacy in allowing a medical intervention against the patient's will.[37]

If we follow an external definition, we approach health problems by reference to a standard that is defined, for example, by reference to medical professionals' consensus on health. This may be a scientific standard or one held by other actors, such as government actors. As applied with reference to proper medical treatment, the propriety of a diagnosis or intervention is established by, first, establishing how the external standard is arrived at, and, second, ensuring that it is soundly applied. If this sort of concept of health were instituted, we would see a wide (though not necessarily always compelling all things considered) means of legitimising imposed medical decisions, even against the will, or at least without the consent, of the patient. The most benign (and almost universally rejected!) face of this idea is the unquestioning 'doctor knows best' understanding of legitimate medical practice, to which the fields of medical ethics and law have responded so forcefully over the past decades.

There are, I argue, significant problems with arriving at a concept of health that was either purely internally or externally defined.[38] Sen convincingly argues that it would be most appropriate to work with a concept that entails both internal and external perspectives.[39] And in the context of English health care law's framing, that is precisely what happens when establishing what would constitute proper medical treatment, as indicated in Miola's chapter. This point presents itself, in particular, in judicial analyses of best interests (albeit that in practice the principle does not always present itself, as argued by Kitzinger and Kitzinger). In this context, the courts, and the Mental Capacity Act 2005, require that there be both a clinical or external component, and a wider, particularised moral, social, familial, welfare, and potentially religious component. Regarding the former, we have what is widely viewed as the *Bolam* aspect of the decision.[40] Here, we look to professional opinion and do not agree on legitimacy if there is not a sufficiently strong body of responsible medical opinion in favour of an intervention. Regarding the latter, we

37 At least as regards the patient. Potentially there could be legitimacy for the sake of protecting others.

38 This is not to deny that some libertarian theorists, such as Illich (n 18) and Skrabanek (n 19), would wish to see health as defined simply by the patient. Equally, one can imagine collectivist accounts that might claim legitimacy to a pure, externalist account. I will not address these here, but I suggest that arguments against each of these two extremes could be soundly formulated. For the purposes of conceptual analysis, it is in no way pivotal that my *normative* assertion here be accepted; simply, if Illich is right then we should apply his concept of health rather than the concept that I defend.

39 Sen (n 36).

40 *Bolam v Friern Hospital Management Committee* [1957] 2 All ER 118.

look to wider aspects of what would fulfil the patient's well-being. Although these assessments are, in practice, also circumscribed by external concepts of welfare, for example, in the very strong presumption in favour of life,[41] they are informed by attributes that are particular to the individual patient, such as her religious or moral beliefs.

These two separate assessments, to which Kennedy alluded in his dissection of the medical decision, have the potential to bring considerable conceptual clarity in relation to the idea of proper medical treatment. As well as allowing relevance to different perspectives in relation to any given decision, they also allow for matters outside of 'the medical' to be included when assessing what is proper; and they allow for clear understandings of why proper for one patient may not be proper for another. As such, I would encourage future works in this area to build on analyses such as Kennedy's, using the lens of the philosophy of health to gain a sound view of the interests that are supposed to be served by medical treatments. And I would stress that in different situations different substantive concepts of health will necessarily prevail. While this is justifiable, it means that we will not have a universally applicable, singular concept of health to apply in an analysis of proper medical treatment.

Drawing from rights theory

The second area of theory that I wish to highlight as useful for analyses of the idea of proper medical treatment is rights theory. As with the previous section, I aim to establish why and how I think approaches from this area of theory lend both explanatory and evaluative potential. While the ideas expressed here are intended to have very general application within health care law, they are derived from consideration of a means to complement and expand on Lewis's method of dissecting interests and rights in relation to the medical exception, and from there to a positive presentation of the idea of proper medical treatment. It should become clear that this approach would operate well in association with the philosophy of health discussion in the previous section.

If the idea of *proper* medical treatment is not to be read as suggesting a tautology (a point that seems to be held by all contributors to this collection), we cannot, as outlined above, assess propriety by reference simply to a treatment being medical. 'Medical' does not automatically imply legitimate. The justification for, or permissibility of, a practice cannot be established simply by demonstrating that it is medical. The term medical, as Kennedy intimates, may mean (something like) conducted by a physician in the course of her professional practice, or (something like) involving methods or techniques derived for application by physicians. Beyond establishing an answer to what medical means, a conceptual analysis of proper medical treatment also requires that we analyse what is meant by 'proper', and who has a stake in making that designation. Given the ideas explored in

41 See e.g. *Re M (Adult Patient) (Minimally Conscious State: Withdrawal of Treatment)* [2011] EWHC 2443 (Fam).

relation to the philosophy of health and their instantiation in health care law, we have seen that our answer to the question will not be limited to medical questions. And I have highlighted how Lewis has added a great deal by analysing law and theory, and separating justifications that are rooted in benefits respectively to patients and the public, and ones that are rooted in their recognition as sound professional standards.

Lewis, Kennedy, and the contributors to this book look to a range of areas of health care law to help substantiate and explain their views, from the paradigm case of a medical decision to areas that seem more problematic; for example, because they offer no therapeutic benefit to the individual patient (as in abortion for social reasons) or no direct benefit whatsoever (as in the case of live organ donation). I suggest that this project can be advanced further if we look to how the law does and might give substance to, or deny, an arguable right to health care in different circumstances. By looking at the right, we can see, as I put it above, who has what stake in the decision. So doing, we can cut across quite distinct areas of contestation, including judicial reviews of funding decisions, claims concerning controversial or innovative interventions, and claims regarding negligence in clinical conduct.

It is worth re-emphasising Lewis's summary of two criteria for *proper* medical treatment. First, there is the patient's consent, or some other means of authorisation for a patient who lacks capacity. Second, there is the need for a public stamp of legitimacy. These are necessary, and when both are present, sufficient conditions for a judgement that a medical intervention is legitimate. The two categories, which embrace respectively respect for autonomy and the safeguarding of an interest, feature in debates throughout health care law. For example, in an evaluation of Court of Protection jurisprudence, Charles Foster and Michael Dunn frame disputes as pitting autonomy against welfare.[42]

While health care law may be seen as containing efforts to resolve disputes between autonomy and welfare, it is interesting to reflect that a large body of debate in rights theory is the disagreement between choice theorists, who essentially share the view that all rights serve to protect autonomy, and interest theorists, who essentially share the view that all rights are justified because of the benefits they secure.[43] These debates are directly reflected in theoretical health care law where theorists disagree radically about whether patient autonomy should be *the* guiding principle. The philosophy of health literature can help us to explain *what* proper medical treatment obtains in. Rights theory can help us to take this further and explain *which* actors, patients, health care professionals, funders, and so on, have which entitlements, and face *which* constraints, in a given situation.

If we accept my characterisation of the argument here as being about who owns the judgement of what proper medical treatment is, then we have seen above that the ownership is shared. Clinicians may be said to hold the *Bolam* aspect, for

42 M. Dunn, C. Foster, 'Autonomy and welfare as *amici curiae*' (2010) 18 *Medical Law Review* 86.
43 See M. Kramer, N. Simmonds, H. Steiner, *A Debate Over Rights* (Oxford University Press, 1998).

example.[44] Even a brief review of different sorts of cases shows how different parties might claim some ownership of a decision. There are cases where there is a clash between the content of an apparent right, as compared with that of a right that a person would wish to assert. This may be down to a dispute about funding, for example. Here, we have concerns about defining a person's interests as well as about prioritisation within a system that distributes benefits. It may, alternatively, be down to a dispute about what is clinically appropriate. Here, we may find disagreement about whether *medically* a course of action is justifiable in the context of concerns for professional responsibility. In different situations, most notably mental health and public health, we find examples of rights to health care that cannot be waived. The idea of a right that cannot be waived is not conceptually problematic (I have a right to pay taxes on my income). Similarly, we might look at rights that a person has but cannot exercise, for example, because there is no health care professional willing to comply.

But to make sense of, say, compulsory detention and the normative foundations that justify it, a list of the involved parties and the nature of their stake in the process is needed. There is not space here to elaborate further on this point, but I hope it is clear how it offers an approach that, in the first instance, can help us expose which stakeholders assert which claims. Depending on the nature of analysis, it may be of benefit to spell out the respective parties' stakes in the process by reference to a matrix such as that provided by a Hohfeldian analysis of jural relations.[45] For the remainder of this chapter, I move from approach to application, with a view to establishing that the breadth of the medico-legal question 'what is proper medical treatment?' coherently demands a plurality of answers.

Against a single concept of proper medical treatment

As I have noted above, medical law, health care law, and health law are characterised by a common practical thread of health care provision and attention to health, rather than any given legal approach. As such, and as reflected by the contributors to this collection, the field boasts scholars from across legal subdisciplines and beyond, such as torts, human rights, crime, constitutional and administrative law, jurisprudence, sociology, and health economics. Equally, as evidenced in the chapters, there is an enormous variety of practical contexts that fall within the field. It is my contention that this variety in approach and context naturally leads to variety in how and why we come to the view, in any given instance, that a treatment should be considered proper. If this is correct, it means that we should be wary of thinking that just because something has been deemed proper medical treatment in one setting, that it, or its apparent analogues, is proper in another. It also suggests a need to be alive to a possible rebuttal of the default in any situation,

44 I do not forget, when stipulating this, that analyses such as Frith's and Lyons's, in particular, remind us to test the soundness even of this as a guiding presumption.

45 D. Campbell, P. Thomas (eds.), *Fundamental Legal Conceptions As Applied in Judicial Reasoning by Wesley Newcomb Hohfeld* (Ashgate Dartmouth, 2001).

whether that default is that something is, or is not, proper medical treatment. To substantiate these points, I will not refer directly to the cases and examples used in the chapters in this collection. It should be clear how these have already had an impact on my understanding. Rather, I will leave those in the background and refer in some detail to a medical law case that is pertinent but is not a general point of discussion in analyses of proper medical treatment. Taking that example, and considering the other cases discussed in this book, I suggest that while each case may be categorised as a medical law case, the *rationale* for finding that there should be a legal designation of proper medical treatment in some cases is (potentially) sufficiently distinctive that we would not wish simply to say that in every medico-legal context they should be considered proper medical treatment.

The case that I will examine, *Allen Carr's Easyway (International) Ltd v Revenue and Customs Commissioners*,[46] is one that I am not aware of having featured in any works in medical law. It is, in many respects, unremarkable, and it falls far from the dizzying controversies of questions such as abortion and euthanasia, or truth-telling and clinical negligence. It is a First-Tier Tribunal (Tax Chamber) ruling on whether a smoking cessation service should be designated as a medical service and thus exempted from value added tax (VAT). The appellant company was contesting the decision that it was liable for VAT on the basis that its services themselves should be considered to be medical because their purpose was to serve health and they were directly supervised by a medical practitioner. Before explaining how the Tribunal came to the view that the exemption should apply, it is important to emphasise that it is clear, in this situation, how the rationale for finding that the services constituted medical treatment would fall far from a similar consideration in, for example, the context of a medical negligence case or a judicial review of a decision not to fund provision of the service on the National Health Service (NHS). This is not to say that in such instances an apparently contrary finding would necessarily arise, but that the *rationale* for it would rightly differ.

I will briefly explain this with reference to my preceding analysis and then refer to the tribunal's process of reasoning. Producing even the sketch of a rights matrix allows us to see that the interested parties are the taxman and a private company. Although a doctor and wider expert opinions may be considered relevant, and in a sense a set of patients can also be identified, the key stakeholders are not the same as those considered elsewhere in this collection. The different rights-holders necessarily raise distinct questions about what should be considered proper. And in relation to the philosophy of health, we are equally not (directly) interested here in the subjective views of patients. Nor is our concern about mediating a contest between expert and ethical concepts. Rather, we are interested in how the tribunal, unmoved by these concerns, established who should designate a service as a health intervention that should be considered medical treatment. Our analysis of what happened in the case is, in short, enhanced by being clear on who the stakeholders are and what their investment is, and is deemed properly to be, in the understanding of medical treatment in this context.

46 [2009] UKFTT 181 (TC).

So let us consider how the case is addressed. Easyway Productions, the appellant company, runs smoking cessation clinics which employ a 'method'[47] developed by Allen Carr, a qualified accountant. The tribunal said of the method that:

> Whilst it has not been subjected to independent scientific evaluation, nor is it specifically endorsed by the NHS, the Department of Health, or other statutory bodies in the health sector, it was acknowledged by the Commissioners in their Statement of Case that the method is generally accepted to have a high success rate, on the basis of testimonials from both satisfied customers and individual health professionals.[48]

In terms of understanding whether the company provided medical services, the salient factual points are that a registered medical practitioner is appointed to supervise therapists at the clinics,[49] notwithstanding that the therapists themselves could have any background, with no need for medical or psychological expertise.[50]

The Tribunal summarised the respondents' position as follows:

> The Commissioners' case in essence is that the sessions given are not medical in nature, not involving the exercise of any medical expertise. It is not sufficient to qualify as 'medical care' for the Appellant to claim that its services have a health benefit and a therapeutic aim, they must also be medical in nature. The sessions are not a supply of medical care provided by a medical practitioner in the exercise of his profession, nor are they directly supervised as such. The method is neither formally recognised nor regulated; the therapists have no formal qualifications and no medical training.[51]

The decision continues from this with an interesting conceptual debate over the idea of medical care. The respondent suggested that while prevention or treatment of disorders was a necessary condition of medical care, alone it was not sufficient.[52] An analogy was considered between what the Allen Carr clinics do and what a personal trainer at a gym does. Drawing from European Court of Justice authorities, the appellants, by contrast, aimed to present a characterisation of medical services established precisely by reference to their aims:

> [The appellants] submitted that we should derive the conclusion that the purpose of the service determined whether or not it should be exempt, and that

47 Within the decision, the tribunal puts the word 'method' in quotation marks, *Allen Carr* (n 46) paras 7–8.

48 *Allen Carr* (n 46) para. 8, also para. 20.

49 *Allen Carr* (n 46) para. 11.

50 *Allen Carr* (n 46) para. 14.

51 *Allen Carr* (n 46) para. 22.

52 *Allen Carr* (n 46) para. 24. Note that this 'necessary' condition would (possibly correctly) preclude many non-therapeutic interventions that are widely recognised *as* medical care.

> services with the objective of reducing the cost of healthcare were within the exemption. Because smoking itself is an illness, namely nicotine addiction, and the Appellant's method prevents the development of illnesses, it comprises medical care.[53]

In reaching its decision, the Tribunal considered whether the service, as provided under medical supervision, should be deemed to be medical care. It did not look at the method alone.[54] While accepting that an aim of providing a therapeutic service was insufficient to qualify as medical care, the Tribunal held that 'these matters take the Appellant a long way towards satisfying the legal requirement'.[55] With the recognition of the method and, crucially, the input and oversight of the medical supervisor who provides a 'medical input',[56] the Tribunal ultimately found a sufficient combination of factors to rule that the services constituted medical care.

This case is, of course, not concerned with proper medical treatment in the sense used in reference to the medical exception employed in criminal law. Yet the aim of the Tribunal was to determine whether a particular intervention was properly considered as medical treatment, and thus properly subject to distinct legal treatment that affords a privileged outcome. As such, it falls within this collection's wider project of examining what is proper medical treatment. Although in a more sustained analysis I would take issue with aspects of the Tribunal's reasoning, my purposes here do not rely on our agreeing with the specific reasons or the final outcome. Rather, my aim is to demonstrate that we have a significant area of law and social policy whose determination requires a considered rationale that hinges on the very question of how, legally, we should conceive of something as being a legitimate medical practice. And having done that, I suggest that the rationale in this case is, quite self-evidently, distinct from the sort of rationale that should guide the rules and principles underpinning a very different sort of medico-legal decision. For example the rationale for allowing experimental treatment in the case of *Simms v Simms*[57] would properly be built on concerns for the patients and, potentially, with a view to developments in scientific understanding of a rare disease. Or the rationale for allowing that non-therapeutic termination of pregnancy be considered a medical intervention, or that assisted-dying be considered a matter best provided in a medical context, might be built on concerns about the best forum for regulatory oversight. In short, when looking for the concept of proper medical treatment in different contexts, we may be looking for different things. As such, in our analysis we should not let the same term, *medical*, lead to false analogues or misplaced concerns about apparent contradictions. We do well, in different instances, to examine the legitimacy of medical treatment by reference to standards that can account for their local context, and employing approaches that allow us to do that.

53 *Allen Carr* (n 46) para. 31.
54 *Allen Carr* (n 46) para. 34.
55 *Allen Carr* (n 46) para. 35.
56 *Allen Carr* (n 46) para. 40.
57 [2002] EWHC 2734 (Fam).

Conclusions

In this concluding chapter, I have demonstrated some of the salient aspects raised in the exercise of understanding the different ideas that fall under the heading of proper medical treatment. Given that such a range of ideas is present, as demonstrated by my own reference to an *apparently* outlying and unremarkable case, I argue that we have important work to do in approaching the question, but should not suppose that there is, or ought to be, a single, right concept of proper medical treatment. Drawing from literatures on rights theory and the philosophy of health, I have suggested how we might demonstrate where conceptual boundaries are fuzzy or how they might shift, and move from there to understanding what the law then ought to do. My argument is that we should look for the rationales that determine who has what stake in a given decision, and what purpose is served by determining something to *be* proper medical treatment. The range and degree of complexity goes to the heart of our needing to find a more subtle range of concepts here.

The project encapsulated in this collection puts in sharp relief the question 'does health care law require us to be able to assess whether an intervention or treatment constitutes proper medical treatment?' And the answer is clearly 'yes'. Should we, therefore, be seeking to establish exhaustively what qualities or criteria would combine in any and all situations to render something proper medical treatment or not? In order to remain properly sensitive to context, I would say 'no'. The consequence of my position is that there will be uncertainty and, across different areas of law, inconsistency about the definitive (un)lawfulness of many practices. For the purposes of, say, taxation, something may be a proper medical treatment when it is not for the purposes of, say, a patient's right to NHS funded care. To some this may be an unsatisfactory conclusion, but I suggest that, for the reasons presented above, it is preferable to the alternative.

Bibliography

ABIM Foundation, 'Medical professionalism in the new millennium' (2002) 136 *Annals of Internal Medicine* 243.

A. Aboraya, 'The reliability of psychiatric diagnosis revisited' (2006) 3 *Psychiatry* 41.

P. Alldridge, 'Consent to medical and surgical treatment – The Law Commission's recommendations' (1996) 4 *Medical Law Review* 129.

American Medical Association (AMA), *Opinion 2.06 – Capital Punishment* (1980), updated June 2000, available at http://www.ama-assn.org/ama/pub/physician-resources/medical-ethics/code-medical-ethics/opinion206.page?.

AMA, *Opinion 2.067 – Torture* (1999), available at http://www.ama-assn.org/ama/pub/physician-resources/medical-ethics/code-medical-ethics/opinion2067.page?.

AMA, 'Physician Participation in Lethal Injection Violates Medical Ethics', Press Release, July 17 2006.

G. Anderson, M. Hall, T. Rust Smith, 'When courts review medical appropriateness' (1998) 36 *Medical Care* 1295.

An International Project of the Hastings Center, 'The goals of medicine: Setting new priorities' (1996) 26 *Hastings Center Report* S1.

K. Andrews, 'Letter – Tortuous arguments evade the issue' (1995) 311 *British Medical Journal* 1347.

Anonymous, 'The composition of certain secret remedies' (1911) 1 *British Medical Journal* 1324.

G. Annas, M. Grodin (eds), *The Nazi Doctors and the Nuremberg Code: Human Rights in Human Experimentation* (Oxford University Press, 1995).

N. Armstrong, C. Donaldson, *The Economics of Sexual Health* (Family Planning Association, 2005).

J. D. Arras, 'A method in search of a purpose: The internal morality of medicine' (2001) 26 *Journal of Medicine and Philosophy* 643.

R. E. Ashcroft, 'From public interest to political justice' (2004) 13 *Cambridge Quarterly of Healthcare Ethics* 20.

R. E. Ashcroft, 'Could human rights supersede bioethics?' (2010) 10 *Human Rights Law Review* 639.

A Task Force Report funded by IMAP (The Institute on Medicine as a Profession)/OSF (The Open Society Foundations), *Ethics Abandoned: Medical Professionalism and Detainee Abuse in the War on Terror* (2013), available at http://imapny.org/wp-content/themes/imapny/File%20Library/Documents/IMAP-EthicsTextFinal2.pdf.

B. S. Atiyeh, M. T. Rubeiz, S. N. Hayek, 'Aesthetic/cosmetic surgery and ethical challenges' (2008) 32 *Aesthetic Plastic Surgery* 829.

Lord Justice Atkin responding to Lord Riddell, 'The legal responsibility of the surgeon' (1924–25) 19 *Transactions of the Medico-Legal Society* 93.

Audit Commission, *Reducing Spending on Low Clinical Value Treatments* (Audit Commission, 2011).

D. J. Baker, 'Should unnecessary harmful nontherapeutic cosmetic surgery be criminalized?' (2014) 17 *New Criminal Law Review* 587.

R. Baker, I. Bateman, C. Donaldson, M. Jones-Lee, E. Lancsar, G. Loomes, H. Mason, M. Odejar, J. L. Pinto Prades, A. Robinson, M. Ryan, P. Shackley, R. Smith, R. Sugden, J. Wildman, 'Weighting and valuing quality-adjusted life-years using stated preference methods: Preliminary results from the social value of a QALY project' (2010) 14 *Health Technology Assessment*, available at http://www.journalslibrary.nihr.ac.uk/__data/assets/pdf_file/0011/64748/FullReport-hta14270.pdf.

R. T. Barrett, M. Small, R. D. Smith, 'How much will Herceptin really cost?' (2006) 333 *British Medical Journal* 1118.

B. Barry, *Political Argument* (Humanities Press, 1965).

P. Bartlett, 'Civil Confinement' in L. Gostin, P. Bartlett, P. Fennell, J. McHale, R. Mackay (eds), *Principles of Mental Health Law and Policy* (Oxford University Press, 2010).

P. Bartlett, 'The necessity must be convincingly shown to exist: Standards for the compulsory treatment for mental disorder under the Mental Health Act 1983' (2011) 19 *Medical Law Review* 514.

P. Bartlett, R. Sandland, *Mental Health Law, Policy and Practice* (Oxford University Press, 2014).

M. Barton, K. Walker, B. Wiesner, 'Artificial insemination' (13 January 1945) 1 *British Medical Journal* 40.

T. L. Beauchamp, 'Internal and external standards for medical morality' (2001) 26 *Journal of Medicine and Philosophy* 601.

D. Benatar, *Better Never To Have Been: The Harm Of Coming Into Existence* (Oxford University Press, 2008).

M. Benjamin, *Splitting the Difference: Compromise and Integrity in Ethics and Politics* (University Press of Kansas, 1990).

D. Beyleveld, R. Brownsword, *Law as a Moral Judgment* (2nd edn, Sheffield Academic Press, 1994).

G. Birchley, 'Angels of mercy? The legal and professional implications of withdrawal of life-sustaining treatment by nurses in England and Wales' (2012) 20 *Medical Law Review* 337.

J. Black, 'Proceduralising regulation: Part I' (2000) 20 *Oxford Journal of Legal Studies* 597.

J. Black, 'Proceduralising regulation: Part II' (2001) 21 *Oxford Journal of Legal Studies* 33.

L. Blum, 'An eighteenth century health care provider and medical entrepreneur' (1984) 60 *Bulletin of the New Year Academy of Medicine* 944.

V. Blum, *Flesh Wounds: The Culture of Cosmetic Surgery* (University of California Press, 2003).

G. Bognar, I. Hirowse, *The Ethics of Health Care Rationing: An Introduction* (Routledge, 2014).

S. Bordo, *Unbearable Weight: Feminism, Western Culture and the Body* (University of California Press, 1993/2003).

C. Bosk, *Forgive and Remember: Managing Medical Failure* (University of Chicago Press, 1979).

K. M. Boyd, 'Disease, illness, sickness, health, healing and wholeness: Exploring some elusive concepts' (2000) 26 *Medical Humanities* 9.

M. Brazier, *Medicine, Patients and the Law* (2nd edn, Penguin, 1992).

M. Brazier, 'Do no harm: Do patients have responsibilities too?' (2006) 65 *The Cambridge Law Journal* 397.

M. Brazier, 'Can the common law accommodate moral controversy in medicine: The case of abortion?' in A. Alghrani, R. Bennett, S. Ost (eds), *The Criminal Law and Bioethical Conflicts; Walking the Tightrope* (Cambridge University Press, 2012).

M. Brazier, E. Cave, *Medicine, Patients and the Law* (Penguin, 2011).

M. Brazier, J. Miola, 'Bye-bye *Bolam*: A medical litigation revolution?' (2000) 8 *Medical Law Review* 85.

M. Brazier, S. Ost, *Bioethics, Medicine and the Criminal Law, Volume 3: Bioethics and Medicine in the Theatre of the Criminal Process* (Cambridge University Press, 2013).

British Medical Association (BMA), *Consent, Rights and Choices in Health Care for Children and Young People* (BMJ Books, 2001).

BMA, *Withholding and Withdrawing Life-prolonging Medical Treatment: Guidance for Decision Making* (3rd edn, Blackwell Publishing, 2007).

BMA, *Children and Young People Tool Kit* (BMA, 2010), available at http://bma.org.uk/practical-support-at-work/ethics/children/children-and-young-people-tool-kit.

BMA Ethics Department, *Medical Ethics Today: The BMA's Handbook of Ethics and Law* (Wiley, 2012).

British Medical Journal (BMJ), Special issue on too much medicine (2002) 324(7342) *British Medical Journal* .

British Pregnancy Advisory Service, 'Four good reasons for Britain to decriminalise abortion altogether', *BPAS Reproductive Review: Issues in Abortion, Pregnancy, and Birth* (12 June 2014), available at http://www.reproductivereview.org/index.php/rr/article/1592/.

H. Brody, F. Miller, 'The internal morality of medicine: Explication and application to managed care' (1998) 23 *Journal of Medicine and Philosophy* 384.

C. Brontë, *Jane Eyre* (Service & Paton, 1897).

R. Brook, M. Chassin, A. Fink, D. H. Solomon, J. Kosecoff, R. E. Park, 'A method for the detailed assessment of the appropriateness of medical technologies' (1986) 2 *International Journal of Technology Assessment in Health Care* 53.

R. Brook, K. Lohr, 'Will we need to ration effective health care?' (1986) 3 *Issues in Science and Technology* 68.

R. H. Brook, R. E. Park, J. B. Kosecof, M. R. Chassin, C. M. Winslow, J. R. Hampton, 'Diagnosis and treatment of coronary disease: Comparison of doctors' attitudes in the USA and UK (1998) 331 *Lancet* 750.

R. Broughton, B. Rathbone, *What Makes A Good Clinical Guideline?* (Hayward Publishing, 2001).

S. Buetow, B. Sibbald, J. Cantrill, S. Halliwell, 'Appropriateness in health care: Application to prescribing' (1997) 45 *Social Science and Medicine* 261.

A. Buyx, 'Be careful for what you wish for: Theoretical and ethical aspects of wish-fulfilling medicine' (2008) 11 *Medicine, Health Care and Philosophy* 133.

D. Callahan, *The Troubled Dream of Life* (Simon and Schuster, 1993).

A. V. Campbell, R. Huxtable, 'The Position Statement and its commentators: Consensus, compromise or confusion?' (2003) 17 *Palliative Medicine* 180.

D. Campbell, 'More patients sue plastic surgeons over faulty cosmetic surgery' (*The Guardian*, 8 January 2012), available at http://www.theguardian.com/society/2012/jan/08/patients-sue-plastic-surgeons-faulty.

D. Campbell, P. Thomas (eds), *Fundamental Legal Conceptions As Applied in Judicial Reasoning by Wesley Newcomb Hohfeld* (Ashgate Dartmouth, 2001).

A. Caplan (ed.), *When Medicine Went Mad – Bioethics and the Holocaust* (Humana Press, 1992).

Care Quality Commission (CQC), *Count Me In 2010* (TSO, 2011).

CQC, *Monitoring the Mental Health Act 1983 in 2011/12* (TSO, 2013).

CQC, *Monitoring the Mental Health Act 1983 in 2012/13* (TSO, 2014).

Centre for Economic Performance Mental Health Policy Group, *How Mental Health Loses Out in the NHS* (LSE, 2012).

M. Cesa (ed.), *Machiavelli on International Relations* (Oxford University Press, 2014).

M. Chahal, 'Off-trial access to experimental cancer agents for the terminally ill: Balancing the needs of individuals and society' (2010) 36 *Journal of Medical Ethics* 367.

T. E. Chan, 'Legal and regulatory responses to innovative treatment' (2013) 21 *Medical Law Review* 92.

A. L. Cochrane, *Effectiveness and Efficiency: Random Reflections on Health Services* (Nuffield Provincial Hospitals Trust, 1972).

The Cochrane Collaboration, *Cochrane Handbook for Systematic Reviews of Interventions* version 5.1.0, updated March 2011, available at http://www.cochrane-handbook.org/.

J. Coggon, *What Makes Health Public? A Critical Evaluation of Moral, Legal, and Political Claims in Public Health* (Cambridge University Press, 2012).

J. Coggon, J. Miola, 'Autonomy, liberty, and medical decision-making' (2011) 70 *Cambridge Law Journal* 523.

The College of Social Work, *AMHP Community of Interest: AMHP Practice Survey 2013* (The College of Social Work, 2013), available at www.tcsw.org.uk/uploadedFiles/TheCollege/_CollegeLibrary/.

H. J. Cook, 'Trigge, William (fl. 1630–1656)' in B. Harrisson (ed.), *Oxford Dictionary of National Biography* (Oxford University Press, 2004).

R. Cookson, P. Dolan, 'Principles of justice in health care rationing' (2000) 26 *Journal of Medical Ethics* 323.

P. J. Corfield, *Power and the Professions in Britain 1700–1850* (Routledge, 1995).

Council for International Organizations of Medical Sciences, World Health Organization, *International Ethical Guidelines for Biomedical Research Involving Human Subjects* (Council for International Organizations of Medical Sciences, 2002).

D. Cox, M. Le Caze, M. Levine, 'Integrity' in E. N. Zalta (ed.), *The Stanford Encyclopedia of Philosophy* (2013) available at http://plato.stanford.edu/archives/fall2013/entries/integrity/.

B. Cox White, E. H. Gampel, 'Resolving moral dilemmas: A case-based method' (1996) 8 *Healthcare Ethics Committee Forum* 85.

M. Crowley (ed.), *Connecting American Values with Health Reform* (Hastings Center, 2009).

S. Cruess, R. Cruess, 'Professionalism: A contract between medicine and society' (2000) 162 *Canadian Medical Association Journal* 668.

T. Culyer, 'Need – The idea won't do, but we still need it' in R. Cookson, K. Claxton (eds), *The Humble Economist: Tony Culyer on Health, Health Care and Social Decision-Making* (Office of Health Economics/University of York, 2012).

Daily Mail 'Boy bled to death after home circumcision by nurse who was paid £100 to use scissors, forceps and no anaesthetic' (*Mail Online*, 14 December 2012), available at http://www.dailymail.co.uk/news/article-2248333/Nigerian-nurse-Grace-Adeleye-guilty-manslaughter-after.html.

N. Daniels, J. Sabin, *Setting Limits Fairly: Learning to Share Resources for Health* (2nd edn, Oxford University Press, 2008).

E. Davies LJ, 'A legal look at transplants' (1969) 62 *Proceedings of the Royal Society of Medicine* 23.

T. Davies, *The Promotion and Pursuit of Health, 1780–1880* (Unpublished PhD thesis, University of Leicester, 2009).

K. Davis, *Reshaping the Female Body: The Dilemma of Cosmetic Surgery* (Routledge, 1995).

J. Dawson, 'Psychopathology and civil commitment criteria' (1996) 4 *Medical Law Review* 62.

D. DeGrazia, 'Value theory and the best interests standard' (1995) 9 *Bioethics* 50.

Department of Health (DH), *Research Governance Framework for Health and Social Care* (2nd edn, DH, 2005).

DH, *Mental Health Act 1983 Code of Practice* (TSO, 2008).

DH, *Abortion Statistics, England and Wales: 2010* (DH, 2011).

DH, *Abortion Statistics, England and Wales: 2011* (DH, 2012).

DH, *Abortion Statistics, England and Wales: 2012* (DH, 2014).

DH, *Post-legislative scrutiny of the Mental Health Act 2007: Response to the report of the Health Committee of the House of Commons*, Cmnd 8735, (TSO, 2013).

DH, *Handbook to the NHS Constitution* (DH, 2013).

DH, *Abortion Statistics, England and Wales: 2013* (DH, 2014).

DH, *Closing the Gap: Priorities for Essential Change in Mental Health* (DH, 2014).

Department of Health and Social Security, *Report of the Committee of Inquiry into Human Fertilisation and Embryology*, Cmnd 9314 (Stationery Office, 1984).

M. De Hert, J. Detraux, R. van Winkel, W. Yu, C. U. Correll, 'Metabolic and cardiovascular adverse effects associated with antipsychotic drugs' (2012) 8 *Nature Reviews Endocrinology* 114.

R. DerSimonia, N. Laird, 'Meta-analysis in clinical trials' (1986) 7 *Controlled Clinical Trials* 177.

S. Devaney, 'Autonomy Rules OK' (2005) 13 *Medical Law Review* 102.

Director of Public Prosecutions, *Policy for Prosecutors in Respect of Cases of Encouraging or Assisting Suicide* (Crown Prosecution Service, February 2010, updated October 2014).

N. Dixon, 'On the difference between physician-assisted suicide and active euthanasia' (1998) 28 *Hastings Center Report* 25.

M. Dixon-Woods, K. Yeung, C. Bosk, 'Why is UK medicine no longer a self-regulating profession? The role of scandals involving "bad apple" doctors' (2011) 73 *Social Science and Medicine* 1452.

S. Dodds, 'Choice and Control in Feminist Bioethics' in C. Mackenzie, N. Stoljar (eds), *Relational Autonomy: Feminist Perspectives on Autonomy, Agency and the Social Self* (Oxford University Press, 2000).

C. Donaldson, G. Mooney, 'Needs assessment, priority setting and contracts for health care: An economic view' (1991) 303 *British Medical Journal* 1529.

C. Donaldson, M. Mugford, L. Vale (eds), *Evidence-based Health Economics: From Effectiveness to Efficiency in Systematic Review* (BMJ Books, 2002).

R. Dresser, 'First-in-human trial participants: Not a vulnerable population, but vulnerable nonetheless' (2009) 37 *The Journal of Law, Medicine & Ethics* 38.

R. A. Duff, 'Towards a modest legal moralism' (2014) 8 *Criminal Law and Philosophy* 217.

M. Dunn, C. Foster, 'Autonomy and welfare as *amici curiae*' (2010) 18 *Medical Law Review* 86.

C. Durrieu-Diebolt, 'Chirurgie esthetique' *Droit pour tous* ('Plastic surgery' Law for All), available at http://sos-net.eu.org/medical/chirgurg.htm.

G. Dworkin, 'The law relating to organ transplantation in England' (1970) 33 *Modern Law Review* 353.

R. Dworkin, *Life's Dominion* (Harper Collins, 1993).

R. H. Ebert, 'A Twentieth Century Retrospective' in E. Ginzberg (ed.), *Medicine and Society – Clinical Decisions and Societal Values* (Westview Press, 1987).

D. Eddy, 'Clinical decision-making: From theory into practice: Guidelines for policy statements: The explicit approach' (1990) 263 *Journal of the American Medical Association* 2239.

T. Elliott, 'Body dysmorphic disorder, surgery and the limits of consent' (2009) 17 *Medical Law Review* 149.

E. J. Emanuel, M. P. Battin, 'What are the potential cost savings from legalizing physician-assisted suicide?' (1998) 339 *New England Journal of Medicine* 167.

T. Engelhardt, K. Wildes, 'The Four Principles of Health Care Ethics and Post-Modernity' in R. Gillon (ed.), *Principles of Health Care Ethics* (Wiley, 1994).

T. Engelhardt, *The Foundations of Bioethics* (2nd edn, Oxford University Press, 1996).

Ethical Opinion Paper, *Ethical Considerations in Relation to Female Genital Cosmetic Surgery* (British Society for Paediatric and Adolescent Gynaecology, 2013).

T. Exworthy, D. Mohan, N. Hindley, J. Basson, 'Seclusion: Punitive or protective' (2001) 12 *Journal of Forensic Psychiatry* 423.

F. Fatah, 'Should all advertising of cosmetic surgery be banned? Yes' (2012) 345 *British Medical Journal* (2012) 7489.

P. Fennell, *Treatment without Consent* (Routledge, 1996).

P. Fennell, 'Doctor knows best? Therapeutic detention under common law, the Mental Health Act, and the European Convention' (1998) 6 *Medical Law Review* 322.

P. Fennell, 'Convention compliance, public safety, and the social inclusion of mentally disordered people' (2005) 32 *Journal of Law and Society* 90.

P. Fennell, 'Mental health law: History, policy and regulation' in L. Gostin, P. Bartlett, P. Fennell, J. McHale, R. Mackay (eds), *Principles of Mental Health Law and Policy* (Oxford University Press, 2010).

The Earl of Feversham, *Report of Departmental Committee on Human Artificial Insemination*, Cmnd 1105 (HMSO, 1960).

M. Field, K. Lohr (eds), *Clinical Practice Guidelines: From Development to Use* (Institute of Medicine, 1992).

M. Fineman, A. Grear (eds) *Vulnerability: Reflections on a New Ethical Foundation for Law and Politics* (Ashgate, 2013).

I. G. Finlay, V. J. Wheatley, C. Izdebski, 'The House of Lords Select Committee on the Assisted Dying for the Terminally Ill Bill: Implications for specialist palliative care' (2005) 19 *Palliative Medicine* 444.

J. Finnis, *Natural Law and Natural Rights* (Clarendon Press, 1986).

A. Ford, 'The concept of exceptionality: A legal farce?' (2012) 20 *Medical Law Review* 304.

C. Foster, *Choosing Life, Choosing Death: The Tyranny of Autonomy in Medical Law* (Hart, 2009).

C. Foster, J. Miola, 'Who's in charge? The relationship between medical law, medical ethics and medical morality' (online advance access, DOI: 10.1093/medlaw/fwv004).

S. Fovargue, 'Oh pick me, pick me: Selecting participants for xenotransplant clinical trials' (2007) 15 *Medical Law Review* 176.

S. Fovargue, *Xenotransplantation and Risk: Regulating a Developing Biotechnology* (Cambridge University Press, 2012).

S. Fovargue, 'The (ab)use of those with no other hope? Ethical and legal safeguards for recipients of experimental procedures' (2013) 22 *Cambridge Quarterly of Healthcare Ethics* 181.

S Fovargue, M Neal, '"In good conscience": Conscience-based exemptions and proper medical treatment' (2015) 23 *Medical Law Review* 221.

S. Fovargue, S. Ost, 'Does the theoretical framework change the legal end result for mature minors refusing medical treatment or creating self-generated pornography?' (2013) 13 *Medical Law International* 6.

M. Fox, M. Thomson, 'Short changed? The law and ethics of male circumcision' (2005) 13 *International Journal of Children's* Rights 161.

M. Fox, M. Thomson, 'A covenant with the status quo? Male circumcision and the new BMA guidance to doctors' (2005) 31 *Journal of Medical Ethics* 463.

B. Freedman, 'A meta-ethics for professional morality' (1978) 89 *Ethics* 1.

H. Freeman, 'Can a woman shave her armpits and still call herself a feminist?' (*The Guardian*, 15 July, 2013), available at http://www.theguardian.com/fashion/2013/jul/15/woman-shave-armpits-still-feminist.

E. Freidson, *Professional Dominance: The Social Structure of Medical Care* (Aldine, 1970).

E. Freidson, *Professionalism Reborn: Theory, Prophecy and Policy* (Polity Press, 1994).

L. Frith, E. Blyth, 'Assisted reproductive technologies in the US: Is more regulation needed?' (2014) 29 *Reproductive Biomedicine Online* 516.

L. L. Fuller, *The Morality of Law* (revised edn, Yale University Press 1969).

A. Furedi, 'Are there too many abortions?' (Winter 2008/9) Special Edition 2 *Abortion Review Special Edition: Abortion and Women's Lives (Papers from the BPAS conference, London 25–26 June 2008)* 3, available at http://www.abortionreview.org/images/uploads/AR_SpecialEdition_2.pdf.

A. Furedi, 'Abortion is safe, and it should be as available as easily as contraception: The time has come to decriminalise it altogether' (*The Independent*, 21 October 2014).

J. Gallager, 'Plastic surgery "booming" in the UK' (*BBC News*, 3 February 2014), available at http://www.bbc.co.uk/news/health-25986840.

L. Ganzini, 'Artificial nutrition and hydration at the end of life: Ethics and evidence' (2006) 4 *Palliative & Supportive Care* 135.

General Medical Council (GMC), *Seeking Patients' Consent: The Ethical Considerations* (GMC, 1998).

GMC, *Good Medical Practice* (GMC, 1998).

GMC, *0–18 Years: Guidance for All Doctors* (GMC, 2007).

GMC, *Patients and Doctors Making Decisions Together* (GMC, 2008).

GMC, *Treatment and Care Towards the End of Life: Good Practice in Decision Making* (GMC, 2010).

GMC, *Good Practice in Research and Consent to Research* (GMC, 2010), updated 2013.

GMC, *When a Patient Seeks Advice or Information about Assistance to Die* (GMC, 2013).

GMC, *Good Medical Practice* (GMC, 2013), updated 29 April 2014.

Genetic Alliance UK, *New Medicines for Serious Conditions: Weighing the Risks and Benefits – The Verdict of a Jury of Patients* (Genetic Alliance UK, 2011).

S. Gibb, C. Donaldson, R. Henshaw, 'Assessing strength of preference for abortion method using willingness to pay' (1998) 27 *Journal of Advance Nursing* 30.

D. Giesen, *International Medical Malpractice Law: A Comparative Study of Civil Responsibility Arising from Medical Care* (Martinus Nijhoff, 1988).

R. Gillon (ed.), *Principles of Health Care Ethics* (Wiley, 1994).

D. Gimlin 'Cosmetic surgery: Beauty as commodity' (2000) 23 *Qualitative Sociology* 1.

D. Gimlin, 'Imagining the other in cosmetic surgery' (2010) 16 *Body and Society* 57.

S. Giordano, 'Is the body a republic?' (2005) *Journal of Medical Ethics* 470.

S. Giordano, 'ICD-11 reforms. Where should gender identity disorder go?' in B. Miller (ed.), *Gender Identity: Disorders, Developmental Perspectives and Social Implications* (Nova Publisher, 2014).

M. J. Goldacre, S. Fazel, F. Smith, T. W. Lambert, 'Choice and rejection of psychiatry as a career: Surveys of UK medical graduates from 1974–2009' (2013) 202 *British Journal of Psychiatry* 228.

L. Gostin, 'The Ideology of Entitlement: The Application of Contemporary Legal Approaches to Psychiatry' in P Bean (ed.), *Mental Illness: Changes and Trends* (Wiley, 1983).

L. Gostin, 'Contemporary social historical perspectives on mental health reform' (1983) 10 *Journal of Law and Society* 47.

J. Graham, *A Private Advice, Formerly Sold at the Temple of Hymen, By the Doctor Himself, For One Guinea* (London, 1783).

J. Graham, *A Lecture on the Generation, Increase and Improvement of the Human Species*, (London, 1784).

J. D. Graham, *Memorandum to the President's Management Council, Benefit-Cost Methods and Life-Saving Rules* (Office of Information and Regulatory Affairs, Office of Management and Budget, Executive Office of the President, 2003).

R. Grey, D. Rofail, J. Allen, T. Newey, 'A survey of patient satisfaction with and subjective experiences of treatment with anti-psychotic medication' (2005) 52 *Journal of Advanced Nursing* 31.

J. Griffiths, H. Weyers, M. Adams, *Euthanasia and the Law in Europe* (Hart, 2008).

J. Grimshaw, A. Hutchinson, 'Clinical practice guidelines: Do they enhance value for money in health care?' (1995) 51 *British Medical Bulletin* 927.

A. Grubb, 'Editorial: Who decides? Legislating for the incapacitated adult' (1998) 5 *European Journal of Health Law* 231.

D. Gurnham, 'Legal authority and savagery in judicial rhetoric: Sexual violence and the criminal courts' (2011) 7 *International Journal of Law in Context* 117.

E. Haiken, *Venus Envy: A History of Cosmetic Surgery* (John Hopkins University Press, 1997).

J. Halliday, N. Vekaria, 'Ashya King to have cancer treatment with 70% chance of survival' (*The Guardian*, 9 September 2014).

L. Halpin, J. Savulescu, K. Talbot, M. Turner, P. Talman, 'Improving access to medicines: Empowering patients in the quest to improve treatment for rare lethal diseases' (2013) *Journal of Medical Ethics* (online advance access, DOI: 10.1136/medethics-2013-101427).

C. Ham, 'Health care rationing' (1995) 310 *British Medical Journal* 1483.

J. Harris, 'Moral enhancement and freedom' (2011) 25 *Bioethics* 102.

J. Harris 'Reproductive liberty, disease and disability' (2005) 10 *Reproductive Medicine Online* 13.

H.L.A. Hart, 'Review: Fuller, The Morality of Law' (1965) 78 *Harvard Law Review* 1281.

R. Harvey, *Making it Better: Strategies for Improving the Effectiveness and Quality of Health Services in Australia* (National Health Strategy Unit, 1991).

I. Heath, 'Role of fear in over diagnosis and over treatment' (2014) *British Medical Journal* 349:g6123 (online advance access, DOI: 10.1136/bmj.g6123).

P. Healey, J. Samanta, 'When does the "learning curve" of innovative interventions become questionable practice?' (2008) 36 *European Journal of Vascular and Endovascular Surgery* 253.

D. Healy, *Pharmageddon*, (University of California Press, 2013).

Health Committee, *First Report Post-Legislative Scrutiny of the Mental Health Act 1983*, Session 2013–14, HC 584 (House of Commons, 2013).

Health and Social Care Information Centre (HSCIC), *In Patients Formally Detained in Hospitals Under the Mental Health Act 1983, and Patients Subject to Supervised Community Treatment* (HSCIC, 2014).

V. Held, *The Public Interest and Individual Interests* (Basic Books, 1970).

W. H. Helfand, *Quack, Quack, Quack: The Sellers of Nostrums in Prints, Posters, Ephemera & Books* (Grolier Club, 2002).

HM Government, *Valuing Every Voice: Making the Case for the Mental Capacity Act* (HM Government, 2014).

J. Herring, *Medical Law and Ethics* (5th edn, Oxford University Press, 2014).

K. Hodkinson, 'The need to know – therapeutic privilege: A way forward' (2013) 21 *Health Care Analysis* 105.

House of Commons/House of Lords Joint Committee on the Draft Mental Health Bill, *Draft Mental Health Bill Session 2-004–5: Volume I Report, together with formal minutes and annexes* (HL Paper 79; HC Paper 95; March 2005).

House of Lords/House of Commons Joint Committee on Human Rights, *Legislative Scrutiny: Mental Health Bill Fourth Report of Session 2006–07* (HL Paper 40, HC Paper 288; 4 February 2007).

E. C. Hughes, *Men and their Work* (Gencoe Free Press, 1958).

Human Fertilisation and Embryology Authority, 'Fertility Treatment in 2013: Trends and Figures' (2014), available at www.hfea.gov.uk/docs/HFEA_Fertility_Trends_and_Figures_2013.pdf .

Human Fertilisation and Embryology Authority, *Mitochondria Replacement Consultation: Advice to Government* (2013), available at http://www.hfea.gov.uk/docs/Mitochondria_replacement_consultation_-_advice_for_Government.pdf.

D. Hume, *An Enquiry Concerning Human Understanding*, in PH Nidditch (ed.) (Clarendon Press, 1975).

R. Huxtable, *Euthanasia, Ethics and the Law: From Conflict to Compromise* (Routledge-Cavendish, 2007).

R. Huxtable, 'Autonomy, best interests and the public interest: Treatment, non-treatment and the values of medical law' (2014) *Medical Law Review* (online advance access, DOI: 10.1093/medlaw/fwt035).

I. Illich, 'Medical nemesis' (1974) 303 *The Lancet* 918.

I. Illich, *Limits to Medicine – Medical Nemesis: The Expropriation of Health* (Marion Boyars, 1976).

Information Services Division (ISD) Scotland, *Statistical Disclosure Control Protocol Version 2.3* (ISD, 2012), available at http://www.isdscotland.org/About-ISD/Confidentiality/DISCLOSURE-PROTOCOL-VERSION-2-3_FULLVERSION.PDF.

ISD Scotland, *Abortion Statistics: Year ending 31 December 2010* (ISD Scotland/ National Statistics, 31 May 2011) 12, available at http://www.isdscotland.org/Health-Topics/Sexual-Health/Publications/2011-05-31/2011-05-31-Abortions-Report.pdf.

ISD Scotland, *Abortion Statistics: Year ending 31 December 2011* (ISD Scotland/ National Statistics, 29 May 2012) 13, available at http://www.isdscotland.org/Health-Topics/Sexual-Health/Publications/2012-05-29/2012-05-29-Abortions-Report-2011.pdf.

ISD Scotland, *Abortion Statistics: Year ending 31 December 2012* (ISD Scotland/ National Statistics, 28 May 2013) 13, available at http://www.isdscotland.org/Health-Topics/Sexual-Health/Publications/2013-05-28/2013-05-28-Abortions-Report.pdf.

ISD Scotland, *Abortion Statistics: Year ending 31 December 2013* (ISD Scotland/ National Statistics, 27 May 2014) 14, available at https://isdscotland.scot.nhs.uk/Health-Topics/Sexual-Health/Publications/2014-05-27/2014-05-27-Abortions2013-Report.pdf?14501589537.

D. S. Irvine, A. Templeton, 'Donor insemination' in T. B. Hargreaves (ed.), *Male Infertility* (Springer, 1994).

E. Jackson, *Regulating Reproduction: Law, Technology and Autonomy* (Hart, 2001).

E. Jackson, *Medical Law: Text, Cases and Materials* (3rd edn, Oxford University Press, 2013).

M.S.R. Jenner, P. Wallis, 'The Medical Marketplace' in M.S.R. Jenner, P. Wallis (eds), *Medicine and the Market in England and its Colonies, c.1450-c.1850* (Palgrave McMillan, 2007).

J. Johnson, W. Rogers, 'Innovative surgery: The ethical challenges' (2012) 38 *Journal of Medical Ethics* 9.

K. Jones, *A History of Mental Health Services* (Routledge, Keegan and Paul, 1972).

M. Jones, 'Informed consent and other fairy stories' (1999) 7 *Medical Law Review* 103.

L. R. Kass, 'Regarding the end of medicine and the pursuit of health' (1975) 40 *Public Interest* 11.

R. Kendell, A. Pearce, 'Consultant psychiatrists who retired prematurely 1995 and 1996' (1997) 21 *Psychiatric Bulletin* 741.

I. Kennedy, *The Unmasking of Medicine* (George Allen & Unwin, 1981).

I. Kennedy, *Treat Me Right: Essays in Medical Law and Ethics* (Clarendon Press, 1988).

I. Kennedy, A Grubb, *Medical Law* (3rd edn, Butterworths, 2000).

J. Keown, *The Law and Ethics of Medicine: Essays on the Inviolability of Life* (Oxford University Press, 2013).

E. L. Keyes, 'The Joanna Stephens Medicines for the Stone: A faith that failed' (1942) 18 *Bulletin of the New York Academy of Medicine* 835.

K. Keywood, 'Psychiatric injustice? The therapeutic presumption of behaviour management in mental health law' (2005) 7 *The Journal of Adult Protection* 25.

M. King, C. Thornhill, *Niklas Luhmann's Theory of Politics and Law* (Palgrave Macmillan, 2005).

C. Kitzinger, J. Kitzinger, 'Withdrawing artificial nutrition and hydration from minimally conscious and vegetative patients: Family perspectives' (2015) 41 *Journal of Medical Ethics* 157.

J. Kitzinger, C. Kitzinger, 'The "window of opportunity" for death after severe brain injury: Family perspectives' (2013) 35 *Sociology of Health and Illness* 1095.

R. Klein, P. Day, S. Redmayne, *Managing Scarcity* (Open University Press, 1996).

R. Klein, J. Maybin, *Thinking About Rationing* (King's Fund, 2012).

M. Kramer, N. Simmonds, H. Steiner, *A Debate Over Rights* (Oxford University Press, 1998).

E. Krause, *Death of the Guilds: Professions, States, and the Advance of Capitalism, 1930 to the Present* (Yale University Press, 1996).

J. M. Laing, 'Perspectives on monitoring mental health legislation in England: A view from the front line' (2014) *Medical Law Review* (online advance access, DOI: 10.1093/medlaw/fwu029).

J. Laing, N. Glover-Thomas, 'Mental Health Professionals' in L. Gostin, P. Bartlett, P. Fennell, J. McHale, R. Mackay (eds), *Principles of Mental Health Law and Policy* (Oxford University Press, 2010).

R. D. Laing, *The Divided Self: An Existential Study in Sanity and Madness* (Penguin, 1960).

E. Lancsar, J. Wildman, C. Donaldson, M. Ryan, R. Baker, 'Deriving distributional weights for QALYs through discrete choice experiments' (2011) 30 *Journal of Health Economics* 466.

M. Latham, 'The shape of things to come: Feminism, regulation and cosmetic surgery' (2008) 16 *Medical Law Review* 437.

M. Latham, 'A poor prognosis for autonomy: Self-regulated cosmetic surgery in the United Kingdom' (2010) 18 *Reproductive Health Matters* 47.

J. Laurance, 'IVF clinics accused of putting money before safety' *The Independent* (London, 14 May 2012), available at http://www.independent.co.uk/life-style/health-and-families/health-news/ivf-clinics-accused-of-putting-money-before-safety-7743505.html.

Law Commission, *Mentally Incapacitated Adults and Decision Making: An Overview. Consultation Paper No. 119* (HMSO, 1991).

Law Commission, *Mentally Incapacitated Adults and Decision-Making: An New Jurisdiction. Consultation Paper No. 128* (HMSO, 1993).

Law Commission, *Mentally Incapacitated Adults and Decision-Making: Medical Treatment and Research. Consultation Paper No. 129* (HMSO, 1993).

Law Commission, *Mentally Incapacitated Adults and other Vulnerable Adults: Public Law Protection. Consultation Paper No. 130* (HMSO, 1993).

Law Commission, *Criminal Law: Consent and Offences Against the Person: A Consultation Paper*, Consultation Paper No 134 (HMSO, 1994).

Law Commission, *Criminal Law: Consent in the Criminal Law: Consultation Paper No. 139* (HMSO, 1995).

Law Commission, *Mental Incapacity. Consultation Paper No. 231* (HMSO, 1995).

P. Lewis, 'Feeding anorexic patients who refuse food' (1999) 7 *Medical Law Review* 21.

P. Lewis, 'Withdrawal of treatment from a patient in a permanent vegetative state: Judicial involvement and innovative "treatment"' (2007) 15 *Medical Law Review* 392.

P. Lewis, 'Legal change on contraceptive sterilisation' (2011) 32 *Journal of Legal History* 295.

P. Lewis, 'The medical exception' (2012) 65 *Current Legal Problems* 355.

R. J. Lifton, 'Doctors and torture' (2004) 351 *New England Journal of Medicine* 415.

M. O. Little, 'Suspect Norms of Appearance and the Ethics of Complicity' in I. De Beaufort, M. Hilhorst, S. Holm (eds), *The Eye if the Beholder: Ethics and Medical Change if Appearance* (Scandinavian University Press, 1997).
'London's first non-medical approved clinician' (23 May 2013), available at www.oxleas.nhs.uk/news/2013/5/londons-first-non-medical-appr/.
I. Loudon, *Medical Care and the General Practitioner 1750–1850* (Clarendon Press, 1986).
N. Luhmann, 'Operational closure and structural coupling: The differentiation of the legal system' (1992) 13 *Cardozo Law Review* 1419.
D. Lupton, *Medicine as Culture. Illness, Disease and the Body in Western Societies* (Sage, 2003).
A. MacIntyre, *After Virtue* (Notre Dame Press, 1981).
A. MacIntyre, *After Virtue* (3rd edn, University of Notre Dame Press 2007).
H. R. Magee, 'Doctors in satirical prints and cartoons' (2007) 187 *Medical Journal of Australia* 596.
L. Martin, S. L. Williams, K. B. Haskard, M. R. Dimatteo, 'The challenge of patient adherence' (2005) 1 *Therapeutics and Clinical Risk Management* 189.
J. K. Mason, R. A. McCall Smith, G. T. Laurie, *Law and Medical Ethics* (6th edn, Butterworths, 2002).
J. K. Mason, G. T. Laurie, *Law and Medical Ethics* (8th edn. Oxford University Press, 2011).
J. K. Mason, G. T. Laurie, *Mason and McCall Smith's Law and Medical Ethics* (9th edn, Oxford University Press, 2013).
G. Matthew, 'Measuring Need and Evaluating Services' in G McLachlan (ed.), *Portfolio for Health* (Oxford University Press, 1971).
D. McGovern, 'Randomized Controlled Trials' in D. McGovern, R. Valori, W. Summerskill, M. Levi, *Key Topics in Evidence-Based Medicine* (BIOS Scientific Publishers, 2001).
A. McHarg, 'Reconciling human rights and the public interest: Conceptual problems and doctrinal uncertainty in the jurisprudence of the European Court of Human Rights' (1999) 62 *Modern Law Review* 671.
T. McIntosh, *A Social History of Maternity and Childbirth* (Routledge, 2013).
R. S. McIntyre, 'Psychotropic drugs and adverse events in the treatment of bipolar disorders revisited' (2002) 63 *Journal of Clinical Psychiatry* 15.
S. McLean, *Old Law, New Medicine: Medical Ethics and Human Rights* (Pandora Publishing, 1999).
A. McNicol, 'The pilot scheme that could shatter the glass ceiling for mental health social workers' *Community Care* (27 November 2013), available at www.communitycare.co.uk/2013/11/27.
Medical Research Council, 'Experimental Medicine', available at http://www.mrc.ac.uk/research/initiatives/experimental-medicine/
Medicines Healthcare Products Regulatory Agency, 'Early Access to Medicines Scheme (EAMS)', available at http://www.mhra.gov.uk/Howweregulate/Innovation/Earlyaccesstomedicinesscheme EAMS/index.htm.
Mental Health Act 2007 Explanatory Notes (TSO, 2007).
Mental Health Act Commission, *Risk, Rights, Recovery Twelfth Biennial Report 2005–2007* (TSO, 2008).
Mental Health Foundation (MHF), *The Fundamental Facts: The Latest Facts and Figures on Mental Health* (MHF, 2007).
D. Meyers, *The Human Body and the Law: A Medico-Legal Study* (Edinburgh University Press, 1970).
Mid Staffordshire NHS Foundation Trust Public Inquiry (2013), available at http://www.midstaffspublicinquiry.com/.

Mid Staffordshire NHS Foundation Trust Public Inquiry, *Report of the Mid Staffordshire NHS Foundation Trust Public Inquiry – Executive Summary* (HC 947, 2013), available at http://www.midstaffspublicinquiry.com/sites/default/files/report/Executive%20summary.pdf.

S. H. Miles, 'Physician-assisted suicide and the profession's gyrocompass' (1995) 25 *Hastings Center Report* 17.

F. G. Miller, H. Brody, 'Professional integrity and physician-assisted death' (1995) 25 *Hastings Center Report* 8.

F. Miller, H. Brody, 'The internal morality of medicine: An evolutionary perspective' (2001) 26 *Journal of Medicine and Philosophy* 581.

F. Miller, H. Brody, 'Enhancement technologies and professional integrity' (2005) 5 *American Journal of Bioethics* 15.

F. G. Miller, H. Brody, K. C. Chung, 'Cosmetic surgery and the internal morality of medicine' (2000) 9 *Cambridge Quarterly of Healthcare Ethics* 353.

Mind, *Mental Health Crisis Care: Physical Restraint in Crisis. A Report on Physical Restraint in Hospital Settings in England* (Mind, 2013).

J. Miola, 'Medical law and medical ethics: Complementary or corrosive?' (2004) 6 *Medical Law International* 251.

J. Miola, *Medical Ethics and Medical Law: A Symbiotic Relationship* (Hart, 2007).

J. Miola, 'On the materiality of risk: Paper tigers and panaceas' (2009) 17 *Medical Law Review* 76.

G. Mitchell, 'Therapeutic lying to assist people with dementia in maintaining medication adherence' (2014) 21 *Nursing Ethics* 844.

C. Mitton, C. Donaldson, *The Priority Setting Toolkit: A Practical Guide to the Use of Economics in Health Care Decision Making* (BMJ Books, 2004).

C. Mitton, S. Patten, H. Waldner, C. Donaldson, 'Priority setting in health authorities: A novel approach to a historical activity' (2003) 57 *Social Science and Medicine* 1653.

H.-G. Moeller, *Luhmann Explained: From Souls to Systems* (Open Court, 2006).

R. Momeyer, 'Does physician assisted suicide violate the integrity of medicine?' (1995) 20 *Journal of Medicine and Philosophy* 13.

J. Montgomery, *Health Care Law* (2nd edn, Oxford University Press, 2002).

J. Montgomery, 'Law and the demoralisation of medicine' (2006) 26 *Legal Studies* 185.

G. Mooney, S. Jan, V. Wiseman, 'Staking a case for claims: A case study of resource allocation in Australian Aboriginal Health Care' (2002) 54 *Social Science and Medicine* 1657.

D. Morgan, R. Lee, *Blackstone's Guide to the Human Fertilisation and Embryology Act 1990* (Blackstone Press, 1991).

M. E. Moran, *Urolithiasis* (Springer, 2014).

S. Morse, 'Crazy behaviour, morals and science: An analysis of mental health law' (1978) 51 *California Law Review* 527.

A. Mullock, 'The Supreme Court decision in *Nicklinson*: Human rights, criminal wrongs and the dilemma of death' (2015) 31 *Journal of Professional Negligence* 18.

R. Nachtigall, 'Secrecy: An unresolved issue in the practice of donor insemination' (1993) 168 *American Journal of Obstetrics and Gynecology* 1846.

NHS Choices, 'Availability of Cosmetic Surgery' (16 May 2013), available at http://www.nhs.uk/Conditions/Cosmetic-surgery/Pages/Availability.aspx.

NHS England, Transforming Participation in Health Care (2013), available at http://www.england.nhs.uk/wp-content/uploads/2013/09/trans-part-hc-guid1.pdf.

NHS Choices, 'Height/weight chart', available at http://www.nhs.uk/Livewell/healthy-living/Pages/height-weight-chart.aspx.

NHS Executive, *New Drugs for Multiple Sclerosis*, EL 95 (97 (DH, 1995).

NHS Executive, *Priorities and Planning Guidance for the NHS: 1995/96* (NHS Executive, 1994 (EL(94)55).

NHS Management Executive, *Improving Clinical Effectiveness* (NHS Management Executive, 1993, (EL(93)115)).

NHS, *The NHS Atlas of Variation in Healthcare* (NHS, 2010).

National Infertility Awareness Campaign (NIAC), 'Assisted conception needs assisted implementation: A report into the status of fertility services in England' (NIAC, 2014), available at http://www.infertilitynetworkuk.com/uploaded/NIAC/Assisted%20Conception%20Needs%20Assisted%20Implementation.pdf.

National Institute for Clinical Excellence, *A Guide to Our Work* (NICE, 1999).

National Institute for Health and Care Excellence (NICE), *Violence: The Short-Term Management of Disturbed/Violent Behaviour in In-Patient Psychiatric Settings and Emergency Departments* (NICE Guideline CG25, February 2005).

NICE, *Trastuzumab for the Treatment of Early Stage HER-2 Positive Breast Cancer*, Technology Appraisal 107 (NICE, 2006).

NICE, *Common Mental Health Disorders: Identification and Pathways to Care*, (NICE Guideline CG123, May 2011).

NICE, *Service User Experience in Adult Mental Health: Improving the Experience of Care for People Using Adult NHS Mental Health Services* (NICE Guideline CG136, December 2011).

NICE, *Fertility: Assessment and Treatment for People with Fertility Problems* (NICE Guideline CG156, 2013), available at https://www.nice.org.uk/guidance/CG156.

D. Neuhauser, A. M. Lewicki, 'What do we gain from the sixth stool guaiac?' (1975) 293 New *England Journal of Medicine* 226.

B. New, J. LeGrand, *Rationing in the NHS: Principles and Pragmatism* (King's Fund, 1996).

D. Nicholson, *The Year: NHS Chief Executive's Annual Report 2008/09* (DH, 2009).

O. Norheim, 'Healthcare rationing – Are additional criteria needed for assessing evidence based clinical practice guidelines?' (1999) 319 *British Medical Journal* 1426.

S. Ost, 'The de-medicalisation of assisted dying: Is a less medicalised model the way forward?' (2010) 18 *Medical Law Review* 497.

S. Pamboukian, *Doctoring the Novel: Medicine and Quackery from Shelley to Doyle* (Ohio University Press, 2012).

E. M. Papper, 'Satire of medicine: The 18th century and beyond' (1990) 83 *Journal of the Royal Society of Medicine* 524.

L. A. Parapia, 'History of bloodletting by phlebotomy' (2008) 143 *British Journal of Haematology* 490.

T. Parsons, *The Social System* (Routledge & Kegan Paul, 1951).

K. Pauly Morgan, 'Women and the knife: Cosmetic surgery and the colonisation of women's bodies' in S. Sherwin, B. Parish (eds), *Women, Medicine, Ethics and the Law* (Ashgate, 2002).

S. Peacock, D. Ruta, C. Mitton, C. Donaldson, A. Bate, M. Murtagh, 'Using economics for pragmatic and ethical priority setting: Two checklists for doctors and managers' (2006) 332 *British Medical Journal* 482.

J. Peay, *Decisions and Dilemmas: Working with Mental Health Law* (Hart, 2003).

M. Peckham, 'Research and development for the National Health Service' (1991) 338 *Lancet* 367.

The Peel Committee, 'Annual Report of the Council: Appendix V: Report of the Panel on Human Artificial Insemination' (1973) Suppl. 2 *British Medical Journal* 3.

E. D. Pellegrino, 'The internal morality of clinical medicine: A paradigm for the ethics of the helping and healing professions' (2001) 26 *Journal of Medicine and Philosophy* 559.

E. D. Pellegrino, 'Toward a reconstruction of medical morality' (2006) 6 *The American Journal of Bioethics* 65.

N. Pfeffer, 'Artificial insemination, in-vitro fertilisation and the stigma of infertility' in M. Stanworth (ed.), *Reproductive Technologies: Gender, Motherhood and Medicine* (Polity Press, 1987).

C. Phillips, *What is a QALY?* (Hayward Publishing, 2009).

E. Pilkington, 'Doctor involved in botched execution "experimented" on inmate, suit claims' (*The Guardian*, 14 October 2014).

V. Pitts-Taylor 'Becoming-being a cosmetic surgery patient: Semantic instability and the intersubjective self' (2009) 122 *Studies in Gender and Sexuality* 3.

D. Porter, R. Porter, *Patient's Progress: Doctors and Doctoring in Eighteenth-Century England* (Stanford University Press, 1989).

R. Porter, 'The patient's view: Doing medical history from below' (1985) 14 *Theory and Society* 188.

R. Porter, *Health for Sale: Quackery in England, 1660–1850* (Manchester University Press, 1989).

R. Porter, *Quacks: Fakers & Charlatans in English Medicine* (Tempus Press, 2000).

R. Porter, 'Graham, James (1745–1794)' in B. Harrisson (ed.), *Oxford Dictionary of National Biography* (Oxford University Press, 2004), available at http://www.oxforddnb.com/view/article/11199.

Press Association, 'Breast implant register for the UK in the wake of the PIP scandal' (*The Guardian*, 29 December 2013), available at http://www.theguardian.com/world/2013/dec/29/breast-implant-register-established-pip-scandal.

D. Price, *Legal and Ethical Aspects of Organ Transplantation* (Cambridge University Press, 2000).

D. Price, 'From Cosmos and Damien to Van Velzen: The human tissue saga continues' (2003) 11 *Medical Law Review* 1.

D. Price, 'Remodelling the regulation of postmodern innovation in medicine' (2005) 1 *International Journal of Law in Context* 121.

L. Putowskiemail, D. Darmochwal-Kolarz, J. Rolinski, J. Oleszczuk, J. Jakowicki, 'The immunological profile of infertile women after repeated IVF failure' (2004) 112 *European Journal of Obstetrics and Gynecology and Reproductive Biology* 192.

R. Quain, 'The harveian oration: On the history and progress of medicine' (1885) 2 *British Medical Journal* 775.

J. Raach, 'English medical licensing in the early seventeenth century' (1944) 16 *Yale Journal of Biology and Medicine* 267.

J. Rawls, *Political Liberalism* (Columbia University Press, 1993).

M. Rawlins, D. Barnett, A. Stevens, 'Pharmacoeconomics: NICE's approach to decision making' (2010) 70 *British Journal of Clinical Pharmacology* 346.

E. G. Raymond, D. A. Grimes, 'The comparative safety of legal induced abortion and childbirth in the United States' (2012) 119 *Obstetrics & Gynecology*.

W. J. Reader, *Professional Men: The Rise of the Professional Classes in Nineteenth-Century England* (Weidenfeld, 1966).

Report of the Expert Committee, Review of the Mental Health Act 1983 (London, 1999).

Review Committee, *Review of the Regulation of Cosmetic Interventions: Final Report* (DH, 2013).

R. Rhodes, 'Two concepts of medical ethics and their implications for medical ethics education' (2002) 27 *Journal of Medicine and Philosophy* 493.

C. Richie 'What would an environmentally sustainable reproductive technology industry look like?' (2014) 10 *Journal of Medical Ethics* 1136.

N. Rose, 'Unreasonable rights: Mental illness and the limits of the law' (1985) 12 *Journal of Law and Society* 199.

C. Rosenberg, 'AMA opposes forced feedings at Guantánamo' (*Miami Herald*, 30 April 2013), available at http://www.miamiherald.com/news/nation-world/world/americas/guantanamo/article1950859.html.

D. J. Rothman, *Strangers at the Bedside: A History of How Law and Bioethics Transformed Medical Decision Making* (Transaction Publishers, 1991).

Royal College of Physicians (RCP), *Doctors in Society: Medical Professionalism in a Changing World* (RCP, 2005).

RCP, *Guidelines on the Practice of Ethics Committees in Medical Research with Human Participants* (4th edn, RCP, 2007).

RCP, *Prolonged Disorders of Consciousness: National Clinical Guidelines* (RCP, 2013)

The Royal Liverpool Children's Inquiry (Stationary Office, 2001).

T. W. Ruger, 'Health law's coherence anxiety' (2008) 96 *Georgetown Law Journal* 625.

D. Rush, E. MacAskill, I. Cobain, A. Yuhas, O. Laughland, 'Rectal Rehydration and Waterboarding: The CIA Torture Report's Grisliest Findings' (*The Guardian*, 10 December 2014), available at http://www.theguardian.com/us-news/2014/dec/09/cia-torture-report-worst-findings-waterboard-rectal.

S. Saarni, H. Gylling, 'Evidence based medicine guidelines: A solution to rationing or politics disguised as science?' (2004) 30 *Journal of Medical Ethics* 171.

J. Sabin, 'Individualism, solidarity and US health care' (2012) 14 *Virtual Mentor* 415.

D. L. Sackett, W.M.C. Rosenberg, J. A. Muir Gray, R. B. Haynes, W. S. Richardson, 'Evidence based medicine: What it is and what it isn't' (1996) 312 *British Medical Journal* 71.

J. Sanchez Taylor, 'The power of breasts: Gender, class and cosmetic surgery' (2012) 35 *Women's Studies International Forum* 458.

G. Santayana, *The Life of Reason: The Phases of Human Progress* (MIT Press, 2011).

B. Saunders, J. Kitzinger, C. Kitzinger, 'Anonymising interview data: Challenges and compromise in practice' (2014) *Qualitative Research*, available at http://qrj.sagepub.com/content/early/2014/09/23/1468794114550439.refs.

W. Schleiner, *Medical Ethics in the Renaissance* (Georgetown University Press, 1995).

E. Schuster, 'Fifty years later: The significance of the Nuremberg Code' (1997) 337 *New England Journal of Medicine* 1436.

F. Scott Fitzgerald, *Tender is the Night* (Charles Scribner's Sons, 1934).

C. Seale, 'National survey of end-of-life decisions made by UK medical practitioners' (2006) 20 *Palliative Medicine* 3.

A. Sen, 'Health Achievement and Equity: External and Internal Perspectives' in S. Anand, F. Peter, A. Sen (eds), *Public Health, Ethics, and Equity* (Oxford University Press, 2004).

Senate Select Committee on Intelligence, *Committee Study of the Central Intelligence Agency's Detention and Interrogation Program. Findings and Conclusions* (SSCI, 2012), available at http://www.intelligence.senate.gov/study2014/sscistudy1.pdf.

L. Servitje, 'If it looks like a duck' (2013) 34 *Journal of Medical Humanities* 407.

S. Sheldon, 'The Abortion Act's paternalism belongs to the 1960s' (*The Guardian*, 22 March 2012).

S. Sheldon, S. Wilkinson, 'Female genital mutilation and cosmetic surgery: Regulating non-therapeutic body modification' (1998) 12 *Bioethics* 263.

Shipman Inquiry, *Shipman: The Final Report* (TSO, 2005).

R. Sifris, 'Restrictive regulation of abortion and the right to health' (2010) 18 *Medical Law Review* 185.

A.W.B. Simpson, *Cannibalism and the Common Law* (University of Chicago Press, 1984).

P.D.G. Skegg, 'Medical procedures and the crime of battery' [1974] *Crim LR* 693.

P.D.G. Skegg, 'Medical procedures and two offences against the person' (1976) 16 *Medicine, Science and the Law* 264.

P.D.G. Skegg, *Law, Ethics and Medicine: Studies in Medical Law* (Clarendon Press, 1984).

B. Skeggs, *Formations of Class and Gender: Becoming Respectable* (Sage, 1997).

P. Skrabanek, *The Death of Humane Medicine and the Rise of Coercive Healthism* (St Edmundsbury Press, 1994).

R. C. Smith, 'Body Integrity Identity Disorder: A Problem of Perception?' in A. Alghrani, R. Bennett, S. Ost (eds), *Bioethics, Medicine and the Criminal Law Volume 1: The Criminal Law and Bioethical Conflict: Walking the Tightrope* (Cambridge University Press, 2013).

R. Snowdon, G. D. Mitchell, E. M. Snowdon, *Artificial Reproduction: A Social Investigation* (George Allen and Unwin, 1983).

S. Sontag, *Illness As Metaphor* (McGraw-Hill Ryerson, 1978).

B. Southgate, *What is History For?* (Routledge, 2006).

M. St. Peter, A. Trinidad, M. S. Irwig, 'Self-castration by a transsexual woman: Financial and psychological costs: A case report' (2012) 9 *Journal of Sexual Medicine* 1216.

P. Starr, *The Social Transformation of American Medicine* (Basic Books, 1982).

M. Stauch, K. Wheat, with J. Tingle, *Text, Cases and Materials on Medical Law and Ethics* (4th edn, Routledge, 2012).

A. Stevens, 'IVF women prefer risky pregnancy to no pregnancy' (2007) 412 *Bionews*, available at http://www.bionews.org.uk/page_13157.asp.

H. Stolberg, G. Norman, I. Trop, 'Randomized controlled trials' (2004) 183 *American Journal of Roentgenology* 1539.

W. Sullivan, 'Medicine under threat: Professionalism and professional identity' (2000) 162 *Canadian Medical Association Journal* 673.

D. P. Sulmasy 'What is conscience and why is respect for it so important?' (2008) 29 *Theoretical Medicine and Bioethics* 135.

Report of the Surgical Practice Working Party, *Professional Standards for Cosmetic Practice* (Royal College of Surgeons, 2013).

J. Swift, *Gulliver's Travels* (Jones & Company, 1826).

K. Syrett, *Law, Legitimacy and the Rationing of Health Care: a Contextual and Comparative Perspective* (Cambridge University Press, 2007).

K. Syrett, 'NICE and the problem of "postcode prescribing" in the English National Health Service' in A. den Exter, M. Buijsen (eds), *Rationing Health Care: Hard Choices and Unavoidable Trade-Offs* (Maklu, 2012).

K. Syrett, 'Courts, expertise and resource allocation: Is there a judicial "legitimacy problem"?' (2014) 7 *Public Health Ethics* 112.

L. Syson, *Doctor of Love: James Graham and His Celestial Bed* (Alma Books, 2008).

T. Szasz, *The Myth of Mental Illness: Foundations of a Theory of Personal Conduct* (Harper and Row New York, 1961).

T. Szasz, *The Theology of Medicine: The Political-Philosophical Foundations of Medical Ethics* (Syracuse University Press, 1988).

S. Taber, 'Should all advertising of cosmetic surgery be banned? No' (2012) 345 *British Medical Journal* 7508.

G. Teubner, 'Autopoiesis in law and society: A rejoinder to Blakenburg' (1984) 18 *Law and Society Review* 291.

G. Teubner, 'Substantive and reflexive elements in modern law' (1983) 17 *Law and Society Review* 239.

D. P. Thomas, 'The demise of bloodletting' (2014) 44 *Journal of the Royal College of Physicians of Edinburgh* 72.

N. Timmins, 'NHS wastes £1 billion on ineffective treatments' (*The Independent*, 2 January 1996).

M. Tran, 'Jeremy Hunt calls for the end of cosmetic surgery on the NHS' (*The Guardian*, 18 June 2014) http://www.theguardian.com/politics/2014/jun/18/jeremy-hunt-end-cosmetic-surgery-nhs.

W.-S. Tseng, J. Streltzer, *Cultural Competence in Health Care: A Guide for Professionals* (Springer, 2008).

US Department of Health and Human Services, Food and Drug Administration, Center for Drug Evaluation and Research, Center for Biologics Evaluation and Research, *Guidance for Industry Expedited Programs for Serious Conditions – Drugs and Biologics* (2014) OMB Control No. 0910–0765.

C. Unsworth, *The Politics of Mental Health Legislation* (Clarendon Press, 1987).

R. Veatch, 'The impossibility of a morality internal to medicine' (2001) 26 *Journal of Medicine and Philosophy* 621.

K. Veitch, *The Jurisdiction of Medical Law* (Ashgate, 2007).

A. J. Viseltear, 'The last illnesses of Robert and Horace Walpole' (1983) 56 *Yale Journal of Biology and Medicine* 131.

I. Waddington, 'The struggle to reform the Royal College of Physicians, 1767–1771: A sociological analysis' (1973) 17 *Medical History* 107.

I. Waddington, 'General Practitioners and Consultants in Early Nineteenth Century England: The Sociology of an Intra-Professional Conflict' in J. Woodward, D. Richards (eds), *Health Care and Popular Medicine in Nineteenth-Century England* (Croon Helm, 1977).

M. Warnock, *A Question of Life: The Warnock Report* (Basil Blackwell, 1985).

H. Weiss, 'Complications of circumcision in male neonates, infants and children: A systematic review' (2010) 10 *BMC Urology* 1186.

G. Welch, L. Schwartz, S. Woloshin, *Over-Diagnosed: Making People Sick in the Pursuit of Health* (Beacon Press, 2011).

W. L. Whitwell, 'James Graham, Master Quack' (1977–8) 4 *Eighteenth-Century Life* 43.

M. Wicclair, 'Conscientious objection in medicine' (2000) 14 *Bioethics* 205.

M. Wicclair, 'Is conscientious objection incompatible with a physician's professional obligations?' (2008) 29 *Theoretical Medicine and Bioethics* 171.

J. W. Willcock, *The Laws Relating to the Medical Profession* (J. & W. T. Clarke, 1830).

A. Williams, 'Intergenerational equity: An exploration of the "fair innings" argument' (1997) 6 *Health Economics* 117.

G. Williams, *The Sanctity of Life and the Criminal Law* (Faber and Faber, 1958).

G. Williams, 'Consent and public policy' [1962] *Crim LR* 74, and [1962] *Crim LR* 154.

G. Williams, *Textbook of Criminal Law* (Stevens & Sons, 1978).

S. M. Wimalawansa, J. P. Fox, R. M. Johnson, 'The measurable cost of complications for outpatient cosmetic surgery in patients with mental health diagnoses' (2014) 34 *Aesthetic Surgery Journal* 306.

R. Winston, 'Why we need to experiment' (*The Observer*, 10 February 1985).

P. Wintour, 'Nick Clegg promises £120m boost for mental health care waiting time targets' (*The Guardian*, 8 October 2014), available at http://www.theguardian.com/society/2014/oct/08/mental-health-care-120m-funding-waiting-time-targets-nick-clegg.

S. Woods, P. McCormack, 'Disputing the ethics of research: The challenge from bioethics and patient activism to the interpretation of the Declaration of Helsinki in clinical trials' (2013) 27 *Bioethics* 243.

Lord Woolf, 'Are the courts excessively deferential to the medical profession?' (2001) 9 *Medical Law Review* 1.

S. Woolf, R. Grol, A. Hutchinson, M. P. Eccles, J. M. Grimshaw, 'Potential benefits, limitations and harms of clinical guidelines' (1999) 318 *British Medical Journal* 527.

D. Wooton, *Bad Medicine: Doctors Doing Harm Since Hippocrates* (Oxford University Press, 2004).

World Health Organization Regional Office for Europe, *Appropriateness in Health Care Services: Report on a WHO Workshop* (Copenhagen, WHO EUR/00/5022388, 2000).

World Health Organization, ICD-10 Version:2015 (2015), available at http://apps.who.int/classifications/icd10/browse/2015/en.

World Medical Association, *Declaration of Helsinki Ethical Principles for Medical Research Involving Humans* (1964, amended 2013).

World Medical Association, *Guidelines for Physicians Concerning Torture and other Cruel, Inhuman or Degrading Treatment or Punishment in Relation to Detention and Imprisonment*, Adopted by the 29th World Medical Assembly, Tokyo, Japan, October 1975, and editorially revised by the 170th WMA Council Session, Divonne-les-Bains, France, May 2005 and the 173rd WMA Council Session, Divonne-les-Bains, France, May 2006.

M. Wurm-Schaar, M. Fato, 'The professionalism movement: A pause might not be sufficient' (2004) 4 *The American Journal of Bioethics* W1.

T. Wynn, 'Psychiatric inpatients experiences with restraint' (2004) 15 *Journal of Forensic Psychiatry* 124.

Index

For Product Safety Concerns and Information please contact our EU
representative GPSR@taylorandfrancis.com
Taylor & Francis Verlag GmbH, Kaufingerstraße 24, 80331 München, Germany

www.ingramcontent.com/pod-product-compliance
Ingram Content Group UK Ltd.
Pitfield, Milton Keynes, MK11 3LW, UK
UKHW010958180926
475701UK00004B/444
* 9 7 8 1 1 3 8 0 9 8 1 7 6 *